Ace the Technical Interview

Ace the Technical Interview

Fourth Edition

Michael Rothstein
Daniel Rothstein

McGraw-Hill

New York San Francisco Washington, D.C. Auckland Bogotá
Caracus Lisbon London Madrid Mexico City Milan
Montreal New Delhi San Juan Singapore
Sydney Tokyo Toronto

McGraw-Hill

A Division of The McGraw-Hill Companies

2 3 4 5 6 7 8 9 0 DOC/DOC 0 5 4 3 2

ISBN 0-07-212622-1

The executive editor for this book was Steven Elliot, the associate editor was Franny Kelly, the editorial assistant was Alexander Corona and the production manager was Clare Stanley. It was set in Century Schoolbook by MacAllister Publishing Services. LLC

Printed and bound by R. R. Donnelley & Sons Company.

This book is printed on recycled, acid-free paper containing a minimum of 50 percent recycled de-inked fiber.

To my father, Michael Rothstein, the creator and author of the "ACE" series who passed away before the completion of this book and Blanche who made him happy these past years.

He was a kind and generous person who always thought of others.

We miss him and cherish his memory in our hearts.

Daniel Rothstein

Contents

Contributors

Chris Bailey is a Principal Systems Developer in the Research and Development Division of SAS Institute Inc. He is currently working on e-commerce solutions with emphasis on Java and distributed programming. He formerly co-authored a proprietary language called SCL and developed a grammatical analysis system while at AT&T. He has a degree in Computer Science from North Carolina State University and studied Mathematics at the Universität Heidelberg in Germany. He now lives and works in Cary, North Carolina. (CHAPTER 3)

Carl H. Burnham is a Web developer and hosting consultant, with more than 15 years of information technology experience in the public/private sectors. Previously, he was senior network administrator with Healtheon. Mr. Burnham is founder of Southpoint.com, a travel destination guide. He is coauthor of *Professional JSP*. (CHAPTER 2)

Valentin Carciu is the Unix System and Informix Data-Base administrator for Lazare Kaplan, Inc. He has been heavily involved in developing a complex software package using Informix for the company's plant in Botswana, Africa. This Unix system supports a diamond-cutting factory with more than 500 workers. Mr. Carciu currently is responsible for the analysis, design through implementation of a complex interface between the Botswanan system and Lazare Kaplan's New York central office applications. (Chapter 12)

David Dodge, Vice President, Professional Services. David joined Idapta in April 2000 and offers more than 22 years of experience in the field. Recent positions include director of business development for Ballantyne Consulting Group, and vice president of professional services for *Internet Security Systems, Inc.* (ISS), where David was tasked with establishing and growing ISS' national consulting capabilities. He was also U.S. vice president of ERP integration services for IBM Corporation. At IBM, he built and managed an organization of more than 1,200 consultants. For more than 12 years, David was a senior principal for American Management Systems, where he was responsible for new technology consulting initiatives. Prior to joining the private sector, David was an officer in the U.S. Navy and an instructor at the U.S. Naval Academy. A published author, David is a graduate of the Naval Academy, and holds a Master of Science degree and a Juris Doctorate from George Washington University. (CHAPTER 13)

Charles Fisher is a Systems Analyst at a national media company based in the Midwestern United States. Under the UNIX platform, he has served as webmaster, system administrator, and developer. Mr. Fisher has a degree in electrical and computer engineering, and has published *Red Hat Linux Administration Tools* with McGraw-Hill. (CHAPTERS 11 and 12)

Dov Gilor began his career in computing at the Federal Reserve Bank of New York. He started as a trainee and was soon a project leader and Supervising Analyst. He and his family moved to Israel in 1973 where Dov worked as an advisory systems engineer for IBM for some 20 years. Since the introduction of DB2 in 1981, Dov was responsible for DB2 support on various IBM platforms. He was also a member of the DB2 and CICS training staff. After taking early retirement from IBM, Dov worked as a DBA and consultant for NASA, Met Life, Morgan Stanley; IBM, BEZEK-Israel Telephone, Javits Convention Center, Detroit Edison, and many others. Dov has published a book on SQL performance. (CHAPTERS 5 and 7)

Donna Matthews holds a Bachelor's Degree in Computer Science/ Business from Roosevelt University in Chicago, Illinois and a Masters in Business Administration with a concentration in Technology Management. Donna is also an Oracle Certified Database Administrator designation. She has over 12 years IT experience primarily with relational databases including: SQL Server, Oracle and Sybase. She has used Oracle v 7.3, 8.0 and v 8.1.5 in a developer role and as a Database Administrator. Donna currently works as a computer consultant to Fortune 500 companies and local and federal government. (CHAPTER 6)

David McMahon is a Microsoft Certified Visual Basic and Microsoft Access developer. He works as a Visual Basic instructor at private colleges teaching Visual Basic courses. He is also a software engineer for an optics company where he develops scientific and engineering software using Visual C++, as well as database front-ends designed with Visual Basic. (CHAPTER 8)

Arthur D. Rosenberg specializes in analyzing and translating business requirements into software applications, producing accurate and readable documentation, designing and conducting training programs, and developing RFPs and proposals. His positions have included project leader, analyst, trainer, and documentation specialist. For a major media corporation he hired and managed a team of eight consultants in testing, documenting, and training customized A/R installation. Mr. Rosenberg has conducted classes and training seminars in PC hardware and software, mainframe applications, and methodology to staffs at several client companies, including The Port Authority of New York and New Jersey, Viacom/MTV, Deutsche Bank, Berlitz School (Paris), University of Stockholm, and U.S. Department of Education. (CHAPTER 1)

Michael Rothstein is the founder and president of Automated Systems Process Corp., which developed proprietary software for year 2000 conversions. He has also worked at IBM and Motorola Inc. and acted as a consultant to organizations such as Citibank and Metropolitan Life Insurance Co.Blue Cross/Blue Shield. Mr Rothstein has authored several computing books for McGraw Hill including the three previous editions of this bestseller, as well as other books on various aspect of system analysis, programming and information technology.

Travis Niedens is currently a network engineer for Microsoft. Before coming to Microsoft, he was employed at IBM Global Services as an I/T Specialist working on the Tier 2 network support team for a state government account. Travis started working in the IS/IT industry at the age of 16 by doing tech support for Sykes Enterprises. He is a CCNP and CCDP and working towards the Routing/Switching CCIE. He currently resides in Bellevue, WA with partner, Rachel, and two tabby cats, Catbert and Merlin. "I would like to thank God for giving me the many gifts that have taken me this far so fast. Thanks to Rachel for being there through my writing, taking time out to help me review and create new content for this chapter, and cooking dinner at odd hours of the early morning after I finished my chapter work. I would also like to thank my friends at Microsoft and IBM Global Services for helping me grow into the Networking field and to understand all the fine aspects involved therein." (CHAPTER 14)

Rama Tamachandran is the Director of Technology with Imperium Solutions, a Microsoft Solution Provider Partner. He is a Microsoft Certified Solution Developer and Site-Builder and designs and develops web and e-commerce applications using ASP, COM, Visual Basic, SQL Server and Windows 2000. He also has extensive experience with building database systems using Visual Basic, Visual InterDev, Access, and FoxPro. Rama is the contributing author of Professional Visual InterDev 6 Programming (Wrox) as well as co-author of four books on Visual Basic from Que Publishing. Rama is also the ASP Pro at Fawcette's www.inquiry.com web site where he answers ASP related questions. He teaches Visual Basic and Web Development at Fairfield University as well as at the University of Connecticut. He lives in Stamford, Conn., with his wife, Beena, and their sons, Ashish and Amit. Rama can be reached at his e-mail address: rama@imperium.com. (CHAPTER 4)

Marc Temkin became involved with computer programming during courses in electronic music synthesizers and computer music while studying for a graduate degree in music at Northwestern University in 1985. He has been active in programming desktop, client-server, distributed and Internet applications using C++, Java, Visual Basic and other languages. He plays string bass, electric bass and guitar in various orchestral, jazz and popular music ensembles. (CHAPTER 9)

Raghu Vullaganti is currently a senior consultant with Hitachi Data Systems Solutions. He has extensive experience with ERP systems, EDI, relational databases, and distributed environments. His responsibilities include requirements gathering, analysis, specifications design, data modeling, database design, development and deployment of various applications. Mr. Vullaganti has provided his consulting services for various fortune 500 companies including accounting firm KPMG, telecommunications, government, and technology industries. "I am always gratitude to the Supreme God, who has been a real guide in my life. I would like to thank Vani, my wife, for her support. I would also like to thank my parents, Narasimha Rao and Syamala Devi, and my brother, Murali, for their support, and encouragement all the time in my life". Mr. Vullaganti can be reached at his e-mail address: vullaganti@yahoo.com. (CHAPTERS 10 and 16)

Glynn Williams is a SAP R/3 Systems Analyst, specializing in the Sales and Distribution module of SAP. He has worked on numerous international projects. He is currently part of a team upgrading a 3.1h system release 4.6c for Hewlett Packard, a Fortune 20 company with annual turnover of 46 Billion USD. Prior to that, he implemented release 4.6b for Honeywell, a Fortune 50 company with turnover in excess of 25 Billion USD. In 1998/99, Glynn was part of a team implementing release 4.0b for Avnet, a company with an annual turnover in excess of 6 Billion USD—the worlds largest electrical component supplier across 12 countries in Europe. He has worked on other projects, such as SADIA, the world's third largest poultry supplier, a company with an annual turnover in excess of 3 Billion USD. He has worked on releases 2.2e through to 4.6c across 17 countries. He is the author of 500+ page, best selling book, *Implementing SAP- R/3 Sales and Distribution*. (CHAPTER 15)

Preface

"What a great world we live in."

When I was born, some sixty years ago, radio was still fairly new, TV was in its theoretical stages and computers were unknown. Medicine was fairly primitive, life was simpler and much more difficult and the "good old days" were old but not that good.

You are living in the exciting generation of computer power, communication and automation. People all over the world have become connected. Distances have evaporated and it is almost impossible to keep truth and information from flowing freely around the world to anyone who wants it. Advances in glorious technology outpaces our ability to absorb and integrate what is available in our daily lives.You have the good fortune to be a contributor to this communication revolution. Obtaining a good job is the primary step in reaping the rewards of your capability.

This book is designed to give you an advantage against your competition for a technical job. It will enable you to prepare for that very critical moment when you are facing the technical interviewer. Many of the authors of the chapters are those who give the technical interviews for their companies. They can provide you with an insight into how to prepare yourself and how to answer technical questions. The knowledgeable impression you make by being prepared will give you an advantage and assist you in getting the job you deserve.

As my friend, Mike Rothstein, wrote in the previous edition; "And that is what this book is all about . . Preparing and Succeeding." The author of each chapter has worked hard to enhance this book and to update the data.

New topics have been added to give you the benefit of the many years of experience of the authors. The Internet web, client-server, interconnectivity and relational databases have all moved to center stage in computing and are covered in several chapters. Each author is experienced in his subject area and you will be the beneficiary of this amassed technical knowledge.

Mike Rothstein worked hard to integrate all of the elements into his very successful series. He spent days and weeks searching for the best authors and cajoling them to finish their part of the book within the allotted time frame, even as he knew that his time on this earth was limited. Each of the authors hope that we have succeeded, in Mike's memory, to give you the reader the best information available to help you succeed.

Good luck.

Dov Gilor

Acknowledgements

A few months ago my father was hospitalized. During one of my visits to the hospital, I made a promise to my father to help him complete the forth edition of "Ace The Technical Interview". We sat for hours and he told me everything there is to know about the book. At the time, non of us knew that he won't be around to see the publication of his book. I couldn't have accomplished this without the help and support of the McGraw Hill staff, especially Steven Elliot and Franny Kelly, who labored on my fathers behalf. Their sensitivity and caring enabled me to keep my promise and publish this edition. I would also like to thank all the co-authors, especially Dov Gilor, a dear friend, for contributing to the success of the book.

Again to all of you....Thank you.

Daniel Rothstein

Introduction

We live in a very advanced technological world and our goal should be to make it the best and most advanced place possible for the good of all mankind. Future generations, where computers respond to the spoken word, are self-programming and control every aspect of society, may look back upon us as primitives. Compared to recent generations, however, we have achieved fantastic breakthroughs in most areas of science and technology and have been blessed with instant data and communication.

You are going to contribute to and enjoy the fruits of these advances, and your skills are still needed so that you can make a significant contribution to the future of our world. With your computer knowledge, you will travel the leading edge of technology as it grows and expands, and this volume, which has much of the latest computer information between its covers, will help you achieve your goal of finding the best job for your skills. Maybe our great grandchildren will have phone and computer implants inserted at birth and their biological systems may be integrated into their implanted data processing systems so they can be hooked into a national or international communications grid, but it will be our dreams, skills, and projects that will allow the next generation's dreams to become reality.

As you may be aware, the concept of the "ACE" series was dreamed up by its editor, Michael Rothstein (of blessed memory). Mike was hard at work putting the finishing touches on this edition when he was cruelly struck down by cancer. Mike was unaware until close to the end, as he labored to finish another of his dreams, that the cancer was growing within him. When he learned the sad news, Mike tried to rush the book to completion, but it was not to be. When he left us, he willed the completion of the task to his son, Daniel, and to his many friends. All we have done is fulfill his wishes.

Mike was a dreamer. He and I worked together for a while at IBM Israel and later as programming and database consultants for MET Life in New York City. Many years ago, Mike suggested that I use my love for SQL performance tuning and write a book about it. I laughed at the thought but am so pleased that he kept kidding me until I finally took him seriously and wrote the book. What a great experience that was and I am ever grateful that he pushed me to do it.

Mike dreamed many dreams and he was often juggling several potential projects at the same time. His projects kept him happy and his happiness was infectious. While some may have doubted, those who knew him were sure that his dreams would reach fruition.

Mike lived a rich and full life. Those who loved Mike's huge smile and cheerful disposition will sorely miss him. He often made us laugh and he gave joy and happiness to his family, children and grandchildren. We, who he left behind staring into that black void, mourn that precious soul who touched our lives and gave us dreams and is no more. No, the ache in our hearts will not disappear, but our faith teaches us to express our pain and longing though love and respect and to eventually be consoled.

May Mike's memory be blessed and may he serve as an advocate in heaven to send a blessing of peace and happiness to us all. May those who knew him keep his memory alive by continuing to dream and to succeed. May you as a reader of Mike's work have the success that he would so dearly want you to have.

Dov Gilor

Ace the Technical Interview

1
The Technical Interview: What You Need to Know, Say, and Do

Arthur D. Rosenberg

Gaining the Competitive Edge

The purpose of this chapter is to help you gear up for—and ace—the information systems interview. Even in today's job market, the competition for the best full-time positions and the choice consulting contracts is fierce. The pros are out there knocking on the same doors as you, and you need every available advantage to come in first! It is no secret that interviews are a key element in winning jobs, and knowing how to present yourself will give you a leg up into the winner's circle.

Our focus is on preparation—doing your homework prior to the interview—and successfully handling different types of interviews. We'll show you how to market your skills and talents while avoiding the *faux pas* that can kill an otherwise successful meeting. You will learn to exercise more control over the people who interview you, to anticipate, recognize, and respond effectively to their questions and tactics. You will be positioned to receive your share of offers, and enabled to better evaluate which jobs you want and which ones to pass up. From now on, you'll go to important interviews with a feeling of confidence and leave them with a smile.

Getting Interviews

Before preparing for an interview, you have to *get* the interview. This is usually accomplished via personal contacts, agencies, postings, and advertisements. Don't get discouraged if they don't come fast and furiously at times, and never take the brush-offs personally. Most of the reasons you don't get potential interviews have absolutely nothing to do with you, so keep your head and spirits up. Sometimes it's a numbers game: the more contacts you make, the more interviews you get, and, inevitably, the more job offers you receive.

Agencies

Placement and consulting agencies often have valuable contacts with clients who are seeking employees and/or consultants. Most are experienced at evaluating and matching skills such as yours with client needs. Bear in mind, though, that the agency traditionally receives its fees from the employer, and so its loyalties are naturally inclined in that direction.

When you negotiate a salary or rate with an agency, you have to balance two opposing facts of life: the less you agree to, the less you will have to live with; and the more you demand, the more attractive the competition may appear.

The Résumé

Your résumé is your emissary to everyone you want to meet. It is also the initial link in the job chain you hope to join, a voice that speaks for you until you have a chance to introduce yourself. Whether you go through an agency or contact the client directly, you need a current résumé to help you stand out among the hundreds of others who may be competing with you for the job. According to the *Résumé Handbook* (Arthur D. Rosenberg and David V. Hizer, Bob Adams, Inc., 3d edition, 1996), only one interview is granted for every 245 résumés received.

Orient your résumé specifically toward a full-time position or a consulting contract. Your résumé should include a summary of experience and at least two or three job-related accomplishments. The full-time position résumé should also have a chronologically organized section (filling in any significant gaps) to show growth, responsibility, and consistency. A consultant's résumé should feature technical and related skills, applications, experience, and clients; it can be as long as necessary. Employee résumés should be limited to two or three pages (one for recent graduates and people with limited work experience); lists of publications, patents, and other relevant credits should be attached. It doesn't hurt to maintain your résumé on a word processor to keep it up to date, and to quickly produce variations that emphasize any specific skills and applications that may be of interest to a potential client.

Your résumé must be clearly organized and detailed without being cumbersome. Particularly for consultants, it also helps to have professional business cards, an answering machine, a fax, and an e-mail address.

Preinterview Preparations

If you are seeking a full-time position, be prepared not only for questions about the job for which you are applying, but also for more personal inquiries, such as why you left your last (or are considering leaving your current) employer, why you'd like to join their company, and more subtle queries intended to reveal your character. If you are a consultant, potential clients are more concerned with your job-related track record—specifically, the hardware, software, and applications you have mastered. Regarding the latter, it is important to be candid and objective, for it is difficult to fool people for long in a data processing environment.

Doing Your Homework

The first step in getting ready for an interview is preparing for the kinds of questions you are likely to be asked. Ask your contact or intermediary about the specific job requirements and related issues. Job requirements may include hardware, software, applications, and responsibilities such as design, installation, supervision, and management. Related issues cover location, hours, and potential future to career-minded applicants. If a technical skill is required, update your memory and knowledge by referring to the appropriate chapter of this book. Ask yourself what you would ask a candidate if you were conducting the interview, and be prepared to answer no less than that.

Try also to find out who your interviewer is likely to be—the president of the company, the MIS director, a project leader or manager, or someone from the personnel department (see "Different Types of Interviewers" in this chapter). Is the interviewer a decision maker, or merely screening for someone else? If you are going to meet a decision maker, be ready to meet some of the members of the team as well.

Objectives

Just as the objective of a résumé is to get the interview, the objective of an interview is to convince the screener to pass you on to the decision maker, or to convince the decision maker to offer you the job. When you go on an interview, always give it your best shot, with confidence and enthusiasm. Don't waste the interviewer's time—or your own—with an *I don't really want this job* attitude. And don't shoot yourself in the foot with a *you probably won't offer me the job* air because, in that case, they probably won't. Whether you are seeking a career position or a consulting assignment, the bottom line is winning the offer. You may later decide not to accept the job if you feel it isn't right for you, or if something better is available, but that decision lies in the future. At worst—if they do not offer you the job—you will have gained the experience of the interview for the investment of your time.

Refresh

Whether you are a rookie or a seasoned professional, you need to be ready for the interview in order to be at your impressive best. When everything else is equal (i.e., when two or more candidates are of comparable skill and experience), then confidence and enthusiasm for the job may serve as the tiebreaker.

Of course, if you're an unusually heavyweight tech, a guru among experts, clients may be lined up for your services despite your coffee stains, frumpy clothes, or passive attitude. They put up with you because they have to. But if you haven't yet outdistanced the competition, your appearance and attitude can work for or against you. Nobody wants to work with a negative individual, a complainer, or a slob when there are more agreeable alternatives available.

Personal Appearance

While we are cautioned not to judge others by *their* personal appearance, we should nevertheless make sure that ours is appropriate. Notwithstanding recent trends toward casual dress, personal appearance still influences the expectations of people who meet us for the first time.

Common sense dictates that the closer you conform to the norm (what you see around you), the more you look the part. Although data processing groups and departments have grown less conservative in recent years, the environment in which you work (especially finance) may not be ready for men with long hair and earrings, women with flashy makeup and clothing, or anyone unusually adorned or dressed. The bottom line is that this is likely to divert attention from their skills and may cause them to be taken less than seriously.

If you have reason to anticipate an extended interviewing process that could last for several hours, wear clothing that will maintain its neatness throughout the day.

References

Give references that will enhance your credibility as an employee/consultant in the job for which you are interviewing. Former employers, supervisors, and colleagues count for more than friends and casual acquaintances. By all means, offer academic recommendations if you are a recent graduate, but try to avoid using any references with whom you have had no contact for a number of years. It is customary to ask permission of the person involved to use his or her name. Besides being the polite thing to do, it alerts the person to expect calls. If you are uncertain of what someone may say about you, check them out by having a friend call them as a potential employer, or just don't use them. Remember, a poor reference is worse than no reference at all.

Disabilities

If you have any handicaps that might interfere with your ability to perform activities normally associated with the job for which you wish to interview, reveal them up front. In this manner, you are more likely to overcome any doubts the interviewer may have (but may be hesitant to ask) about your ability to perform.

Different Types of Interviewers

Before getting into the personalities of individual interviewers, let's take a moment to identify the two major camps by objectives: screeners and deciders.

Screeners

The screening interview is usually a formal, impersonal meeting conducted by a professional interviewer. It is most often required for a career position, occasionally for a consulting assignment. The purpose of this process is to weed out the more obviously inappropriate candidates by verifying their background, credentials, appearance, and any overt characteristics.

The screening interviewer is likely to be skilled at the kinds of techniques that encourage you to put your foot in your mouth by revealing facts you'd rather not discuss (e.g., discrepancies between what you say and what is written on your résumé, or perhaps the real reason why you left a certain company). The screener probably doesn't know a whole lot about the job for which you are interviewing, so he or she is unlikely to ask any technical questions. The screener's purpose is to gather enough relevant information about you to make a safe decision as to whether to pass you on to the decision maker or show you the door.

Since this is likely to be the only time you ever meet the screeners (even if you get the job), they are less interested in you personally than would be a potential supervisor or colleague. In a very real sense, screeners are primarily focused on uncovering reasons to stop you from getting any further. So it is more important that they find nothing wrong with you than that they like you.

Your objective in a screening interview is to pass. This means providing the screener with solid facts that fit into a wholesome picture. You need only to satisfy screeners, not impress them. Avoid any hint of suspicion or controversy. Respond clearly and fully to all questions while volunteering absolutely nothing. If the screeners are not impressed with you, you won't be able to charm or fast-talk your way past them; and if they are satisfied with your credentials, the more you talk, the wider and deeper the potential pitfall.

Deciders

The decision (hiring) interview is commonly conducted by a department head, project leader, supervisor, or any combination of these. Unlike screeners, decision makers tend to know more about the job and related technical details than about interviewing techniques. They are concerned with your ability to do the work, and how you will fit into the environment. They may have to deal with you on a daily basis, and so it matters, to some extent, that they are comfortable with you.

Since the decision-making interviewer isn't usually a professional interviewer, the decision interview tends to be a less structured affair. This is where you must be prepared for technical questions and informal conversations on a more personal level. This is where you may have to convince potential supervisors and colleagues that you are—in addition to being competent—a reasonably agreeable person. This is where you may use your interpersonal skills to direct the interview in a positive (for you) direction. And this is where you get the information and the *vibes* that help you to make up your own mind about the job.

Personalities

Whenever people with different objectives get together, potential hazards come into play. Despite the best of intentions, objectivity can give way to conflict when certain types of individuals confront each other. A few of the more obvious examples include status and authority, male-female, short-tall, and older-younger. Differences of national origin, accent, and style (e.g., flamboyance versus restraint) may also influence an interaction. This is especially true of job interviews.

While confidence and attention are assets in most interview situations, the following conditions call for heightened sensitivity. Since we cannot cover all of the possible personality combinations in a single chapter, we offer these examples as representative of the kinds of efforts that may be needed on both sides of the interview.

Upper management. The president, the chairperson, and certain department heads may have large egos. When you interview with a bigwig, treat that person with the respect to which he or she is accustomed. Manifest your confidence within the confines of your arena, and tread lightly on their comfort zones.

Consultant-employee. Interviewing with a manager or project leader who may know (and possibly resent) how much you're getting paid is not uncommon. The best way to deal with this is to focus on the job to be done and your ability to do the job, and downplay any reference to your lifestyle. Your task is to convince the interviewer that you are a reliable team player who will make the interviewer look good, not to let them know about your Lamborghini or indoor swimming pool.

Male-female. Be careful to avoid any innuendo that might be interpreted in a suggestive manner. Both male and female candidates should keep their eyes up to face level and feel free to manifest their natural self confidence while avoiding remarks that could possibly be "sexually" misconstrued.

Short-tall. People whose physical dimensions are considered to be within the norm are often unaware of the sensitivities of exceptionally tall, short, overweight, and otherwise visually unusual individuals. Avoid making any references to these characteristics—your remarks may be misinterpreted.

Older-younger. When there is a significant difference in age, the elder interviewee should strive to be energetic and careful not to condescend. The younger interviewee should be calm, respectfully confident, and an especially good listener.

One-on-One

As mentioned earlier, personal predispositions can be difficult to avoid, even during a professional interview. Focus your attention on the interviewer rather than on the impression you are trying to make. Listen carefully to what interviewers say, and try to read their reactions to you. If they appear to lose interest in what you're saying, change course by asking them a question. For example,

"Have I answered the question to your satisfaction?"

"Was there something else you wanted me to address?"

"Do you want me to go into (technical) detail?"

"How many people are there in your department?"

"When do you plan to make a decision on this position?"

Outnumbered

When you are being interviewed by two or more potential employer/clients, it may be useful to have some samples of your work, or extra copies of your résumé, to divert their attention. Try to learn, if you don't already know, who has the most authority, and be sure to address that individual at least as often as the others. Pay attention to them all by looking at them, one by one, as you talk. Get them to do most of the talking, if you can, by asking questions based on what they tell you. Answer every question as accurately and completely as you can.

If someone asks a stupid question, focus on any aspect of it that may be sensible; or divert it toward relevancy, if possible, without embarrassing the one who asked it. Example: You are interviewing for a three-to-six-month assignment, and someone asks, "Why are you interested in working for our company?" Even if the question seems inappropriate or out of context, try to come up with a face-saver, like, "I've been hearing about your company's accomplishments/innovations in recent months, and this is a chance to learn more about it/them," or "I've been learning a good deal about CASE (DB, etc.), and this looks like an excellent opportunity to apply that knowledge." The point is that even if the individual who asked the silly question does not recognize or appreciate your tact, the others will.

The Interview

When you succeed in getting the interview, be punctual. Plan to arrive early enough that unforeseen delays will not make you late. Excuses for arriving late are just that—*excuses*—even if they are true. Being late is failing to arrive on time. You don't want a potential employer's initial experience with you to be tainted with any kind of failure.

If you are going to be unavoidably delayed, call the interviewer before the time of the scheduled interview to apologize for inconveniencing him or her and ask if it would be more convenient to delay the interview or reschedule it.

Credibility is the most important impression to create during an interview. This is accomplished by appearing honest, confident, enthusiastic, courteous, and inoffensive. Speak in a manner that is natural for you; if you have memorized a bunch of technical details, deliver them in a conversational manner, not as if reading from a list. Avoid slang ("like, real cool," "right on," etc.); bad English ("so he goes, 'well, yeah,' and I go, . . ."); profanity of any kind; and criticism (especially of a past employer or someone known to the interviewer). Avoid frequent use of "well," "umm," "y'know," and such.

Try to enjoy the interview; this can help you to relax and make a positive impression. Memorize the interviewer's name, and be sure to pronounce it correctly when addressing him or her. And—forgive us for adding the obvious—do not smoke, chew gum, or eat food or candy during an interview. It's OK to accept coffee, tea, or water if offered, although it may be safer to decline. Remember that the interviewer—especially the professional interviewer—is watching you and evaluating your behavior.

Body Language

Eye contact is the dominant feature in nonverbal communications. The way you meet or avoid someone's gaze can reveal volumes about your character and feelings. Consciously and unconsciously, our eyes contribute to the messages we give out. For example, looking away from the listener while speaking means *don't interrupt me even if I pause for a moment;* looking at the listener when you stop speaking is a signal that you're finished; and looking away from the person who is speaking suggests impatience or dissatisfaction with whatever that person is saying.

It has been estimated that as much as 70 percent of all face-to-face communication is nonverbal. While volumes have been written on this subject, we have summarized the function into a few action verbs:

- *Reach out* to potential employers and clients with a firm handshake on arriving and departing.
- *Smile* as pleasantly as your personality allows.
- *Look* at people when they speak, and make eye contact with each of them in turn when you are talking.
- *Relax* your body, especially your head and hands; avoid abrupt or jerky motions, fidgeting, crossing your arms, or covering your mouth with your hands.
- *Lean* slightly forward, without slouching.
- *Nod* affirmatively to show attention and agreement, and to encourage the interviewer to continue talking, but avoid nodding when they say something with which you disagree.

Evaluating

Winning teams are those that make quick adjustments to what their opponents are doing. A successful interviewee pays attention to what the interviewer says and does, and reacts accordingly. For example, if you are describing your last job or assignment, and the interviewer's eyes begin to wander around the room, it's time to change the topic or to ask a question. If the interviewer glances frequently at the clock on the wall or his or her watch, it may be wise to keep your answers brief. When you do manage to catch the interviewer's interest, hold to that subject, and to similar topics, as long as may be reasonable.

Always listen carefully to what the interviewer says, whether it is what you want to hear or not. Skilled interviewers tell you precisely what they want you to know; unskilled interviewers may reveal more than they realize. In either case, the information an interviewer provides can help you to evaluate the interviewer, the company, and the job, and to respond in an appropriate and relevant manner.

If the interviewer is terse, tense, or unpleasant, don't take it personally. He or she may be having a bad day, or perhaps that's just the personality of the interviewer. Continue to conduct yourself with professional courtesy and enthusiasm, and hope for the best. Unless you experience this sort of unpleasantness often, chances are it isn't worth a second thought.

Responding

Make an effort to answer every question clearly, accurately, and thoroughly without overexplaining or repeating yourself. Maintain consistency between different questions. This is most easily achieved by telling the truth. Be ready for open-ended questions like, "Tell me about yourself," or "What do you consider to be your major strengths and weaknesses?" In such cases, represent yourself in a believable and work-related manner; discuss your assets in a matter-of-fact manner without embellishment. (Please refer to **Fielding Hard-to-Handle Questions** later in this chapter.)

And, above all, assume that if you are telling the truth, you are being believed. With a skilled interviewer, the way you respond to questions can be even more important than the answers; clear, decisive answers contribute to the image of intelligence and credibility.

- *Qualify.* Ask questions that help to define or clarify what is being asked of you. Example: "Are you more interested in how I designed the system, or in how I applied the methodology?" This keeps you from taking a false path, and gives you a few extra moments to prepare your answer.
- *Clarify.* After answering a question, check the interviewers' demeanor. If they seem to be satisfied (e.g., they smile or nod), then pause to let them comment or ask another question. If they do not appear comfortable, ask if you have answered the question to their satisfaction and if there are any additional points they would like you to address.
- *Specify.* Tell what *you* did in your last job, or in your last job related to the position/assignment for which you are applying, aside from the team on which you worked.
- *Quantify.* Try to put your accomplishments in a meaningful context. Examples: "I wrote a hundred programs averaging half a million lines of code in two years," "We were the only group to complete our project on schedule," or "When my assignment was completed, I was assigned another task by the project leader."
- *Don't lie.* Plausible exaggeration is the outer limit of creative expression when describing your experience and accomplishments. Employers tend to check up on their prospective employees thoroughly, and a consultant's reputation is his or her lifeline to success. Never tell a verifiable lie to a potential employer/client—even the possibility of its discovery will haunt you.

Controlling the Interview

Projecting an Image

There are three separate aspects of your behavior of which you need to be aware: how you really feel, the image you would like to project, and the interviewer's perception of your behavior.

Your personal feelings are private. You may choose to reveal a few of them, but most of us prefer to filter out at least some of our innermost views and characteristics.

"Image control is how you represent yourself to the world. It requires recognition of the image you are projecting, a clear picture of the image you would like to project, and an understanding of how to bring these into harmony" (*Career Busters—22 Things People Do to Mess Up Their Careers and How to Avoid Them* [Arthur D. Rosenberg, McGraw-Hill, 1997]). Projecting an image requires an awareness of how others perceive us. Alas, many otherwise clever individuals harbor self images which are not uniformly shared by those who meet them.

To compensate for potential discrepancies, we suggest the following kind of reality check: ask three or four trusted friends and colleagues of both genders what they consider to be your two or three strongest personality characteristics, both positive and negative. Examples: nice smile, good speaking voice, nervous hand gestures, avoiding eye contact. Use these lists to make up your own list, emphasizing traits which were mentioned more than once, plus any negative traits of which you are already aware. Do not delete any negatives, no matter how strongly you may disagree, or this exercise will be worthless. Remember, you are focusing on how others perceive you, aside from what you may see in yourself. Next, ask three or four of your closest friends and family members to rearrange the list, beginning with your strongest tendencies. The combination of the rearranged lists will likely give you some idea of your public image, pro and con. Then it's up to you to work on what you want to do about it. Note that even positive qualities, when carried to excess, can be negative.

Influencing the interviewer's perception of you, as discussed earlier under "Evaluating," depends on paying careful attention to what the interviewer says and does, perceiving what he or she wants and does not want, and adjusting your approach accordingly. Always bear in mind that what the interviewer wishes to hear is more important than what the interviewee would like to say. The closer you come to emphasizing those qualities that relate specifically to what the interviewer is looking for, the more successful you will be. Just as it may be counterproductive to ramble on about your Sybase background in an Oracle environment, don't push any skills in which the interviewer appears uninterested.

Turning the Interview Around: Interviewing the Interviewer

Note: this tactic is intended primarily for the decision interview; it is rarely successful with a professional screening interviewer.

One of the most successful interviewing tactics is getting the interviewer to do most of the talking. It is a given that people who talk a lot enjoy talking. So even if you do not get to make all the points you'd like to make, avoid the temptation of interrupting a chatty interviewer. An interview dominated by the interviewer is likely to leave that interviewer with a comfortable feeling about the interviewee.

When interviewers show a tendency to talk about themselves, their company, the surf at Malibu, Bogart movies, or any other subject, let them do so with a minimum of interruption. One way to discover what makes them tick is to politely ask semipersonal questions, such as: "How long have you been working here, if you don't mind my asking?" or "Do you have a long commute?" or (in response to their question) "We have three children; how about you?" You never know what might get them going.

On the other hand, don't get too personal, avoid politics, and stay clear of references to any unusual physical characteristics. Remember, small talk can be a double-edged sword.

Fielding Hard-to-Handle Questions

Before responding to a difficult question, pause just long enough to check your body language and compose your thoughts.

If you get a technical question for which you are unprepared, tell what (if anything) you know, and admit your ignorance in a straightforward manner (e.g., "I have relatively little background in Oracle—is it essential to this position?" or "I would welcome the opportunity to sharpen my skills in Delphi" or "I was not aware that C++ was a prerequisite for this assignment"). Then try to draw attention to an area in which you are more knowledgeable.

The majority of these queries break down into six major categories: *Tell me about yourself . . . , What are your strong/weak points?, How do you feel about . . . , Why did you leave your last job/do you want to leave your present job?,*

Why do you want to join our company?, and *What do you want to be doing two/five/ten years from now?*

Example 1:

Q: *Tell me a little about yourself.*

Prepare a two- to five-minute mini-profile in advance for this open-ended query to avoid fumbling for words or revealing something you'd prefer not to mention. Make sure it is in no way inconsistent with your résumé. Smile, as if you welcome the opportunity. One smooth line of conversation is the progression of events in your childhood, youth, education, or earlier career that led you to your current professional level. Some of the topics you might use are your ambitions, hobbies, leisure activities, and family, but that's strictly up to you and what you're comfortable talking about.

A: In my last two jobs my responsibilities were primarily research oriented. Although I'm pretty good with numbers, I was beginning to feel isolated and would like to be more involved in customer relations.

A: I enjoy collecting stamps. My grandfather used to let me search for the right place to stick the stamps in the books when I was a kid, and he gave me his collection when I graduated from high school. By the time I finished college, I had the whole collection computerized, which is what got me interested in computers.

A: Although I have a technical background, I'm very interested in management. That's why I've been taking evening classes toward a possible MBA.

A: My husband and I are joggers, and we enjoy listening to classical music.

A: My wife and I enjoy traveling together. We like to take advantage of the chance to visit different parts of the country before starting to raise a family.

Example 2:

Q: *What are your strongest/weakest attributes?*

When you have a chance to showcase your strengths, provide two or three examples that have some relevance to your profession.

A: My manager at Gigo told me I was a very good analyst. She assigned me to establish the design standards for an important project and was very pleased with the results. I also had a reputation for picking up new programming languages quickly.

Experienced interviewers won't let you get away with stock answers and clichés these days, like "I used to get a little impatient when people held me back, but I've learned to be a team player." They know that nobody's perfect, and they want an honest answer. The best way to respond is by admitting to a (minor) human weakness within the context of how you are improving it.

A: I missed a couple of deadlines by a week or two because I wasn't very good at delegating work to other members of my team, but I've been improving. In fact, two of my last three projects were on time, which is above average in my department.

A: I was not a natural with computers in college, and so I tended to avoid them for a while. I finally wised up to the reality that computers are a fact of life and completely changed my attitude toward them. In fact, I'm signing up for an evening computer course this coming semester.

Example 3:

Q: *How would you feel about one of your subordinates being promoted to a position above yours?*

It's O.K. (and very believable) to admit to human emotions, so long as you don't go overboard.

A: I guess it would depend on who it was and the circumstances in which it happened. If I honestly felt that the person deserved the promotion, I might be a little jealous, but I'd also be among the first to congratulate him or her. But if I had reason to believe that it was due to backroom politics or personal favors, I'd probably be very angry.

Example 4:

Q: *Why did you leave your last job?*

The overwhelming majority of people who aren't terminated by their employers leave their jobs for better opportunities (more money and prestige), because they're bored or dead-ended (no room to move up), or due to a conflict with a boss, colleague, or assignment. Responding to this question is tricky because you don't want to be in the position of complaining or bad-mouthing others. Having a personal problem doesn't necessarily label you a loser, but it's hard to look good when you paint yourself into a negative picture. Even if an interviewer encourages you to reveal the gory details, you're better off presenting your move, or willingness to move, in a positive light.

A: I've been programming for over three years and am ready to move ahead to the next stage of my career.
A: I was typecast as a "techie" and would like to explore managerial opportunities..
A: When they merged the two divisions, it was clear that there would be heavy cuts in marketing. Frankly, I'm a lot better at promoting products than at playing politics.

However, if you were ousted because of a personality conflict that cannot be hidden, you may need to discuss it in a straightforward manner.

A: When I transferred to the central region, I found that the regional manager had a very different set of priorities than my former boss and I. He was totally production oriented, whereas I feel very strongly about quality. It was clear to both of us early on that we weren't comfortable working together.

Example 5:

Q: *Why are you interested in joining our company?*

This is the flip side to question #4, and some of the same answers may be appropriate. It's your chance to demonstrate your knowledge of the interviewer's company and their activities.

A: The innovations your company has been making in high-speed performance convinced me that this was the place to be.
A: A large organization like yours has far more opportunity for people with solid line experience.
A: A small company like yours is much more personal.
A: Your company's track record demonstrates a level playing field for women executives.

Example 6:

Q: *Where do you see yourself two/five/ten years from now?*

You are expected by your employers and potential employers to have goals. Prepare a goal description that is likely to sound reasonable: junior accountant to senior accountant (not directly to controller); upper management to vice president. Of course, you are advised to edit out your plans to leave the company for any reason. Also, it is best not to define a precise time frame that could embarrass or pressure you unreasonably. The safest ground is ambition that doesn't border upon arrogance.

A: With the courses I am taking and the experience I expect to gain in this position, I am aiming at becoming a project leader when the opportunity arises.
A: I am definitely interested in upper management, although I know I've got a long way to go. My first step is to show my manager that he or she made a good decision in adding me to the team.
A: My goal is to become a supervisor. How long has it taken other people who entered at my level to get promoted?

Managing Uncomfortable Situations

The *pressure interview* is more frequently encountered by potential employees than consultants, but every interviewee should be prepared for it. Most often, pressure interviews are devised to find out how the candidate will respond to unexpected circumstances; occasionally, they may be inadvertent, the result of internal pressure, an incompetent interviewer, etc. But generally they are intentional, premeditated ploys to see how you react to stress.

The rule of thumb when under pressure is courtesy, tact, and confidence. Don't blow your cool; never let yourself be baited into rudeness, anger, impatience, or agreeing with a point of view with which you really disagree. You can acknowledge the interviewer's point without agreeing ("I understand your point"), and you can politely disagree ("Your point is well taken, although I find that . . .").

If the interviewer stares at you strangely (e.g., in apparent disbelief), don't feel that you must justify whatever you just said. If your statement is challenged, don't back down; show confidence in your position without arguing or becoming flustered. If the interviewer lapses into a prolonged silence after you have finished talking, just sit there calmly, meeting his or her stare as pleasantly as possible, until the interviewer resumes. Don't let interviewers lure you into qualifying, overexplaining, taking back what you have told them, or fidgeting. If they haven't asked a question, you don't have to answer one. If you have been honest with interviewers, you have nothing to feel guilty about. When experienced interviewers behave strangely, their purpose is to see how you respond. Tell yourself that they are testing you, and you will very likely pass the test. If the interviewer asks you if you're nervous, there's nothing wrong with smiling and admitting to being human: "I haven't done a lot of job interviewing and I'm not very experienced at it. I guess I'm a lot better at balancing budgets than talking about my achievements," or "I was just thinking about some of the people I have interviewed in the past, and how they may have been feeling."

In the following scenarios, you are presented with stressful situations and a number of sample options. The choices are yours. There are no right or wrong answers, only a range of options. It is important to be aware of these potential courses of action, and to be ready to exercise them in time of need. The likely consequences of these options are fairly obvious; your choice is a reflection of your personality and values.

Scenario 1. You arrive for an interview and are seated by a secretary/receptionist in a typical meeting room containing a table and chairs. This person tells you that Mr./Mrs. Something-or-Other will be there shortly, and leaves. The minutes pass, and no one shows up. You recognize that you are being tested, or that the interviewer has other priorities. How long do you wait (15 minutes? 30? an hour or two or three?) before:

1. Asking the secretary to contact the interviewer
2. Telling the secretary that you have to leave at a certain time
3. Jotting a note on the back of your card and leaving
4. Just leaving

Or do you just sit back and wait, no matter how long it takes? To what extent are you influenced by how badly you want the job? How much are you willing to put up with in order to get the job? One answer is that you should wait until you begin to feel annoyed or that you are being put upon. Why? Because it is better to reschedule the interview than to have your annoyance interfere with the interview—and interfere it will, because it is difficult to hide annoyance.

Scenario 2. After keeping you waiting for an hour or more, the interviewer arrives without apologizing, complaining that there isn't enough time to do all the things he or she needs to do (as if you are responsible for the inconvenience). Throughout the interview the interviewer takes obvious and frequent time checks and repeatedly interrupts you before you can finish what you're saying. What do you do?

1. You ignore the interruptions and continue as if everything were perfectly normal. *If interruptions really do not bother you, no problem!*
2. You ask the interviewer if it might not be preferable to reschedule the interview for a more convenient time. *This is a polite way of letting the interviewer know that you are not prepared to continue.*
3. You tell the interviewer that you do not believe you are receiving a proper opportunity to present your credentials for the job. *There are times when a degree of aggressiveness may be appropriate, as long as it suits your personality.*
4. You suggest (preferably without sarcasm) that both of you might be more comfortable if someone else continued the interview with you. *This is likely to impress the interviewer, although the impression may be negative. On the other hand, there's an outside chance that this was just what the interviewer was looking for.*
5. You refuse to put up with it and leave. *Of course, this will probably end any chance of your getting the job.*

Scenario 3. You arrive for an interview in a conference-room-sized office. The interviewer, who is seated to one side of the room behind a desk, tells you that he or she will be with you in a minute. The only chairs in the room, aside from the interviewer's, are around the table at the opposite end of the room. What do you do?

As in the preceding scenarios, your choice should be the one with which you are most comfortable and for which you are prepared to accept the consequences.

1. You quietly wait for the interviewer to tell you what to do. *After all, the interviewer is running the show.*
2. You ask the interviewer where to sit. *This is the polite thing to do.*
3. You wander around the office, waiting for the interviewer to act. *The interviewer will get around to you when he or she is ready; meanwhile, you'll do your thing.*
4. You invite the interviewer to join you at the table. *This is a polite way of asserting yourself.*
5. You bring a chair from the table to the desk and sit down. *This is an aggressive way to assert yourself.*

6. You sit in a chair at the table, and wait. *Patience is a virtue.*
7. You sit in a chair at the table and read a newspaper (pretend to make notes in a notebook, etc.). *Two can play that game.*
8. You sit on a corner of the table and glance at your watch from time to time. *You are not intimidated, and you haven't got all day.*
9. You turn around and leave. *You don't need this.*
10. You tell the interviewer off, and then leave. *Who do they think they are, anyway?*

Postinterview Follow-Up

Communicating

If your interview was arranged by an agency, call your contact no later than the afternoon following a morning interview, or the very next morning after an afternoon interview (unless the interviewer calls you first). Avoid the temptation to call or write directly to the interviewer, unless he or she is expecting you to follow up with information.

Negotiating for a Salaried Position

Do your best to find out the going rate for the job you want, and how much you can reasonably expect them to pay you. Then consider the least you are willing to accept. Now you're ready to negotiate.

Never bring up the question of salary yourself; try to avoid revealing what you are currently earning, unless they insist, with a comment like, "I would rather not discuss that." If they say they need to know what you are earning in order to make you an offer, you can suggest a figure that you know to be within their range. Once you ask for a certain amount, unless you are willing to negotiate, be prepared to stick to it. If their offer is final but a little on the low side, you could ask that, if they are satisfied with your performance after six months (for example), they then give you a salary review (i.e., more money). It never hurts to try.

Negotiating for a Consulting Contract

Once your qualifications for the job have been established, try to find out what the client/agency is willing to pay. Of course, agencies are skilled negotiators, and they may have alternative resources from which to choose. Typically, they will ask you your rate. If you give them a precise number, there is little chance of their offering you more; if you give them a range, there may be room for discussion without scaring them away. If you are adamant, obviously there is no room for negotiation.

To negotiate your rate successfully, you must be aware of what the market will bear in your specialty. Your willingness to accept a lower rate than you would like, for a period of time, depends upon your need.

Managing Your Expectations

Just as you convinced the interviewer—and yourself—that you wanted the job during the interview, consider afterward the possibility that you may not get it. Try not to let any one position or contract become so important that you will be severely disappointed if it doesn't work out. Conversely, don't talk yourself into believing that you did a bad job at the interview.

Remember that—whether you get it or not—it's only a job.

Summary

The job interview is an unavoidable part of earning a living. Interviewing is hard work. The bad news is that a lot of otherwise talented people are surprisingly poor interviewees; the good news is that it is a skill you can improve—and well worth the effort. Consider it an investment not only in obtaining a job but also in keeping a job and moving on to better jobs. Keep in mind that the fundamental principles of successful interviewing (preparation and presentation) are the building blocks of nearly every aspect of your professional career.

Sure, interviewing is hard work, but like most things, it gets easier when you get better at it. You can improve your interviewing skills by practicing on family members and friends. Every morning, before you pick up the phone or leave for an interview, tell yourself that *today may be the day.* Interviewing is a tough job, and getting yourself psyched up is an essential part of preparing to succeed. When you show up for an interview, present the most confident and enthusiastic candidate you're capable of being.

Bibliography

Harper, John J. Marcus, *The Complete Job Interview Handbook,* 3d ed., Perennial, 1994.

Medley, Anthony, *Sweaty Palms: The Art of Being Interviewed,* Tenspeed Press, 1993.

The National Business Employment Weekly, a weekly journal published by the *Wall Street Journal* oriented toward every aspect of seeking jobs and improving careers.

2
HTML and XML

Carl Burnham

Introduction

The *Hypertext Markup Language* (HTML) and the *eXtensible Markup Language* (XML) share a common beginning with the Standard Generalized Markup Language (SGML) a descriptive language created for the publishing of large documents. Both HTML and XML are together evolving rapidly to enable innovative presentations on the Web. XML is being built into most new software versions and operating systems. The potential Web developer/designer needs to be aware of these changes and how to effectively use these languages each in current and future browser versions and applications.

An Introduction to HTML

Tim Berners-Lee, a *European Particle Physics Laboratory* (CERN) scientist, originated the World Wide Web in 1989. A year later, he went on to write the first Web browser and called it the "World Wide Web." Since that time, the World Wide Web has continued to evolve and expand at a phenomenal rate to become the information resource that it is today. The markup language for the Web, which has been used since the beginning has been HTML.

HTML is a non-proprietary language, consisting of an ASCII text file augmented with standard markup tags that enable content to be viewed within a browser. At its most basic, an HTML document will consist of the following structure:

```
<HTML>
<HEAD>
<TITLE>This is the title of the document</TITLE>
```

...Within this section other head elements such as metatags, descriptive tags, author, and copyright information can be found...

```
</HEAD>
<BODY>
```

...The body section typically includes content, which is marked up to represent the text data, along with font, background, and linkage attributes. It may also contain code snippets for other scripting languages (which may also be in the head section) ...

```
</BODY>
</HTML>
```

HTML can be written using a text-based program, such as Notepad in Windows. Those who need to maintain a Web site consisting of numerous HTML files may find that popular Web editing programs such as Microsoft Frontpage, Macromedia Dreamweaver, Adobe GoLive, NetObjects Fusion, or SoftQuad HotMetal Pro can assist with developing. It is critical, though, that a candidate for a position as a Web developer/designer know how to program in HTML in order to know what happens behind the scenes in the actual HTML code. In addition, several Web editors are known to add their proprietary tags to coding, which can cause problems with certain browser versions.

The latest version of HTML is HTML 4.0. It is defined by the *World Wide Web Consortium* (W3C) standards body and supported by the latest version web browsers.

An Introduction to XML

Since its introduction in 1996, XML has continued to develop rapidly, with the introduction of XML-based applications and new meta-language features. Its widespread adoption can be attributed to the descriptive way that XML can be used to mark up data for browsers and devices, even within databases and e-commerce applications.

XML, like HTML, is a non-proprietary language. It can also be written using a text-based program, although it is more structured than HTML. XML is based on the Unicode character set, which allows more characters to be defined than can be defined in an ASCII text file. XML documents typically use either a *Document Type Definition* (DTD) or a Schema to determine the type of structure that data in the XML document will have. The very first XML application was *Channel Definition Format* (CDF), a Microsoft technology that became available in February of 1997. The current version of XML is version 1.0 (a W3C Recommendation as of February 1998).

In the next version of HTML, the features of XML 1.0 are combined with HTML 4.0 to provide much more functionality; a key feature enables direct access to Web content via wireless devices. Called XHTML 1.0 (Extensible HyperText Markup Language), it is a W3C Recommendation as of January 2000. The benefits of XHTML are numerous, including the addition of new elements to HTML, greater scalability, and adaptability with wireless devices. The first browser to be able to utilize the features of XHTML is Microsoft Internet Explorer 5.0.

Existing HTML documents (even if HTML 4.0-compliant), will need to make changes in order to be a "well-formed" XHTML document and in order to work properly. Other changes include the requirements that tags and attributes be in lower case, that attributes values be within quotes, and that empty tags have matching closing tags. XHTML tools that can assist with the conversion of existing documents are beginning to appear.

Level of Expertise

The questions and answers listed here begin at the novice level (a knowledge level equal to between six months and one year of use) and progress to an advanced level (a knowledge level equal to two years or more of use, accompanied by the completion of coursework, including advanced HTML/XML and scripting languages). The topic questions listed here have been designed to cover some but not all of the key areas with which a Web developer/designer candidate needs to be familiar for each technology discussed in this section. The section includes questions and answers for both HTML and XML. Depending upon the position, the candidate might also need to have a working knowledge of Internet protocols and some familiarity with the use of programming languages within HTML and XML, including JavaScript, Java, JSP, or ASP.

Questions and Answers - HTML

HTML - Novice Level

Q: *HTML stands for what?*

A: It stands for HyperText Markup Language, which is used to design Web pages.

Q: *What is the tag that is placed at the beginning of a file?*

A: An HTML file begins with the <html> tag. A closing tag (</html>) is placed at the end of the file.

Q: *HTML tags must be uppercase. True or false?*

A: False. HTML tags are not case-sensitive.

Q: *What are the two types of imagemaps?*

A: The two types of imagemaps are server-side and client-side.

Q: *What is a common alternative to using imagemaps?*

A: Image slicing, where an image is sliced and put into closely corresponding cells of a table, is a commonly used alternative.

Q: *What are the two main parts of an HTML document called?*

A: The head and the body. The head contains descriptions of the content, and the body contains the code that is displayed by the Web browser.

Q: *Where is the title of a document placed in an HTML document?*

A: The title is located in the header section between the opening and closing tags (<head> . . . </head>). This section can also contain descriptive <meta> tags, which are used by search engines to find and categorize the document on the Web.

Q: *Encode the following text as the title for an HTML document:* The Business of the Web

A: `<HTML><HEAD><TITLE>The Business of the Web</TITLE></HEAD>`

Q: *What is the tag used to add a link to the Website* `www.mcgraw-hill.com` *so that when users click on "McGraw-Hill Books" (without the quotes) on a web page, they will be taken to the site?*

A: `<A HREF="http://www.mcgraw-hill.com">McGraw-Hill Books</A>`

Q: *What is the tag parameter that refers to a hyperlink's color when clicked?*

A: The ALINK (active link) refers to the hyperlink's color.

Q: *What tag parameter refers to the color of a hyperlink that has been clicked on before?*

A: The tag parameter is VLINK (visited link).

Q: *Name at least two Web authoring tools that provide a WYSIWYG (What You See Is What You Get) approach to designing Web pages.*

A: Microsoft Frontpage and Macromedia Dreamweaver are two leading tools. Another is Adobe PageMill. These authoring tools assist with the learning process, allowing users to view the HTML code and to test different page layouts prior to production.

Q: *Name a disadvantage of using a Web-authoring program for designing Web pages.*

A: The disadvantages of using an authoring program include the extra proprietary code that is added to HTML in some cases, the concern that the code generated may not match the current HTML version specifications, and the fact that a solid foundation is needed in HTML to gain a clear understanding of Web page design. The author needs to know what is going on under the hood in order to make manual changes to coding when they are needed.

Q: *What type of list does <ul>..</ul> reference?*

A: It refers to a bulleted list.

Q: *What new typographic feature is supported by HTML 4.0?*

A: It supports *Cascading Style Sheets* (CSS).

Q: *Which of the following tags gives the correct syntax for representing an image:*

a. `<IMG> ="images/house.jpg">This is the house</IMG>`
b. `<IMG SRC=images/house.jpg>`
c. `<imgsrc="images/house.jpg">`
d. `<IMG SRC="images/house.jpg">`

A: The correct answer is d.

Q: *What is CGI short for?*

A: CGI stands for Common Gateway Interface. CGI is a method of running a program (typically written in Python, C, C++, or PERL) on a Web server. The typical location of the program is in the cgi-bin subdirectory of the Web server.

Q: *What is the disadvantage of using CGI?*

A: Disadvantages include lack of maintenance (the server creates a new process on every single instance where the program is called), slow performance, lack of security, and portability issues when moving files to other Web server platforms.

Q: *What are some alternatives to CGI for server-side processing?*

A: Alternatives include ASP, JSP (and Java servlets), PHP, and SSI. Technologies, such as JSP run once (instead of every instance with CGI), and are run in protected memory mode on the Web server.

Q: *What is <P> and <BR> used for?*

A: <P> is used when starting a new paragraph, and <BR> is used to add a line break within your HTML file.

Q: *What does the parameter SRC stand for in your coding?*

A: SRC refers to the source URL; it is used with frames, images, media files, and links.

Q: *What do you use to control how text and background colors appear when using links?*

A: The <BODY> tag is used to control the color used for links.

Q: *What color is referenced (and where) by bgcolor="#FFFFFF"?*

A: The white background of a page is referenced.

Q: *How do you center a paragraph?*

A: Use <P ALIGN=CENTER>.

Q: *Which organization is responsible for proposing HTML and XML standards?*

A: The World Wide Web Consortium (W3C). The W3C consists of over 400 member organizations involved with setting Web standards.

Q: *What does <HR> stand for?*

A: This is a horizontal rule tag that is used as a separator on a page.

HTML - Intermediate Level

Q: *How would you create a link to the graphics file newgraphic.jpg with no borders?*

A: You would include within the anchor tag <A HREF="filename.html"> <IMG SRC="newgraphic.jpg" BORDER=0></A>

Because you have specified no border, the text color will not be around the image.

Q: *How would you add the HTML coding to link to an FTP site called anftpsite.com, with general being the default directory?*

A: Within your code, add: <A HREF=ftp://ftp.anftpsite.com/general">an ftp site</A>

Q: *Give two examples showing when an alt attribute would be used within your HTML code.*

A: The alt attribute can be used with a Java applet and with describing images. The alt attribute can display text if a Java applet tag (<applet>) cannot be displayed within a browser. In addition, it can be used as part of the image tag (<img>) to describe the image for search engines, and also to display text if an image cannot be displayed.

Q: *A detailed table with graphics may sometimes take time to load in a browser. What is the primary method used to ensure that a table loads optimally?*

A: When placing graphics within a table, make sure that each includes WIDTH and HEIGHT tag attributes.

Q: *What is the process of using multiple tags on a single element?*

A: This process is referred to as nesting. The secondary tags must be contained within the initial tag, or errors may occur.

An example:

The party is starting at <I><BIG>9:00</BIG></I>, not 8:00. (This is correct.)

The party is starting at <I><BIG>9:00</I></BIG>, not 8:00. (This is not correct.)

Q: *Where is the <FRAME> tag always placed?*

A: It is always placed within the <FRAMESET> tag when using frames.

Q: *You want to place two frames, with the first column being 150 pixels wide. You want to name the first frame "main.html", and the second frame "details.html." How would this be represented in code?*

A:
```
<FRAMESET COLS="150,*">
<FRAME SRC="main.html">
<FRAME SRC="details.html">
</FRAMESET>
```

The first window will be 150 pixels wide, containing "main.html." The second one will contain "details.html" and will take up the remaining portion of the page.

Q: *If using frames, what must be added for older browsers that do not support frames?*

A: Within the <FRAMESET>..</FRAMESET> brackets, add the following:
<NOFRAMES>This page uses frames, your browser version does not support. </NOFRAMES>

Q: *How do you ensure that frames can be indexed by search engines?*

A: Within the <NOFRAMES>..</NOFRAMES> brackets, include a link to a page containing the same content as the frame so that search engines can index properly.

Q: *Name the two parameters used in a <FORM> tag.*

A: The two parameters are ACTION and METHOD.

Q: *What value within a <FORM> tag sends any form results through the URL?*

A: The Get value, in the METHOD parameter of the <FORM> tag, sends form results.

Q: *Where is the URL (usually a cgi-bin directory) placed within a <FORM> tag?*

A: The URL is placed in the ACTION parameter section.

Q: *In adding a form to your HTML document, what is the best way to make sure that it is aligned properly?*

A: Your form will be more structured if placed in a table.

Q: *What is a <TD> tag, and where is it placed?*

A: The <TD> tag is used to denote an element within a table.

Q: *What comes before a <TD> tag in a table?*

A: A <TR> tag, which represents a table row, should come before a <TD> tag.

Q: *How would a cell within a table be listed if it were 300 pixels wide?*

A: The cell would be listed as follows: <td width="300">.

Q: *What is another way to represent the <applet> element?*

A: You can use the <object> element, which is included as the suggested method from version HTML 4.0 forward.

Q: *When designing a page, you want to have the background color as dark blue. Which of the following lines of code would be the better choice?*

a. `<BODY BGCOLOR="darkblue">`

b. `<BODY BGCOLOR="000099">`

A: If the goal is to accommodate the greatest number of users, select choice b, which is supported by older browser versions.

Q: *What is the standard tag included at the beginning of an HTML document if it claims to be a "valid" HTML 4.0 document?*

A: A line similar to the following is used to claim validity:

```
<!DOCTYPE HTML PUBLIC "-//W3C//DTD HTML 4.0//EN">
```

Q: *What version of HTML uses the <object> element?*

A: The <object> element element is an alternative way to represent <applet> or <embed> tags, as of HTML 4.0.

Q: *How would you reference the email address agriffith@mays.com in your code and provide the link "Email Us" (without the quotes) to it?*

A: You would reference it as follows:

```
<A HREF="mailto:agriffith@mays.com">Email Us</A>
```

Q: *How would you list a radio button tag whose value is "fifth-wheel," with the group name being "RV," and with text to the right of the button?*

A: <INPUT TYPE="radio" VALUE="fifth-wheel" NAME="RV">fifth-wheel would be the correct method of listing this radio button tag.

Q: *How do you put a heading in a table?*

A: Use the <TH> tag to put a heading in a table.

Q: *What is another function, besides defining a hyperlink, of the <A> tag?*

A: To move to another location within a page, a bookmark or "anchor" can be defined with an <A> tag. An examble would be `<A HREF="#reference">reference material</ A:.`

Q: *What is another way to represent the <center> element?*

A: <DIV align=center> is the suggested method in HTML 4.0. As older browsers do not recognize this command, text marked this way will have a left alignment instead. Both tags can be nested together, though, to accommodate older browsers, if needed.

Q: *Can JavaScript code be referenced in the beginning of a document?*

A: Yes. JavaScript can be located in the head section of an HTML document, as well as in the body. Any JavaScript document declarations and subroutines are placed here.This also applies to VBScript.

HTML - Advanced Level

Q: *How does using alt attributes within your HTML code in your Web site help in attracting visitors?*

A: Many search engines use alt attributes when analyzing a Web site, and using descriptive alt tags can contribute to a Web site being rated higher in search results .

Q: *What is the <EM> tag used for?*

A: The <EM> tag is used to emphasize text. This is usually represented by italics within most browsers.

Q: *Provide four examples of the use of <EMBED> tag.*

A: The <EMBED> tag is used when representing Macromedia Flash files, audio (such as mpeg, wav, midi, or Shockwave) files, or when streaming video (such as ra, mp2, or mov files). When the tag is included in the HTML, it works with a browser plug-in to handle the media file. In some cases, especially if an older browser is used, a plug-in may need to be downloaded before it will work properly.

Q: *What is an alternative tag that can be used in place of the <EMBED> tag?*

A: The <OBJECT> tag can be used in place of the <EMBED> tag. It is also used with ActiveX controls, although it is not supported by WebTV, and it is not recognized by browsers prior to version 4.0. It is likely, though, to become more prevalent than the <embed> tag as it is more widely supported by industry leaders.

Q: *How would you embed an avi file named movie.avi within a page and how would you program for browsers that may have problems?*

A:
```
<EMBED SRC="movie.avi">
<NOEMBED>
<A HREF="movie.avi">Movie</A>
</NOEMBED>
```

Q: *When is the <NOEMBED> tag used?*

A: Some older browsers (Internet Explorer 1.0, 2.0, and Netscape 1.0) do not support the <EMBED> tag. Keep this in mind when trying to code for older browsers.

Q: *To add a comment that would appear for older browsers that can't run a Javascript or Visual Basic client-side script, what element would you need?*

A: <NOSCRIPT>This Web page requires JavaScript 1.1 in order to run correctly. </NOSCRIPT>

The text is shown that is within the opening and closing NOSCRIPT tag area, if an older browser is unable to run the <SCRIPT> element.

Q: *For browsers that do not support it, what is the most common method of hiding JavaScript?*

A:
```
<SCRIPT LANGUAGE="JavaScript">
  <!–
  … JavaScript code goes here  …
  … is hidden from non-enabled browsers …

  //–>
</SCRIPT>
```

Q: *Other than using the BGCOLOR attribute, how could an author represent the background color of a page?*

A: Using *Cascasing Style Sheets* (CCSs) is the method suggested from version HTML 4.0 forward.

Q: *What is a key limitation (as of this printing) of using CCSs for Web designers?*

A: Although the technology has potential for the presentation of HTML documents, CSS is not fully supported by existing or older browser versions. In addition, different browser implementations (namely Microsoft Internet Explorer and Netscape Navigator) currently support different CSS features.

Q: *Name the three types of CCS.*

A: The three types are embedded, inline, and linked.

Q: *What kind of CSS is represented by the following:*

```
<STYLE TYPE="text/css">
<!- A.blue {color: #0000FF} >
</STYLE>
```

A: Embedded.

Q: *What is considered the most efficient CSS for a Web site to use?*

A: The linked stylesheet, where a single file can contain all the definitions for each page on a Web site, is the most efficient CSS.

Q: *Name a form of HTML that uses CSS and a DOM (Document Object Model)?*

A: *Dynamic HTML* (DHTML) is able to produce visually attractive Web pages, somewhat similar to those produced by Flash. DHTML also uses JavaScript.

Q: *What are some drawbacks to using the above technology?*

A: DHTML is currently supported only by browser versions 4.0 and higher. The learning curve for DHTML is higher than that for HTML, and it is also not protected from being copied, as with Flash technology.

Q: *How would the coding be added for the following definition list?*

Router

A device which forwards packets from one network to another, based on destination address.

Routing Table

A table that a router uses to track internetworking traffic.

A: Note that the closing tags are not required:

```
<DL>
<DT>Router
<DD>A device which forwards packets from one network to
  another, based on destination address.
<DT>Routing Table
<DD>A table that a router uses to track internetworking traf-
  fic.
</DL>
```

Q: *How do you open a second browser window from a link that allows the current browser window to remain open?*

A: Using the TARGET="_blank" attribute will accomplish this.

For example, <A HREF=http://www.southpoint.com/ TARGET="_blank"> will open a new browser window.

Q: *How would the coding be added to make the following into an ordered list?*
Sacramento
Denver
Charleston
San Antonio
Biloxi
Savannah
Orlando
Phoenix

A:
```
<OL TYPE="1" START="1">
<LI>Sacramento
   <LI>Denver
   <LI>Charleston
   <LI>San Antonio
   <LI>Biloxi
   <LI>Savannah
   <LI>Orlando
   <LI>Phoenix
   </OL>
```

Q: *Which graphic format is usually used if the graphic contains text?*

A: The gif format is typically used for displaying text graphics. Other formats, such as png, are beginning to be used by designers who desire more flexibility in this area, though png is limited to browser versions 4.0 and higher.

Q: *You want to add an image (sunrise.jpg) to your page, with the dimensions 600x400. You want the image to have no border. The file that the image will be linked to is new.htm. When the mouse goes over the image, you want the text "The mountain view at sunrise" to display. Since the image is large, a low-resolution photo named sunrise1.jpg will be loaded initially, until sunrise.jpg loads. What would your code look like?*

A:
```
<a href="new.htm"><img
src="sunrise.jpg" width="250" height="180" alt="The moun-
tain view at sunrise"
lowsrc="sunrisel.jpg" border="0"></a>
```

Q: *How would you code the text "This is it" as a Times New Roman font set to 5, with the color being blue?*

A:
```
<font face="Times New Roman" size="5" color="#0000FF">This
is it</font>
```

Q: *How would the following be coded for display on a page?*

© July 2000

A:
```
&copy; July 2000
```

The & ESCAPE SEQUENCE is used to display symbols, along with < (less than) and > (greater than).

Q: *What HTML tag is used to denote a server-side JavaScript?*

A: The tag for server-side JavaScript would be <SERVER>. If client-side, the tag would be represented as <SCRIPT>.

Q: *How would you embed a file called designdetails.pdf as a plug-in, located in the newdrawings folder at* `www.thisisnotawebsite.com`?

A:
```
<A
HREF="http://www.thisisnotawebsite.com/newdrawings/design-
details.pdf">
```

Q: *How would you add coding to an HTML file to load the URL* `www.mcgraw-hill.com after five seconds?`

A:
```
<meta http-equiv="refresh" content="5;URL=www.mcgraw-
hill.com">
```

Questions and Answers - XML

XML - Novice Level

Q: *Why use XML?*

A: *XML (eXtensible Markup Language) allows data to be structured in a way that can be presented in a wide range of formats. Most new software developments are based on the expanded flexibility which XML brings to data, and it will be a part of the next version of HTML (XHTML).*

Q: *Will XML replace HTML?*

A: No, according to the W3C organization, version 5 of HTML will be called XHTML (a combination of XML and HTML).

Q: *What does DTD stand for?*

A: A Document Type Definition (DTD) is a file that defines how XML tags can be shown with the correct syntax for XML documents.

Q: *Name at least four types of markup that can be found in XML documents.*

A: These markup types include elements, DTDs, entity references, marked sections, processing instructions, and comments.

Q: *What language are both HTML and XML based on?*

A: Both languages are based on Standard Generalized Markup Language (SGML), which was an early standard meta-language recommended by the W3C for use in structuring documents for the publishing industry.

Q: *Consider the following:*

<state><city/></state>. What is the state element in relation to the city element?

A: The <state> element is the parent element of the <city>. In other words, the city element is nested within the state element.

Q: *What is the typical declaration at the beginning of an XML document?*

A:
```
<?xml version="1.0"?>
```

This statement specifies that the document complies with version 1.0 of the XML specification.

Q: *With which browser versions does XHTML work?*

A: It works with browsers 4.0 and higher.

Q: *What is XHTML?*

A: *EXtensible HyperText Markup Language* (XHTML) is a W3C Recommendation for version 5 of HTML, which blends the features of XML tags with HTML presentation as part of one file.

Q: *What is the most common form of markup in an XML document?*

A: Elements are the most common form of markup.

Q: *What is <list> as it is referred to in XML?*

A: The <list> element is an example of a root element, which is not a part of any other element.

Q: *How else could you describe a root element?*

A: A root element can also be described as a document element.

Q: *How does the title "New Method for Designing" appear in the XML markup for a page?*

A: `<TITLE>New Method for Designing</TITLE>`

This is the same as for HTML.

Q: *What is Microsoft's Web translation service and schema for XML called?*

A: It is called BizTalk.

Q: *An XML document can be well formed without elements. True or false?*

A: False; an XML document must contain at least one element.

Q: *What term is used to describe the placement of a secondary tag inside another tag?*

A: Nesting, which works the same in XML as it does in HTML.

Q: *Name at least two ways that you can make changes to your HTML file to turn it into an XML file.*

A: Changes that can be made to a file include making sure that every element includes an ending tag (for example, <hr> requires a closing tag </hr>), putting attribute values in quotes (" "), adding an XML declaration (denoted by <?xml version="1.0" standalone="yes"?>), matching case for all tags, and using escape for any markup characters (such as replacing & with &).

Q: *An element always has an opening angle bracket < > and closing </>. True or false?*

A: False. If an element is empty, it can have an opening < > only.

Q: *If an XML document doesn't include a DTD, it is said to be what? And if it does, what is the term used to describe it?*

A: If it does not include a DTD, it is considered well formed. If an XML document does include a DTD, it is considered to be valid.

Q: *What is a DOM and when is it used?*

A: A Document Object Model (DOM) is a parser that turns text into an XML tree format, which can then be further modified.

Q: *What are some different types of XML parsers?*

A: *Simple API for XML* (SAX) is a parser that is typically centered around the parsing of events in large XML documents.

DOM is a parser that turns text into an XML tree format, which can then be further modified.

A validating parser is one that reads from an XML Schema or a DTD to verify the resulting XML document matches with the schema.

Q: *In order to reference a URL within your XML document, it must first be defined within a CDATA section. True or false?*

A: False, the correct location for the reference is within a DTD.

Q: *What is another name for an element?*

A: A tag.

Q: *XML is similar to SGML in that both are well formed. True or false?*

A: False, SGML was not designed to be well formed.

Q: *XML ignores white space. True or false?*

A: False, white space is not ignored with XML. There are attributes that can define how it is handled.

Q: *How, other than with a DTD, can you describe an XML document?*

A: Schemas can also be used to define how a document is structured.

Q: `<guides_utah></guides_utah>`

What is another way that this element can be stated when it contains no data?

A: `<guides_utah/>`

Q: *<listing_new/> and <LISTING_NEW/> reference the same elements. True or false?*

A: False, XML is a case-sensitive language.

Q: *A well-formed document always starts with a declaration. True or false?*

A: The above statement is true.

Q: *When an XML document is stated to be valid, it means that it references a DTD. True or false?*

A: This is true.

XML - Intermediate Level

Q: *What is XSL?*

A: XSL stands for EXtensible Stylesheet Language; it controls how XML is presented on the Web by using templates to describe patterns in a document.

Q: *How would an XSL stylesheet called "newsletter.xsl" be referenced within an XML document?*

A:
```
<?xml:stylesheet type="text/xsl" href="newsletter.xsl"?>
```

This line tells the browser to reference newsletter.xsl as the stylesheet for the XML document. This line is listed in an XML document after an XML declaration.

Q: *For the following code snippet in XSL, what is heading in relation to newsletter?*

```
<xsl:template match="newsletter/heading">..</xsl:template>
```

A: The heading is a direct child of the newsletter element.

Q: *What is XSLT?*

A: *XSL Transformations* (XSLT) is a part of XSL, which controls how XML is output and which allows elements to be used for different functions.

Q: *Name at least two XML standards that have been proposed for a Business To Business (B2B) exchange of data.*

A: Those that have released specifications include BizTalk by Microsoft, cXML by Ariba, and CBL by Commerce One.

Q: *What are two ways to allow XML to work closely with databases?*

A: The use of a SAX or parser would allow this. A SAX is typically used to parse events in large XML documents. DOM (available with browsers 5.0 and higher) deals with inheritance, typing, and constants in a hierarchical-tree manner for XML documents in general.

Q: *What is > an example of?*

A: This is an example of a character entity for the greater than sign (>).

Q: *Show an alternative way that > can be represented in an XML document such that the output shows the following: The sum is > than the parts.*

A:
```
<xml>
    <! [CDATA[The sum is > than the parts.] ] >
</xml>
```

By placing them in a CDATA section of your XML, these special characters can be displayed correctly on the page.

Q: *Within an XML document, all elements that are in your DTD must be declared. True or false?*

A: This is true.

Q: *For the following, which is correct?*

A. <div class="heading">

B. <div "class =heading">

C. div class="heading"

D. <div class>"heading"</div>

A: The correct answer is A.

Q: *What is class in relation to div in the question above?*

A: Class is an attribute of the div element, which has the value heading.

Q: *What does xmlns within coding represent?*

A: It represents a namespace.

Q: *Where is a namespace declared when used in a DTD?*

A: A namespace element must first be declared within an ATTLIST declaration.

Q: *The following code can be referred to as a declaration; what else could it be called?*

```
<?xml version="1.0" ?>
```

A: It could also be called a *processing instruction,* (PI). This is represented by <?...?> within an XML document, and it allows the sending of specific instructions to an application.

Q: *When using namespaces or elements, a colon can be used. True or false?*

A: False, a colon can only be used with namespaces.

Q: *A DTD for an XML document is always referenced from another document. True or false?*

A: False, a DTD can be referenced from within an XML document or as a separate document.

Q: *Name at least two entities that are reserved as character entities.*

A: Character entities include

the less than sign (<), which is represented by <
the greater than sign (>), which is represented by >
the apostrophe, which is represented by '
the quote, which is represented by "e; and
the ampersand (&), which is represented by &
They are represented this way so as to keep out of markup.

Q: *How would an image file described as "Arches National Park" and called arches.jpg be referenced within an XML document?*

A: <IMG SRC="arches.jpg">Arches National Park</IMG>

Q: *When XML documents that contain the same element names are combined, what is used to keep elements from colliding and to be sure that they are identified?*

A: Namespaces are used to make sure that element names are unique and are denoted by xmlns: within XML.

Q: *How does an XML Schema differ from a DTD?*

A: Although both serve the purpose of defining the content of an XML document, an XML Schema provides more detail about how the data will be organized and defined by way of Schema Definitions. The W3C has released a specification for a standard XML Schema.

Q: *What does PCDATA stand for?*

A: PCDATA stands for Parsed Character Data.

Q: *How would you specify that elements named Guide and Newsletter are child elements of the <Southpoint:Website> element?*

A:
```
<!ELEMENT Southpoint:Website (Southpoint:Guide,
Southpoint:Newsletter)>
```

XML - Advanced Level

Q: *Besides being able to work on multiple platforms and with new WAP wireless devices, what is another advantage of XHTML?*

A: XHTML can extend an XML file by adding additional elements without having to modify the DTD to which the file refers.

Q: *How would the following be coded within XML?*

Fred & Alice

A:
```
<ampersand>
    Fred &amp; Alice
</ampersand>
```

The & symbol cannot appear (nor can < or >) within the markup unless it is well-formed.

Q: *If wanting to directly reference http://www.southpoint.com/updates/traveltips.xml within an XML document, how would it first be declared as an external entity?*

A:
```
<!ENTITY traveltips SYSTEM
"http://www.southpoint.com/updates/traveltips.xml">
```

Q: *How would the above be referenced within an XML document?*

A:
```
<document>
    <heading>Travel Tips</heading>
    &traveltips;
</document>
```

Q: *What are two other methods for coding links within XML?*

A: XLink and XPointer, two relatively new XML technologies, can also code links.

Q: *Consider the following:*

```
<!DOCTYPE Santana:Music SYSTEM "reference.dtd">
```

What does Santana:Music represent?

A: This is the root element for the XML document.

Q: *If a document is well formed without a DTD, what are the attributes?*

A: All attributes will be of type CDATA, which stands for character data.

Q: *Which attribute is used if white space must be added to an element?*

A: The reserved attribute xml:space must be added.

Q: *Which attribute is used to designate that a specific language is to be used with an element?*

A: The reserved attribute xml:lang is used.

Q: *CSS and XSLT are not capable of working together. True or false?*

A: False; they are capable of working together.

Q: *If you want to change an XML document into a table, which is best to use: CSS or XSLT?*

A: XSLT. Other formats that an XML document can be changed into, in addition to tables, include lists, modified elements, or formats such as HTML. CSS is designed to work well with the appearance of the source document.

Q: *Name at least one XML method that can be used to add fields from a database to a document.*

A: A database can be accessed through a DOM API, after being loaded as an object. Another method would involve creating an XSL stylesheet.

Q: *Name two XML database products.*

A: XML database products include eXcelon, DataChannel, Tamino, and Poet.

Q: *When using XPointer, what is used to search for elements that have similar attributes?*

A: attr( )

The attribute name will appear within parenthesis.

Q: *What is SOAP?*

A: *Simple Object Access Protocol* (SOAP) uses HTTP to transfer XML documents in a platform-independent manner via the Internet.

Q: *Where are notations usually used when describing attribute types?*

A: Notations are used with unparsed entities (usually binary files), which are defined in the DTD.

Q: *What is SMIL?*

A: *Synchronized Multimedia Integration Language* (SMIL) is based on XML and it allows multimedia to be controlled and edited easily.

Q: *Within an XML declaration, if not specified, what type of encoding is used?*

A: UTF-8 encoding is used. This specifies the use of the Unicode character set.

Q: *With Internet Explorer version 5.0, what are two ways that XML can be embedded within HTML?*

A: XML can be embedded through the use of <XML>...</XML> inline tags and by using the SRC attribute to denote an external XML document. With this browser version, these two methods are referred to as data islands.

Q: *The version 4.0 browsers provide native support for XML. True or false?*

A: False. At the time of this writing, Internet Explorer version 5.0 is the only browser that provides this support.

Q. What character set does XML have in common with Java?

A: Both XML and Java are based on Unicode instead of on ASCII text, which allows for a much wider range of characters.

Q: *What is needed in order for a Web server to recognize XML?*

A: Verifying that the mime-type includes text/xml for files ending with .xml to be recognized. This will allow access to the full Unicode character set.

3
Java

Chris Bailey

Introduction

Java is the programming language of choice. No other language can claim to have been as wildly successful, going from inception to a million users in only a few years. In a majority of business environments, client, server, mid-tier, or special purpose, Java is the language in which systems developers must be proficient. When embarking on a career in information technology, it is necessary to be familiar with Java, unless you are maintaining a legacy system. Because Java developers are in such great demand, supply has not kept up and the salaries of Java developers continue to rise.

One simple metric of the success of a new product or service often used by those at Javasoft is the amount of Java documentation for sale. In 1996, it was difficult to find books on Java. In 1997, bookstores had a few bookshelves filled with Java books. Now, nearly any bookstore with a technology section will have many bookshelves filled with books on Java. Clearly, authors would not write such books were there not a great demand for the language. To this end, when interviewing, we need to see which candidates have read of the literature, used the language, and understand the topic.

As the vice president of Javasoft told us on a recent visit, one of the primary development principles in creating the Java language was to ensure that the language and its usage stayed very simple. Thus, even though the class libraries are extensive, and continue to grow, the core language is both easy to use and fairly error free during execution. This has doubtless contributed to the success of the language, now known as Java, originally called OAK, which had very modest goals, certainly not to be the programming language of choice for nearly all aspects of development today.

My name is Chris Bailey and I'm a Principal Software Developer at SAS Institute Inc., where I have been working since 1984. My areas of expertise include Java, C, distributed programming and EJB, and a proprietary commercial language I co-authored called SCL. I am frequently called upon to do technical interviews, to assess a candidate's technical competency. In assessing technical competency, it is common to use a few categories, including basic knowledge, advanced in-depth knowledge, and, at the highest level, "deployment" knowledge. Basic knowledge determines whether the item should have appeared on the candidate's resume as a skill set. In-depth knowledge determines a deeper knowledge of the "specification," and deployment knowledge is "why will this work or not work in real life.

When determining the level of Java expertise within our organization, the following would be typical of the types of question we would ask.

Questions and Answers

Q: *Do you like Java, and, if not, why not?*

A: As obvious as this seems, if you're applying for a job harvesting apples, don't tell the foreman you dislike it and would rather shine shoes. In any large organization there are almost always multiple technologies at play, and we don't want anyone in the Java development group squarely on the other side of the C++/Java fence telling us what is wrong with the tools we are using. Conversely, if an applicant were to claim that he loves Java, but cannot include a rationale other than "because it will get me a job at your company", that too is, not the best approach. A good answer for this would be: "because it is a fairly well thought out language, easy to develop in, and catches many more mistakes than other languages I have used, both at compile and at run-time."

Q: *How would you compare Java to C++?*

A: C++ is generally faster at execution because it compiles to native code. C++ has #includes. C++ has more mature development environments, larger libraries, and has much better debuggers. Java stills wins hands-down because it is a well-designed language, not compatible with a legacy language (C++ compatibility with C is its strength and weakness). Java also has garbage collection, is easier to read and is portable. Java does not allow overloading which is frequently misused, the syntax is consistent, and the threads are better. Further, there is no uncertainty as to whether a char is signed or unsigned, an integer is 2, 4, or 8 bytes, and both compile and run-time checking are superior.

Q: *What does "virtual" mean in C++ and why do you not have it in Java?*

A: Virtual means that every method to call to an object must go through an extra offset in the v-table in case it is being overridden by a subclass. In Java every method is implicitly virtual.

Q: *What is an object?*

A: Because everything in Java except a primitive is an object, candidates should be familiar with this term. One possible answer is, "a black box containing data and surfacing the operations that will be performed on that data." Any answer where the candidate roughly describes encapsulation and polymorphism will suffice.

Q: *What is garbage collection?*

A: Java does not have the notion of new/delete or malloc/free, because there are two things a programmer can do wrong with allocated memory: free or not free it. If the programmer frees it, someone else will invariably want to use it. If the programmer cannot free it, the program will leak memory. Java solves this with a notion called "garbage collection" where the programmer only creates objects. When no other objects are referencing a particular object, it can be freed automatically by the virtual machine. This solves the "do, do not" free/delete dilemma, and many claim it is the only viable way to solve "programming in the large."

Q: *What is compaction in relation to garbage collection?*

A: Since all memory references are indirect, Java can maintain a table of what memory is currently being referenced and release those that are not. This is garbage collection. However, in doing so, it may create many "holes" in heap memory. The collector can coalesce these holes, moving the object up into free territory, thereby decreasing fragments and possibly releasing large chunks of contiguous memory at the end back to the operating system.

Q: *If you needed multiple inheritances, for example to extend an event class and a UI class, how would you do this in Java?*

A: The wrong answer, as was stated by one job candidate recently, is "That's easy; you just extend both classes." This made it clear that the candidate did not understand Java, résumé claims not withstanding. One possible answer is to use interfaces, implement the interfaces, extend one of the classes and delegate to the other.

Q: *Why isn't "virtual" needed in Java like it is in C++?*

A: Because everything in Java is virtual. All methods go through the extra cost of indirection for overriding in a subclass.

Q: *Please explain your class hierarchy in a sample project you have done.*

A: An example of an incorrect answer is "I just open and close sockets." A correct answer would be something like, "My Collection extends Vector which extends Objects." What you are looking for in this answer is to confirm that the candidate understands overriding and inheritance, basic object-oriented concepts.

Q: *What's an interface?*

A: It is a list of methods often used as a contract between the caller and the person being called. It is probably also one of the best ideas in Java.

Q: *What's an abstract class?*

A: An abstract class is a class that cannot be instantiated but can have implementation for as many methods as needed.

Q: *Please explain the difference between an interface and an abstract class.*

A: An abstract class can have implementation for some of its methods. Thus, when extending an abstract class, the superclass is known and defined and possibly has some implementation. An interface allows multiple inheritance, and does not mandate what superclass is used. This is a huge advantage, as someone can take an arbitrary class, subclass it, and make it implement an interface simply by adding methods.

Q: *What is the purpose of a Java subclass? What would you use it for and how would you do it in Java?*

A: A subclass is used to inherit the implementation of a superclass to optionally override some of the methods and optionally augment the list of methods. This is done in Java with use of the "extends" keyword.

Q: *How would you make a class that cannot be extended?*

A: Declare the "final." This means that the implementation is exactly known, which might, for example, be useful for security purposes. If someone could simply subclass the "permission checker," then they could add their own class to violate all of the security designed into the system.

Q: *What is variable scoping within Java?*

A: A variable is visible; that is, it can be accessed without any qualifiers, in the scope which it was defined, its containing block, a fancy term for the braces and any nested braces, until something at a deeper nest level hides it with a similar name then there must be a qualifier present, for example:

```
{
  int x;

  // outer x visible, not overriden
  void baz(int y) { x = y; }

  // outer x gets value of inner x
  void foo(int x) { this.x = x; }

}
```

Q: *How do you call a call method in a superclass, especially ones you have overridden in a subclass?*

A: Use the keyword "super" before the call. For example:

```
void foo() { super.foo(); }
```

Q: *In a large system, how does Java avoid name collision?*

A: All large systems can be broken down into groupings and these can be further broken down into categories. Different categories would be put into different Java entities called "packages." Names are unique within packages. For example, if you had two Util classes, then they would be put into unique packages to avoid collision like My Company.My Package.Util and BubbasCompany.BubbasPackage.Util.

Q: *How would you make an array of 10 primitive integers in Java with an initial value of zero?*

```
int[] x = new int[10];
```

A: Although this seems really simple, people that have experience in other languages can easily make a mistake here. For example:

```
int x[10];
```

Another typical mistake would be to add code to initialize the value, which in Java is unnecessary.

Doing so, while writing a program snippet that will work, probably indicates a lack of understanding of the language.

Q: *Most languages define boolean true as either the mathematical value non-zero or explicitly one. What does Java do?*

A: Java explicitly differentiates between boolean, which can only have values of true and false, and mathematical quantities. Unlike many other languages, since this is explicit, you cannot assign from one to the other.

Q: *How would you make an array of ten Integer objects in Java with zero as the value?*

```
Integer[] iv = new Integer[10];
for(int i=0;i<iv.length;i++)
  iv[i] = new Integer(0);
```

A: This is different than the above example creating primitives. In Java, when an array of objects is created, it only creates that many "slots" in a vector but does not initialize them. They must be explicitly set to point to object or subclasses of the object, as in the example code.

Q: *How big can an array be in Java?*

A: Almost all items in the Java language compiled code are limited by 4-byte integers. Arrays are one of these, so the number of elements is limited by the size with which the array was allocated. The size is limited by the language to the maximum value of an integer, which in turn is defined as 32 bits with one sign bit, or 2^{31}-1. Many of the Java internals even have 16 bit limitations, for example, branching instructions, but they can branch to nearby "wide go to" byte codes with 32 byte offsets.

Q: *What are the primitive data types in Java?*

A: The primitive data types in Java are boolean, byte, short, int, long, float, double, and char. It would be incorrect to include "String" which is an object, not a primitive, so it would have the allocation rules examined above.

Q: *Why is a Java char two bytes?*

A: So that it can hold Unicode characters.

Q: *Are Java characters signed or unsigned?*

A: In contrast to C++, where they are "undefined" with either a range of –128 to 127 or 0 to 255, in Java they are unsigned to hold the full range of Unicode characters from 0 to 65535.

Q: *What happens if you assign a character primitive to an integer primitive?*

A: The compiler complains. To circumvent this, if it is truly intentional, use a cast.

Q: *What is the difference between "public static void main(String[] x)" and "public static void main(String x)?"*

A: Not only does the former use an array instead of a simple Object, it is also the default entry point when the class is invoked via "java classname." Even though that is not the specific question, if the candidate has done any Java programming, he will know this.

Q: *Who is the "father" of Java?*

A: James Gosling. Among Java converts, he is the father of the movement, much like Linus Torvalds is for Linux.

Q: *What was Java first called?*

A: Oak. This question is a bit trickier, and more for history buffs (although one could ask how much history a four year old language can have). If the candidate knows anything more than this, then the candidate has either read this book or worked at Sun Microsystems and should be hired immediately.

Q: *What does "transient" mean?*

A: It means that the item in question does not need to be serialized, thus in remote calls or persistence it will not be copied out to the socket or written to disk.

Q: *Why would you make a method final?*

A: You would make a method final so it cannot be overridden by a subclass. This is similar to the reason you would make an object final, but at a more granular level.

Q: *Are there any other advantages to making a method final other than not allowing a subclass to override it?*

A: Absolutely. A final method tells the compiler that, because it does not need to indirect and search for an override in a subclass, it is free to inline the method and make the access as fast as possible. This is heavily used in the base classes in Java, for example, in String, which we want to be as fast as possible because it is used in nearly all programs.

Q: *Is Java an interpreted language?*

A: This is a trick question. In the past, the answer was "yes," but is now "mostly." Almost all vendors supply "just-in-time" compilers to compile Java byte code, once loaded into memory, into native machine code.

Q: *What does the keyword "private" mean?*

A: It means that no other class can see the item in question, whether it is a field or a method, other than the class which defines it. This is crucial to object oriented development. Those outside of the specified class do not care about the details, just a crisp clear presentation. In object oriented programming, this means the "how" of what you do is separated from the "what." "Private" enables the programmer to publicly surface, for example, a "sort," but privately hide whether it is a bad bubble-sort or a more reasonable but also more complex heap or quick sort. The OO term for this is separating the implementation from the interface. In Java this also means that those on the outside of your object can neither see your implementation, nor can make unauthorized changes, but they can usually override the methods and rewrite it.

Q: *Are there any other advantages to private other than information hiding?*

A: Absolutely. Just like final, because the compiler does not have to go through indirection tables to get overrides in a subclass. It can inline these methods for faster access.

Q: *What does Java provide with "native?"*

A: The ability to write optimized code for performance in other languages like assembler, C, and C++. There are a few example of this, very tight loops doing intense mathematical operations, (although the usefulness of this is decreasing), access to devices to surfaced in Java (how does one check IRQ7 on a PC in Java).

Q: *What are the first and last elements of an array and how do you access them?*

A: a[0] and a[a.length-1]. The candidate must know that Java is 0-based, like C, not 1-based, like Basic.

Q: *Why can Java garbage collection be a bad thing?*

A: Garbage collection occurs randomly, so a real-time program may slow down unexpectedly when the garbage collector starts. This would be bad if the space shuttle were landing at exactly that time. More importantly, and this is not so much the fault of the garbage collector, but its very existence often encourages quite sloppy programming. This was even true of the basic Java class libraries, which would allocate thousands of Point objects as the cursor was tracked across the screen, rather than simply changing the X and Y coordinates. Class instantiation, memory, and garbage collection is expensive. Objects are also expensive. Changing X and Y is cheap. In this context expensive refers to space and time or memory and cpu.

Q: *What is encapsulation with respect to Java?*

A: Encapsulation is the building of self-contained units. It is crucial to understanding object-oriented programming. An encapsulated object, Java's primary work unit, should not be linked like spaghetti to all the other units in a program. Instead it should "put on a face" for the outside world via ints interface and public methods, and have a private implementation that does not change or surface itself to the callers.

Q: *What is inheritance in terms of Java, both syntactically and semantically?*

A: Inheritance is subclassing. This is when one Java object extends to another, thereby augmenting the functionality. An example would be a Double extending Number. It has all the characteristics of a number, and augments them with double precision floating point operations. Even if candidates are unclear as to the terms syntactic and semantic, they should always immediately respond by saying, "Extends" to a question referring to "inheritance in Java."

Q: *What Java class would you use to store an arbitrary collection of things indexed by name?*

A: Restating the question or using different terminology makes it even easier, but key-value pairs in Java are managed any of the classes that implement java.util.Map, such as TreeMap, HashMap, or Hashtable.

Q: *When would you use Java primitives instead of their object counterparts?*

A: Here I am looking for an answer like, "when it is not necessary to put the item into a hash table as an Object." To perform any basic mathematical operation, cheap primitives are used, and

```
int x,y = 10,z = 25;
x = y + z;
```

is cheaper than

```
Integer x = null,y = new Integer(10),z = new Integer(25);
x = new Integer(y.intValue() + z.intValue());
```

Q: *How do you change the size of an array?*

A: You have to reallocate the array, and make the old pointer "garbage." For example, if you have

```
int[] x = new int[10];
```

the only way to add two more elements to the array is

```
x = new int[12];
```

which means, if you want the items to maintain their value, you would have to use:

```
temp = new int[12];
for(int i=0;i<10;i++)
  temp[i] = x[I];
```

or, if the candidate is very sharp, the candidate will replace the above with System.arraycopy().

Q: *What is the finalize method used for in Java?*

A: The finalize method in Java is used to do any clean up when the garbage collector runs and notices that there are no outstanding references to this object. Its memory is returned to the available heap, and this is a chance for the object to "clean itself up."

Q: *How do you open a file in Java?*

A: If the candidate has done any serious Java programming, this is an easy question. There are a number of right answers, but what we are looking for is:

```
try {
  java.io.FileInputStream x=new
    java.io.FileInputStream(name);
}
catch(java.io.IOException e) {
  e.printStackTrace();
}
```

With the example the candidate shows that they know the IO package library in Java and understands that Java propagates errors through try/catch rather than return codes.

Q: *When would you use* instanceof *in Java?*

A: The keyword instanceof in Java is an operation to see if a particular object is either the object in question, a subclass of the object in question, or implements the interface in question. For example:

```
Float f = new Float(0.0); boolean b = f instanceof Number;
```

would assign the value true to b.

Q: *What is a runtime exception? Do you catch these in your program?*

A: A RuntimeException means something has gone wrong that should cause the program to terminate and the situation should be handled by the programmer. A mistake would be:

```
try{x[n] = 3;}
catch(ArrayIndexOutOfBoundsException e) {}
```

where the correct code would be

```
if(x != null and x.length > n)
  x[n] = 3;
```

Intermediate Questions

Q: *What does it mean to "pass an array" to a method?*

A: The answer should be that the "pointer" to the array is passed, and the entire array is "not" copied to the stack. The only exception to this would be an array of primitives or serializable objects being passed to an out-of-process Java VM.

Q: *What is the difference between a class method and an instance method, both semantically and syntactically?*

A: Syntactically, class methods are preceded by the keyword static. They can be called anytime by any caller if the access is public. However, instance methods are local to and operate on data contained within that particular instance of the class. Even if the candidate can echo this near "double-speak," the candidate should be able to easily present an example showing the difference, such as the following:

```
public class a
{
  static int x;
  int y;
  public static int addX(){return ++x;}
  public int addY(){return ++y;}
  public static void main(String[] args)
  {
    // prints 1
    System.out.printIn(""+a.addX());
    // prints 1
    System.out.printIn(""+(new a()).addY());
    // prints 2
    System.out.printIn(""+a.addX()); //
    // prints 1
    System.out.printIn(""+(new a()).addY());
  }
}
```

where the reason is that each addY() operates on a local copy of the data to that instance, where the global addX operates on a single copy of the data, the "class" copy, and there is always only a single class.

Q: *How would you convert a character string to a number in Java?*

A: Here again the candidate must be careful. A good candidate well-versed in Java and linguistics would either ask about the kind of String and number (floating point or integral) or would simply code to handle all cases. A weaker candidate with some experience should nonetheless be able to quickly answer,

"`Integer.parseInt(string) ;`"

or

"`Double.valueOf(string).doubleValue();`"

Q: *What kind of debugger do you use in Java?*

A: If the candidate purchased an IDE or worked with one previously, like VisualJ++, then those have debuggers in the standard toolset integrated into the editing, compiling and testing of the source code (hence the term Integrated Development Environment). The standard "free" debugger (which is of great value) comes from Sun and is called "jdb." This is one case where the candidate can legitimately say "I do not use one" simply because the toolsets are so weak in their current state that "eyeball" debugging and insertion of "println" trace statements are as effective as the debugger. This is especially true when multiple Java VMs are used, such as networked applications, or when debugging time/slice GUI, such as how fast and where the user moves the mouse. If every time they move the mouse they have to slowly enter a debugger command, that would completely change the running characteristics of the program, thereby often hiding the problem.

Q: *What's a Java applet?*

A: An applet is a subclass of java.applet.Applet that is used to present highly interactive visuals on a Web page.

Q: *When would you use a Java application rather than a Java applet?*

A: An application, since it is pre-installed on the target machine, does not require the wait time for download of an applet, nor does it have to follow the same very restrictive security guidelines. Thus, if the program must start quicker, cannot be dependent on a browser, or must read or write to the local file-system, then an application is more appropriate than an applet. An application is also used to solve non-visual problems, server side or batch computing, whereas an applet is strictly used for a *graphical user interface* (GUI).

Q: *What's the difference in event handling between JDK1.02 and JDK1.1?*

A: Anyone who has been programming Java for some time and done anything visual should know this. In JDK1.0 events were handled by the generic handleEvent(Event). In JDK1.1 they were encapsulated where each event is not a general purpose entity, but only deals with "itself," and an object has listeners.

Q: *To what does the term "sandbox" refer?*

A: The Java sandbox describes the earliest Java security model, that an applet was self-contained in its sandbox like a small child playing, and could not climb outside the high walls to do any damage. This means, for example, that an applet cannot read or write to or from the local file system. It is free to query and change its own values and items in the sandbox, but it is not free to go outside the sandbox without violating the security model and throwing an exception. This was a huge benefit to Java in the early days; it meant that users could download and run highly interactive Java applets without having to worry about compromising their system.

Q: *What is a Java bean?*

A: Simply put, a Java bean is an in-process Java object that adheres to some programming conventions. For example, if it wanted to surface an entity that could be queries or modified name Bubba of type BubbasFavouriteType, it would do so by:

```
BubbaFavouriteType  getBubba();
void  setBubba(BubbaFavouriteType value);
```

This means that any other program could inspect this object and using simple rules "infer" what properties this object had and display them in property sheets and customizers.

Q: *When do Java programmers get together?*

A: Obviously there could be a lot of cute answers to this question, but the annual bash-Microsoft-geek-fest formally known as the JavaOne Developers Conference in California at the beginning of summer every year should be well-known to all.

Q: *Is Java a public language?*

A: The answer is, quite clearly, yes and no. Yes, you can get Java free of charge, and you are free to use it. No, any changes to the language are not public, where the public or recognized industry experts have a say, but rather at the whim of the few people at Sun Microsystems and Javasoft that make the decisions, not a recognized standards body. This is a marketing faux-pas that will hopefully clear itself up shortly.

Q: *Where is Java used?*

A: Java is used nearly everywhere. For example, in a distributed computing system, Java may supply the client interface, the mid-tier technology, and the backend database. In addition to desktop and industry computers, Java is now gaining prominence in ever smaller devices, such as smartcards.

Q: *How would you run another command, like an operating system command, from within your Java program?*

A: `Runtime.getRuntime().exec(command_to_run);`

Q: *If you use* `Runtime.getRuntime().exec(command_to_run);` *where does the output from the command go?*

A: Unless you specifically request that the output of the executing program be re-directed to your code, it will go in to the bit-bucket.

Q: *What's a Java servlet?*

A: A Java servlet is "Web-server-side" Java, a program that typically sends HTML to browsers, but resides inside a Java virtual machine on the web server.

Q: *What happens when you pass an array of integers to a method and it changes their values?*

A: This will quickly show if the candidate understands the difference between call-by-reference and call-by-value. Because the "pointer" to the array is passed "call-by-value" and not returned, but not changed, then changes to the contents will be reflected in the original caller. An example of this would be:

```
void baz()
{
  int[]xvec = new int[10];
  foo(xvec);
  System.out.printIn("Element 3 is " + xvec[3];
}

void foo(int[] zz)
{
  zz[3] = 14;
}
```

Here the value of the third element of the array is assigned the value 14.

Q: *What happens when you pass an array of integers to a method and it changes their values?*

A: Just like the previous question, this is call-by-value versus call-by-reference. However:

```
  void baz()
  {
  int[]xvec = new int[10];
  foo(xvec);
  System.out.printIn("Length is " + xvec.length);
}

void foo(int[] zz)
{
  zz = new int[12];
}
```

will not show the value of 12 but rather 10. What happened is crucial to understanding Java.

- First, xvec is created and points to heap storage with ten slots.
- Second, the pointer is passed to a method.
- Third, the variable zz is assigned that value and now points to the same location.
- Fourth, the variable zz is made to point to a different location; in other words, xx still points to the old 10 element array, and zz now points to the new 12 element array.

Q: *What happens if you pass a primitive to a method and the method that was called modifies that value?*

A: The method that was called modified its variable slot, which had a separate copy of the value leaving the original value unchanged as used by the caller.

Q: *How would you write a "swap(a,b)" routine in Java?*

A: You are not able to do so. C and C++ supply many tricks to do this; templates, macros, pointers, and so on. In Java, if 'a' and 'b' are primitives, like int, short, then you must do it inline:

```
temp=a;a=b;b=temp;
```

But if 'a' and 'b' are objects, then it becomes more difficult. You can either do it inline as shown in the previous example, or write a method using recursive deep-copy if that is supplied, for example:

```
void painfulSwapMethod(SomeType a, SomeType b) {
SomeType c = new SomeType(a);
a.setContents(b);
b.setContents(c);
}
```

Q: *What is an inner class?*

A: An inner class is a class defined within a class, and, in general, only "instantiable" by the outer class, for example:

```
class outer
{
  class inner
    {
    {
    void foo()
    {
      new inner();
    }
```

```
{
```

The example will create two classes on disk, a.class, and a$b.class.

Q: *How would you make an anonymous inner class?*

A: An anonymous inner class is an inner class that is not named. For example, within class "a":

```
void foo()
{
  //anonymous inner class
  Runnable runner = new Runnable()
    {
      public void run(){}
    };
}
```

is the same as using named inner classes with

```
class RunBubbaRun implements Runnable
{
  public void run(){}
};
void foo()
{
  Runnable runnable = new RunBubbaRun();
}
```

The difference comes in the creation of the class files during compilation. The former will create a$1.class and the latter will create a$RunBubbaRun.class.

Q: *If you compile a Java program on a PC and try to run it on Unix, what will happen?*

A: According to theory and Java's advertising, this is the great strength of Java, that it is "write-once-run-anywhere." However, theory does not hold true in practice, and it usually becomes "write-once-test-everywhere." There are also pitfalls of using Java that lets you do "nonportable" things which will not run on other hosts. In addition, moving between different incompatible levels of Java can cause problems., for example, if your PC has JDK1.2 and your Unix machine has JDK1.1.3.

Q: *When do you throw things or catch them in Java?*

A: Java has changed the paradigm for handling failure. In previous languages, items similar to the following constructs were common:

```
if(open() == OK) { if(read() == OK) if(close() == OK) ...
```

Java changes the above to the much cleaner construct seen below.

```
try { open(); read(); close(); } catch(IOException e) ...
```

Q: *What is an exception in Java?*

A: An exception is an object that can be passed from the caller, which detects the problem condition, to anyone listening. The caller only knows that it is "throwing it out," not who, if anyone, will receive it and handle it appropriately. This makes it very easy to write "clean" code with well-defined interfaces.

Q: *Why and how do you propagate an exception in Java?*

A: If the subsystem you use throws exceptions and that is consistent with the type of information you want to surface, especially with respect to leaving the handling to someone else, then propagating the exception is the appropriate thing to do. A simple example would be:

```
class MyIOClass { void openSomething() throws IOException
```

Here, usually the class that does the low level thing that can cause the exception is not the same class as the one that is responsible for putting up nice error messages, logging them to a file, or doing whatever is appropriate. To propagate an exception in Java, declare it when the method is declared. For example:

```
void snooze(int secs) throws InterruptedException
{Thread.sleep(secs*1000);}
```

Here since sleep() can throw an InterruptedException, it is declared in the throws clause of the method which means it will be automatically propagated.

Q: *What ramifications does using exceptions have on Java subclasses?*

A: Any exception that is thrown by a superclass is implicitly in the subclass override method signature. However, and this is very important, a subclass cannot "add" an exception to a method signature, as this would violate the contract between the superclass and the objects which use it. In other words the following is illegal:

```
class a { void foo() {} }
class b extends a { void foo() throws IOException {} }
```

Here we have violated the contract between "a" and its callers. They do not expect to have to handle IOException and now suddenly must plan for it, or anything else a subclass wants to change.

Q: *If an array, let's say "int[]x" has ten elements, and you assign a 5 to the 10th element via x[10]=5, what really happens?*

A: The Java Virtual Machine will throw an ArrayIndexOutOf BoundsException and if no one is listening, it will stop the program.

Q: *When would you override a method in Java instead of overloading it?*

A: You overload a method, add different sets of parameters to the signature, when it is convenient for the caller or has some benefit to the implementation. You would overload a method or implement a different behavior in a subclass, when you want to change the method for that specific level of subclass.

Q: *What is reflection?*

A: Reflection is the means by an Object can inspect the methods and fields of another Object. It is supplied in the `java.lang.reflect` package.

Q: *How could you determine the node name of the networked computer on which a piece of Java code was running?*

A: Java supplies a package for Internet Addressing called java.net.InetAddress and you could simply call

```
java.net.InetAddress.getLocalHost().getHostName()
```

Q: *How would you pass a class instead of an instance as a parameter?*

A: Given the instance, you could simply call instance.getClass(), or given the class name, you could append ".class" to the name, as in

```
foo(bazInstance.getClass());
foo(baz.class);
```

Q: *How could you create an instance of a class if you only had its name?*

A: You would use

```
{ Object o = Class.forName(class_name).newInstance(); }
catch...
```

Q: *What's a thread?*

A: A thread is a possibly concurrently executing piece of Java code residing in the same Java virtual machine as its creator. The syntax of the language makes concurrency quite simple.

Q: *Are there any problems using threads in Java?*

A: There are many. Behavior is not guaranteed for threads of equal priority; they could time-slice, run concurrently, or even run sequentially. They also make program much more difficult to debug.

Q: *How do you start a thread in Java? And how do you start it after stopping it?*

A: This is normally the straightforward call thread.start(). However, after a thread has been stopped, it cannot be restarted. The only way to restart a stopped thread is not to restart it at all, but rather to create a new thread and run the same section of the program.

Q: *How can you write thread safe code in Java?*

A: Writing thread safe code in Java is easy if you either insure complete atomic self-contained units that can either do nothing harmful or nothing at all, although some might debate whether that is harmless. Or you "synchronize" blocks of code, which will guarantee, albeit at a cost, sequential behavior.

Q: *When would using the keyword "synchronize" still be unsafe code for threads? For example, would*

```
public synchronized int getX() { return ++x; }
```

always be safe or could it be unsafe and return undefined values, or return the same value when called twice?

A: If the value being modified had class scope rather than instance scope, then synchronizing multiple instances guarantees that each instance gets called sequentially in its own right, but not with respect to the others. For example, here behavior would be undefined because each instance modifies the single class scope variable:

```
static int x;
public synchronized int getX() { return ++x; }
```

The circumvention is to lock the class scope variable rather than the instance method. In other words you would have the following:

```
public int getX()
{
  int r=0;
  synchronized(getClass())
    {
      r = ++x;
    }
  return r;
}
```

Q: *What are some of the benefits associated with using threads?*

A: The programs can be "multi-user" enabled, like a Web server. The programs can distribute work to multiple processors concurrently, like Hybrid OLAP. The programs can put timeout conditions on any operation.

Q: *Is calling* stop() *the best way to terminate a thread?*

A: This is the least effective way to terminate a thread. Here's a simple analogy. One of the worst ways to end someone else's phone call is to pull the cord out of the wall. One of the best ways is to politely ask someone to end a call. Threads in Java behave in the same way. The best way, if it is available to the caller, is to ask the thread, for example, by setting some stop-request flag, so the thread can cleanly prematurely end its execution. Calling stop() is just like pulling the phone cord out of the wall: sudden and with no notice, as no request was made and no preparations were undertaken. Thread.stop() is depreciated in JDK1.2.

Q: *If someone called stop() how could you force cleanup, or are there any exceptions thrown and why?*

A: Because "stop()" doesn't give a thread the chance to cleanup, it will throw a ThreadDeath that the caller can catch. The caller can then call any cleanup routines necessary.

Q: *Why would you use implements Runnable instead of extends Thread?*

A: If your class already had a superclass but needed to run in parallel with other classes, then, rather than changing the superclass, which you cannot, you would simply implement the Runnable interface. This is the Java means to allow multiple inheritance "functionality" without multiple inheritance "headaches."

Q: *What is the difference between the Error and the Exception classes?*

A: Both classes are direct subclasses of Throwable. Almost no errors, but all exceptions excluding RuntimeException should be caught. For example, a program is expected to catch and handle IOException but is probably not expected to handle, and can do almost nothing useful with OutOfMemoryError.

Q: *What if you need to add exceptions "after-the-fact," that is, after the class hierarchy and interfaces have been defined and the code is compiled and cannot be changed?*

A: Hopefully you will never be in this situation and can always design a clean system from the ground up. In this unfortunate circumstance, you can make the new exceptions subclasses of RuntimeException so the code using them is okay. When development has you in a difficult bind, this is the best of the various options. The others choices, letting the program fail or rewriting the system and delaying the product for a long time, are often unacceptable to the consumer or management.

Q: *If a method I am calling throws multiple different exceptions, is catch (Exception) an effective and convenient way of handling all the exceptions that method throws?*

A: It is very convenient, but not a wise programming practice. While saving a few keystrokes, this also makes the program catch conditions that it is not prepared to handle, like when the method that threw the exception had a RuntimeException. This should be ignored rather than one of its own exceptions.

Q: *After you throw an exception, or return from a method, will any of the remaining code in your method body be executed?*

A: Absolutely, but only if the code to be executed is in a finally section and the return or throw occurred in the corresponding try section. For example:

```
try {
if(need_to_return) return;
if(need_to_throw_exception) throw new
RuntimeException("uh-oh");
} finally {
do_stuff();
}
```

will always execute do_stuff()

Q: *If you launched many threads to do work, and wish to await their completion, how would you do so?*

A: For each of the threads you launched, call the join() method on that thread. This will cause the caller to yield and wait until the thread in question dies. If the other threads die during that time, then when you call their join() methods, they will become no-ops, returning immediately.

Advanced Questions

Q: *What is the "finally" clause in Java?*

A: It is code that is guaranteed to run even if an Exception gets thrown or propagated. For example:

```
try { do_dangerous_stuff(); }
catch(DeepDarkDangerousSecretException dddse) { throw
xxx; }
finally { free_willy(); }
```

Here, even though the processing of the method may be "short-circuited" by the exception, Willy will be freed no matter what.

Q: *How do you relinquish processor control in a Java thread?*

A: By calling yield(). Yield() will either temporarily stop the current thread and switch control to a waiting thread, or, if there is none waiting, simply continue processing in the current thread.

Q: *How can you kill a thread in Java?*

A: Traditionally by calling stop(), but that is changing with Java2. There are also other ways threads can die of their own accord. One fairly typical example is to throw an Exception for which no one is listening.

Q: *What is preemptive threading in Java?*

A: Preemptive threading means the system has the choice when to force a thread to yield and to give control to other threads. Non-preemptive threading means that a thread must explicitly give up control. Neither one of these is perfect in this simplistic fashion. For example, preemptive may always kick mission critical items off the CPU, and non-preemptive may never allow other users into a system if the single one doing processing never explicitly yields. Java gets around this with priorities.

Q: *What are some ways to make two separate classes execute concurrently?*

A: Make both classes extend Thread, and call start() on both. Further, make both classes implement Runnable and create a new thread passing the classes to the constructor.

Q: *What exactly does "synchronized" do?*

A: For the first call in to a synchronized method, or recursive calls within the same thread, it does nothing. However, if another thread, thread 2, tries to call this method while thread 1 is executing, the Java Virtual Machine will prevent execution by the second thread until the first thread completes its usage. In other words, it forces a "single-threaded" behavior on a multi-threaded system.

Q: *What is the difference between Runnable and Thread?*

A: Runnable is an interface; Thread is a class. Any object hierarchy can be made "Runnable" but almost none can be made to change its superclass to Thread. For example, if we have

```
class a extends b implements Runnable
{
  public void run(){}
}
```

Q: *What does thread deadlock mean?*

A: A thread deadlock is when two threads are waiting on the same piece of information and on each other. In this case, the system will simply "shut down" and have each thread wait its turn until infinity. In other words, it will block forever, and nothing can occur to release the block. This is called a deadlock.

Q: *What is volatile?*

A: The volatile modifier tells the compiler that the variable modified by volatile can be changed unexpectedly by other parts of the program. This is important in multithreaded programming. For the master copy of the variable to always reflect its current state, simply specify the variable as being volatile. This will force the compiler to "write-to-memory" rather than leave in registers, for example. A much more typical way of doing this in Java is via synchronized so that groups of variables can be written together instead of listing each as volatile.

Q: *What is AWT?*

A: AWT is Java's Abstract Window Toolkit. It has also commonly been called "the Awful" or the "Abominable Windowing Toolkit" because, in trying to be all things to all viewers in a portable fashion, it does nothing very well. But it is portable!

Q: *What is Swing?*

A: Swing is the answer to everything that was wrong with AWT. It is the newer more powerful visualization toolset from Java. AWT was Java1, where Swing is Java2.

Q: *If you were writing a game or simulation in Java, how would you have the program pick a random number between 1 and 10?*

A: `(int)(Math.random()*10+1)`

Q: *What is a stream in Java?*

A: It is a flow between source and target, for example, the contents of a file between the file and its reader, or the contents of a socket between a Web browser and a Web server.

Q: *What are some of the common stream classes in Java for reading?*

A: Here we are looking for the common subclasses of java.io.InputStream which are used in nearly all programs (because most programs are more useful when they get some data in). Some answers would be FileInputStream to read flat files on disk, ByteArrayInputStream to handle in-memory streams, DataInputStream to handle reading all the primitive types, just as long, directly from a stream source, and, one of the most useful, BufferedInputStream to read efficiently in large blocks.

Q: *Anyone that has had to insert trace statements into Java code to debug it is familiar with "println()". Where does "println()" come from?*

A: System.out.println() comes from the out field of the java.lang.System class and is of type java.io.PrintStream supporting methods like print() and println().

Q: *How do distributed programs communicate?*

A: Almost always through TCP/IP sockets, the java.net.Socket class. Most remote protocols are based on this as well.

Q: *Most Java distributed communication streams are based on TCP/IP sockets. Does Java also support UDP (datagram) sockets?*

A: Absolutely, via java.net.Datagram Sockets. A datagram socket is the sending or receiving point for a connectionless packet delivery service. Each packet sent or received on a datagram socket is individually addressed and routed. Multiple packets sent from one machine to another may be routed differently, and may arrive in any order.

Q: *What benefits would there be in using a MulticastSocket in an applet?*

A: Because you're not allowed to use them, none. It is a very fast and efficient messaging mechanism. More specifically, when a socket subscribes to a multicast group/port, it receives datagrams sent by other hosts to the group/port, as do all other members of the group and port. A socket relinquishes membership in a group by the leaveGroup(InetAddress addr) method. Multiple MulticastSockets may subscribe to a multicast group and port concurrently, and they will all receive group datagrams.

Q: *What is JDBC?*

A: Interestingly enough, and despite widespread acceptance, JDBC is not "Java Database Connectivity." It is simply a trademarked name. JDBC is a set of classes for executing SQL and is used to communicate with databases. Almost every database today supports JDBC drivers, so a Java program does not have to write special code for the different DBMSs; rather it simply uses fast, portable, efficient JDBC.

Q: *What is JMS?*

A: Java Messaging Service. This is supplied in the javax.jms classes.

Q: *How would you read a Web page in Java?*

A: There are many correct answers to this question. For example, you read create a URL and open an input stream from it, or, for a low-level nuts and bolts type program. You could open Socket 80 on the host where the web server resides, and send an HTTP header and read the response.

Q: *What is a URL?*

A: A URL is a Uniform Resource Locator. The java.net.URL class is most often used to read a Web page. However, a URL can also be used to read local files, databases, or any types of resources with common protocols.

Q: *If you are inside a firewall, how do you read an external Web page in Java?*

A: Either set the system properties in your local VM environment for the proxy or send the HTTP GET request to the firewall to force the indirection.

Q: *In the base Object class in Java, there is a clone() method. What is it for and what are the pitfalls?*

A: The clone() method is used to make a copy of an object For example:

```
Object copyObject = originalObject.clone();
```

However, an object may choose not to suport clone(), and instead may throw a CloneNotSupportedException. And even if the object does support clone, the caller must be careful of a deep versus a shallow clone. Deep means that it is recursively copied making an entirely new item, and shallow means there is another object that points to the same data show changing the data on the original changes the data on the clone. This topic is more in depth than it seems at first. In fact, there are entire seminars on this topic. A well-versed candidate with a good understanding of OO concepts should be able to address this topic effectively.

Q: *What is the Java Virtual Machine?*

A: The Java Virtual Machine is a program adhering to a rigidly defined specification for interpreting Java byte codes. Most Web browsers and, many web servers and most operating systems come with a Java Virtual Machine (JVM).

Q: *What is a Java plugin?*

A: It is a means of hosting another vendor's Java Virtual Machine (JVM) within a browser. For instance, Netscape™ and InternetExplorer™ both support Java, but Javasoft supplies a plugin, also called an ActiveX control for IE, that allows them both to use the same JVM. This way they do not run their own, possibly incompatible JVMs, just point to the same one.

Q: *If Java is portable, why does it often not work when you copy a Java applet from one Web server to another and then load it on to browsers, which then complain about security errors?*

A: Java applets are usually only allowed to, by default, connect back to the host from which they came. Thus, if the Web server where the applet originally resided also had a database that the applet connected to, when the applet is moved to another Web server, it cannot connect from the client back to the original Web server without violating the default security model.

Q: *Who is Duke in relation to Java?*

A: Duke is the official Java mascot, prevalent in all the advertisements, logos, documentation, and shipped products. It is a little creature that looks like a one-eyed penguin with three fingered hands wearing a glove and often waving or doing cartwheels.

Q: *What is Java RMI?*

A: RMI is Java's Remote Method Invocation either based on JRMP, Java Remote Method Protocol, or CORBA, Common Object Request Broker Architecture with RMI-IIOP, over RMI over Internet Inter Orb Protocol.

Q: *What is the Reaper?*

A: The Reaper is used by RMI to make distributed garbage collection possible.

Q: *How do you make something call-by-value with RMI?*

A: If an object implements, or extends a class that implements java.io.Serializable, then it will be call-by-reference.

Q: *How do you make something call-by-reference with RMI?*

A: If an object extends java.rmi.server.UnicastRemoteObject and implements an interface that extends java.rmi.Remote and has had Stubs generated by "rmic," then the object is call by value.

Q: *Is there a situation where you would use both call-by-reference and call-by-value with RMI?*

A: In almost all situations, using both together is appropriate. For example, if five CEOs of large corporations were viewing spreadsheets and the data were remote and changed remotely, the clients (the CEOs) need to have passed call-by-reference handles to the server (the data provider) so it can trigger an event to them on an interrupt. Granted, this example is a bit of a stretch because five CEOs would probably never read spreadsheets at the same time. Otherwise they have to poll. However, once they are notified, then they can retrieve the entire data collection in large Collection chunks passed by value. We wouldn't want the network tied up with getCell(1,2), getCell(1,3), etc. Instead we should passed back the call-by-reference serializable Collection getAllCells().

Q: *When using RMI, does the caller of the methods have to do anything special?*

A: Absolutely. All RMI methods may throw java.rmi.RemoteException. This makes perfect sense, because the methods are actually executing on the other side of a socket, and, as such, are subject to socket failures for which the client must be prepared.

Q: *What are some of Java's greatest weaknesses?*

A: Java is usually interpreted and often slower than C/C++ or any language that hosts OS native libraries for visualization. It is not a good language for writing a graphical user interface (GUI).

Q: *Is checking the size of the vector against a loop variable to prevent going beyond the limits a good practice, as in for(i=0;i<vector.size();i++)?*

A: Yes. You should always check bounds conditions, but the above code example is typical of poor programming if the vector size is invariant, i.e. fixed. The code will force a possibly expensive method call to be made through every iteration of the loop when the invariant, the size, could be calculated outside the loop.

Q: *What is the Java appletviewer?*

A: The appletviewer is a small tool to test applets that are interactive pieces of Java code to be run inside browsers and downloaded from a Web server. It does so without the need for a browser or a Web server by providing its own container, like a browser, and reading from a local file or URL but not relying on a Web server. This also helps the author of the Java programs focus on the content rather than the deployment. Content refers to the appearance and function, whereas deployment focuses on the packaging for the Web server, the firewalls, and browser incompatibilities.

Q: *What is the difference between a short and a char in Java?*

A: They are both two-byte entities, but short is used for holding small integral values, and char for character values. Short is also signed and has the range of 15 bits plus sign bit, -2^{15} to 2^{15} and char is unsigned and has a range from 0 to 2^{16}.

Q: *What are some popular Java IDEs that you have used?*

A: If candidates have written any Java programs, they have either used the JDK from Sun, or IDEs such as Microsoft's VisualJ++™, Symantec's VisualCafe or Inprise's (formerly Borland) JBuilder. The alternate train of thought is that "real programmers can write Fortran programs in any language" and that the Java Language Specification (JLS) and an editor are all one needs.

Q: *When are other languages, such as Perl or JavaScript, better choices?*

A: It depends. If the task at hand is very simple, such as a server-side dynamically generated Web page or a client side field validation, then Java is often overkill, bringing with it additional associated costs in the form of the JVM which needs to be fired up. For the Web-server-side example, Perl is very popular, and for simple client-side, JavaScript is very popular and often appropriate.

Q: *What is J2EE?*

A: Java 2 Enterprise Edition. This is Sun and Javasoft's latest incarnation, an attempt to make Java an industrial strength language.

Q: *How can you see the threads in a Java program?*

A: This is actually a difficult problem. For instance, if running on a PC you can use the Task-Manager and view the Threads column, but that will only tell you that the Java process has a large number of threads. Often something simple, typically pressing Control-Break, will give thread tracebacks for each of the current threads. But if the program has hundreds of threads running concurrently, this will not give a clear indication of which thread is running with the highest priority, who is going to get the next time slice and to which thread a yield will relinquish control.

Q: *Does Java have pointers?*

A: No, Java does not explicitly have surface pointers. However, every object in Java is actually a pointer, and by maintaining tables of all the pointers, Java can do other things, like provide garbage collection. In other words, nothing is "called" a pointer, but everything "is" a pointer with the associated costs and benefits, like garbage collection versus indirect slower memory addressing.

Q: *If your method seems slow, how would you determine how long it is taking?*

A: Either by invoking java –prof and by looking at the log or using some other tool that does profiling. If none of these is available, for example in a servlet environment, then you can record the elapsed time spend via:

```
long startTime = System.currentTimeMillis();
doit(); // whatever takes so long
long stopTime = System.currentTimeMillis();
System.out.println("doit took"+(stopTime-startTime)+
"milliseconds");
```

Q: *What is a JAR file?*

A: A JAR file is a Java Archive file. It is simply a zip file with an extra file, called a manifest, added to it. When you want to bundle all the classes and extra resources like images for an applet or application, you typically put them in a jar file. To load them off of a web server, you must specify the ARCHIVE= tag for your applet.

Q: *What is an example of something you found extremely hard to debug in Java?*

A: Distributed processing and multithreaded processing are very easy to write but tend to be very difficult to debug in Java. Many of the other things are "tedious" but not "difficult" and should not stump a good Java programmer.

Q: *What are come of the common socket ports used by Java programs for common protocols?*

A: HTTP commonly uses port 80, and HTTPS port 442 for java.net.URL.
RMI commonly uses port 1099 for java.rmi.
LDAP commonly uses 389 for javax.naming.
TELNET commonly uses port 23 for rlogin.

Q: *What is JCE?*

A: The JavaTM Cryptography Extension (JCE) 1.2 provides a framework and implementations for encryption, key generation and key agreement, and Message Authentication Code (MAC) algorithms.

Q: *What is RMI-IIOP?*

A: Remote Method Invocation (RMI) over Internet Inter-Orb Protocol (IIOP) delivers Common Object Request Broker Architecture (CORBA) compliant requests, which makes it possible for Java programs to call non-Java programs. An example would be C++ running on a machine in another country on different architecture.

Q: *What is JSSE?*

A: *Java™ Secure Socket Extension* (JSSE) is used to enable secure Internet communications using SSL and TLS.

Q: *What is JNDI?*

A: *Java Naming and Directory Interface™* (JNDI), which, as the name implies, is for naming and directory services, and is often used as a means of accessing LDAP servers.

Q: *What's the difference between a JavaBean and an Enterprise JavaBean?*

A: JavaBeans are fast because they run in-process. *Enterprise JavaBeans* (EJB), conversely, run out of process and use RMI calls over sockets verifying authorization. This means that EJBs are much slower, but the indirection allows them to be automatically persisted and restored and to support fail-over and parallelism. This is the same type of cost/benefit that happened to Java originally when it was decided that all object references would be indirect, which made them slower and more expensive than C++, but provided hooks for automatic garbage collection and dynamic class verification. Just as the Java VM provided these, the EJB container and Application Server extend the functionality to the EJBs.

Q: *What is a just-in-time compiler or Java HotSpot™?*

A: A *just-in-time* (JIT) compiler starts with interpreted code, and, during execution, changes control from the interpreter to segments of code compiled that were compiled during their earlier passes. The Sun Microsystems product to do this is called HotSpot™. Peter Deutsch originally invented the technique for another language called Smalltalk.

Q: *What is JTA?*

A: JTA is the Java Transaction API, standard interfaces between a transaction manager and distributed transaction system elements, such as a resource manager, the application server, and the transactional applications.

Q: *What is JSP?*

A: JSP is Java Server Pages, a combination of HTML and Java servlets in a single source file. The programmer typically switches from HTML-mode to Java-mode by using the special tags <% to enter Java mode and %> to exit it. The most typical example would be something similar to the following:

```
<html>
Hello,
<% out.println("today's date is "+ new java.util.Date());
%>
and goodbye
</html>
```

Q: *What is JTS?*

A: JTS is Java Transaction Service which specifies the implementation of a Transaction Manager supporting JTA.

Q: *What is JAAS?*

A: The Java Authentication and Authorization Service.

4
Active Server Pages

Rama Ramachandran

Active Server Pages (ASP) is Microsoft's Web application programming environment that enables you to combine HTML, scripting, and COM components to create powerful Internet applications. Since its inception, ASP has taken the world by storm. Because the underlying scripting language, Visual Basic Script or VBScript, is similar to Visual Basic, hordes of VB programmers have migrated naturally to writing ASP applications. Several large e-commerce sites, including Dell.com, Priceline.com, MotherNature.com, PlanetRX.com, and thousands of others have built enormously popular Web applications using ASP technology.

The market for ASP programmers is exploding with more and more companies switching to Microsoft technologies for their e-commerce platforms. Knowing ASP, VB, Windows NT, and Microsoft's *Structured Query Language* (SQL) Server will make you a sought-after professional in today's marketplace. This chapter provides you with the most common questions asked by interviewers when seeking candidates with such skills. Before proceeding into an ASP interview, you should be prepared in the following areas:

- ASP's background, setup, and environment
- ASP scripting, especially using VBScript
- Database access in ASP using ActiveX Data Objects (ADO)

- COM component usage in ASP
- Performance enhancement techniques in ASP

We'll cover all these topics in the series of questions and answers provided later. I am a Microsoft Certified Solution Developer and a Microsoft Certified Site-Builder, and have been using ASP since Microsoft introduced it. I am the Director of Technology at Imperium Solutions, a Wesport, Connecticut-based Microsoft solution provider partner. I have successfully launched several Web sites including www.letseatout.com, a premier online restaurant guide, and www.ct.org, the Web site for the Connecticut Technology Council. I am also the ASP Pro at www.inquiry.com where I answer ASP-related questions and post articles that teach ASP. I also teach Web development for the Masters Degree in Software Engineering at Fairfield University, Connecticut. I am not only involved in conducting technical interviews for candidates for my company, but also for my clients.

If you are looking for a career in ASP, you are on the right track. I wish you all the best and hope that these questions and answers will strengthen your skill and help you prepare.

Questions and Answers

Q: *What is ASP?*

A: ASP stands for *Active Server Pages.* It is a server-side scripting technology that enables you to create dynamic and interactive Web sites and Web applications.

Q: *What is a server-side script?*

A: When a browser requests a Web site, the Web server "serves" the page back to the browser. If the browser requests for an ASP page on the Web server, the Web server first executes the script within the .asp page and sends the results back to the browser. This script that is executed on the server is called a server-side script.

Q: *What is an ASP page?*

A: An ASP page is a standard HTML Web page with an .asp extension. Embedded within the HTML text is ASP scripting code. When a browser requests the ASP page, the ASP script code is executed and pure HTML text is sent back to the browser.

Q: *Which tags are used to enclose ASP script code?*

A: The <% and the %> tags enclose ASP script code and separate it from HTML text within an ASP page.

Q: *What language can you use to write ASP script code?*

A: You can either use VBScript or Microsoft's version of JavaScript (Jscript) to write server-side ASP script code. In addition, third-party products are available that will enable you to write script using other Web languages such as Perl and the Tool Command Language (TCL).

Q: *How do you define which language is being used within a specific ASP page?*

A: The ASP primary scripting language is used to process commands within the ASP tags <% and %>. By default, this is VBScript. In addition, you can also specify the scripting language on a page-by-page basis. To do so, you use the preprocessor directive <%@ LANGUAGE="ScriptingLanguage" %> at the top of your ASP page. By doing so, this directive overrides the default scripting language used in the Web application. For example, to use VBScript, you would code

```
<%@ LANGUAGE="VBSCRIPT"%>
```

To use JScript, you would use

```
<% @ LANGUAGE="JSCRIPT"%>
```

Q: *How would you specify the default scripting language for all ASP pages within your Web application?*

A: To set the primary scripting language for all pages in a Web application, set the Default ASP Language property on the App Options tab in the Internet Information Services management console snap-in.

On Windows 2000, choose Start, Programs and navigate to the Internet Services Manager, the Internet Information Service (IIS) management server. Then right-click on your Web application and choose Properties. On the Properties dialog box that appears, click on the Configuration button within the Home Directory tab. In the Application Configuration dialog box that pops up, navigate to the App Options tab. Set the language under the Default ASP Language Property text box (see Figure 4-1).

Q: *What are the two tools you can use to debug an ASP script?*

A: To debug an ASP script, you can use the Microsoft Script Debugger or you can use Microsoft Visual InterDev.

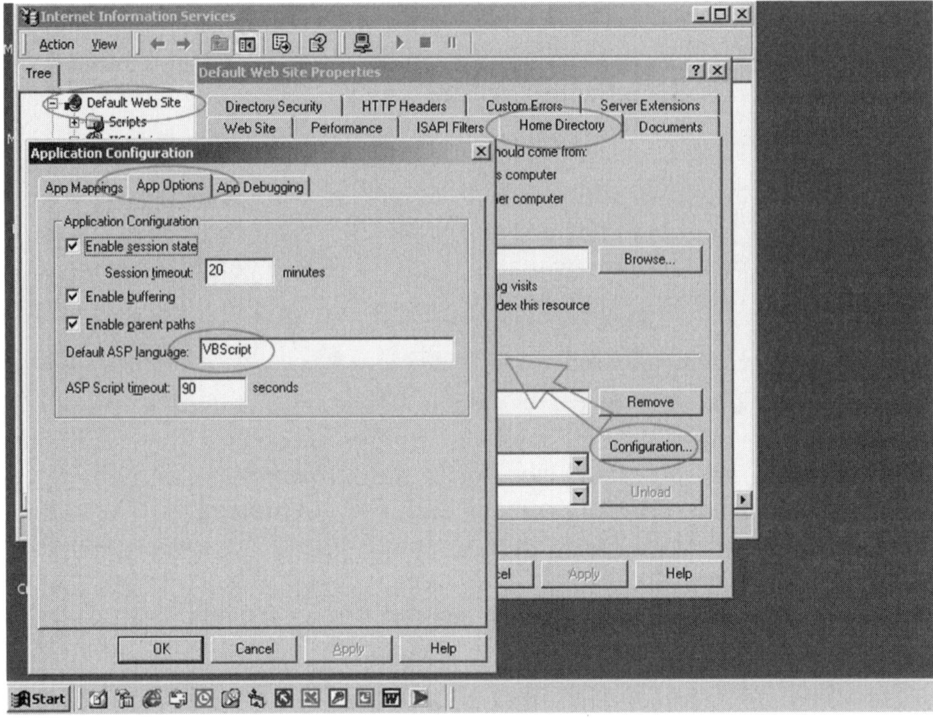

Figure 4-1 Setting the default ASP scripting language for your Web application

Q: *How can you turn on Script Debugging for an ASP Web application?*

A: In the Application Configuration dialog box for the ASP Web application properties, under the App Debugging tab, check the box that says Enable ASP server-side debugging. This allows you to debug an ASP Web application using either the Microsoft Script Debugger or Microsoft Visual InterDev (see Figure 4-2).

Q: *Which Web server does ASP work with?*

A: Microsoft has developed ASP to work with its own *Internet Information Server* (IIS). IIS is a free Web server that ships with Windows NT 4 and Windows 2000.

Q: *Which version of IIS ships with Windows 2000?*

A: Windows 2000 ships with Microsoft IIS Version 5. Versions prior to 5 shipped with Windows NT 4.

Q: *Which is better, an in-process application or an out-of-process application?*

A: The answer depends on the Web application. An in-process application runs in the same process thread as ASP, and is therefore the

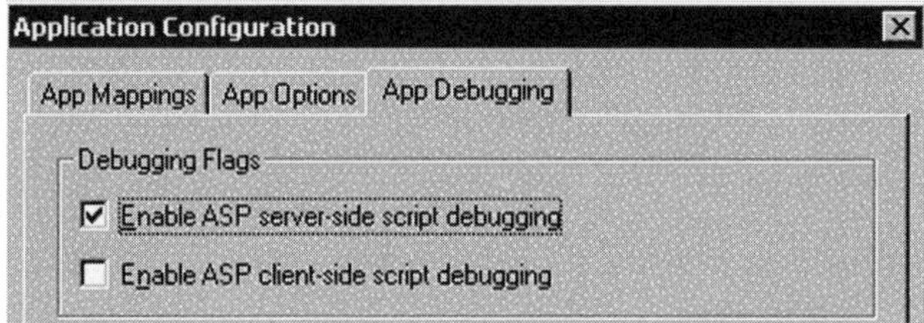

Figure 4-2 Turning on Script Debugging for an ASP Web application

fastest in performance. However, since it runs in the same process as ASP, if the Web application fails for some reason, it can bring down your Web server. An out-of-process application runs in its own process. This makes it poorer in performance but provides better Web server protection. If the application fails, it does not shut down the Web server. If you desire the best performance but can afford the Web server shutdown on failure, use in-process applications. If you cannot afford to shut down the Web server because other mission-critical applications are running on it, then run the applications out-of-process.

Q: *How do you output information to the browser from an ASP page?*

A: To send output (strings) back to the browser, you use the Write method of the built-in response object in ASP. So the statement

```
Response.Write "Hello World"
```

would output the string "Hello World" on the browser. Using this technique, you can send text, numbers, and HTML tags to the browser. This enables you to dynamically generate Web page content.

Q: *How would you send information to the browser without using the Response.Write method?*

A: Another technique for sending data back to the browser is to enclose it within the ASP tags and precede it with an equals sign. For example, <%= "Hello World" %> would be equivalent to writing Response.Write "Hello World." When the ASP page code is executed, the ASP script engine converts all <%= ... %> script code to its equivalent Response.Write statements.

Q: *How will you transfer the control of code execution to a different page from an ASP page? That is, how will you send a user to a different page from server-side script?*

A: In ASP, you can use the Response.Redirect method to send the user to a different page. So, if you want to force the user to view the login.asp page, you can use the following code:

```
Response.Redirect "login.asp"
```

This forces the browser to request the login.asp page, sending the user to the login page.

Q: *How has this behavior changed in ASP 3 that ships with Windows 2000?*

A: In ASP 3, we have two new control flow mechanisms. In addition to the Response.Redirect statement, you can use the Server.Transfer and the Server.Execute statements. The Server.Transfer statement is an optimized version of the Response.Redirect statement.

```
Server.Transfer "login.asp"
```

The previous statement causes the ASP code to stop executing on the current page. It then loads and executes the login.asp. This is better than the Response.Redirect method because it does not require the server to inform the browser to go to the login page, thereby reducing one round trip for the request.

```
Server.Execute “page2.asp”
```

The Server.Execute statement pauses execution in the current page and then loads and executes the page2.asp page. When it has finished executing the second page, it returns back to the line in the first page and continues execution. This is the equivalent of making a subroutine call in a different module.

Q: *What are the built-in objects in ASP?*

A: ASP ships with the following objects that are intrinsic to ASP:

- Application object
- Request object
- Response object
- Server object
- Session object
- ObjectContext object
- ASPError object

Q: *What can you do to an Image tag (IMG) to ensure that it appears to load faster?*

A: Specify the Width and Height attribute of an IMG tag. This enables the browser to keep space on the page while it is rendering the page and requesting the image in a background process. This renders the page faster.

```
<IMG SRC="graphic.gif" HEIGHT="40" WIDTH="200">
```

Q: *How can you produce a tool tip when the user hovers his/her mouse over an image?*

A: Specify the tool tip text as the ALT attribute of the Image (IMG) tag. When the user hovers over the image, the ALT text appears as a tool tip.

```
<IMG SRC="login.gif" HEIGHT="40" WIDTH="200" ALT="Login">
```

Q: *How can you produce a tool tip when the user hovers over a hyperlink?*

A: Specify the tool tip text as the TITLE attribute of the Anchor (A) tag.

```
<A HREF="destinationpage.htm" TITLE="View for more info">
```

Q: *What does Response.Buffer do in ASP?*

A: Response.Buffer enables ASP to complete the execution of all the code within an ASP before sending output to the browser. If buffering is on (Response.Buffer = True), output is sent to the browser only when the entire page is processed. If buffering is off, each Response.Write statement actually sends the output to the browser before continuing to process the next line. By using buffering, it is possible to redirect the user to another page halfway during the execution of the ASP page's code. If buffering is not on, then a Response.Redirect will fail if any output has been sent previously to the browser.

Q: *What are the default states for buffering in IIS 4 and IIS 5?*

A: In IIS 4, buffering is off and the programmer must manually turn it on. In IIS 5, buffering is on by default.

Q: *What is the comment character used in VBScript code? What is used in JScript?*

A: In VBScript, the apostrophe (') is used for a comment. All content to the right of the comment character up to the end of the line is considered as a comment. In JScript, a set of two slashes (//) is used as a comment character for a line. To add comments to a block of code in Jscript, the /* and */ tags are used to enclose the block. VBScript does not have a block code comment character.

Q: *Which scripting language is case-sensitive among the languages used in ASP pages?*

A: VBScript is not case-sensitive, while JScript is.

Q: *How do you declare a variable in VBScript, and how do you do it in JScript?*

A: In VBScript, you use the Dim statement to declare a variable:

```
Dim strName
```

In JScript, you use the var statement to declare a variable:

```
var x;
```

Neither VBScript nor JScript enables typed variables. That is, you cannot declare a variable to be of a particular type as you would do in Visual Basic. By default, all variables are of type "variant" and are capable of storing any kind of data, such as strings, numbers, dates, and so on.

Q: *How can you make sure that the value of a variable in one ASP page is available to other ASP pages for the same user during the time he spends accessing your Web application?*

A: In order to enable one ASP page to view the contents of a variable set in another ASP page for the same user, you would use the Session object. The Session object holds a collection of variables that are available to all pages of a Web application for the same user during the same session. To place a variable in the Session object, use the following code:

```
' — Declare the variable
Dim strName
' — Assign value to the variable
strName = "Rama Ramachandran"
' — Place it in the Session object
Session("uname") = strName
```

In another Web page (or in the same Web page at a later time), you can access the value of the variable uname stored in the Session object:

```
Dim strUName
strUName = Session("uname")
```

Q: *How can you make sure that the value of a variable is available to all Web pages in an application for all users to your Web site?*

A: In order to share variables and give them an application-wide scope for all users, store the variables in the Application object. All ASP pages in your application for all users then can access this variable. Store the variable in the Application object the same way you would store it in the Session object.

Q: *What should you do to the Application object before assigning a value to an application-level variable?*

A: You should lock it to prevent the application-level variable from being accessed by another ASP page at the exact same time. Once you have finished assigning the variable value, you should unlock the Application object. This enables other ASP pages to access the variable's value:

```
Application.Lock
Application("ConnString") = "DSN=blah"
Application.UnLock.
```

Q: *How do you declare a constant in an ASP page?*

A: In VBScript, you would declare a constant by using the const statement:

```
const APP_NAME = "My Web Application"
```

In Jscript, you use the var statement:

```
var APP_NAME = "My Web Application";
```

Q: *How do you declare and use arrays in an ASP page?*

A: In VBScript, you declare a variable to be an array by adding parentheses at the end of the variable name. You can include the number of items in the array within the parentheses:

```
Dim aryNames(10)
```

This creates an array variable called aryNames with indices that range from 0 to 10. You can then access and use these items by using the following syntax (notice the box brackets instead of the parentheses):

```
AryNames[3] = "Rama Ramachandran"
```

In JScript, you declare a variable to be an array by using the Array statement:

```
var aryNames = new Array(10);
```

You can then refer to the items by using the following syntax:

```
AryNames(3) = "Rama Ramachandran";
```

Q: *What would you use to iterate through all the items of a collection?*

A: You would use the For Each...Next loop to iterate through all the items of a collection. The following code iterates through the Cookies collection and dumps their contents on to the browser:

```
For Each c in Request.Cookies
 Response.write c.Name & " = " & c.value
Next
```

Q: *Which HTML tag or control is used to obtain input from the user?*

A: You can obtain input from the user by using an HTML FORM. Use the HTML <FORM> tag to create a form on a Web page.

Q: *What are the two methods that send a FORM's data back to the Web server?*

A: You can instruct an HTML FORM to send data back to the Web server using one of two methods, GET or POST. You specify this by using the METHOD attribute of the FORM tag:

```
<FORM METHOD="GET">
<FORM METHOD="POST">
```

When you use the GET method, all form data is appended to the URL query string and sent back to the Web server. When the POST method is used, the form data is sent as invisible headers along with the browser's request.

Q: *How do you access FORM data in your ASP page?*

A: By using either the Request.QueryString collection or the Request.Form collection. If the FORM is encoded using the GET method, you need to use the Request.QueryString collection:

```
strName = Request.QueryString("name")
```

If the FORM is encoded using the POST method, you need to use the Request.Form collection:

```
strName = Request.QueryString("name")
```

If you are not sure what encoding is used on the form, you can access the Form's contents by directly querying the Request object:

```
strName = Request("name")
```

Q: *How would you declare a text box on a FORM that accepts a password so that the user cannot see what he/she is typing?*

A: You declare the input field of type PASSWORD:

```
<INPUT TYPE="PASSWORD" NAME="password" SIZE="10">
```

Q: *How would you make sure that the user has entered some text in a text box on the FORM without allowing them to submit a form with a blank field?*

A: By using client-side JavaScript code. You would write a function that checks to see if the text box contains valid data or not. You would invoke this function on the ONSUBMIT event of the form. When the form is submitted, it first executes the client-side code. If the function returns a False return value, the form is not submitted.

Q: *How do you use include files in ASP pages?*

A: You can use include files in ASP pages to share common code between ASP pages. If your common routines are in a single file, then that file can be included in other ASP pages. At run time, the ASP script engine combines all the include files with the main page and executes the code. To include a page (page2.asp) within another page (page1.asp), you would use the following syntax:

```
<!- #include virtual ="page2.asp" ->
```

or

```
<!- #include file ="page1.asp" ->
```

Q: *Why would you use the virtual keyword in an include statement?*

A: When you want to refer to an include file in a virtual directory, you would use the virtual keyword in an include statement. If you are referring to a file in the same directory or within the same physical directory structure (a relative path), you would use the file keyword in the include statement.

Q: *Can you substitute dynamic names for include files in ASP pages?*

A: No. Since include files are gathered together and combined before any ASP code execution takes place, they cannot contain ASP variables. The name of the include file cannot be a variable.

Q: *Can you place an include statement within the ASP tags <% and %>?*

A: No, the include statement is a preprocessor directive and needs to be outside the ASP tags.

Q: *What are the events that occur when a session begins and ends?*

A: When a session begins, the Session_OnStart event is fired and when the session ends, the Session_OnEnd event is fired.

Q: *Where would you write code to execute when the Session events fire?*

A: Since these events occur on a Session-wide level, you cannot write code for the Session_OnStart and Session_OnEnd in any ASP page.

However, ASP looks to a special page to when these events are fired. This is the Global.asa page. The Global.asa is a special ASP page that is placed in the root of your Web application. It contains the code to be executed when the Session and Application events fire.

Q: *How do you use cookies in ASP pages?*

A: You can access the cookies on a user's computer by accessing the Cookies collection of the Request object. To set the value of a cookie, you access the Cookies collection of the Response object using

```
Response.Cookies("UserID") = 897
```

or

```
Dim strUserID
StrUserID = Request.Cookies("UserID")
```

Q: *How do you make sure that a cookie value persists on the user's computer even after the browser is shut down?*

A: To check that the value of the cookie persists for a predetermined amount of time, you set the Expires property of the cookie to a future date. The cookie value exists until that date and then it is automatically deleted:

```
Response.Cookies("UserID").Expires = "December 31, 2001"
```

Intermediate Questions

Q: *How do you delete a cookie from an ASP page?*

A: To delete a cookie, simply set its Expires property to a date that is past:

```
Response.Cookies("UserID").Expires = "December 31, 1999"
```

Q: *How would you find out what kind of browser your Web site visitor is using from an ASP page?*

A: In ASP, you can use the Request object's ServerVariables collection to obtain this information. To find the browser agent being used, you would access the HTTP_USER_AGENT variable:

```
Dim strBrowser
strBrowser = Request.ServerVariables("HTTP_USER_AGENT")
```

Q: *Suppose you need to find out which Web site is referring your visitors to your site. How could you do this with ASP?*

A: You can use the Request objects's ServerVariables collection to obtain this information. To find the URL of the page that your user visited before coming to your Web site, examine the HTTP_REFERER variable. Use the following line of code in the first page a Web site visitor would acess from another Web site (a search engine or an affiliate Web site) to access their URL:

```
Dim strReferer
strReferer = Request.ServerVariables("HTTP_REFERER")
```

Q: *A form requires the name of a page as part of its ACTION attribute. If a form page needs to load itself, how can you dynamically substitute the name of the page itself as part of the ACTION attribute without hard-coding it each time?*

A: You can use the Request objects's ServerVariables collection to obtain this information. Instead of hard-coding the name of the ASP page, use the SCRIPT_NAME variable as the ACTION attribute of the FORM tag:

```
<FORM ACTION="<%= Request.ServerVariables("SCRIPT_NAME")
%>">
```

At run time, if this is in Page1.asp, the above line is resolved to

```
<FORM ACTION="Page1.asp">
```

Q: *If you do not plan to use session variables, you can turn off session state for your Web page. How do you do this for your ASP page?*

A: You can use the @ENABLESESSIONSTATE preprocessor directive to turn off session tracking for an ASP page. By doing so, the Web server does not need to maintain additional information about the session and therefore Web page performance is enhanced:

```
<% @ENABLESESSIONSTATE = FALSE%>
```

Q: *Given a currency value, how can you format it properly in ASP so that it displays with a dollar sign, commas, and two decimal places?*

A: Use the FormatCurrency function to format a number into a currency value. Also specify the number of decimal places you want in your output. Given the number 1,234,567, the following code would return $1,234,567.00:

```
Response.Write FormatCurrency("1234567",2)
```

Q: *How would you format the current date so that it returns the long date format?*

A: Use the FormatDateTime function to format an expression as a long date format:

```
Response.Write FormatDateTime(Date, 1) ' 1 returns long
date time
```

Q: *How would you be able to present the number 0.05 as a percentage (5%)?*

A: Use the FormatPercent function to format a number as a percentage. The FormatPercent function returns an expression formatted as a percentage (multiplied by 100) with a trailing percent character:

```
Response.Write FormatPercent(0.05, 0) ' returns 5%
```

Q: *On a particular page in the application I'm developing, I'd like to display some numbers in ####.#### format. How do I go about doing that in ASP?*

A: Use the FormatNumber function in VBScript. This returns an expression formatted as a number:

```
FormatNumber(Expression [,NumDigitsAfterDecimal
[,IncludeLeadingDigit [,UseParensForNegativeNumbers
[,GroupDigits]]]])
```

For example, FormatNumber ("123.45",4) would return 123.4500.

Q: *What is the database technology that is used to access databases from an ASP page?*

A: ASP uses Microsoft's *ActiveX Data Objects* (ADO) to access databases. ADO provides a simple and powerful means for accessing OLE DB-compliant databases including relational databases, spreadsheets, sequential files, or e-mail directories. ADO is scalable and provides high-performance access to back-end databases.

Q: *How would you know the number of elements in an array variable?*

A: Use the UBound and LBound functions to find out the upper and lower levels of an array. This tells you how many elements are present within an array variable.

Q: *With DAO, before you could open a recordset, you needed to open the database. How is this done with ADO?*

A: In ADO, there is no such thing as a database. Instead, ADO relies on a Connection object. A Connection object represents a connection to a back-end database and performs the role that a database object used to do in DAO.

Q: *How do you open a connection to a database using ADO?*

A: To open a connection to a database, ADO needs to be provided with a connection string. This is a series of semicolon-delimited arguments within a string that identifies the back-end database and the mechanism used to access it. Once a connection string is provided, you can use the Open method of the Connection object to open a connection to the database. ADO inspects the connection string to figure out which provider to use to access the back-end database. With ADO, you can use two kinds of providers that provide connection services to databases: OLE DB and ODBC.

The following table lists OLE DB connection strings for several common data sources:

Data Source	OLE DB Connection String
Microsoft® Access	Provider=Microsoft.Jet.OLEDB.4.0;Data Source= physical path to .mdb file
Microsoft SQL Server	Provider=SQLOLEDB.1;Data Source=path to database on server
Oracle	Provider=MSDAORA.1;Data Source=path to database on server
Microsoft Indexing Service	Provider=MSIDXS.1;Data Source=path to file

To provide for backward compatibility, the OLE DB provider for ODBC supports the ODBC connection string syntax. The following table lists commonly used ODBC connection strings:

Data Source Driver	ODBC Connection String
Microsoft Access	Driver={Microsoft Access Driver (*.mdb)};DBQ=physical path to .mdb file
SQL Server	DRIVER={SQL Server};SERVER=path to server
Oracle	DRIVER={Microsoft ODBC for Oracle};SERVER=path to server
Microsoft Excel	Driver={Microsoft Excel Driver (*.xls)};DBQ=physical path to .xls file; DriverID=278
Microsoft Excel 97	Driver={Microsoft Excel Driver (*.xls)};DBQ=physical path to .xls file;DriverID=790
Paradox	Driver={Microsoft Paradox Driver (*.db)};DBQ=physical path to .db file;DriverID=26
Text	Driver={Microsoft Text Driver (*.txt;*.csv)};DefaultDir=physical path to .txt file

continues

Data Source Driver	ODBC Connection String
Microsoft Visual FoxPro(r) (with a database container)	Driver={Microsoft Visual FoxPro Driver};SourceType=DBC;SourceDb=physical path to .dbc file
Microsoft Visual FoxPro (without a database container)	Driver={Microsoft Visual FoxPro Driver};SourceType=DBF;SourceDb=physical path to .dbf file

Q: *What is needed in order to use ODBC to access a back-end database?*

A: In order to use ODBC, you need to install the ODBC drivers for the back-end database on the Web server. In addition, ODBC requires a User, System, or File *Data Source Name* (DSN) to be set up on the Web server.

Q: *How do you create an ODBC DSN?*

A: To create an ODBC DSN, use the ODBC administrator program available under Control Panel (or Control Panel, Administrative Tools), as shown in Figure 4-3. To create a new User, System, or File DSN, click Add under the User, System, and File DSN tabs respectively. Then choose the kind of database you are connecting to and click Finish. This launches the ODBC data source administrator specific to your back-end database (see Figure 4-4).

For example, if you choose to create a DSN for an Access database, the ODBC Microsoft Access Setup dialog box pops up, allowing you to select an existing Access MDB file (see Figure 4-5).

On the other hand, if you choose to set up a DSN for a SQL Server database, the dialog box in Figure 4-6 enables you to set up the server and, within that, choose the database to connect to (see Figures 4-7 through 4-10).

Q: *What is a System DSN and how is it different from a User DSN?*

A: A System DSN is available to all users on a computer even when no user is logged on to the computer. A User DSN, however, is specific to and is only available to the user for which it is created. In a Web environment, since a Web server usually does not have any users logged on at all times, a System DSN is much better than a User DSN.

Q: *What is a File DSN and how is it different from a System DSN?*

A: A File DSN is a DSN description encoded in a physical file. A System DSN resides within the system registry, while a File DSN is available as a file. This makes the File DSN extremely portable. If you want to

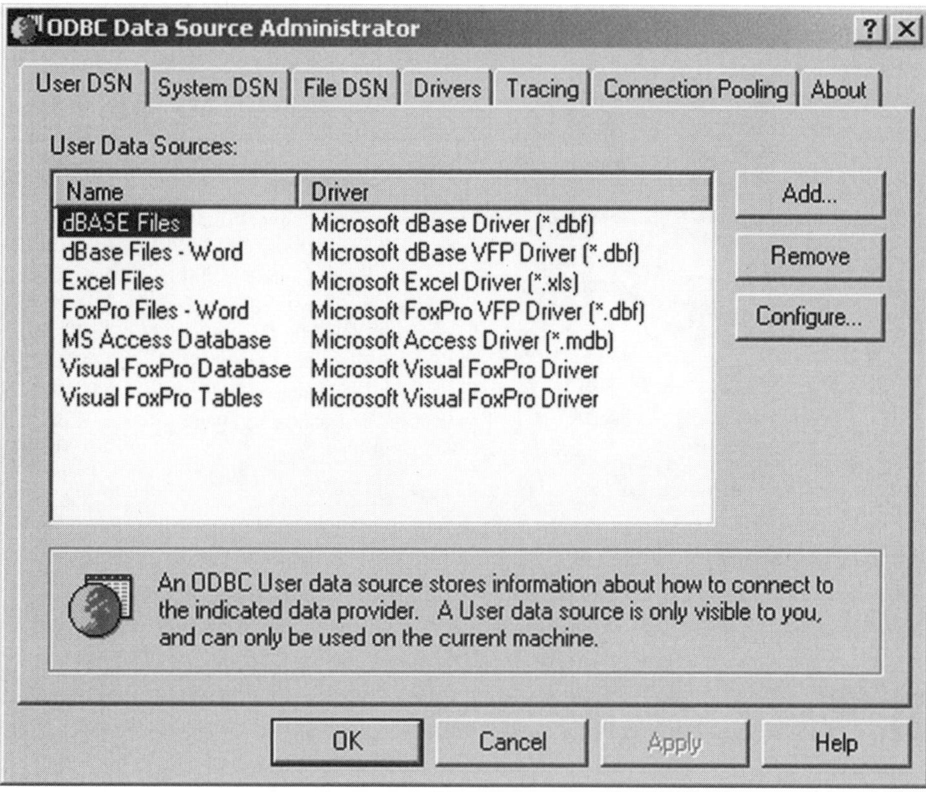

Figure 4-3 Creating an ODBC DSN

move your DSN from your development machine to your production machine, and you use a System DSN, you must physically create the System DSN on the production machine. This means that you need to have access to the production machine itself. If you use a File DSN, all you need to do is copy the File DSN file over from one machine to the other. The production machine does not need any registry manipulation if you are using a File DSN. To that extent, a File DSN is portable. However, a System DSN provides slightly better performance than a File DSN.

Q: *What are the network protocols available to access Microsoft SQL Server from ADO?*

A: ADO can access Microsoft SQL Sever using TCI/IP sockets, named pipes, or multi-protocols. TCP/IP sockets provide the best performance, since a Web server machine can connect directly to a SQL

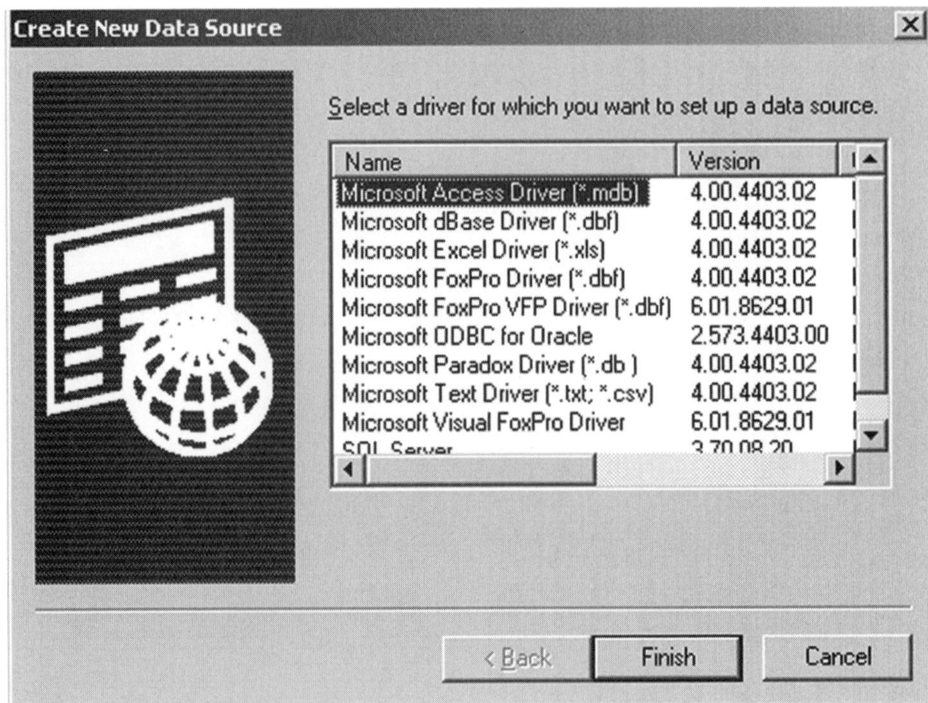

Figure 4-4 Creating a new data source

Server machine using TCP/IP sockets. If the Web server is using named pipes, database clients need to be authenticated by Windows before establishing a connection. This may cause the remote SQL Server computer running named pipes to deny access to a user who does not have a Windows account on that computer. Connections made using TCP/IP sockets connect directly to the database server without connecting through an intermediary computer, as is the case with named pipes.

Q: *What is ODBC Connection Pooling and how do you set it up?*

A: Connection Pooling is the technique by which the ODBC system manages multiple open connections to a database and pools them together. As new connections are requested, instead of creating a new one, an existing open connection from the pool is provided. This reduces the time and overhead of creating and destroying new connections and therefore improves performance. Prior to ODBC 3.0, Connection Pooling had to be set up manually by tweaking the

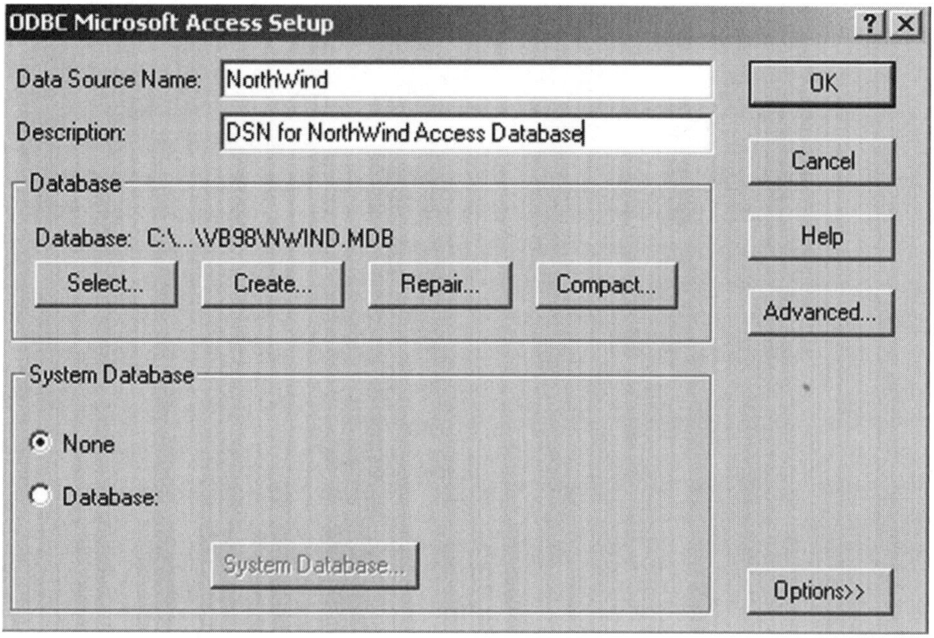

ODBC Microsoft Access Setup

Data Source Name: NorthWind

Description: DSN for NorthWind Access Database

Database

Database: C:\...\VB98\NWIND.MDB

Select... Create... Repair... Compact...

System Database

None

Database:

System Database...

OK

Cancel

Help

Advanced...

Options>>

Figure 4-5 Selecting an existing Access MDB file

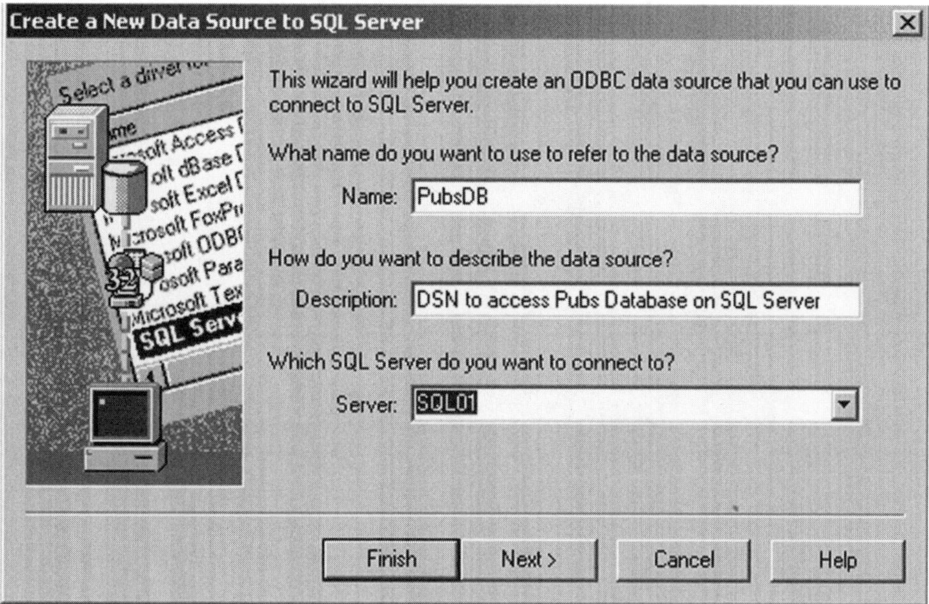

Figure 4-6 Setting up the server and choosing the database

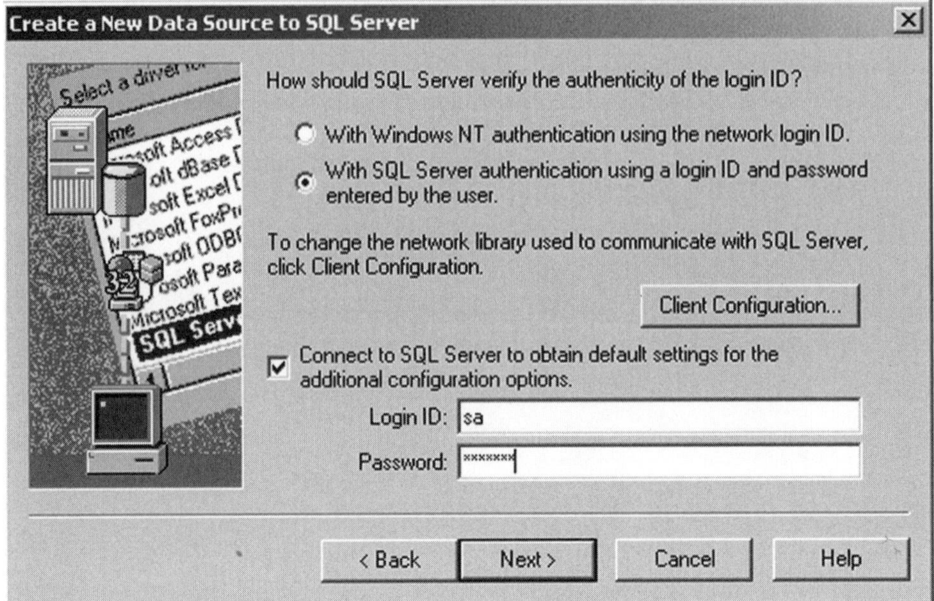

Figure 4-7 Verifying authenticity and connecting to SQL Server

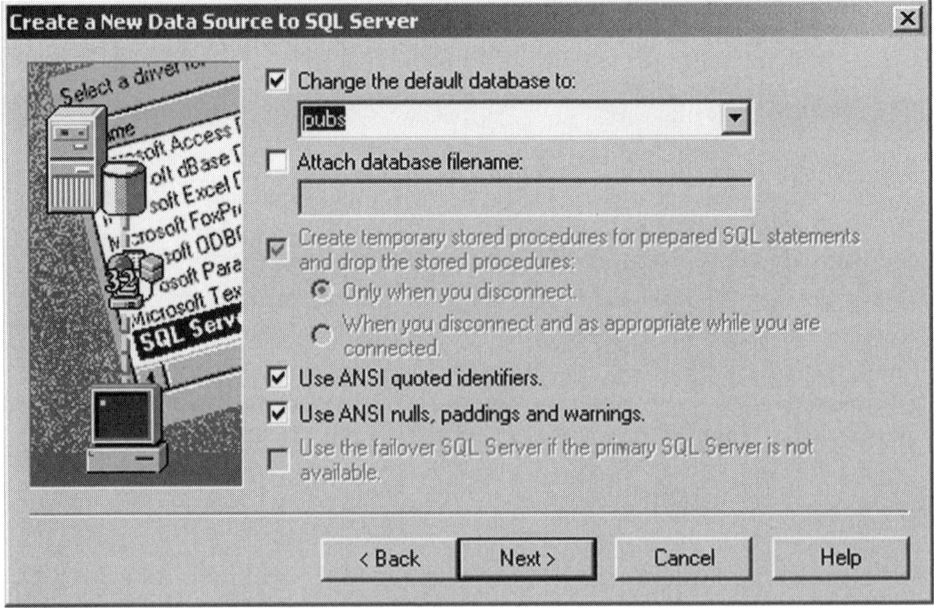

Figure 4-8 Changing the default databases

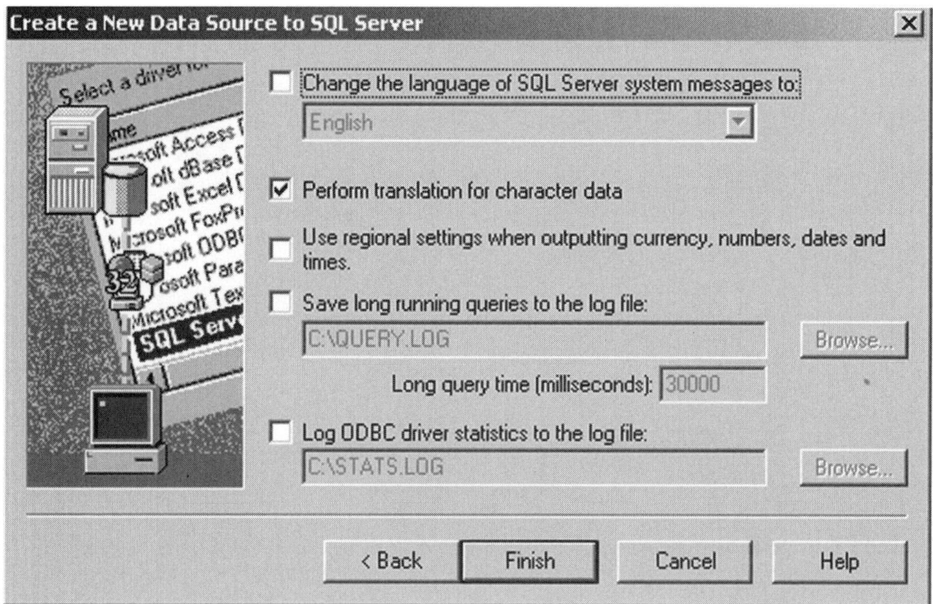

Figure 4-9 Performing translations for character data

registry settings. With ODBC 3.0 and later, Connection Pooling is turned on by default. To utilize connection pooling, the ASP programmer should open a connection at the very last moment when he/she needs the data and should close the connection as soon as possible after data retrieval.

Q: *How do you perform an action query in ADO using just the Connection object?*

A: To carry out an action query (a query that does not return any records), you use the Execute method of the Connection object after you have opened a connection to the database:

```
<%
Dim strConnString, objConn, strSQL
'Define the OLE DB connection string.
strConnstring= "Provider=Microsoft.Jet.OLEDB.4.0;" & _
      "Data Source=C:\Data\NWind.mdb"
' open a database connection.
Set objConn = Server.CreateObject("ADODB.Connection")
objConn.Open strConnectionString
```

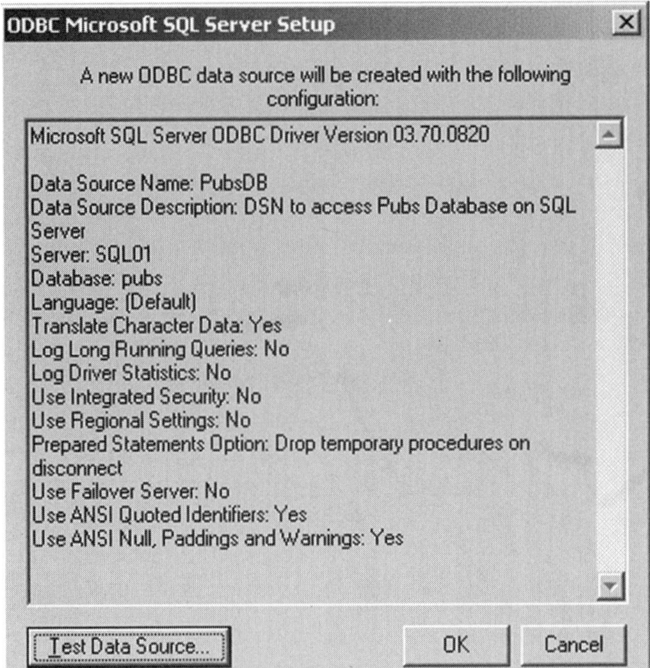

Figure 4-10 The final configuration settings

```
' Define our Action query
strSQL = "INSERT INTO Customers (FirstName, LastName) VAL-
UES ('Bill','Gates')"
' Execute the Action Query
objConn.Execute strSQL
' Close the Connection
objConn.Close
set objConn = Nothing
%>
```

Q: *What is the Command object in ADO?*

A: A Command object is the definition of a specific command you want to execute in ADO. If you plan to run the same query over and over again in your Web pages, it is better to place it in a Command object.

The first time the Command object is executed, the database engine parses and compiles the query. You can then specify that the database engine should store the compiled results. The subsequent execution of the Command object performs much faster since the database engine does not have to recompile the query each time, but rather can use the saved compiled results. A Command object also is useful when you want to execute a query that accepts parameters that change at each execution. You can use the Parameters collection of the Command object to pass parameters to your query and obtain different results.

Q: *In a Command object, how would you specify that a particular parameter is a return value and not an input parameter?*

A: Use the Direction property of the parameter to specify that it is an output parameter and not an input parameter. Use the intrinsic constant, adParamOutput, to specify that it is an output parameter or a return value.

Q: *How do you create a disconnected recordset?*

A: Before opening the recordset and fetching the data, set the CursorLocation property to adClient. This creates a client-side cursor. Once you have opened the recordset using a specific Connection object, immediately break the connection by setting the recordset's ActiveConnection property to nothing. This results in a disconnected recordset.

Q: *How do you define a transaction using ADO?*

A: To begin a transaction, use the Connection object's BeginTrans method. When the transaction is complete, if it is successful, invoke the Connection object's CommitTrans method. If the transaction is unsuccessful, invoke the Command object's RollBackTrans method.

Q: *What is the advantage of a disconnected recordset?*

A: Since a disconnected recordset does not hold an active connection to the database, you can take as long as you want to analyze and read the contents of the recordset in your ASP page without affecting the database's performance. All the data in the recordset resides on the client, and the database connection has been broken. This enables the database to accept other connections, thereby improving database access performance.

Q: *If you want to display the current time on your Web site and also display the time in New York, which is three hours ahead of you, how would you do it?*

A: To display the current time, use the FormatDateTime function with the current time, available from the function Now:

```
Response.Write FormatDateTime(Now(),3)
```

To display the time in New York, which is three hours ahead of you, add three hours to the current time by using the DateAdd function and then display the output. For the DateAdd function, you can specify "h" to indicate we need to add hours and three to indicate three hours.

```
Response.Write FormatDateTime(DateAdd("h", 3, Now()),3)
```

Q: *Which keyword is required to assign a value to an object variable?*

A: The SET keyword is required to assign a value to an object variable. You can assign a value to a regular variable by simply using the assignment operator (the equals sign):

```
X = 5
```

However, when you want to assign a value to an object variable, you need to precede the variable name with the SET keyword. Otherwise, you will get a run time error:

```
Set objRS = Server.CreateObject("ADODB.Recordset")
```

Q: *How will you know if a given variable is an array or not?*

A: Use the IsArray function to determine if a given variable is an array or not. IsArray returns true or false depending on whether the argument is an array or not.

Q: *If you have an array with 60 elements in it, how would you delete all the items from the array with a single line of code?*

A: Use the Erase statement to completely delete all the contents of an Array.

Q: *How can you define a new line character in ASP so that the output wraps around to the next line?*

A: In VBScript, you can use the intrinsic constant vbCrLf. This causes your output to wrap to the next line. In Jscript, you can use the \n characters to cause the output to wrap to the next line:

```
StrValue = "Hello" & vbCrLf & "World"
```

Q: *Which statement would you use in your ASP page code to tell the script engine to ignore any errors and continue processing?*

A: Use the statement "On Error Resume Next" at the top of your code to ensure that code continues to execute even when errors occur. This is not a good idea, since an error in one part of the code can cause more errors later on.

Q: *If you use the On Error statement to continue code execution even if an error occurs, how would you know later on if an error occurred?*

A: Inspect the value of the Err object. If an error has taken place in your code, the Err object will contain the error number and its text description. If no error occurs, the error number is zero.

Q: *When you have finished using an object variable, how do you ensure that the object variable is destroyed and its resources are returned to the operating system?*

A: When you are done with an object variable, set its value to "Nothing." By doing so, the object is physically removed from memory and you regain the resources used by the object.

```
Set objRS = Nothing
```

Q: *How would you generate a random number in your ASP page?*

A: Use the Rnd function to generate a random number. The Rnd function returns a random number between 0 and 1. To make sure you get a different set of random numbers each time, use the Rnd function with the value of the Timer function. To do so, use the Randomize Timer statement.

Q: *How do you generate a random number between 50 and 100 on your ASP page?*

A: To generate a random number between A and B, use the formula:

```
Random Number = Int((Upper Value - Lower Value + 1)* Rnd +
Lower Value)
```

To get a value between 50 and 100, use the following code:

```
Int((100 - 50 + 1) * Rnd + 50)
```

Q: *Which statement would force you to declare all variables in your ASP page?*

A: The Option Explicit statement placed at the top of the ASP page can force the programmer to explicitly declare all variables before using them. This is a good practice to ensure that typos in variable names do not cause problems. It also forces the programmer into a discipline of declaring variables before using them.

Q: *Which function would you use to find the location of a particular character within a string?*

A: Use the InStr function to find the location of a specific character or string within a larger string, as in the following:

```
strString = "Hello\World\How\Are\You"
IntPos = InStr(strString, "\")
' - IntPos will be 6, the first "\" from the left
```

Q: *How would you find the location of the last occurrence of a particular character within a string?*

A: Use the InStrRev function to find the location of a specific character or string within a bigger string, but search in the reverse order. Because this function searches from right to left, you can use this function to find the last occurrence of a particular character within a string:

```
strString = "Hello\World\How\Are\You"
IntPos = InStrRev(strString, "\")
' - IntPos will be 20, the first "\" from the right
```

Q: *If you wanted to substitute all occurrences of the word "morning" with the word "evening" in a block of text in a variable, what would be the quickest way to do so on an ASP page?*

A: Use the Replace function to quickly replace text within a string. This is much faster than inspecting each character of the text block and performing a substitution. Here's an example:

```
strString = "Good morning, isn't this a lovely morning?"
strString = Replace(strString, "morning", "evening")
' - Substitute evening for morning
''- strString value will be "Good evening, isn't this a
lovely evening?"
```

Q: *When you use ADO code in ASP pages, frequently you get the error message "Data Source not found or no ODBC provider found," yet the Web application works fine on your development machine. How can you fix this error?*

A: This error is happening because ADO is using a System DSN to access the database. On the development machine, this System DSN has been set up and therefore the code works. On the Web server where the page ultimately resides, no matching System DSN can be found, and therefore the page produces this error. Thus, create an identical

System DSN on the Web server and your code should work. Better still, use an OLEDB provider string within your code so you do not need to rely on ODBC DSNs.

Q: *What would be a technique for caching lookup data that displays in a combo box on your HTML page so that you do not have to access the database for each user?*

A: Instead of accessing the database for each user to produce a SELECT list based on a recordset, generate the HTML for the SELECT list using a recordset only once. Then place the generated HTML within an application-level variable. All subsequent requests for the lookup data can be accessed from the application-level variable, leading to vast performance improvements. Since no database access is involved the second time onwards, the ASP page is rendered much faster.

Q: *Let's say you are being asked to evaluate an existing ASP Web application in which the programmer is opening a connection to the database, obtaining the data in the form of a recordset, and then storing the recordset in a Session variable so that it can be reused over and over again. The logic is that the database needs to be accessed only once, so it is better for performance. What are your comments to this technique?*

A: This is a poorly designed application. The programmer is placing an ADO recordset in a session variable with the mistaken assumption that by doing so he/she is saving a round trip to the database each time the user needs the data. However, by placing a COM object (an ADO recordset is a COM object) in a session variable, the programmer cripples IIS. IIS and ASP run under a multithreaded environment. By placing a COM component in a session variable, it forces ASP to always seek the same thread where the COM component is residing in memory, thereby forcing it into a single-threaded application. This causes poor performance. Also, since the Recordset object maintains an open connection to the database, it consumes precious database resources. The net effect of this technique is poor performance and poor scalability, especially in a busy Web server environment.

Q: *How can you force the browser to think that the data you are sending from an ASP page is not plain HTML text, but rather an Excel Spreadsheet?*

A: A browser relies on the MIME type of the response it receives to determine what kind of data is coming down the data stream. A browser looks for the ContentType header to determine this. You can manipulate the *Multipurpose Internet Mail Extensions* (MIME) content type of your response by changing the ContentType property of the Response object. The ContentType property specifies the HTTP content type for the response. If no content type is specified, the default is text/HTML. To change it so that the browser thinks you are sending an Excel spreadsheet, use the following code before you send any content:

```
<%
Response.ContentType = "application/vnd.ms-excel"
%>
```

Q: *When you are executing sections of code that take a long time to process, it is important to know if your user is still waiting for the results or has moved off of the page. If the user has moved off, then you can stop processing. How will you know from server-side script if your user has moved off of your Web page?*

A: You can know from the IsClientConnected property of the Response object. This new property was introduced with ASP 3 on Windows 2000. This property gives you greater control over circumstances when the client may have disconnected from the server. For example, if a long period of time has elapsed between when a client request was made and when the server responded, it may be beneficial to make sure the client is still connected before continuing to process the script. This property returns false if the user has moved off of the Web page, and therefore you can stop processing.

Q: *What is a Component Object Model (COM) component?*

A: A COM component is a reusable, programmatic building block that contains code for performing a task or a set of tasks. A component can be invoked by another calling program. You use components to reuse code, distribute proprietary functionality, and improve performance. A component that is built according to Microsoft's COM standards is a COM component.

Advanced Questions

Q: *What kinds of COM components are created using Visual Basic?*

A: Using Visual Basic, you can create ActiveX DLLs and ActiveX EXEs. ActiveX DLLs run as in-process COM components, while ActiveX EXEs run as out-of-process COM components.

Q: *Which threading model is used by Visual Basic COM components?*

A: Visual Basic supports the creation of Apartment-Model-Threaded COM components.

Q: *Which is better, a COM component with a lot of properties and a single method, or a COM component where all property values are passed as arguments of a single method call?*

A: The single method call with property values as arguments is better. Each call to assign a property value of a COM component from an ASP page requires a trip to be made to the COM component in memory and back. If all the property values are passed as arguments to a single method call, a single round trip would accomplish the task of setting all the property values and invoking the method. Since this eliminates numerous round trips, the performance is significantly better.

Q: *How would you instantiate a COM component in your ASP page?*

A: Before using a COM component, it has to be registered on the Web server. You also need to know the Class ID for the COM component. If you know it, you can use the Server.CreateObject statement to create an instance of the COM component. The following code creates an instance of the ADO Recordset COM component, which has a class ID of ADODB.Recordset:

```
Dim objRS
Set objRS = Server.CreateObject("ADODB.Recordset")
```

Alternatively, you can also use the <OBJECT> tag to declare an instance of a COM component. To ensure that it is instantiated on the server and not on the client, you need to add the attribute RUNAT=SERVER:

```
<OBJECT ID="objRS" PROGID="ADODB.Recordset"
RUNAT=SERVER></OBJECT>
```

Q: *Why is it that you need to use the CreateObject function to create an instance of a COM component, but you do not need to do this for the built-in objects in ASP?*

A: Unlike using the objects provided by a COM component, you do not need to create an instance of an ASP built-in object to use it in your scripts. These objects are automatically created for you when the ASP request starts processing.

Q: *How can you refer to constants built into DLLs (such as the ADO constants) without using an include file on an ASP page?*

A: Normally, to be able to refer to constants built into DLLs including ADO constants (such as adOpenKeyset or adLockOptimistic for example), you would need to manually write each constant's name and value in a separate include file that you would need to include in your ASP page using the #include statement. However, there is a better way.

Use the METADATA statement to include the name of a type library within a DLL. ASP then parses the type library and has access to all constants declared within the type library:

```
<!— METADATA TYPE="typelib" _
FILE="c:\program files\common
files\system\ado\msado15.dll"—>
```

The previous line includes the ADO type library within your ASP page. You then can refer to intrinsic ADO constants without having to declare them:

```
objRS.ActiveConnection = ..your connection object...
objRS.CursorType = adOpenKeyset
objRS.LockType = adLockOptimistic
```

Q: *Which is better, using Server.CreateObject to create a COM component when required, or defining a COM component in an ASP page (or the Global.asa page) using the <OBJECT RUNAT=SERVER> tag?*

A: If you are going to be using a COM component in specific areas of your ASP application, use the <OBJECT> tag rather than the Server.CreateObject statement. The Server.CreateObject statement immediately creates the COM component. If later on, you do not end up using the COM component, then you have wasted valuable resources. The <OBJECT> tag, on the other hand, does not create a COM component when the code is executed. It instead defines a variable. The actual COM component is instantiated only when you use its properties or methods for the very first time.

Q: *Which is better, Server.Transfer or Response.Redirect?*

A: Always use Server.Transfer. It does a direct transfer on the server side from one ASP page to another. The Response.Redirect statement sends an instruction to the browser to return back and request a different ASP page. This extra round trip is eliminated with the Server.Transfer statement and is therefore faster.

Q: *How do I format my numbers in the format ######, where a number of 123 would display as 000123?*

A: Concatenate a string of zeros to the left of your number and then call the NumberFormat function on the right "n" portion of it. So, if your variable intValue had 123 in it, the following would produce 000123:

```
Response.write FormatNumber(Right
("0000000000" & Trim(intValue),6),0)
```

The Trim() would get rid of leading and trailing spaces. The ampersand would concatenate the zeros to the number and then the Right would return the rightmost n numbers. Finally, the FormatNumber function would make sure that you have no decimal places.

Q: *How would you be able to access the last modified date of a file from an ASP page?*

A: You would need to use the FileSystemObject component to access a file and then use the File Object's DateLastModified property to access the last modified date for the file.

Q: *How would you send an e-mail from an ASP page?*

A: You can use the *Collaboration Data Objects for NT Server* (CDONTS) to quickly and easily send e-mail from an ASP page. Make sure the *Simple Mail Transfer Protocol* (SMTP) service is set up in Windows NT/2000 and then use the following code:

```
Dim myMail
Set myMail = Server.CreateObject("CDONTS.NewMail")
myMail.From = "rama@imperium.com"
myMail.To = visitor@mywebsite.com
myMail.Subject = "Thank you for visiting my site"
myMail.Body = "I hope you enjoyed the site. Please come
again."
myMail.Send
Set myMail = Nothing
```

Q: *What is a Web farm?*

A: A Web farm is the name of a Web architecture where multiple Web servers service the same URL. Intermediary software or hardware determines which Web server has the least load at run time and transfers the URL request to that Web server. This technique is called *load balancing*. A Web farm enables a Web site to satisfy hundreds and thousands of concurrent Web site users and is usually the architecture of choice for large e-commerce sites.

Q: *What is NLBS or WLBS?*

A: NLBS stands for *Network Load Balancing Service* and WLBS is its previous name, *Windows Load Balancing Service*. It is the load balancing service that ships with the Windows NT Server operating system. WLBS shipped with Windows NT 4, and NLBS ships with Windows 2000 Advanced Server.

Q: *Which HTML statement enables you to upload a file from the client's desktop to your Web server?*

A: The <INPUT TYPE=FILE> statement is used to upload a file from the user's machine to the Web server. This statement presents a text box and a default Browse button that enables the user to choose a file from the local machine. When the form that contains the statement is submitted, the file is sent from the user's machine to the Web server.

Q: *If you have a recordset containing data, how can you jump directly to the fifth page of records, assuming each page has 20 records?*

A: Use the recordset's PageSize and the AbsolutePage properties. The PageSize property determines how many records comprise a page. Set this to 20. Then set the AbsolutePage property to 5. The record pointer will then be the first record of the fifth page, where each page has 20 records.

Q: *What is the best cursor type to use for read-only data that will be dumped on a Web page within an HTML table?*

A: Since we are dumping the data on an HTML table and proceeding in one direction within the recordset, a forward-only, read-only cursor will provide the fastest performance.

Q: *What is MTS?*

A: MTS stands for *Microsoft Transaction Server*. It is a component and transaction management service that runs under Windows NT 4. In Windows 2000, MTS morphed into COM+, a part of the Windows Component Services.

Q: *What can you do within your MTS COM components to improve your component's performance?*

A: Make sure that you are calling the SetComplete and SetAbort methods when your component code finishes executing successfully or fails respectively. This enables MTS to release the component quicker and manage it better, leading to better performance and scalability.

Q: *How can you obtain the Windows NT login name for an intranet application in an ASP page?*

A: Use the ServerVariables collection to find the Windows NT Login name. Access the REMOTE-USER or the LOGON-USER variable within the ServerVariables collection:

```
StrName = Request.ServerVariables("REMOTE-USER")
If InStr(strName, "\") > 0 Then
 StrWindowsLoginName = Mid(strName, InStr(strName, "\")+1)
End If
```

Q: *How can you force a session to close?*

A: Use the Session.Abandon method.

Q: *How do you prevent ASP from producing a timeout error when processing a long section of code?*

A: Increase ASP's script timeout time by setting the Server.ScriptTime Out property to a sufficiently large number.

Q: *How can you obtain the list of all the tables in a database using ADO?*

A: Use the Connection object's OpenSchema method with an argument that specifies that it will return to only tables. The resulting recordset contains a list of tables, their names, and their attributes:

```
Set rstTables = objConn.OpenSchema(adSchemaTables)
```

Q: *What is a DSN-less connection?*

A: When you use a Connection object and open it by providing the connection information in a string, rather than within an ODBC data source name, it is called a DSN-less connection. Instead of creating an ODBC File, User, or System DSN and then providing the name of the DSN as the connection string of the Connection object, you can provide the DSN details directly:

```
ObjConn.Open "DRIVER={Microsoft Access Driver
(*.mdb)};DBQ=C:\DATA\NWIND.MDB"
```

Q: *What is a cookie?*

A: A cookie is a piece of text information that is stored on a user's computer by the browser and is available for future visits to the Web site. On the server, the Web application can access this cookie and manipulate it.

Q: *How would you know the physical path of a specific file on your Web server?*

A: Use the Server.MapPath() method to obtain the physical path of a file.

Q: *How would you make sure that a user can select only one out of three radio buttons on a form?*

A: Make sure all three radio buttons have the same name.

Q: *What is the easiest way to provide a single-line border around an HTML table without having any borders around the individual table cells? That is, how can you create a border for a table without creating borders for its cells?*

A: Place the table within an outer table. Set the outer table's background color to the border color and the inner table's background color to white. The inner table is then framed within the outer colored table.

Q: *How can you make sure that when a hyperlink in a frame is clicked, the contents of another frame are refreshed with the target of the hyperlink?*

A: Make sure that the hyperlink has its TARGET="" set to the name of the other frame.

Q: *How can you make sure that a user can only enter a maximum of 10 characters within a Zip code text field on a HTML form?*

A: Use the TextBox's MAXLENGTH attribute and set it to 10:

```
<INPUT TYPE="TEXT" NAME="zipcode" MAXLENGTH="10">
```

Q: *A list box and a combo box in HTML both use the SELECT tag. What makes one a list box and the other a combo box?*

A: The SIZE attribute. If the SIZE is set to 1, it becomes a combo box. If the SIZE is greater than 1, it becomes a list box.

Q: *When you created a recordset and then attempted to get its recordcount, it returns a value of -1. How can you find out the number of records within the recordset?*

A: Perform a Recordset.MoveLast before accessing its RecordCount property.

Q: *Is there a better way to obtain the recordcount without having to move to the last record?*

A: Yes. Before opening the recordset, make sure that you define it to be a Dynamic, Keyset, or Static cursor type by setting the recordset's CursorType property. Of the above, a Static cursor type is the slowest in performance.

Q: *What is the technique used to dump the contents of a recordset into an array?*

A: Use the recordset's GetRows method. This transfers all the contents of the recordset into an array in memory.

Q: *What would you use to dump the contents of a text file on your Web server onto the browser?*

A: Use the FileSystemObject to read the contents of the text file and send it to the browser.

Q: *If you want to stop ASP code execution in the middle of your ASP page, how would you do it?*

A: Use the Response.End method. When this line is executed, all ASP code execution halts.

Q: *You want to send the contents of a database record as the arguments of a hyperlink's URL using its QueryString. How do you make sure that spaces and punctuations in the data do not cause problems with the hyperlink's URL?*

A: Encode the data before attaching it to the hyperlink. You can encode in ASP by using the Server.URLEncode method.

Q: *In VBScript, how can you include a double quote within a string that is itself enclosed in double quotes?*

A: Use two double quotes for every single double quote within the string.

Q: *How would you break out of a loop in VBScript?*

A: Use the Exit statement. Within a Do loop, use Exit Do. Within a For loop, use Exit For.

Q: *What would be an ideal location to store a database connection string: a Session object or an Application object?*

A: You can use either one. An Application object is better since it needs to be set only once for the entire application rather than setting it up for each session.

Q: *Can you store the contents of an ADO recordset in an XML format?*

A: Yes. Use the Save method of the ADO recordset. The Save method uses two arguments: a destination and an optional format type. Specify adPersistXML as the format type for saving the ADO recordset to save the data in an XML format.

```
ObjRS.Save "C:\ADORS.XML", adPersistXML
```

Q: *How can you pass data between forms without the Web site user being able to view it?*

A: Use a HIDDEN form field on the form and populate it with data. The Web site user cannot view the data, but it is available to the server-side script as part of the form's contents.

Q: *How would you send a date value to SQL Server within a SQL statement?*

A: Enclose the date within single quotes. If you are using Microsoft Access, enclose the date within the Number (#) character.

Q: *How can you restrict the number of records returned by a recordset to 100 only?*

A: Either use the Top N statement within your SQL statement or use the MaxRecords property of the recordset and set it to 100 before opening the recordset.

Q: *What is MSMQ?*

A: MSMQ stands for *Microsoft Message Queuing Service*. It is a technology that enables reliable messaging between COM components.

Q: *How would you parse and place the contents of a comma delimted string into an array?*

A: Use the Split function to quickly and easily parse a string and place its contents within an array.

Q: *What makes a function different than a subroutine?*

A: A function executes code, always returns a value, and is always called on the right-hand side of an equals sign in an assignment. A subroutine executes code but does not return any values.

Q: *Can you use session variables on a Web farm?*

A: Session variables cannot be used on a multiserver Web farm. Certain load-balancing techniques can force all requests from a specific user to always be routed to a specific Web server. In this case, session variables can be used since the same Web server services a single session's Web page requests.

Q: *Is ASP the right solution for all Web applications?*

A: No. Like any other programming environment, it has to be used judiciously. Do not use ASP simply because you like to see all your Web pages have an .asp extension. ASP requires work on the server side, so if most of your Web site contains static Web pages, do not use ASP; simply use HTML pages. ASP is useful when you want to add interactivity to your Web site. Because of its tight integration with Microsoft's IIS and Microsoft SQL Server (via ADO), it is the environment of choice when designing e-commerce sites on the Windows platform.

5
Structured Query Language (SQL)

Dov Gilor

Structured Query Language (SQL) is a powerful language for creating and manipulating relational databases. It has become the standard throughout the database industry. Almost every database system in use today claims to be based on one form or another of SQL. Those systems that are not true *Relational Database Management Systems* (RDBMSs) offer SQL functionality by simulating the execution of SQL statements.

People with SQL expertise are in great demand in the computer marketplace and should receive many requests for interviews. The questions and answers in this chapter should help you ace the technical interview. Please note that Chapter 7, "DB2," will provide the reader with a great deal of additional RDBMS-specific information for DB2.

In the relational model, the database consists of tables that hold data in columns. Each column in a table row should be related to the key and to the other columns. The relationship between different pieces of data is represented by the actual values in the columns rather than by pointers or the record location, as in other non-relational databases. Data is selected and retrieved from the tables and presented in a result table format so that the output of a query is a table. An optimization program is used, usually during the BIND process, to determine how the data will be accessed.

In many installations, applications are given access to views rather than to the base tables to ensure that the modification of a table structure would not require modifying the many applications that use the table. The applications therefore access views that do not necessarily have to be modified when a table structure is modified. Views might also be used to simplify queries that need to access data from columns in many different tables or in a format different from the column. A view can also be used for security reasons to limit the columns and/or rows that are presented to the user. Note that a view can be created at any time after the tables are created.

The SQL statements must be prepared prior to execution either statically or dynamically. During static preparation, which is only possible in an application program, a pre-compiler syntactically checks the SQL statements and converts them into host language statements so that they can be compiled by the host language compiler. Dynamic SQL statements are prepared and executed during the execution of the application and usually not by a pre-compiler. Static SQL statements can be more efficient because they are prepared once (during pre-compile) and the access path is determined once (in a BIND process) in a process separate from the actual execution of the application. With dynamic statements, the preparation and BIND process are done each time the application is executed and it is done as part of the execution, thereby increasing the response time.

SQL statements can also be executed via DB2 utilities or be issued interactively by using the *Query Management Facility* (QMF), *SQL Processor Using File Input* (SPUFI), or other similar products. Statements can be embedded in application programs written in many languages including REXX, COBOL, Assembler, BASIC, C, C++, Java, PL/I, and so on. IBM and non-IBM application generators can also be used to build SQL applications.

In order to execute an application, it must be part of a PLAN. The pre-compile program creates a *database request module* (DBRM) as its output, which consists of the parsed statements in a SQL-usable format. This DBRM is then transformed via a BIND into a package and/or a PLAN that contains the access path. A package contains the SQL statements in their compiled format (known as *sections*) from a single source program. Static SQL sections contain the operational form (bound) of SQL statements. The dynamic SQL statement sections contain a placeholder control structure that will be used at execution time.

SQL is comprised of three elements: the *Data Definition Language* (DDL), the *Data Manipulation Language* (DML), and the *Data Control Language* (DCL).

With DDL, the *database administrator* (DBA) or user can create, delete, and modify the objects that physically and logically contain the data. The DDL commands include the following:

- CREATE, which defines each of the SQL objects (tables, indexes, databases, and so on).
- DROP, which deletes an SQL object.
- ALTER, which modifies an object.

To create a table with a SALARY table with a foreign key and a constraint on salary, for example, the following statement can be used:

```
CREATE TABLE EMPSAL_2001
(EMPNUM                  CHAR(5)      NOT NULL,
DEPTCODE                 CHAR(3)      NOT NULL,
SALARY                   DECIMAL(8,2) NOT NULL WITH
                                      DEFAULT,
COMMISSION               DECIMAL(5,2),
FOREIGN KEY EMPKEY (EMPNUM)
REFERENCES EMP_TABLE ON DELETE RESTRICT,
CONSTRAINT SALMAX CHECK (SALARY  5000)
)
IN SALSPACE
```

DML includes the following:

- SELECT, which retrieves data from the columns of one or more tables.
- INSERT, which adds one or more rows to a table.
- UPDATE, which modifies one or more column values in a table.
- DELETE, which removes one or more rows from a table.

To SELECT the salary information of every employee whose EMPNUM is greater than 10,001 and the SALARY is greater than 75,000, for example, the following statement can be used:

```
    SELECT EMPNUM, SALARY, COMMISSION, DEPTCODE,
SALARY + COMMISSION
    FROM EMPSAL_2001
    WHERE SALARY > 75000 AND EMPNUM > '10001'
    ORDER BY SALARY, 5
```

The control language includes the following:

- GRANT, which authorizes one or more users to use one or more SQL statements on one or more objects.
- REVOKE, which revokes any or all of the previous authorizations.

To GRANT all authorizations on EMPSAL_2001 table to OSHRA and enable her to authorize others, for example, the following statement can be used:

```
GRANT ALL ON EMPSAL_2001
  TO USER OSHRA WITH GRANT OPTION
```

The full syntax of all of the language statements for DB2, for example, can be found in the manuals that are stored at the IBM site, www.ibm.com/software/data/db2/library.

The heart of the RDBMS is a collection of tables known as the catalog or data dictionary. The catalog contains data about statistics, authorizations, and the defined SQL objects (tables, tablespaces, indexes, views, aliases, and so on). The catalog tables are accessed and/or modified whenever an object is selected, modified, created, altered, or dropped. The system automatically maintains the catalog tables and ensures their accuracy where needed, but the user can access the catalog tables by using the standard SQL statements and can even modify several values. When the application tables have already been created, the catalog tables are a source of much of the information about the data and the table structure that might be required by developers.

One of the interesting aspects of working with SQL is that the user specifies *what* needs to be done, rather than the access method that tells the system *how* it should be done (as required in other database systems).

An important aspect of working with relational databases is proper database design. The database should contain all of the data needed by the applications. In theory, databases are designed before applications are designed, but many believe that the applications should be designed first and then the databases should be built to best satisfy the needs of the applications.

Developers must keep the needs of batch and online processing in mind and realize that contention may become a serious problem. Concurrent access requires a separation of batch and online operations, a quick COMMIT online to release resources to other users, and a limited table modification during online prime time.

Another concern for developers is the need for security. Authorizations should not be too easy to bypass, nor should they be so complex that they prevent needed access. Access to large tables might be more efficient if the data were placed in a partitioned table. This is especially true when online and batch, or batch and batch, have to access the same tables at the same time but might access different partitions.

Application design is also an important aspect of database usage and the following tips might be useful. Data, for example, should be accessed in the same sequence in all applications where possible to avoid deadlocks. The COMMIT WORK statement should be issued as soon as possible to avoid contention, even in read-only applications (which also hold locks). When using a cursor defined with the WITH HOLD OPTION, close the cursor as soon as possible rather than waiting for the end of the application to release locks and free the resources held by the cursor.

Use the *cursor stability* (CS) isolation option whenever practical in an application. This ensures that the lock will be released as soon as the program reads the next row or page.

When coding applications, use static SQL whenever possible. After each SQL statement, test the SQL return code to examine the results of the operation.

This chapter is based mainly on the SQL of the DB2 RDBMS, but many other RDBMSs use similar SQL statements. The objects used in SQL are detailed in the DB2 chapter of this manual, but most also apply to other RDBMSs. The following questions and answers are listed by category and should help you ace the technical interview.

Datatypes

Q: *Which datatypes can be used in SQL statements?*

A: SQL only enables specific datatypes unless the user defines new datatypes. These datatypes include Char, Varchar, Graphic, Numeric (Decimal, Integer, Small integer, Float, and so on), Date, Time, Timestamp, a *Binary Large Object* (BLOB), user-defined datatypes, datalink types, and so on.

Q: *How are large, complex structures stored in SQL tables?*

A: The *Large Objects* (LOB) datatype is used to store such structures (video, voice, music, or images) represented in SQL tables. They can occupy up to two GB of storage.

Q: *What is a BLOB?*

A: A BLOB is a Binary Large Object. It is only compatible with other

BLOBs. A BLOB scalar function can convert other datatypes to be treated as BLOBs.

Q: *What are the size limits of some of the newer type fields?*

A: The BIGINT value is an eight-byte integer that contains 19 digits and a sign. It can contain from -9,223,372,036,854,775,808 to + 9,223,372,036,854,775,807. The CLOB can hold up to 2,147,483,647 bytes. The BLOB may hold up to 2,147,483,647 bytes.

Q: *What is graphic data and mixed data?*

A: SQL can use *single-byte character data* (SBCS) or *double-byte character data* (DBCS). Character sets for English and European languages, for example, use the SBCS and all characters are represented by one byte of memory. The 4,095 different characters that can be represented by one byte cannot represent the Japanese language with its large variety of characters. It therefore uses the DBCS for its character set. In a graphic data string, each character requires two bytes. The length of the string therefore is half the number of bytes in the string. *Mixed data* (MBCS) can contain both SBCS and DBCS characters. Mixed data can only be represented in an MBCS database.

Q: *When should a column be defined as a Binary string?*

A: The Binary string type is used to contain non-traditional (non-text) data such as pictures. Note that a character string defined as holding bit data can also be used for this type of data.

Q: *What is the difference between single-precision floating-point (REAL) and double-precision floating-point (DOUBLE or FLOAT)?*

A: The single-precision number is a 32-bit approximation of a real number, while the double-precision number is a 64-bit approximation of a real number. These numeric types are used for engineering and scientific calculations. The REAL number may be zero or may range from −3.402E+38 to −1.175E-37, or from 1.175E-37 to 3.402E+38. The double-precision number can be zero or can range from −1.79769E+308 to −2.225E-307, or from 2.225E-307 to 1.79769E+308.

Q: *What is a user-defined distinct type?*

A: A user-defined distinct type is a type that is incompatible with other types but has an internal representation similar to an existing type. A MYVIDEO type, for example, might be defined as CREATE DIS-

TINCT TYPE MYVIDEO AS BLOB (2M). This BLOB is not compatible with any other BLOB, even though it may have the same datatype.

Q: *What is a user-defined structured type?*

A: A user-defined structured type is a type that has its structure defined in the database. A structured datatype can be used as a table or view type but not as a column type. It will contain several data types in a sequence of named attributes. It may be a subtype of a super-type (from which it inherits all of the attributes) and may also have its own attributes. This super-type may also be a subtype of another super-type until a root type of the hierarchy is reached.

Q: *What is a user-defined reference type?*

A: A user-defined reference type is a type that uniquely identifies a row in a typed table or view. This target row is uniquely identified by an instance of a scoped reference type. The reference type is similar to distinct type and shares a common representation with one of the built-in datatypes.

Q: *What is a DATALINK value?*

A: When files are stored outside of the database, a reference from the database to the file is needed. The DATALINK value stored in the database is a value that contains this logical reference. This value has the attributes of the complete address of the file server, the type of link (currently only the *Uniform Resource Locator* (URL) is supported), the identity of the file within the server (the file path), the scheme of the link (whether a file or HTTP), and other information.

Q: *When two different datatypes are used in an operation, what are some of the rules for the result datatype?*

A: The result type of an operation is determined by considering the type of operands in the operation. When more than one pair of operands is used, each set of operands, starting with the first pair to be executed, is considered. The result datatype of the first operation is then considered with the next operand to determine the next result type, until all operands are considered. The last operand and the previous result type determine the final result type for the operation.

When both operands are character strings (CHAR), for example, the result is a character string with the length of the largest of the two strings. With numeric operands, the general rule is that the result takes on the form and size of the larger of the two operands. When one operand, for example, is an INTEGER and the other is a SMALL-INT, the result is an INTEGER.

Q: *When compared, do date, time, and timestamp operands behave as the previously mentioned datatypes?*

A: The date operand is compatible only with another date operand, a time operand is only compatible with another time operand, and a timestamp is compatible with another timestamp. Each is also compatible with any expression that contains a valid string representation of that type of operand. The result datatype for date operands is DATE, for time operands it is TIME, and for a timestamp it is TIMESTAMP.

Q: *What are some of the size limits on names in SQL?*

A: Most systems have to limit the sizes of names. It is always advisable to use the standard size that would enable the application to be portable across platforms, rather than use the maximum size that a particular SQL database management system enables. In DB2 version 6, for example, names within the database are usually up to 18 bytes long (user-defined type, statement, cursor, constraint, and so on) and external names (program, schema, server, and package) sent to the system are usually eight bytes long, while certain identifiers may be up to 128 (table, view, index, tablespace, trigger, correlation, and so on) or 255 bytes (host identifier).

Creating, Altering, and Dropping

Q: *Which SQL objects are specified by the CREATE statement?*

A: The SQL CREATE statement is used to create the SQL objects. The following objects, for example, can be created:

- STOGROUP: A list of *Direct Access Storage Devices* (DASDs) to be used to store data.
- DATABASE: A logical collection of tables and indexes.
- TABLESPACE: A physical storage space (VSAM in DB2).
- TABLE: The data structure of columns and rows with data.
- INDEX: A list of keys address pointers used as an efficient path to the data.

- VIEW: An alternate representation of columns from one or more tables.
- ALIAS: An alternate name for a table.

Q: *What are some of the parameters in the CREATE TABLE statement?*

A: The definition of a table can be specified by a user with at least CREATETAB authority and must include its name and the names and attributes of its columns. The stogroup, database, and tablespace must already be defined before the table is defined. Other elements such as a primary key, foreign keys, and/or check constraints (which limit the values that can be entered into the table) can also be defined in the CREATE TABLE statement or with the ALTER TABLE statement.

The creator can include the name of the tablespace that will hold the table's index. The column attributes can include the Standard or the new attributes (such as BIGINT, BLOB, CLOB, DBCLOB, DATALINK), or user-defined column types. The table can contain unique constraints, referential constraints, check constraints, and check conditions.

A table can also be created like another table by using the following example:

```
(CREATE TABLE name AS
(SELECT * FROM table2)
```

Note that the CREATE command creates the table definition but will not load it with any data. The INSERT statement or the LOAD utility should be used to load the table.

Q: *When a table is created, what privileges are automatically granted to the creator?*

A: The creator of a table has all of the CONTROL type privileges. The creator can thus grant privileges to other users, restrict the use of the table, create views and indexes, and delete the table. He or she can also select, insert, delete, and update the table data.

Q: *What types of constraints are available to the user?*

A: The constraint is a rule that is enforced by the database manager. The unique constraint, for example, disables duplicate values in one or more columns of a table (and is enforced via a unique or primary index). The referential constraint limits the values in one or more columns of a table (the dependent table) to those that match the values existing in another table (the parent table) and is enforced via primary and foreign keys. The table check constraint will set restrictions on data added to a specific column or columns of a table. For example, the maximum number of students in a class may be limited to 35. Commands are available to turn the referential and table check constraints on or off.

Q: *What is the role of the schema in the definition of DB2 objects?*

A: A schema is an explicitly created object in the database. It is a collection of named objects and can include tables, nicknames, triggers, views, functions, and packages. Schemas provide a logical classification of objects in the database.

Q: *Can a table be part of a schema that does not yet exist?*

A: When a table is created with a schema name that does not exist, the schema is implicitly created.

Q: *How are database objects deleted?*

A: Objects can be deleted using the DROP statement. If an object that has dependents is deleted, the dependents are also deleted. For example, if a table is dropped, its indexes and views are dropped and the packages using the table are invalidated.

Q: *What is the difference between a simple and a segmented tablespace?*

A: A simple tablespace is usually not recommended and is available because of compatibility requirements with earlier versions. In a simple tablespace, each page in the tablespace can contain rows from multiple tables. When a data page contains rows from more than one table, the *input/output* (I/O) will read fewer table rows into memory (buffer) of the needed table, and the buffers will, therefore, usually hold unneeded rows. In addition, if the entire table needs to be locked, a table lock is not possible because there is no way of easily knowing which pages hold rows from only one table. To lock a table in a tablespace, the user must use a tablespace lock that would lock the rows of all the tables in the tablespace.

A segmented tablespace segments the available pages and assigns specific pages to specific tables. This way, no page holds rows from more than one table and a table lock would be possible.

Q: *What is a partitioned table and how is it specified?*

A: When a table will have a huge number of rows and there is a logical way to divide the table into physical units, a partitioned table can be specified. The one partitioned table is physically placed in multiple tablespaces. They form one logical table but can be administered separately. To specify that the table is partitioned, specify a PARTITIONING key in the CREATE TABLE statement or place the table in a multiple partition nodegroup. The partitioning key, for example, can be a range of dates on a date column or a range of item numbers in the ITEM column of an inventory table.

Q: *What is the function of the ON UPDATE clause?*

A: This clause in the CREATE TABLE specifies what is to take place on the dependent tables when a row of a parent table is updated. The options are ON UPDATE NO ACTION (which is the default) and ON UPDATE RESTRICT.

Q: *Why would the user define the DATA CAPTURE parameter in the CREATE TABLE?*

A: DATA CAPTURE defines whether or not extra information for interdatabase data replication is written to the log. NONE requests that no extra information be logged, while CHANGES requests that extra information regarding SQL changes to this table be written to the log. This is needed when the table is replicated and the capture program is used to capture changes from the log.

Views

Q: *When a view is created, where is the data stored?*

A: Data is never stored in a view. A view is a logical representation of the existing base tables. The CREATE VIEW statement is used to specify which columns of which tables are represented in the view, but all of the data remains in the base tables. The view is just an alternate label used to access data.

Q: *If the view is just an alternate label used to access data, why not use the actual base table and the column names in the SQL statements?*

A: Using views has many advantages. One advantage is the ability to specify a constraint using the WITH CHECK OPTION. This constraint specifies that every row that will be inserted or updated via the view must satisfy the search conditions of the view. If the WITH CHECK OPTION is not specified, the definition of the view is not used to check when an insert or update operation is performed via the view. Also, a new parameter, CASCADED, specifies that when an insert or update is done, the CHECK OPTION of any view that this view is dependent on is also checked.

A view can also be used to simplify complex queries for end-users or programmers. It can also be used to enable users to access only specific rows and columns. Views can give different names to the same columns to make it easier to use for different users. Many companies only use views and do not grant users access to base tables.

Q: *Can a view include a union of two SELECT statements?*

A: In later versions, a view may contain a UNION statement. Two types of UNION statements exist: UNION and UNION ALL. The UNION statement causes a SORT and eliminates duplicates, while the UNION ALL does not. When more than two SELECT statements are combined via UNION statements and the duplicates need to be eliminated, it is more efficient to use UNION ALL for the first unions and only use the UNION statement (and have the data sorted) for the last UNION. This will eliminate unnecessary sorting at each step.

Q: *Can all views be used to modify base tables?*

A: No, any view that is read-only cannot be used to modify the base tables. The factors that will make a view read-only include when the view involves a join, when column functions are in the view, when sorting is done in the view, when scalar functions are used, and so on. The rule is that the modifiable view must be a simple view and cannot include any derived or calculated columns. It also cannot involve joins, unions, or any parameter that would require the creation of a temporary table.

SQL Statements

Q: *Are most SELECT statements simple selects?*

A: No, a SELECT statement can be and often is complex, and it can consist of several pages of coding. It can contain multiple sets of conditions to fully filter all aspects of the data. A SELECT statement can contain joins, subqueries, and UNION processing. The rule usually is "keep it simple," but a better rule is "let SQL do the filtering rather than reading everything and let the application do the filtering."

Q: *What is the most efficient coding method of specifying the selection of a value based upon the evaluation of one or more conditions?*

A: The CASE expression is the easiest way, and it enables a value to be selected based upon the evaluation of one or more conditions. The value of the first case expression that evaluates to TRUE is used. The ELSE keyword is used if none of the cases evaluate to TRUE. If no ELSE keyword is used and none of the cases evaluates to TRUE, then the result is NULL. When a case expression evaluates to NULL, the case is not true and is treated as false.

An example of a case expression is

```
SELECT PARTNO, PARTNAME,
CASE SUBSTR(STORE,1,2)
WHEN 'NY' THEN ' New York'
     WHEN 'NJ' THEN ' New Jersey'
     WHEN 'CA' THEN ' California'
     WHEN 'FL' THEN ' Florida'
END
FROM PARTSTORE
WHERE . . . . . . . . . . .
```

Q: *How is an AS clause used in a SELECT statement?*

A: The AS clause is used to temporarily name an expression or to rename a column in the output within an SQL statement. This might make it easier for the user to understand what data is in the column when its original name is not too descriptive. The new name is only valid within the SQL statement and can be used in the ORDER BY (sort) clause.

Q: *What needs to exist for the EXISTS keyword to be evaluated as true?*

A: The EXISTS parameter tests for the existence of certain values in certain rows. A SELECT is used and the result of the condition is true only if the number of row values that would be returned by the select is greater than zero.

Q: *How is the IN condition (and the ANY or ALL condition) different from most other conditions?*

A: Most conditions compare a column to a single value. The IN condition compares a column value with a collection of values. These values can be in the query, such as COLA IN (value1, value2, value3), or in a table, such as COLA IN (SELECT COLx FROM TAB1 WHERE ...).

Q: *The COUNT column function indicates the number of values in the answer set, but what is COUNT_BIG?*

A: The COUNT_BIG serves the same function as COUNT, but it can be used to count a much larger number of rows. The COUNT value must fit into an integer. The COUNT_BIG can return a decimal number with a precision of 31 and a scale of zero.

Q: *How does a LIKE condition differ from an ordinary compare?*

A: The LIKE condition does not compare a column to a specific value but rather searches for a specific pattern string. The pattern string is specified using the underscore (_) and percent sign (%), each of which have a special meaning. The percent sign (%) represents an unknown string with a length of zero or more bytes. The underscore (_) represents one and only one unknown byte. For example, the condition WHERE COLA LIKE '%NY_ _ %' means the criteria is met if anywhere in COLA are the letters NY followed by at least two additional characters. The following data values match the criteria: NYPD, ABCNY10, and AAABBBNYCCCDDD. The value BKLYNNY does not match the criteria.

Q: *What if a check for the symbol "%" or "_" is required in a LIKE comparison?*

A: An optional escape character will specify that a _ or % can be found in the character string. This enables the LIKE condition to be used to match strings that contain the percent or underscore characters. When an escape character is used, the _, %, or escape character can represent either a literal of itself or an unknown value. For example, to retrieve all rows where COLA has a % in the first position and unknown characters following the %, use the following:

```
SELECT * FROM TAB1 WHERE COLA LIKE '*%%' ESCAPE '*'
```

The * is the escape symbol, the first % after the * is a real percent sign, and the second % means that any number of characters can follow the percent sign in the column value.

Q: *What is the function of the concatenation operator* (CONCAT)?

A: CONCAT creates a single-string expression by combining two-string datatype operands. The operands of concatenation must be compatible. The length of the result is the sum of the lengths of the two operands. When CONCAT is used and one of the operands is null, the result is null. A binary string cannot be concatenated with a character string.

Q: *What is the function of a GROUP BY clause?*

A: When the user is not interested in individual rows but rather in a summary of a group of rows, the GROUP BY parameter is used. To request, for example, the average salary in a department, the user specifies that the output is to be grouped by department. Each row of the output would contain the department number and an average salary for that department. The output can be grouped by more than one column and the user can specify some complex groupings.

Q: *Which clause requests that the output of a SELECT is sequenced?*

A: The ORDER BY clause specifies the sequence of the query output. More than one column can be specified in the ORDER BY clause. The column to be sorted can be identified by name, by its numbered position in the SELECT list, and by its name in the AS clause. If duplicate values are in the columns of the sort key, rows with duplicate values are displayed in an arbitrary order. The output rows can be sorted in an *ascending sequence* (ASC) or *descending sequence* (DESC). The null value sorts to the highest value.

Q: *What type of data does a user-defined function work with?*

A: A user-defined function is similar to system built-in functions and can be a column function, a scalar function, or a table function. A column function returns a single value each time it is called, the scalar function returns a single value for the column value in each row, and the table function returns a table. The user-defined scalar or column function can be referenced in the same manner as any built-in function. A user-defined table function can be referenced only in the FROM clause of a SELECT.

Q: *What SQL statement is used to update the values of a column?*

A: The UPDATE statement is used to update one or more values in specified columns of specified rows in a table. Two types of UPDATE statements exist: the searched and positioned UPDATEs. The searched UPDATE specifies a search condition that is used to identify the row(s) to be updated. The positioned UPDATE is available only in an application and is used to update exactly the one row currently pointed to by a cursor.

Q: *Which SQL statement is used to insert values into a table row?*

A: The INSERT statement is used to insert one or more rows into a table or via a view. To insert using a view, all the NOT NULL columns of the base table must be in the view.

Q: *What is a subquery and how is it executed?*

A: A subquery is a SELECT statement within the condition of a SELECT statement. If, for example, a list of all employees who earn more than the average salary for the entire company is requested, the developer has at least two options. Issue a SELECT to retrieve the average salary for the company and then issue a second SELECT using the average previously retrieved to retrieve those who earn more. The best alternative is to code the subquery:

```
SELECT employee and salary information
FROM the employee (JOIN) and salary table(s)
WHERE SALARY > (SELECT AVG(SALARY) FROM salary table)
```

In this case, the second (inner) select is executed first and only once, and the value retrieved will be compared against every employee's salary. This is called *a non-correlated subquery.*

Q: *What is a correlated subquery?*

A: A correlated subquery is similar to a non-correlated one, but at least one column in the subquery relates to a column in the outer query table. If, in the previous example, the average salary to be compared should be the average of the department rather than the average of the whole company (engineers should be compared to engineers and not clerks or others), then each inner query requires the department number of the employee in the outer query before the inner query can be executed:

```
SELECT employee and salary information
FROM the employee (JOIN) and salary table(s)
WHERE SALARY     >        (SELECT AVG(SALARY) FROM
salary table
WHERE DEPTNO = this employee's department)
```

In this case, the system reads a row from the table in the outer select, extracts the department number, and passes it to the inner select for processing. The DB2 system is sophisticated enough to try to reduce the processing by utilizing an in-memory table used to store the results of the executions of the subquery in case they can be reused for other employees in the same department. The process is repeated for each employee satisfying any other conditions that might be present.

Note that DB2 may automatically transform a subquery into a join when it is possible and when it will improve the access path. It might be better when a transformation is possible if the developer tests the options and transforms the query rather than depend upon the system to do it.

Q: *How big can the data page size be in a table?*

A: The size of the data page in a tablespace can be defined as 4K, 8K, or 16K. If a table is created with a 4K page size, it may have a maximum of 500 columns. The 8K, 16K, and 32K page size may have a maximum of 1,012 columns.

Q: *Are there functions for converting numeric data to character data and character data to numeric data?*

A: Yes, the CHAR scalar function, for example, can be converted to a string and the DIGITS scalar function can convert numeric data to character data for comparison. If one column, for example, has data in numeric form and another column has the data in character form, the predicate may be

```
WHERE charcolumn = DIGITS(numericol)
```

Date, Time, and Timestamp

Q: *What is a labeled duration?*

A: A labeled duration represents a specific number of microseconds, seconds, minutes, hours, days, weeks, months, or years. It uses one of the following keywords: YEARS, MONTHS, DAYS, HOURS, MINUTES, SECONDS, or MICROSECONDS. A labeled duration can be used as an operand only where the other operand is a DATE, TIME, or TIMESTAMP. An example would be WHERE STRTDATE + 10 YEARS = TOTDATE.

Q: *Is a DATE duration, a TIME duration, and a TIMESTAMP duration similar to labeled durations?*

A: No, these durations are the result of subtracting two date, two time, or two timestamp values from each other. The date duration, for example, represents a number of years, months, and days and is in the format of a DECIMAL (8,0) number representing yyyymmdd. A date duration of 1000, for example, means 10 months and no days, while 100001 means 10 years, no months and one day. The time duration represents the number of hours, minutes, and seconds (hhmmss) in the format of a DECIMAL (6,0) number. The timestamp duration represents the number of years, months, days, hours, minutes, seconds, and microseconds (yyyymmddhhmmss.zzzzzz) in the format of a DECIMAL (20,6) number.

Q: *What is the value of these date, time, and timestamp operators?*

A: These operators enable date, time, and timestamp arithmetic calculations. When addition is desired and one operand is a date, the other operand can be a date; a labeled duration of years, months, or days; or a date duration. When one operand is a time, the other operand can be a time operand; a labeled duration of hours, minutes, or seconds; or a time duration. When one operand is a timestamp, the other operand can be any type of duration.

The first operand, however, cannot be a duration. A date, time, or timestamp value cannot be subtracted from a duration, but a duration can be subtracted from a date, time, or timestamp.

Triggers

Q: *What is the function of a trigger?*

A: A trigger defines the actions to be taken when an update, deletion, or insertion is performed for a specific table. These operations trigger a set of actions. The trigger can be set to operate prior to or after a modification to the table. Triggers are used to enforce business rules by placing the logic in the database, thereby relieving programmers of the responsibility of coding the logic in each application program.

Q: *How are triggers defined?*

A: Triggers are defined using the CREATE TRIGGER statement. In the CREATE statement, the developer specifies when the trigger is to be activated (before or after the modification of the table), which type of modification (an update, deletion, or insertion) will trigger the action, and the name of the table. A condition statement can also be part of the trigger definition to indicate that the actions should only be executed if the condition is satisfied.

Q: *Which type of command can be part of the triggered action?*

A: When the trigger executes after the table modification, the actions can include updates, insertions, deletions, and selections, and can set SQLSTATE. If the trigger action executes prior to the modification, the actions can only include selections. They can also set SQLSTATE and transition variables.

Q: *Can triggers be used with other special mechanisms?*

A: Triggers can be used with CHECK constraints and with referential constraints.

Q: *What are transition variables?*

A: These are variables that can be used by a trigger to modify a column value that will be updated or inserted. These variables use the table column names qualified by an identifier. This identifier indicates whether the reference is to the new column value (after the modification) or to the old value.

Q: *How many actions can be triggered by one trigger?*

A: A trigger can cause the activation of other triggers. The trigger "cascading" can even trigger itself again. The trigger can also activate other triggers due to referential integrity actions. Be aware that this may result in significant database activity, all as a result of the modification of one or more rows in the subject table.

Application Programming

Q: *How are the structures needed by SQL embedded into an application program?*

A: The structures that are not automatically inserted by the precompiler can be added using the INCLUDE statement that inserts declarations into an application source program. The SQLDA, for example, and any table descriptions created via the DCLGEN command can be inserted. Remember that the INCLUDE statement should be placed in the application where it is acceptable for the source statements to be placed.

Q: *What are host variables and how are they used?*

A: A host variable is a field defined in an application program (a host language) such as a COBOL data item or a C++ variable. A host variable is referenced in a SQL statement as the name of a field that holds a comparison value or as the field to receive the column value. The host variable must be declared in the SQL DECLARE section of the application. The SQL DECLARE section begins with BEGIN DECLARE SECTION and ends with END DECLARE SECTION.

Q: *Why are indicator variables used?*

A: It may be necessary to insert a null value into a column or to check if a null value was retrieved from a column. When the indicator variable contains a -1 (or any negative number), a null is in or is to be placed in the column, and the value in the host variable is invalid (it may be left over from a previous operation). A -2 in the indicator variable indicates that an arithmetic expression error or a numeric conversion error occurred. It also can contain other information such as the length of input or truncated values. If a NULL is encountered and no indicator variable is assigned by the programmer, a program error will occur.

Q: *A program usually has only one area to hold the input that is read. How does a program handle an SQL query that returns many rows?*

A: To handle a query result of more than one row, a program uses a CURSOR as a placeholder and reads one row at a time. When the CURSOR is opened, it is positioned as pointing to the beginning of the answer set. When the first FETCH is issued, the cursor is moved to point to the first row to be read and the contents of the row are moved into the application I/O area. The program processes that first record and then issues another FETCH. That FETCH and all subsequent FETCHes move the CURSOR to point to the next record and move the row values into the program I/O area, thereby overlaying the data from the previous FETCH. This process continues until the last row is reached (SQLCODE 100) or until the application stops fetching and closes the CURSOR.

Q: *When the CURSOR has been closed, can the application issue another FETCH?*

A: No, in order to FETCH, the cursor must be opened. When it is reopened, it is repositioned to the beginning of the answer set (and not to the row it was pointing to when it was closed).

Q: *What is the function of the WITH HOLD parameter of the DECLARE CURSOR statement?*

A: The WITH HOLD specifies that the pointer to the current row should not be released when a COMMIT is issued at the end of a unit of work (UOW). On COMMIT, all the locks held by this cursor will be released except for the lock(s) needed to maintain the position (the current row). If a ROLLBACK is issued, however, all open cursors are closed and all locks are released.

Q: *What does the FETCH statement do?*

A: The FETCH statement moves the cursor to the next row and moves the values in the row pointed to by the cursor to the host variables. The cursor must be open. If the cursor is already at the last row of the answer set, the SQLSTATE is set to 02000 and the SQLCODE is set to 100; no values are moved to the host variables.

Q: *How does the FETCH statement know which record to read?*

A: The OPEN statement, which must be executed before the first FETCH, positions the cursor to a point prior to the first row in the answer set. Sometimes this process is speedy because only one table is accessed and an index exists, or the data is read sequentially in the physical sequence of the table. No processing is done and the cursor just points to the proper start of the retrieval. The OPEN process, however, can be slow when a join, sort, or other action is required before the first row is known. The DBMS may have to create a work table to store and sort the answer set prior to executing the first FETCH.

Q: *When is it permissible to use the SELECT INTO statement?*

A: The SELECT INTO can only be used in an application when the result of the SELECT is zero or one and only one row of data. The application developer will code the host variables that will receive the column values in the SELECT statement itself.

Q: *What is the difference between a simple predicate (a WHERE condition) and a complex predicate?*

A: Simple predicates can be indexable and are known as stage 1 predicates. Stage 1 refers to the stage where the RDBMS can compare the predicate value to the table (or index) data values. When predicates are complex, the RDBMS cannot evaluate them in stage 1 processing and has to pass the rows of data to the stage 2 processor before the conditions can be evaluated and the row is accepted or rejected. This transfer of rows requires additional resources and increases the response time. The WHERE clause predicate conditions can be written in multiple ways to achieve the same results. Query tuning and performance involve finding the most efficient predicates.

Q: *Are all stage 1 predicates indexable?*

A: Most stage 1 predicates are indexable, but some are not. For example, COLa <> value and COLa IS NOT NULL are stage 1 predicates and are not indexable. Most other simple predicates involving the NOT operator are stage 1 but are not indexable. The administration manual has a list of indexable stage 1 and stage 2 predicates.

Q: *What are compound predicates and are they stage 1 or stage 2?*

A: A compound predicate occurs when two simple predicates are connected via an AND or OR operator. The execution stage of a compound predicate is usually the same as the simple predicate that is evaluated last. Two indexable predicates that are combined via an OR operator, for example, will be indexable and stage 1. If a stage 1 predicate is combined via an OR operator with a stage 2 predicate, the compound will be a stage 2 predicate.

Q: *What are some general performance rules for coding SQL predicates?*

A: Predicates that are evaluated via an index or in stage 1 are more efficiently executed than stage 2 predicates. This is because earlier stages can filter and reject rows that do not meet the criteria and therefore do not require additional processing. To pass a row from stage to stage to application requires additional processing and *central processing unit* (CPU) time.

Q: *How are dynamic statements prepared and executed?*

A: One method is to use the SQL PREPARE and EXECUTE statements. PREPARE extracts the SQL statement from a character string and creates an executable statement as output. The PREPARE statement is checked for syntax errors and if it is invalid, it will not be executed. The statement string may include parameter markers in the form of question marks (?) to be replaced by appropriate values when the statement is executed. The PREPARE statement can be prepared once but be executed many times in a program run.

An alternative method of specifying dynamic SQL statements is to use the EXECUTE IMMEDIATE statement in the application program, especially if the dynamic statement is executed only once. This statement prepares and executes the character string representation of an SQL statement. The character string cannot contain host variables or parameter markers. The statement is checked for syntax errors prior to execution, and if the dynamic statement is invalid, it is not executed.

Q: *Are host variables used in dynamic statements?*

A: In a dynamic SQL statement, host variables are not used. In dynamic

SQL statements, question marks (?) known as parameter markers are used instead of host variables. The question mark indicates that the application will provide a value.

Q: *Does the OPTIMIZE FOR x ROWS clause ensure that only a certain number of rows will be processed?*

A: No, the OPTIMIZE FOR clause is only a suggestion to the optimizer on how to evaluate an access path. Without the OPTIMIZE FOR clause, the optimizer assumes that the application intends to read all of the rows in the answer set. The clause tells the optimizer that the user intends to fetch only a few of the rows and not all of the rows in the answer set. The OPTIMIZE FOR 3 ROWS clause, for example, enables the application developer to indicate to the optimizer that despite the calculation that a thousand rows will be in the answer set, only three rows are planned to be accessed. The optimizer might choose one access path if only three rows are in the answer set, while it might choose a different access path if a thousand rows are in the answer set. This clause is a non-executable clause, and the information is only utilized during the BIND (when the access path is calculated). This clause does not limit the number of rows that can be fetched. Nothing can prevent the user from deciding to access all thousand rows, but the execution may be less efficient.

Authorizations

Q: *Why is a user required to be authorized to access SQL objects?*

A: The database manager requires that a user be implicitly or explicitly authorized to execute any database operation in order to enforce database security. Two administrative authorities with the highest level of authority exist: SYSADM and DBADM. The SYSADM has the highest authority as the system administrator, and the DBADM has authority over a specific database in the DB2 subsystem. Two system control authorities are also available: SYSCTRL and SYSMAINT. They do not enable access to user data, but they do provide authority over operations affecting system resources.

Q: *Once given access to the database, can the user perform every operation?*

A: No, authority or privileges apply only to those specific operations that the object owner or administrator has given to the user.

Q: *How does a user receive authority to modify the database attributes?*

A: An individual user must have authorization to perform an operation on a database. To modify the database itself, the user must have DBADM authority. Only someone with SYSADM authority can grant DBADM to a user. The DBADM (or the SYSADM) can grant other authorities on the database and tables. The authorities that can be granted to users include creating a table (CREATETAB), implicitly creating a schema (IMPLICIT_SCHEMA), binding an application (BINDADD), and connecting to a database (CONNECT), etc. Authority can be granted to everyone (PUBLIC), to one or more specific users, or to a group of users.

Q: *What authority can be granted on tables?*

A: The authority to perform all operations on a table can be granted, as well as the authority to perform specific operations such as ALTER (including creating or dropping keys or adding columns or constraints), DELETE, INSERT, SELECT, UPDATE, and so on.

Q: *How does a user receive the authority to access or modify a table or view?*

A: The table or view creator, a user who has been granted the authority to grant others authority, or someone with DBADM or SYSADM authority, must grant the user the privilege of using the table.

Q: *How does a user receive permission to grant authority to other users to access a table?*

A: The first user has to be granted the authority WITH GRANT OPTION to be able to grant authority to other users. As long as the person with the GRANT OPTION retains the authority, the second user retains the authority. When the authority is revoked from the first user, the second user will automatically also lose the authority.

Q: *A worker was just fired. How do I make sure that he doesn't access the database?*

A: The REVOKE statement is used to revoke all or part of a user's authority. It can be issued interactively, via a utility, or coded in an application. The user who revokes the privileges from another user must have SYSADM authority, DBADM authority, or the CONTROL privilege on the referenced table, view, or nickname. When a user's authority is revoked, any authority granted by the user to others is also revoked.

Joins

Q: *What are the different types of joins available to users?*

A: The user may specify INNER join, LEFT OUTER join, RIGHT OUTER join, or FULL OUTER join. The result of joining tables is an intermediate result table. In later versions of DB2, the table to be joined can be temporarily created by a SELECT statement (a nested table) or can be the result of a user-defined table function.

Q: *What is the difference between an INNER join and an OUTER join?*

A: The INNER join combines each row of one table (left) with every row of the other table (right). Only when the join condition is satisfied in both tables are the rows made part of the answer set. All other rows are discarded. The OUTER join includes certain rows from a table even when the join condition is not satisfied. The row where the join condition is not satisfied is concatenated with NULLs to represent the missing data.

Q: *How does the RDBMS decide which rows to include in the answer set with an OUTER join?*

A: The left outer join includes those rows from the left table even if there is no matching join row in the right table. The right outer join includes those rows from the right table even if no matching join row is in the left table. The full outer join includes those rows from both the left table and the right table even if no matching join row is in the other table.

Q: *What is the most efficient type of join?*

A: Every join is less efficient than most non-joins, and the join should only be used when it is needed. Simple is best, and the inner join is the most efficient of the joins. The full outer join is the least efficient, but it should be used when it is needed. DB2 tries to automatically simplify a join operation when it can.

Q: *Must two different tables be used to perform a join?*

A: No, a table can be joined to itself. If, for example, personnel is interested in all the male employees whose birthday falls on the same date as that of a female, the personnel table can be joined to itself as follows:

```
SELECT * FROM A.PERSONNEL, B.PERSONNEL WHERE A.BDATE =
B.BDATE AND A.SEX <> B.SEX and A.SEX = 'M'
```

Q: *Are multiple joins permissible in one SQL query?*

A: SQL only knows how to perform a join between two tables. In order to join three tables, a join of two tables is first executed and the result of this join is placed in a temporary (composite) table. A second join is then performed between the composite table and the third table. If a fourth table is to be joined, the composite table output of the join of the third table and the first composite table will be joined with the fourth table. Each two-table join can utilize a different join method.

Q: *Which join methods does DB2 use to achieve a join?*

A: Three join methods exist: a nested loop join, a merge scan join, and a hybrid join. The DB2 optimizer chooses the method it calculates to be the most efficient one to perform the join. A multiple table join can involve more than one join method. The user can check which join method the optimizer chose by looking in the EXPLAIN tables. The nested loop join is method 1, the merge scan join is method 2, and the hybrid join is method 4 in the EXPLAIN tables.

Q: *What is the nested loop join method?*

A: Nested loop is the most common method of performing a join. The first or outer composite table is searched. For each row that satisfies any non-join (local) predicates in the WHERE clause conditions, the RDBMS will search for matching rows in the inner or new table. When a match occurs, the columns requested from the two tables are concatenated together and form the current row of the composite table. When the join is an inner join and no inner rows match the outer row being checked,the outer row is discarded. When the join is an outer join and no inner rows match the outer row being checked, a row of null values is concatenated to the current row. Note that it is the optimizer that decides which join method should be used.

Q: *When is it best to use a nested loop join?*

A: The nested loop method scans the outer table only once and for each row that matches the local predicate criteria, it will repetitively scan the inner table. The nested loop is most efficient when an index on the inner table is clustered so that the values of the join column are in sequence. It is also efficient when the number of rows retrieved from the inner table (via an index) is small. The optimizer also chooses this method when the outer table is small or the local predicates (conditions) significantly reduce the number of qualifying rows in the outer table.

Q: *What is a merge scan join and how is it processed?*

A: The merge scan join is similar to any merge. Both tables must have an index on the join column(s) or be sorted in a join column(s) sequence. A row of the outer table is read and the sorted inner table is searched for a matching row. If a match occurs, the concatenated row is built. The scan of the inner table continues as long as there is a match. When no additional match is found, another row of the outer table is read. If that row has the same value as the inner row, the merge continues as previously for all duplicate records in the inner table. If the value in the outer row is a new value, the inner table is searched to find a new matching value or a lower value. The process then starts again.

When an unmatched row is found, the response depends upon whether the join is an inner join or an outer join. For an inner join, the row is discarded. For a left outer join, the row is discarded if it comes from the inner table and is kept if it comes from the outer table. For a full outer join, the row is kept.

Q: *When is the merge scan join method used?*

A: For the optimizer to choose a merge scan, at least one of the join conditions must be in the form T1.COLa=T2.COLb. When the join column indexes are not clustered or inefficient, the optimizer might choose to sort one or both tables to improve the merge efficiency. When a full outer join is performed, the merge scan method must be used.

This type of scan is often used when the optimizer calculates that the join is a many-to-many join, the tables are large, there is no matching index, and/or the join predicates do not provide much filtering.

Q: *What is a hybrid join?*

A: The hybrid join involves a combination of methods. It is only used with an inner join and requires a usable index on the join columns of the inner table. It is used when the inner table index is non-clustered and many duplicate rows in the outer table match the condition criteria.

The outer table is scanned to extract all the rows that satisfy any local predicates. The rows that match are placed in a temporary table. An index on the inner table is then searched for matching keys, and the row address on *relation IDs* (RIDs) of the matching keys are concatenated to the rows of the temporary output table. The temporary output table is then sorted in a RID sequence and a PREFETCH is used to sequentially read the inner table and finish building the output row by concatenating the data from the inner table.

Q: *What is a cartesian join?*

A: In a cartesian join, every row of the inner table is concatenated to each row of the outer table because no join predicates exist between the two tables to filter the rows. If 100 rows exist in each table, for example, the cartesian join output will have 10,000 rows.

Indexes

Q: *Are indexes created automatically on each table?*

A: No, the system has no way of knowing how you plan to access the data. The table owner usually creates one or more indexes using the CREATE INDEX statement. Indexes need not be unique and can contain duplicates. When the CREATE INDEX statement is issued with the UNIQUE clause, the system checks to ensure that no non-unique values exist. If the table already contains duplicate key rows, the unique index is not created. No non-unique values can be inserted or updated into the key columns of a unique index. NULL values are treated as any other values and when the index is unique, only one row can have a key that is NULL (unless UNIQUE WHERE NOT NULL is specified.)

Q: *What are the elements in an index?*

A: The index contains the key value and the address or RID of the data. The RID includes the data page address and the number of the slot on the page that has a pointer to the location on the data page where the row begins. Logically, for every RID there is a key. When duplicate keys exist, however, only one key exists (unless there is a large number of duplicates) with many associated RIDS. When the optimizer calculates that a sequential PREFETCH is more efficient than the reading of the data pages synchronously via a non-clustered index, the index RIDS can be sorted (LIST PREFETCH) in a data page sequence and the data pages accessed sequentially.

Q: *Can indexes only be searched in the sequence that they were created in?*

A: If the CREATE INDEX includes the parameter ALLOW REVERSE SCANS, the index will be created to support both forward and reverse scans.

Q: *Is the data in the table always in the same sequence as the index?*

A: No. If the data is physically in the same sequence as the index, the index is said to be clustered. Usually, only one index can be clustered. Clustered indexes are usually only useful when large quantities of sequential data must often be retrieved from the table. Trying to maintain a cluster on an active table may prove wasteful and inefficient.

Q: *Once the index is clustered, how do I ensure that it remains clustered?*

A: One index can be designated as the clustering index by using the CLUSTER parameter in the CREATE INDEX statement. When a new row is inserted into the table, this clustering index is accessed to determine which page of data to insert the row on. There must be sufficient free space on the page or on adjacent pages to allow the new row to be inserted. If free space is not available on the data page, the row is inserted at the end of the table, thereby reducing the CLUSTERRATIO of the index. The parameter PCTFREE on the CREATE TABLESPACE statement specifies what percentage of each data page should be left free when the LOAD or REORG utility is used to load the table.

Q: *Is there a way in a unique index to include columns that are not unique so that index-only access is possible?*

A: The INCLUDE parameter can be specified in the CREATE INDEX to enable the developer to include non-unique columns in a unique index. The columns included with this parameter will not be used to enforce uniqueness.

Q: *Is there a way to set a threshold for the reorganization of an index's leaf pages that fall below a specific percentage of utilized space?*

A: The MINPCTUSED parameter can be used in the CREATE INDEX to set the threshold to reorganize a leaf page when many keys have been deleted and the leaf page has very few entries. This reduces the I/O needed to read the index. Note that the DB2 section contains a great deal of additional information on index usage.

Locks

Q: *How is data integrity maintained when more than one application process tries to access the same data at the same time?*

A: Each RDBMS implements a locking mechanism that prevents the modification of the same row by more than one user at a time. The locking is controlled by the system.

Q: *What is the usual mode of operation to maintain integrity?*

A: As a general rule, users can read the same rows that other users are reading (concurrency). The users, however, may not even read data rows that were modified by other users but that have not yet been committed to the database. Modified data is locked exclusively because the second user may be reading the data, for example, in order to fill an order. If the first user has not yet updated the row, the second user may assume that more or less units are available than are actually in stock.

Q: *What is a unit of work* (UOW) *or a unit of recovery* (UOR)?

A: A UOW is a recoverable sequence of operations. When the database manager is required to back out uncommitted changes made by an application program, it backs out all the changes that were made in that UOW or UOR. The UOW begins with the first access to any table by an application and ends when a COMMIT is issued or the application ends (or is rolled back). The COMMIT or ROLLBACK affects only the changes made within the unit of work. Once changes are committed, they cannot be backed out if a ROLLBACK is issued. If an application continues after a ROLLBACK or a COMMIT, a new UOW is begun.

Q: *When can a COMMIT or ROLLBACK statement be issued?*

A: The COMMIT statement terminates a UOW and causes all database changes that were made by that UOW to be written permanently to the database. The ROLLBACK statement causes all the modifications made in a UOW to be backed out. A COMMIT or ROLLBACK can be issued in an application or be issued dynamically. The COMMIT releases all locks that were not opened with the WITH HOLD option and the ROLLBACK releases all locks. A new UOW is initiated when a COMMIT or ROLLBACK is issued, but the program does not terminate. It is usually recommended that an application explicitly end its UOW before terminating. It is not recommended that the implicit end of UOW be depended upon.

Q: *If a COMMIT releases the locks, what is the effect of the WITH HOLD parameter in the DECLARE CURSOR statement ?*

A: When a COMMIT is issued, all the locks of all the cursors in the application are released except for the locks needed to maintain the position in the table referenced by the cursor with the WITH HOLD option. All the locks are released, including the locks held for a cursor with the WITH HOLD option when a ROLLBACK is issued.

Q: *What are the different types of locks?*

A: Locks come in three general categories: share locks (S), exclusive locks (X), and update locks (U). An S lock enables other applications to read the locked data but not modify it. An X lock prevents other applications from modifying or even reading the data (unless the second application is using the UR mode). The U lock is a special case with characteristics of both S and X. The application indicates that it is planning to read the data but requires an option to modify it. In that case, other applications are allowed to read the data, but they may not read it for update or modify it.

Q: *What happens if one application has an X lock on a row and another wants to place an S lock on the entire table?*

A: An application cannot place an S lock on a table when one or more rows are locked exclusively. To ensure that the system is aware that a lower-level object (page or row) is locked, the system places intent locks on higher-level objects (a page, table, tablespace, or database) when any lower-level object is locked.

Q: *Which types of intent locks are used?*

A: An intent lock is available for each type of regular lock. The Intent Share (IS) lock is placed on a page, a table, a tablespace, and a database when a row is locked with an S lock to indicate that a lower-level object has been locked. An Intent Exclusive (IX) lock is placed on higher-level objects when a lower-level is X locked and an Intent Update (SIX) lock is placed on higher-level objects when a lower-level is U locked. As you can imagine, multiples of each type of intent lock can be found on the same or on different level objects.

Q: *When are locks released?*

A: Usually, locks are held until the end of a UOW or the application is terminated, which initiates an automatic end of the UOW.

Q: *What is the reason that "most" but not "all" other applications are prevented from even reading the exclusively locked data?*

A: One particular mode of operation is known as *dirty read* or *uncommitted read* (UR) that can even access data that has been modified but not yet committed to the database. UR is mainly used for statistics gathering where the exact state of every single record is not significant. It should not be used for any other type of operation.

Q: *What defines an application's degree of isolation from other concurrent applications?*

A: It is the isolation level of an application or dynamic query that defines its degree of isolation. Four isolation levels limit the access and ensure the integrity of the data to be selected. This degree of isolation determines whether it can read data being modified (and locked) by other applications and whether other applications can modify the rows being read (and locked) by this application. The isolation level only refers to data selection. Isolation level can be specified as an attribute when a package is generated or it can be modified in the application.

Q: *What are the four levels of isolation?*

A: The four isolation levels are *Repeatable Read* (RR), *Read Stability* (RS), *Cursor Stability* (CS), and *Uncommitted* (or dirty) *Read* (UR). The RR level ensures that none of the rows accessed during a UOW is changed by any other application until the UOW is completed. It also does not allow the application to read any rows modified by another application until they are committed by that application. The application acquires share locks on all the rows it references and keeps them until the end of the UOW.

The RS isolation level is similar to the RR, but the application is not completely isolated from the effects of other applications running concurrently. It does not lock all the rows that it references, but only the rows that satisfy a search condition. An application running with level RS that issues the same query more than once might see additional or "phantom" rows that were inserted after the first selection by another application.

The CS isolation level ensures that only the current row or page being viewed is not changed by another application. A share lock is only held during the time that the application is processing the row or page. When the application moves on to a new row or page, however, the lock previously held is released and that row or page that is no longer locked can be changed by any other application.

The UR isolation level does not check to see if a lock is being held on a row that is to be read and does not place a lock on the row read. It allows any row that is read during the UOW to be changed by any other application.

Regardless of the isolation level, the database manager will place an X lock on every row that is modified, until the UOW is complete. The isolation levels are basically read isolation levels and they ensure that any row that is modified by an application is not modified by any other application until the UOW is complete.

Q: *If the database management system controls locking, what is the function of the LOCK TABLE statement?*

A: The LOCK TABLE statement prevents other applications from modifying or using the table. When this statement is not used, the RDBMS locks each row or page as needed, depending upon what was defined when the tablespace was created. Sometimes the developer needs exclusive access to a table and this statement enables exclusive access. One example of its use is when a table is defined with row-level locking. The developer may be aware that almost every row will be accessed by the application and this LOCK TABLE statement will override row level locking and greatly reduce locking overhead.

Q: *How does the LOCK TABLE statement operate?*

A: The statement can operate in SHARE or EXCLUSIVE mode. In SHARE mode, other applications can read the table but cannot modify it. In EXCLUSIVE mode, most other applications are prevented from even reading the table.

Q: *How many locks can be placed on a table?*

A: Any SQL object can concurrently have multiple locks. Many different users and applications, for example, can read rows from the same table and they each can hold an S lock on the table, page, or row. If an S lock is being held on the entire table, another user cannot lock the table or any of its pages or rows with an X lock because they are incompatible.

Q: *What is the effect of the CLOSE WITH RELEASE option?*

A: The CLOSE WITH RELEASE option negates any guarantees usually applicable with RS and RR isolation modes against phantom and non-repeatable reads. They no longer apply when the cursor is reopened to any previously accessed rows.

Q: *Why would lock escalation occur?*

A: Lock escalation is the process where the database manager replaces multiple row locks with a single table or tablespace lock and releases all of the lower-level locks. It occurs when the number of available locks has been exceeded.

Explain

Q: *The EXPLAIN tables give the developer a good picture of how DB2 will access the data requested. How does an application developer acquire these EXPLAIN tables?*

A: These EXPLAIN tables must be created (usually by the DBA) for the application developers. The DBA defines the following tables:

- EXPLAIN_INSTANCE
- EXPLAIN_ARGUMENT
- EXPLAIN_PREDICATE
- EXPLAIN_STREAM
- EXPLAIN_OBJECT
- EXPLAIN_OPERATOR
- EXPLAIN_STATEMENT
- ADVISE_INDEX
- ADVISE_WORKLOAD

Q: *What is the meaning of Access-type in the EXPLAIN table?*

A: Access-type indicates whether an index was used (I) to access the data, if more than one index was used (Mx), or if a table (space) scan was used (R). When an index is used, the INDEX-ONLY column indicates if there was a need to read the data pages (N) or if the index had all the data needed (Y) in a usable format.

Q: *What is the meaning of match-cols in the EXPLAIN table?*

A: An index can be used in several ways. When the indexable condition in a query or a modification includes the first column in the index, that condition matches the first index column and, assuming the condition is indexable, the query is said to have one matching column. If the second column of the index also appears in an indexable condition (and the first index condition is an equal condition) that second column also matches the index columns and now two matching columns occur. Zero matching columns (when ACCESSTYPE=I) indicates that the optimizer, for some reason, chose to read the entire index even though no matching columns existed.

Q: *Why would an index be used when no matching columns exist in the query conditions?*

A: An index might be used even when no matching columns exist for several reasons. There might, for example, be only 100 pages in the index and 10,000 pages in the data. The index could still be used, even though the first column of the index, for example, is not used in the WHERE clause, but the second and third columns are. The optimizer might calculate that it would still be much more efficient to read the entire index (with a maximum of 100 I/Os) to check for the second and third column values, and only read the few data pages that have these values, rather than to read all 10,000 data pages.

Another possibility is that there may be many rows in the output that need to be sequenced in the same sequence as one of the indexes. The optimizer might calculate that it would be more efficient to read the data in the sequence of the index and avoid a sort of the data.

Q: *What other important information can be found in the EXPLAIN tables?*

A: All the information is important, but several quick indicators are useful to application developers. The ACCESS-NAME column specifies which index was used. Check if it is the one you think it should be. The SORTN columns specify why and when a SORT is required. Creating a proper index might enable the system to avoid a sort. The JOIN_TYPE indicates if a full outer join (F), a left outer join (L), or an inner or no join (blank) is performed. JOIN_TYPE never identifies a right outer join specifically because at execution DB2 converts every right outer join to a left outer join.

Q: *What is a composite table?*

A: A composite table is the first table accessed in a join or it is the output table from a previous step. It is known as the outer table in a join operation. The second table accessed is the new table or the inner table.

Performance

Q: *How does the PREFETCH of pages improve efficiency?*

A: When many data pages have to be read in order to satisfy a query, the processing may take longer than the I/O to read the page, but the system will have to wait while the next page is being read. If the data pages are in sequence, the system can perform advance reads of the pages needed (PREFETCH) asynchronously. When this occurs, no waiting occurs because a page is already available as soon as the application processing of the previous page is complete.

Q: *What is the filter factor* (FF) and how does it affect performance?

A: The filter factor is a decimal value between 0 and 1. It is the estimate of the percentage of the rows in a table that will satisfy the predicate condition. A predicate with a FF of .1, for example, implies that the optimizer estimates that 10 percent of the rows will need to be accessed to satisfy this condition. A smaller filter factor usually means that fewer rows need to be accessed, resulting in fewer I/Os and less CPU resources. When the optimizer can choose between several access paths, the filter factor plays a significant role in its choice.

Q: *If the filter factor is .1, does the optimizer know exactly how many rows need to be read?*

A: No, the filter factor is an estimate. The optimizer does not know how many rows match the criteria, nor does it usually know how many rows are in the table unless the statistics have been recently updated. The filter factor and the calculations of the optimizer both depend upon the statistics, the system defaults, and the estimates. The optimizer is only as good as the accuracy of its estimates.

Q: *What are sargable predicates?*

A: A *sargable* (short for "search argument") *predicate* is another name for stage 1 predicates. Stage 2 predicates are sometimes called *nonsargable* or *residual predicates* because they cannot be applied until the second stage of processing. When the index and stage 1 cannot fully filter the rows, many more rows than match the full criteria must be read and/or passed from stage to stage. This definitely requires additional CPU time and may cause increased I/Os.

Q: *What are the factors that affect the stage that the predicate can be evaluated at?*

A: The main factors are the syntax of the predicate as well as the type and length of constants and columns in the predicate. Constants and columns whose types or lengths do not agree with the column to be compared usually cause the predicate to become stage 2. It is best to make sure that the values compared are of the same length and type. If a column defined as CHAR (3), for example, is compared to BIGGER, a six-byte constant, the predicate is stage 2.

Q: *How does the RDBMS gather statistics and can they be manipulated?*

A: Statistics are not updated or gathered automatically by DB2. The RUNSTATS utility is used by the DBA to update the statistics for a table or tables. When a table is loaded with 500 rows, for example, and statistics are requested, while subsequently over the next three months another million rows are added, the statistics will still indicate 500 rows unless a statistics update is requested.

Q: *Must I therefore always update statistics on a regular basis?*

A: Although the DBA may want to know what the statistics for a table are, the optimizer is the only system function that uses statistics. The optimizer only uses the statistics when an access path is calculated for a package (BIND) or for dynamic access. When all of the access is via static SQL, a BIND is rare, and a good index will usually be chosen by the optimizer, then changes in the statistics is of little consequence. Executing RUNSTATS requires time and resources, and its use should be carefully justified. Too many installations set aside an evening or three and just run RUNSTATS without any plan to determine which tables need statistics update.

Q: *Is there an alternative to running statistics?*

A: Several of the statistics columns in the catalog can be manually updated by the DBA. To simulate a production table in a test database in order to verify the access path, for example, the statistics could be modified to reflect those from the production system and the application bound and EXPLAINed. Care must be exercised when updating catalog columns to ensure consistency. There is no guarantee that the optimizer decisions will be affected by the statistic changes and the results should always be double-checked.

Q: *Which catalog table statistics are the most useful to the optimizer to help choose the access path?*

A: The statistical information available in the SYSTABLES and SYSTABLESPACE catalog tables indicates the number of rows of data in your table and the number of pages that hold the data. The information in the SYSINDEXES table enables the optimizer to estimate which index of the available indexes on a table would be the most efficient for a particular query. The filter factors of predicates can often be estimated from the data in the SYSCOLUMNS and SYSCOLDIST catalog tables.

Q: *How important are statistics to the optimizer?*

A: The general rule is that statistics should be up to date when the BIND process takes place, but statistics gathering takes lots of resources. It should be remembered, however, that if no statistics are available, the optimizer will use predefined default values. These default values, in many cases, cause the optimizer to choose the same access path that it would choose if the statistics were accurate.

6
Oracle

Donna Matthews

The Oracle8*i* software was released in the spring of 1999. It differs from previous releases in its capability to incorporate Internet computing tasks. Oracle8*i* can support relational databases and object-oriented structures.

The current chief executive officer, Larry Ellison, and two fellow programmers, Bob Miner and Ed Oates, founded the Oracle Corporation in 1977. According to *U.S. News & World Report*, Oracle was the second-largest software company in the world as of January 1999, second only to the Microsoft Corporation. The Oracle Relational Database accounts for most of its business. Oracle's products run on numerous operating systems, including Microsoft's Windows NT. The Oracle8*i* database NT version contains *graphical user interface* (GUI) tools to simplify tasks. For example, this version comes with a GUI tool that can generate a new database from the user's responses to a series of required questions.

What Is Oracle?

Oracle is an object-relational database management system. It is called an *object-relational database* because it supports object-oriented structures, such as methods, as well as the relational database model. The database utilizes the relational model created by E. F. Codd, an IBM research scientist, in 1960. Figure 6-1 shows an example of the relational database model. The relational model was created to improve the storage and processing of large quantities of data. A relational database is comprised of multiple *tables* that share a common field that is used to form relationships, or *joins*, between two tables. Tables are used to store data within Oracle. A table

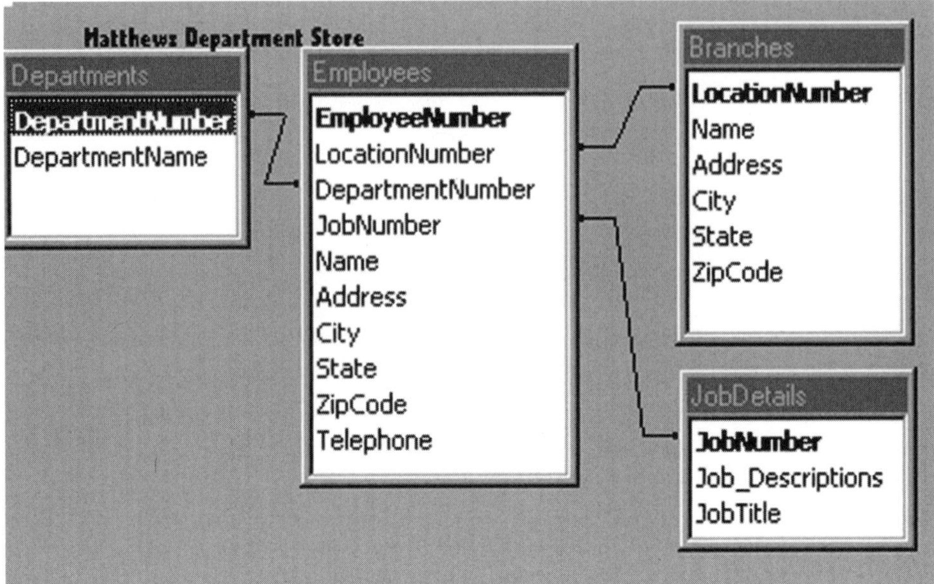

Figure 6-1 Relational database model diagram

consists of columns or fields that describe an attribute. The Name field in the Employees table would contain an employee's full name. Each column has a defined data type, such as character. The data type determines what data the column will contain.

An object-relational database attempts to combine attributes of both relational databases and object orientation programming. Oracle8*i* objects offer an additional set of features that enable the creation and manipulation of user-defined object types. Oracle's database integrates the management of traditional data and such complex objects as time-series and geospatial data, along with diverse binary media such as audio, video, images, and applets. Oracle8*i* enables users to define additional kinds of data, which make it easier for application developers to work with the complex data presented by images, audio, and video.

Some of Oracle8*i*'s object capabilities include the following:

- Scalars, LOB's, objects, references, and collections
- PL/SQL methods, external procedures, and Java methods
- Triggers, constraints, object views, and user-defined operators
- Sorted, hash, bitmap, index-organized tables, and extensible indexing

- Object query optimization and an extensible optimizer
- Object support in export/import, loader, parallel query, and partitioning
- Object support in OCI, C++ (ODD), Pro*C, JDBC, and OO4O

Architecture

An Oracle database consists of both physical and logical structures. This enables the physical storage to be maintained without affecting access to the database. Oracle's logical structure consists of one or more *tablespaces* and schema objects, such as tables, views, and indexes.

The physical structure consists of one or more *datafiles*, two or more *redo logs*, one or more *control files*, and a parameter file.

Datafiles and Tablespaces

Datafiles hold all the data in the database and can associate with one database only. One or more datafiles together form a logical unit called a tablespace. It is not necessary for the Oracle user to know the locations of the datafiles, as the tablespace contains the necessary information about the datafiles. A simple example of the relationship between tablespaces and datafiles is demonstrated in the following command:

```
CREATE TABLESPACE USERS
Datafile 'c:\oracle\data\users.dtf' SIZE 20M;
```

The ALTER TABLESPACE command is used to modify an existing tablespace. For example, to add an additional datafile to the USERS tablespace, the following command would be used:

```
ALTER TABLESPACE USERS
ADD DATAFILE 'c:\oracle\data\users2.dtf';
```

An Oracle database must consist of at least one tablespace, known as the SYSTEM tablespace. The separation of physical and logical storage has several advantages:

- It enables an Oracle database administrator to modify physical storage without affecting database access. For example, if an Oracle programmer had to access a database by indicating the location of the datafiles in a program, the program would have to be modified were the DBA ever to change the name or location of the datafiles. However, with the use of tablespaces, the information about the datafiles is transparent to both user and developer.

- The separation of physical and logical storage in Oracle also allows for backups of specific parts of the database. A specific tablespace can be backed-up without backing up the entire database.
- Tablespaces also enable database data to be divided by functionality. For example, separate tablespaces and datafiles can be created for data and indexes.

Redo Log Files

Redo log files record all the changes made to the data. Each Oracle database consists of two or more redo log files. These files are used to recover data after a system or media failure and can be used to restore a database to the condition it was in immediately prior to the system or media failure. Without redo log files, recovery can be made only to the last backup.

Redo log files are created during database creation. An example of the commands used to create redo log files is as follows:

```
CREATE DATABASE TEMP

CONTROLFILE REUSE
LOGFILE
  GROUP 1 ('diskb:log1.log', 'diskc:log1.log') SIZE 50K,
  GROUP 2 ('diskb:log2.log', 'diskc:log2.log') SIZE 50K
```

Control Files

Control files contain information about the physical structure of the database, including the database name, the locations of the datafiles, the redo log files, and the time stamp of database creation. A control file is accessed when the database is started. If a control file error occurs, the database will not start. Control files are identified in a parameter file called init.ora.

An *instance* is used to access the database and must be created before connection to the database can be established. It is comprised of a set of memory structures and background processes. The parameters of the instance are set in an init.ora file. This file is read during instance startup. An instance contains memory structures called the *system global area* and the *program global area*.

Now let's look at an example of the creation of an instance. An init*.ora parameter file is used to configure the instance. The init*.ora file is a text file that can be modified. An example of an init*.ora file is shown in Figure 6-2. The * in the init*.ora file is usually replaced with the name of the instance. For the instance named ORCL, the name of the init.ora file would be initorcl.ora.

```
###########################################################################
# INITDEPT.ORA file
###########################################################################
db_name = dept
instance_name = dept
service_names = dept
db_files = 1024 # INITIAL
# db_files = 80                          # SMALL
# db_files = 400                          # MEDIUM
# db_files = 1500                          # LARGE
control_files = ("c:\Oracle\dept\control01.ctl",
"c:\Oracle\dept\control02.ctl")
db_file_multiblock_read_count = 8 # INITIAL
# db_file_multiblock_read_count = 8                # SMALL
# db_file_multiblock_read_count = 16                # MEDIUM
# db_file_multiblock_read_count = 32                # LARGE
db_block_buffers = 8192 # INITIAL
# db_block_buffers = 100                     # SMALL
# db_block_buffers = 550                     # MEDIUM
# db_block_buffers = 3200                     # LARGE
shared_pool_size = 15728640 # INITIAL
# shared_pool_size = 3500000                    # SMALL
# shared_pool_size = 5000000                    # MEDIUM
# shared_pool_size = 9000000                    # LARGE
java_pool_size = 20971520
log_checkpoint_interval = 10000
log_checkpoint_timeout = 1800
#processes = 59 # INITIAL
# processes = 50                           # SMALL
# processes = 100                           # MEDIUM
processes = 200                          # LARGE
parallel_max_servers = 5 # SMALL
# parallel_max_servers = 4 x (number of CPUs)          # MEDIUM
# parallel_max_servers = 4 x (number of CPUs)          # LARGE
log_buffer = 32768 # INITIAL
# log_buffer = 32768                        # SMALL
# log_buffer = 32768                        # MEDIUM
# log_buffer = 163840                        # LARGE
max_dump_file_size = 10240 # limit trace file size to 5M each
# Uncommenting the line below will cause automatic archiving if archiving has
# been enabled using ALTER DATABASE ARCHIVELOG.
# log_archive_start = true
# log_archive_dest_1 = "location=c:\Oracle\dept\archive"
# log_archive_format = "%%dept%%T%TS%S.ARC"
# Global Naming - enforce that a dblink has same name as the db it connects to
global_names = true
oracle_trace_collection_name = ""
# define directories to store trace and alert files
background_dump_dest = d:\Oracle\admin\orcl\bdump
user_dump_dest = d:\Oracle\admin\orcl\udump
db_block_size = 2048
remote_login_passwordfile = exclusive
os_authent_prefix = ""
distributed_transactions = 500
compatible = 8.1.5
Once the instance has been created, a user can access the database. For exam-
ple, connect scott/tiger
```

Figure 6-2 Examples of init.ora file

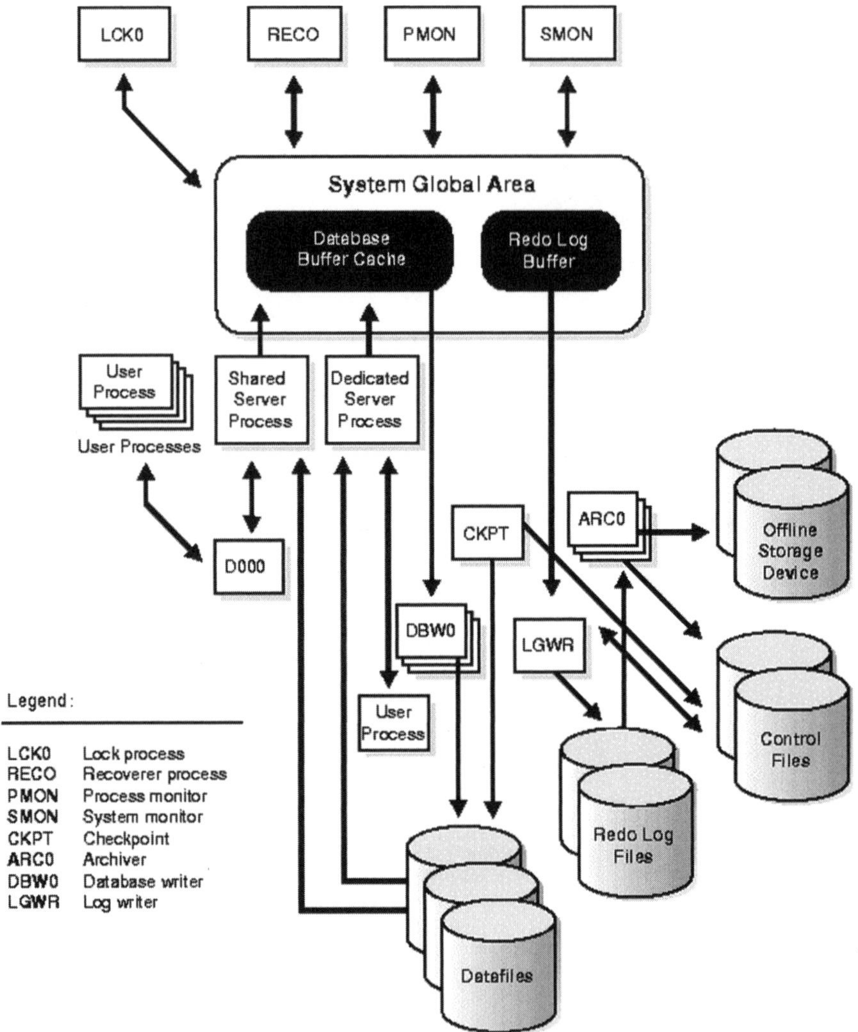

Figure 6-3 Oracle memory structure

Oracle Memory Structures

When an Oracle instance is started, the system global area and program global area memory structures are accessed. Oracle also has a *User Global Area* (UGA), which contains information about the user session. Figure 6-3 displays all the memory structures.

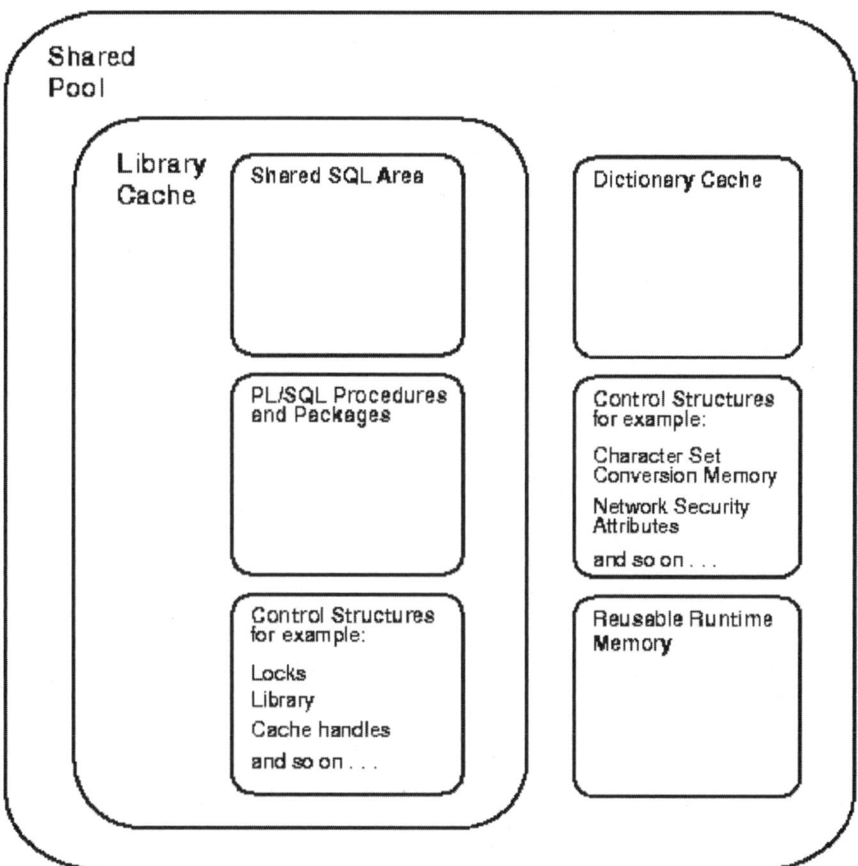

Figure 6-4 SGA components

System Global Area (SGA)

The information stored in the system global area is divided into several types of memory structures, including the *database buffers*, the *redo log buffer*, and the *shared pool*. The size of these areas is configured in the init.ora file. Figure 6-4 displays the components of the SGA.

Database Buffer Cache

The database buffer cache memory stores data recently accessed from the database.

Redo Log Buffer

The redo log buffer memory area stores changes to the database. The changes are stored in the redo log buffer until they are written to the redo log files.

Shared Pool

The shared pool is the area of memory that contains the shared *Structured Query Language* (SQL) area. The shared SQL area contains information on execution plans for SQL statements. This area is very important to developers. Each time an SQL statement is processed, it is placed in memory in the shared pool area. When a new SQL statement is sent to Oracle, Oracle checks to see if it already exists in the shared pool area. If so, Oracle will obtain the information from the shared pool rather than reprocessing the statement. If the SQL statement is found in the shared pool, it can speed up the execution time of the query. The statement must be an exact match to be retrieved from the shared pool area. For example, the SQL statement "Select * FROM Test" would not be equivalent to "SELECT * FROM TEST." The shared pool is set by the SHARED_POOL_SIZE parameter in the init.ora file.

Large Pool

The large pool is an optional area in the SGA that handles backup and restore operations, I/O server processes, and session memory for the multi-threaded server and Oracle XA.

Oracle Background Processes

In this section, we'll examine some secondary processes within Oracle, including the *Program Global Area* (PGA), the *Database Writer* (DBWn), and several others.

Program Global Area (PGA)

The *Program Global Area* (PGA) is used to handle Oracle server processes. Each Oracle instance may use the following background processes: DBWn, LGWR, CKPT, SMON, PMON, ARCn, RECO, Dnnn, LCK0, SNPn, and QMNn. PMON, SMON, DBWn and LGWR are mandatory processes. These processes must be initiated when an instance starts. Figure 6-5 displays the PGA components.

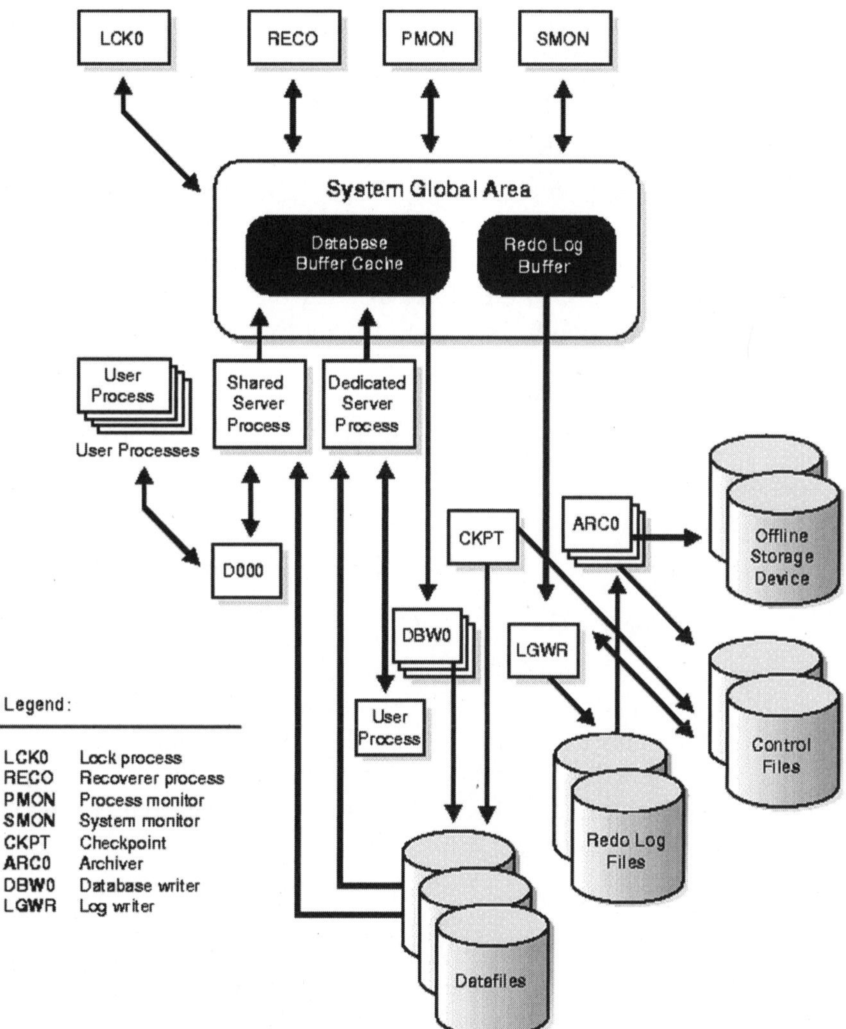

Figure 6-5 PGA components.

Database Writer (DBWn)

The *Database Writer* (DBWn) writes modified data from the database buffer cache to the shared global area. The number of database writer processes can be set by the DB_WRITER_PROCESSES in the init*.ora file for 1 to 9. The n specifies the number of the database writer process, such as DBW2.

Log Writer (LGWR)

The *Log Writer* (LGWR) process writes redo log entries from the redo log buffer in the SGA to the redo log files.

Checkpoint (CKPT)

The *checkpoint* (CKPT) process is responsible for signaling the DBWn process to write changed data from the database buffers to the files. This is done based on the LOG_CHECKPOINT_INTERVAL and LOG_CHECKPOINT_TIMEOUT parameters set in the init.ora file or by a DBA when the command Alter System Checkpoint is issued.

System Monitor (SMON)

The *system monitor* (SMON) performs crash recovery when a failed instance starts up again.

Process Monitor (PMON)

The *process monitor* (PMON) performs recovery when a user process fails.

Archiver (ARCn)

The *Archiver* (ARCn) copies the online redo log files to archival storage, such as disk or tape, when they are full so that they will not be overwritten. The LOG_ARCHIVE_MAX_PROCESSES statement in the init.ora file sets the number of archiver processes (up to ten are permissible). This feature can only be utilized if the DBA has created the database while in archivelog mode.

Recoverer (RECO)

The *Recoverer* (RECO) resolves distributed transactions that are pending due to a network or system failure in a distributed database.

Dispatcher (Dnnn)

Dispatchers (Dnnns) are optional background processes responsible for routing requests on a multi-threaded sever.

Lock (LCK0)

The lock (LCK0) process is used for inter-instance locking in the Oracle Parallel Server.

Job queue (SNPn)

The *Job Queue* (SNPn) is used to refresh table snapshots in a distributed database. Snapshots are duplicate copies of data on a remote system.

Queue Monitor (QMNn)

The *Queue Monitor* (QMNn) is an optional process that monitors message queues for Oracle Advanced Queuing.

Accessing Data

Database objects are maintained in a schema object. Oracle schema objects include such structures as tables, views, sequences, stored procedures, synonyms, indexes, clusters, and database links. Schemas are logical structures that refer to database data. The objects are accessed by the use of SQL. Oracle also includes PL/SQL, an expansion of SQL, which includes such additional programming components as variables, procedures, functions, if statements, and while and for loops.

Oracle8*i* Features (Version 8.1.6)

The addition of internet capabilities, including Java programming, is the most significant enhancement to the Oracle8*i* release. Oracle8*i* allows the user to utilize Java programming wherever PL/SQL code is used, including stored procedures and triggers.

New features of Oracle8*i* include the following:

- The capability to use Java or PL/SQL to manipulate data.
- Java or PL/SQL stored procedures, functions, and triggers.
- A built-in Java Virtual Machine, JServer, which allows the user to store and run Java code within an Oracle database.
- Support for SQLJ, which allows users to embed SQL within Java code.
- Software WebDB, an application development software that assists in the creation of Web-based PL/SQL applications. No programming is needed.
- Support for other Internet features, such as Javabeans, *Common Object Request Broker Architecture* (COBRA), and *Internet Inter-ORB Protocol* (IIOP).
- Oracle interMedia, which allows the user to manage and access multimedia data, such as images, text, audio, video or spatial data. Oracle interMedia includes Oracle ConText, used for processing textual data.
- Enhanced JDBC driver support, which handles connections to the Oracle database from Java.

- Oracle iFS (Internet File System), which provides a simple way of storing different types of files in the database.
- New Java capabilities including JavaServer Pages (JSP) and Java servlets.
- New XML developer kits and utilities.
- Enhanced Internet security.
- Java 2 Enterprise Edition APIs support.

Oracle8*i* is backward-capable with previous versions of Oracle databases.

The following questions for Oracle have been divided into beginning, intermediate and advanced skill levels:

Beginning Skills

Q: *Can you describe Oracle?*

A: Oracle is an object-relational database management system that stores data in a database. An Oracle database consists of logical and physical structures. For example, a tablespace is used to logically define the physical storage of data in datafiles. Oracle data is stored in related tables and SQL is utilized to retrieve information from the tables.

Q: *In the command, "Connect Scott/Tiger@ORCL," the @ORCL is needed for what purpose?*

A: @ORCL, a host string, determines what database instance the user wishes to access. The statement will connect the user, Scott, to the database associated with the ORCL instance.

Q: *Will the database start if the control file is missing?*

A: The database will not start without the control file. The control file contains ncecessary datafile information and transaction control numbers.

Q: *How is SQL*Plus started?*

A: Sqlplus <username><password>.

Q: *What is a sequence?*

A: A sequence is used to provide a sequential unique number. A sequence will provide a numeric value increased by a specified increment. An example of a sequence follows:

```
CREATE SEQUENCE Orderno_Seq
     START WITH 1
     INCREMENT BY 1
     NOMAX VALUE
     NOCYCLE
     CACHE 20;
The preceding statement will do the following:
START WITH 1:      Sets the starting point of the sequence
INCREMENT BY 1:    Specifies the value by which the next
                   sequence value should be increased
NOMAXVALUE:        Sets no maximum value for the sequence
NOCYCLE:           Indicates that the sequence cannot gen-
                   erate additional values after reaching a
                   maximum value that has been set
CACHE 20:          Pre-allocates 20 sequence numbers to
                   memory for faster retrieval
```

A sequence is referenced with the NEXTVAL and CURRVAL pseudocolumns. The NEXTVAL generates a new sequence number. The next example illustrates how to reference a sequence.

```
INSERT INTO PURCHASES(Orderno, Customer)
VALUES(Orderno_seq.NEXTVAL,7021);
```

Q: *What is SQL*Plus?*

A: SQL*Plus, an Oracle tool, is an extension of SQL. SQL* Plus is used to connect to an Oracle database. The user can also use the tool to process SQL queries.

Q: *What is Net8?*

A: Net 8 is used to establish network connections and to transfer data based on networking protocols such as TCP/IP. Net 8 allows clients to connect to remote Oracle databases residing on multiple servers.

Q: *If I need to add data to a table, which SQL command should I use?*

A: The SQL command used to add data to a table is "insert." Here's an example:

```
Insert into employees(first_name,last_name)
VALUES "Donna", "Matthews";
```

Q: *What is the difference between an index created by ASC and an index created by DESC?*

A: The difference is that ASC will create an index with ascending values, such as A, B, C. The DESC index will create an index with descending values, such as C, B, A.

Q: *What is a join?*

A: A join is used to link Oracle tables together through a key field, usually handled by a where condition in the SQL statement. Here's an example:

Select * From Employee, Department where Employee.Deptno= Department Deptno. Additional joins also exist:

Inner Join: An inner join will only return the rows where matches were found

Outer Join: An outer join will return all rows, including rows where a match does not exist.

Union: A union is the opposite of an inner join and returns those rows where no match was found between the tables.

Q: *What is a trigger?*

A: A trigger is a procedure that is executed when a specific event occurs, such as when a table is inserted, updated, or deleted.

Q: *What is a view?*

A: A view is an overlay for tables. Views and tables are queried and accessed in the same way as a table. Views make it possible to hide the actual name of a table as well as fields that a user should not access.

Q: *What is a procedure?*

A: A procedure is a block of PL/SQL statements that is called by applications. A procedure allows the user to store frequently used commands for easy access later.

Q: *What does the distinct clause in SQL statements do?*

A: The distinct clause in an SQL statement will remove any duplicate values. For example, if two last_name values of Matthews exist in a table, only one will be displayed.

Q: *Which one must return a value, a procedure, or a function?*

A: A function must return a value and a procedure may never return a value.

Q: *What is the purpose of the HAVING clause in SQL?*

A: The HAVING clause restricts the group of rows returned. It is similar to the WHERE clause, except that it is employed when a GROUP BY clause has been used in the SQL query. Here's an example:

```
SELECT snum, state, AVG(amount), MAX(amount)
     From salesrep
     GROUP BY snum
     HAVING state = 'IL';
```

Q: *In a relational database, which one of the following describes an attribute?*

A. Field

B. Record

C. Database

D. None of the above

A: The correct answer is A. A record is a combination of fields or attributes. A database is a combination of records.

Q: *Which one of the programming languages below is used in relational databases to manipulate the data?*

A. Visual Basic

B. C++

C. SQL

D. None of the above

A: The correct answer is C. SQL is used to manipulate the data in relational databases. Answer A is incorrect because Visual Basic is usually a front-end to the database, but SQL is used to manipulate the data. Answer B is also incorrect because C++ must use SQL to manipulate the data.

Q: *What is SQL?*

A: SQL stands for structured query language, which is used to access Oracle databases.

Q: *Oracle8*i does not support Java programming.

A. True

B. False

A: The correct answer is B. Oracle8*i* supports Java programming wherever PL/SQL is used. Java programming can be used for stored procedures and functions, as well as for triggers.

Q: _____ *are queries based on tables.*

A. Views

B. Sequences

C. Indexes

D. None of the above

A: The correct answer is A. B is incorrect because sequences generate unique numbers for numeric columns in a table. C is incorrect because indexes are used to speed up the access of data from a database.

Q: *Given the tables "Employee_Information" and "Employee_Resume," what type of relationship do you think exists?*

A. One-to-one

B. Many-to-many

C. One-to-many

A: The correct answer is A. Each employee should have only one resume.

Q: *What does the SQL statement "Select * From Employees where state = 'IL';" do?*

A: This statement will display all the fields in the employee table where an employee is located in the state of Illinois.

Q: *What is the purpose of an index?*

A: An index is used to store data in a specific way in a table which will permit easy retrieval of data. An index to a database is similar to an index in a book; it allows the user to immediately access the information he or she is seeking without having to read every page. Indexes sort one or more fields in a database in ascending or descending order.

Q: *How can a user create a table?*

A: The SQL statement "Create table" is used to create a table in Oracle. An example of the statement follows:

```
CREATE TABLE students (
Student_id NUMBER(5) NOT NULL;
Department CHAR(3) NOT NULL);
```

Q: *How does a user create an index?*

A: The SQL statement "Create index" is used to create an index in Oracle. The syntax is "Create Index "ORCL.employees (empid);" is an example of a create statement. <indexname> on <table_name (column_name(s)>.

Q: *What is data normalization?*

A: The goal of data normalization is to eliminate redundant data in tables. For example, in a payroll table where the hourly rate of $60 per hour is stored in a new field for each and every supervisor, a table can be created that is used to retrieve the hourly rate by the use of a join. This configuration will allow changes to be made once rather than in multiple locations for all supervisors in the table.

Q: *Can you give an example of a one-to-one relationship?*

A: The relationship between an employee table and an employee resume table, where each employee has only one resume, illustrates a one-to-one relationship.

Q: *Can you give an example of a one-to-many relationship?*

A: An example of a one-to-many relationship can be illustrated by the relationship between sales_reps and sales offices. Sales_reps can report to only one office, but an office can have more than one sales rep.

Q: *What does the command "Drop Table Employees" do?*

A: The drop table command is used to delete the employee table and to remove information about it from the data dictionary.

Q: *What is the purpose of an Entity Relationship Diagram (ERD)?*

A: An ERD is used to graphically depict the relationship between tables in an Oracle database.

Q: *What is PL/SQL?*

A: PL/SQL is a programming language used to access Oracle databases. PL/SQL enhances the SQL programming language with additional programming capabilities, such as if-then statements, functions, procedures, and so on.

Q: *In a SQL statement, what is the purpose of the where clause?*

A: The where clause is used to restrict the data returned from a SQL query.

Q: *If the department name for Human Resources were changed to HR in a Departments table, which SQL command would be used to update this information?*

A: The SQL command update would be used to change the department name. The syntax would be:

```
UPDATE Departments
Set Dept_Name = "HR"
Where Dept_Name = "Human Resources";
```

Q: *Based on the previous question, what problem would occur during the update if the Dept_Name Human Resources were not used consistently in the Departments table? How could this problem be avoided?*

A: The problem would be that not all of the occurrences of Human Resources would be updated. This problem could be avoided by creating another table which consists of department_code and department_name. The department_code could be used in a where condition to retrieve the department name. With this configuration, an update would need to be done in only one place.

Q: *The SQL statement,*

```
Select First_name, Last_Name from Employee
Where Last_Name = "Matthews";
would accomplish what task?
```

A: This statement would retrieve data in the fields First_name and Last_name where the value in the field Last_name is "Matthews."

Q: *The SQL statement,*

```
Select First_name, Last_Name from Employee;
would retrieve what from the employee table?
```

A: This SQL statement will retrieve first name and last name data from the employee table.

Q: *Can you describe a primary key?*

A: A primary key is used to identify rows in a table. An example of a primary key is a social security number in an employee table.

Q: *Describe a foreign key in a database.*

A: Foreign keys refer to a primary key in another table. For example, the social security number in the payroll table can be used to refer to the social security number in the employee tables.

Q: *What is the purpose of the order clause?*

A: The order clause is used to sort data by a specific field in a table.

Q: *What are some of the advantages relational databases offer?*

A: Some advantages are: improved data integrity, reduced data redundancy, easier data retrieval, and easier data updates.

Q: *What does the command "commit" do?*

A: Commit makes changes permanent.

Q: *What does the command "rollback" do, and can it be issued after a commit?*

A: The rollback command will return a table to the state it was in before an insert, update, or delete was issued. A rollback can be issued after a commit; however, the changes will not be removed as they will already have been saved in the database.

Q: *What does the command "group by" do in an SQL statement?*

A: The group by statement will group the output over identical values. It is used with aggregate functions such as average. A group by statement can be used to retrieve an average for all 50 states from a table.

Q: *What will the command "Select LENGTH('Donna') from dual;" return?*

A: The command will return the number five for length of 'Donna.'

Q: *What will the command "SELECT substr('DONNA',1,3) from dual;" return?*

A: This SQL query will return 'DON.' The command retrieves the data starting at the first position and retrieves three characters.

Q: *What will the command "SELECT UPPER('donna') from dual;" return?The command will return 'DONNA.' The function UPPER converts the text from lower case to uppercase.*

Q: *"Select count(*) from students;" will retrieve what data from Oracle?*

A: The select count statement will return the total number of records in the student table.

Q: *What will the command "v_numberseats Number:=45;" do?*

A: This command will create a variable named "v_numberseats" with a datatype of Number and set the value of the variable to 45.

Q: *Is there a difference between the two commands that follow?:*

```
DECLARE v_firstname, v_lastname varchar2(20);
And
Declare
V_firstname varchar2(20);
V_lastname varchar2(20);
```

A: Both statements are the same. The only difference between the two is visual.

Intermediate Skills

Q: *The init.ora file is only used when an instance is stopped.*

A. True

B. False

A: The correct answer is B. The init.ora file is used at instance startup to configure the parameters and settings for the instance.

Q: *Which of the following is used to configure an instance when it starts?*

A: redo log files

B: control files

C: tables

D: init.ora files

A: The correct answer is D. The init.ora file is used at instance startup to configure the parameters and settings for the instance. Redo log files are used to store changes to data. A setting in the init.ora file configures the control file. Tables are accessed only after an instance is started and the database is accessed.

Q: *The DBWn background process is used to write data from the database buffer to the redo log files; true or false?*

A. True

B. False

A: False. The DBWR (Database Writer) is used to write data from the database buffer to the database files. LGWR (Log Writer) is used to write data from the Log Buffer to the redo log files.

Q: *Which is not a background process?*

A. DBWR

B: PMON

C: LGWR

D: SGA

A: D is the correct answer. A, B, and C are all components of the background process.

Q: *Increasing the size of the data block parameter in the init.ora file will have what impact on queries?*

A: Increasing the size of the data block parameter will speed up the execution of queries.

Q: *If a match is found in the shared pool for a SQL statement, what will happen?*

A: If this occurs, the SQL statement will not need to be executed. Oracle will use the execution path information from the SQL statement in the shared pool.

Q: *A new service name is created, but the Oracle DBA did not add the entry to the listener.ora file. Will the user be able to make a connection? If not, why?*

A: The user will not be able to make a connection because the listener.ora file is used to establish the services on the server.

Q: *Will typing "connect scott/tiger&orcl" in server manager enable the user to connect to the server from a client machine?*

A: The answer is no. The correct syntax for establishing a connection is connect "username/password@service" name.

Q: *If the listener service is not running on the server, what will happen when a user tries to connect to the service name?*

A: The listener must be running in order for a user to connect to the service name. The listener is used to process a user's request and route the request to the proper database.

Q: *What is the effect if the background_dump_dest parameter in the init.ora file is changed from c:\oracle to c:\temp?*

A: The log files will be written to the c:\temp directory instead of the c:\oracle directory.

Q: *Is the syntax "CREATE USER demo IDENTIFY by test;" correct for creating a user?*

A: The syntax is incorrect. The word IDENTIFIED should be used in place of the word IDENTIFY.

Q: *What impact will it have if the user does not install the sample (starter) database?*

A: It will have no impact at all. The installation of the starter database is used as a guide to setting up an Oracle database.

Q: *What is the purpose of the SQL*Loader?*

A: The SQL*Loader is an Oracle tool that allows the user to load non-Oracle data into a database. It is commonly used when loading an ASCII flat file, which is delimited or non-delimited into Oracle.

Q: *In an Oracle database, should all of the database objects be maintained in the SYSTEM tablespace? Why or why not?*

A: The system tablespace should be reserved for Oracle's use only. The data dictionary is maintained in the system tablespace. Additional tablespaces should be created for a new database.

Q: *Which of the following is used to ensure that the data meets a specific condition before it is inserted, deleted, or edited?*

A. Primary Key

B. Not Null

C. Check

A: The correct answer is C. The primary key is used to set the key that the table information should use as a unique key (for example, a social security number in an employee table). A not null constraint is used to disallow null data in a field.

Q: *What is a package?*

A: A package is used to store procedures and functions in one place.

Q: *What are the two components of the package?*

A: A package consists of a package specification and a package body.

Q: *The command "sysdate" returns what?*

A: This command returns the computer's system date.

Q: *What is the purpose of the redo logs?*

A: Redo logs record all of the changes made to a database. This information is used to perform rollbacks, which are used if it is necessary to recover data, and to help maintain read-consistency of data.

Q: *What is the purpose of the control file?*

A: The control files contain information about the database, such as datafiles, and other physical architecture information about the database.

Q: *How does import/export work in Oracle?*

A: Export reads the database and writes the output to a binary file, which is called an export dump file. The import utility is used to import the exported file back into Oracle. Exports are available for full, incremental, and cumulative database export. The export can be done while the database is up and running.

Q: *What is a tablespace?*

A: A tablespace is a logical division of a database. Each database must at least have a SYSTEM tablespace.

Q: *What is a datafile?*

A: Datafiles physically divide a database. They give, for example, the actual name and location of files used in an Oracle database.

Q: *Describe the relationship between the tablespace and datafiles.*

A: The SYSTEM tablespace, made of the datafiles c:\system.dtf, illustrates the relationship. The tablespace is the physical name and the datafiles are the actual physical files. The tablespace can consist of one or more datafiles. As long as the system tablespace name stays the same, an Oracle DBA can make changes to the datafiles associated with the tablespace.

Q: *What is the difference between the truncate table and delete statements?*

A: Both truncate and delete remove data from a database table. However, truncate also resets the storage to the initial setting.

Q: *What is a cluster?*

A: A cluster is used to store tables that are frequently accessed together. Clusters enable better query performance.

Q: *What is the purpose of the init*.ora file?*

A: The init*.ora file contains the parameters for the Oracle database which that database should use. Some of the parameters in the init*.ora file are DB blocks.

Q: *What is the purpose of the Oracle Application Server?*

A: The Oracle Application Server is a Web server that is available from Oracle. The Oracle Application Server also allows you to easily access Oracle packages.

Q: *What is the purpose of the LGWR?*

A: The LGWR is a background process that handles the writing of the redo log buffer to the online redo log files.

Q: *How many tablespaces are required in Oracle and what is the name of any mandatory tablespace?*

A: Only one tablespace is required in an Oracle database, the system tablespace.

Q: *Is it a good idea to store everything in the system tablespace?*

A: No, the system tablespace should be reserved for Oracle's use to avoid corruption of the Oracle database.

Q: *What occurs during a CKPT in Oracle?*

A: Data is written to the datafiles and redo log files during a CKPT.

Q: *What is contained in the alert log and how often should it be checked?*

A: The alert log records the commands and command results of major events in the database, such as tablespace creation. The alert log should be checked daily to see if any problems are occurring with the database.

Q: *What is the purpose of the DBWn?*

A: The DBWn is the background process that handles writing data from the database buffers to the datafiles.

Q: *What does the not null constraint do on a field?*

A: The not null constraint ensures that the field is not left empty. Data must be entered in any field that has been assigned a not null constraint.

Q: *What is an instance?*

A: An Oracle instance is used to access the data in the database. The parameters are set in the init*.ora file. An instance that could be used to connect to the database is "Connect Scott/Tiger@ORCL." ORCL is the name of the instance.

Q: *What does the describe command do?*

A: The describe command will provide information about an Oracle object. For example, "Describe employees" will provide information on the employee fields and their datatypes in the table.

Q: *What command is used to create a user?*

A: The command is as follows:

```
Create user Rochelle
Identified by "Tasha"
```

This command will create a user "Rochelle" with the assigned password "Tasha."

Q: *What is the purpose of the default constraint?*

A: The default constraint sets a default value if no data is inserted in a column.

Q: *What occurs during shutdown abort?*

A: The shutdown abort command immediately stops the Oracle database and disconnects all connected users without completing any current transactions being performed.

Q: *What occurs during startup nomount?*

A database is created.

Q: *What is the purpose of the check constraint?*

A: The check constraint's purpose is to ensure that values in a specified column meet a certain criteria. It might be used, for example, in a situation where the salary value must be less than $200,000.

Q: *What is a database link?*

A: A database link allows the user to access remote data without providing the fully qualified name of the remote object. This is done by creating public database link cur_link and connecting to an employee identified by matthews using 'TEMP.'

Then, once the user needs to connect to the table the command "Select * from employee@cur_link would retrieve the data.

Q: *If you own the table Employees, what command grants user Rob the ability to select data?*

A: The command "Grant Select on employees to Rob;" gives him access.

Q: *What is contained under a user's schema in Oracle?*

A: The user's schema will contain a set of objects owned by that user, such as tables, procedures, and so on.

Q: *What is the purpose of Oracle Designer?*

A: Oracle Designer allows a user to develop applications quickly. Oracle Designer provides a Rapid Application Development (RAD) environment to model and generate Data Definition Language (DDL), client-server, and Web-based applications.

Q: *What is Oracle WebDB?*

A: Oracle WebDB is a software package that enables users to easily develop Web-based applications from Oracle databases.

Q: *What is a synonym?*

A: A synonym is used to completely identify a database object, such as a table, in a distributed database. The command is "Create public synonym employee for HR. employee;"

Q: *What will the command "drop user ORCL cascade" do?*

A: A user normally cannot be dropped if it owns objects; however, if cascade were added, it would drop the user and all the objects associated with the user.

Q: *The following statement, "Create user matthews identified by MATTHEWS," accomplishes what task?*

A: This command will create the user matthews with a password of MATTHEWS.

Q: *The command "Alter user matthews default tablespace test" will do what?*

A: The command will set the default tablespace for the user matthews to "test." Therefore, whenever the user matthews executes a SQL command that requires storage but does not specify a tablespace, the tablespace "test" will be used.

Q: *The "Grant insert on employees to PUBLIC" command will achieve what end?*

A: This command will give all users who have access to the database the ability to insert data into the employee table.

Q: *What is the default order when an index is created?*

A: The default order of an index is ascending order, as in A, B, C.

Q: *What is the purpose of the dual table?*

A: The dual table comes with Oracle and is owned by the user SYS. The dual table can be used to run SQL queries, such as "Select SYSDATE from Dual;."

Advanced Skills

Q: *Which Oracle feature contains information about the database, including a time stamp of data creation?*

A. None of the following

B. Datafiles

C. Tablespaces

D. Control Files

A: The correct answer is D. The datafiles contain the data contained in the database. Tablespaces are the logical name given to datafiles.

Q: *Execution plans for SQL statements are maintained in the:*

A. Database buffer

B. Redo logs

C. Shared pool

D. None of the above

A: The correct answer is C, the shared pool. The database buffer contains only recently accessed data. The redo logs contain changes to the database.

Q: *The datafile users.dtf, which is part of the users tablespace, is accidentally deleted. Will the database still start? Explain.*

A: The database will not start without the users.dtf. At instance startup, the controlfile is used to check for the database structure information. Because the users.dtf is missing, the users tablespace will be invalid.

Q: *The Oracle database contains a tablespace called users, which consists of the datafile c:\oracle\database\users.dtf. The DBA decides to add a new datafile called users2.dtf to the tablespace. Will this change cause the developer to recreate all of the objects that are currently configured to the user's tablespace?*

A: This change will have no effect on either existing objects under the tablespace or on any other development tasks. Oracle utilizes a database independence environment. This means that the changes to the physical structure (datafiles) have no impact on the logical structure (tablespaces). The changes are transparent to both the user and developer.

Q: *A media failure has occurred while data entry is being done. Which of the following can be used to recover the data that has not been written yet?*

A. Redo log

B. Control file

C. Tablespaces

A: The correct answer is A. The Redo log file contains information on data changes. B is incorrect because the control file is used to provide information only on the database structure. C is incorrect because tablespaces give the logical names assigned to datafiles in Oracle.

Q: *If the background process DBWn does not start, will the instance start?*

A: No, the instance will not start without the DBWn process. DBWn is used to write modified data from the database buffer cache in the shared global area to the datafiles.

Q: *Explain the purpose of the LGWR background process.*

A: The purpose of the LGWR is to manage the contents of the redo log buffer, contained in the shared global area, and of the online redo log files. LGWR writes log entries to the redo log files.

Q: *What is the purpose of the DBWn background process?*

A: The DBWn background process manages the contents of the data buffer cache. The DBWn performs writes of changed data to the datafiles.

Q: *The network administrator has decided to change the name of the server to ORATEST and has also changed the IP address without the user's knowledge. When the user tries to make a connection to the server, will it work?*

A: No. The connection will not work unless the names files are also updated. For example, if the user gains a connection by use of a tnsnames.ora file, the entry will reference the old server name or IP address, which no longer exists and the connection will fail. This example shows the need for the Oracle DBA and network administrators to communicate with each other about any system changes.

Q: *In the tnsnames.ora file, if the SERVICE_NAME=orcl is changed to SERVICE_NAME=dept and a user then tries to connect to the orcl service name, what will happen?*

A: The connection will not work because the tnsnames.ora file will not have an entry for the orcl instance. If the user wants to add the department service name, the entire section for the orcl must be duplicated and the occurences of orcl replaced with dept.

Q: *In the listener.ora file, which section contains information about the service names?*

A. Description

B. Connect data

C. Host

A: The correct answer is B, the connect data section. The description section contains information about the server. The host is a component of the description section, which provides information on the server where Oracle resides.

Q: *Sending multiple sessions to the server at one time is handled by which of the following:*

A. Connection manager

B. Tnsnames.ora

C. Oracle names

A: The correct answer is A. B is incorrect because the tnsnames.ora file exists on client machines to provide information on the services and server residing on the Oracle server. Answer C is incorrect because Oracle names is a method used to allow for client connections.

Q: *Which option would be used to shut down a database without waiting for users to disconnect and which does not roll back uncommitted transactions?*

A. Normal

B. Immediate

C. Abort

A: The correct answer is C, abort. A normal shutdown waits for all currently connected users to terminate their sessions. An immediate shutdown terminates currently executing SQL queries and rolls back uncommitted transactions.

Q: *Which backup can only be performed if the database is in archivelog mode?*

A. Offline backup

B. Online backup

C. Export

A: The correct answer is B, online backup. A and C are incorrect because these backups can be performed even if the database is not in archivelog mode.

Q: *Which one of the following is used to create the data dictionary?*

A. Catalog.sql

B. Init.ora

C. LGWR

D. DBWn

A: The correct answer is A. The init.ora file is read at instance startup to set parameters. The LGWR is a background process that handles writing information to the redo log files. D is incorrect because the DBWn is a background process that writes changes to physical datafiles.

Q: *Describe a cold backup in Oracle.*

A: A cold backup requires that the database be taken down. All files associated with the database are then copied.

Q: *What does maxinstances do in the create database statement?*

A: Maxinstances, in the create database statement, sets the maximum number of instances that can be connected to an Oracle database at one time.

Q: *What exactly are extents?*

A: Extents are continuous sets of Oracle blocks of space. If possible, all of one object should be maintained in one extent.

Q: *Describe a hot backup.*

A: A hot backup occurs while the Oracle database is running. In order for a hot backup to be done, the Oracle database must have the ARCHIVELOG option set. The ARCHIVELOG option is set with the command "alter database archcivelog;." This process will make a copy of the redo log files before they are overwritten. Tablespaces are then taken into backup state, datafiles are backed, and then the tablespaces are returned to an online status.

Q: *What is the purpose of the plan table?*

A: The purpose of the plan table is to provide the execution path for SQL statements.

Q: *What does the archive feature do and how is it set?*

A: The ARCHIVELOG option is set with the command "alter database archivelog;." This process will make a copy of the redo log files before they are overwritten.

Q: *What is the purpose of the tnsnames.ora files?*

A: The tnsnames.ora files contain information on such Oracle instances as names, Network protocols, and IP addresses. This file is used to provide information to connect to Oracle databases.

Q: *What is a role and how is it associated with a user?*

A: A role is used to distribute Oracle database privileges. Dba and connect are examples of some of the roles.

Q: *What is a profile?*

A: A profile is used to place limits on the system and database resources available to a user.

Q: *Can the database block size be changed after a database is created?*

A: No, the only way the database blocks can be resized is if the database is recreated.

Q: *What does the statement "Analyze table employee computer statistics" do?*

A: The command creates information in the form of indexes, such as on the employee computer statistics table in Oracle. This information can be used by Oracle to determine the best execution path for SQL queries.

Q: *What are rollback segments?*

A: Rollback segments are used within a database to construct a before image for uncommitted transactions and are used to roll back data when a rollback command is issued.

Q: *Name a few of the parameters that can be set in the init.ora file.*

A: Two parameters that can be set are OPTIMIZATION_MODE and DB_BLOCK_SIZE.

Q: *What is the difference between privileges and a role?*

A: Privileges are the Oracle commands given to a user, such as "Create Table." Roles consist of privileges and give the DBA a way to easily assign the same privileges to all users with a specific job role.

Q: *What command is used to change a user's password?*

A: The command "alter user" can be used to change a user's password.

Q: *When the DBA sets privileges for a user and adds the command "with grant option," how are the user's privileges altered?*

A: The with grant option clause of the grant command is used to give the grantee the ability to grant privileges to other users.

Q: *Can tablespaces be taken offline?*

A: Yes, tablespaces can be taken offline; this is done when a hot backup is needed.

Q: *What does the command "Alter tablespace coalesce" do and why is this needed?*

A: This command will develop free spaces in tablespaces into larger extents. This will allow larger objects to fit in one extent.

Q: *What does the initial command do in create tablespace commands?*

A: The initial command sets the number of extents that are initially created for a tablespace.

Q: *What is the purpose of the Shared SQL Pool?*

A: The Shared SQL Pool stores information on SQL commands that have been submitted and their execution paths. When a new SQL command is issued, the Shared SQL Pool is checked for a match and the execution path from the Shared SQL Pool is used.

Q: *What will the command "DROP Table" do?*

A: This command will delete the table from the Oracle database and all associated indexes from the table.

7

DB2

by Dov Gilor

DB2 or *Universal Database* (UDB) is IBM's *relational database management system* (RDBMS). Several years ago, each IBM platform had its own variety of RDBMS. The MVS SQL RDBS was called DB2, the VM and VSE systems were called SQL/DS, the AS/400 system was called SQL/400, and so on. While similar, the different varieties were not necessarily compatible. In recent years, the interconnectivity of systems (DRDA) and the need to port applications between platforms has forced a greater stress on compatibility and standardization. All of the IBM SQL varieties are now called DB2 (DB2/MVS, DB2/VM, DB2/400, DB2/VSE, and so on), and the SQL used to access DB2 is very similar (in most cases identical) from platform to platform.

This introduction will discuss some important aspects that will help the interviewee to ace the technical interview. It is assumed that the reader, who is applying for a technical DB2 position, has a basic knowledge of relational technology. Some people believe a database should be designed purely on the basis of the data that exists rather than upon the needs of the applications. This author believes that for performance reasons, the designer should decide how the data will be used before the database is designed. Response time is usually much more important than purity of design.

Like most other computer systems, DB2 is updated regularly. Each new version developed by IBM has enhanced functionality and performance as compared to the previous version. Many of the basic concepts, however, remain the same for several generations so that much of the information in this chapter will be applicable for several years. Version 6, for example, included many enhancements to make DB2 more manageable, reliable, flexible, and accessible from any workstation or via the Internet and local area networks (LANs). Almost one hundred new built-in functions have been added to DB2.

Version 7 has been announced and it delivers improved performance for e-business and data warehouse applications. It provides a full set of tools for building and using a data warehouse. In addition, utility improvements, availability improvements (such as being able to change system parameters, ZPARMS, without stopping DB2), and complex join improvements have been made. The application programming improvements include the ability to issue a subselect within an UPDATE statement and to code the UNION phrase within views. Previous versions added SQL support for REXX, declared temporary tables, externalized savepoints and other features.

In addition to the basic system, IBM will supply a set of optional DB2 tools (at an additional cost) to make the use of DB2 even more user-friendly. The tools include the DB2 Administration Tool, DB2 Bind Manager, DB2 Data Propagator, DB2 Performance Monitor, QMF for Windows, Visual Explain, DB2 Stored Procedure Builder, and many others.

This chapter refers to version 6 and 7 of DB2 and uses OS/390 as its basis. As mentioned earlier, much of the information is also applicable to other platforms. Several of the many changes in version 7 will be discussed in the following pages. The applicant is cautioned to use the information in this chapter to review the various areas usually discussed in an interview and any recent DB2 changes via the latest manuals or via the Internet. The latest DB2 manuals are available over the Web at http://www.ibm.com/software/data/db2/library/

The DB2 market is vast with more than 1,000,000 DB2 licenses sold by IBM. If recent experience is any measure, anyone registering his or her current DB2 resume on the Internet will receive dozens of requests for further information each week.

The questions that are asked depend heavily upon which position an applicant is applying for. The DBA is expected to know many more details than the senior application developer, who, in turn, is expected to know much more than the beginning programmer. Knowledge of some basic performance information is useful to all, and performance tips are included throughout the chapter.

This chapter discusses DB2 and relational database specific features and performance topics. The sample database installed with DB2 has many examples of table and application design that will prove useful once you begin to work. Please note that the SQL chapter of this book provides a great deal of additional information that will prove useful during a technical interview. It discusses the elements of the *Structured Query Language* (SQL) used with DB2, as well as design and performance tips. Good luck in your interviews.

Database Objects:

The major objects in DB2 that may be created, altered or manipulated include

- STOGROUP—a list of DASD drives that will be assigned to hold the other objects.
- DATABASE—an administrative logical structure that allows the DBA to divide the tables in DB2 into easily managed groups and to use the commands and utilities to control these groups as a unit. Each physical DB2 subsystem may contain many databases. No limitations (except that authorization is required) are placed on accessing two tables from different "databases" in the same SQL command.
- TABLESPACE—The physical DASD space that will contain the tables and the indexes (INDEXSPACE).
- TABLE—The logical structure of rows and columns that hold the data. The tables are created by the user or DBA and maintained by the system. Theoretically, no sequence to the rows in the table is required, but performance-tuning requirements may make it worthwhile to maintain some order.
- VIEW—A view is an alternative way of representing a table, but it itself does not contain data. It allows the user to redefine table names or simplify complex queries. It can limit the retrieval and modification of specific rows and columns to specific users. It can involve joins of several tables and unions of multiple queries.
- INDEX—The sequenced set of pointers containing the key and the address of the page and slot on the page that holds the page location of the beginning of the row. The index is built and maintained by the system, and it is used to ensure uniqueness when required and to improve performance.

The Optimizer

A major function of the optimizer is to analyze the SQL statements and choose the most efficient way to access the data. The DB2 optimizer evaluates the WHERE (predicate) conditions, as well as the sort, grouping, join and other conditions; calculates the best method to access the data by using the available statistics and system defaults; and chooses an access path. Knowing how the optimizer works usually assists those who work with databases to design and prepare applications that are more efficient. Once an application is written, for example, it undergoes a BIND step to create an access module. When an index is available and used, performance is usually much better than it would be without the use of an index. The decision to use an index is made by the optimizer during the BIND (optimization) process, based mostly upon the WHERE condition predicates, the sort requirements, and the statistics available. The decision is based on the calculated (I/O and CPU) cost of using a particular access method. Knowing the factors used by the optimizer in its calculations is important to efficient applications.

The available statistics are used by the optimizer to calculate or estimate how significantly a particular index will reduce the number of pages (I/O) that have to be accessed. If the optimizer calculates, for example, that every page in the tablespace will have to be read at least once because of the query conditions, it might decide not to use the index since it would be less costly to scan the entire table than to scan the index and the entire table. If the index is unclustered (data in the table is not in the same sequence as the index), using the index might require that the same data page be read several times. This will occur when a page is read into a page buffer and not used for awhile. The page buffer may be reused and the page purged from memory. When needed again for another key value, the page will have to be reread, thereby requiring another I/O. If, however, the optimizer calculates that it can avoid a large sort because the index is in the sort sequence, the optimizer might decide to use the index anyway.

Some of the decisions that the optimizer has to make may be seen from the following example. Three indexes can be found on the CUSTOMER table:

- SEX, ACCNTYPE, ACCNTNO
- ACCNTYPE, ACCNTNO
- ACCTNO, ACCNTYPE, SEX

```
SELECT   *
FROM DOV01. CUSTOMER
WHERE ACCTNO = :HACCT AND ACCNTYPE LIKE :HV2 AND SEX = :HSEX
ORDER BY ACCNTYPE, ACCNTNO
```

The optimizer has several choices:

- Not to use an index; to scan the entire table
- To use one of the indexes
- To use two or all three of the indexes

When a user believes that a specific index should be used and the user wants to be sure that it is being chosen by the optimizer, the EXPLAIN statement, or the EXPLAIN option of BIND may be used to provide the information.

Index Keys

Indexes are so important to performance that they deserve their own section. Indexes may be used to enforce uniqueness on column values, to contain primary key values, to cluster data, to partition tables, and to provide access paths to data for queries. It is important to understand the structure of DB2 indexes in order to achieve the best possible performance. The index data logically consists of a KEY value and the address known as the relation id (RID) or tuple id (TID), which consists of the data page address and the slot number, which points to the location on the data page where the row with this key is found. With this address, the RDBMS can access the page(s) required directly, rather than be forced to perform a sequential search of all the data pages. When a thousand or several million pages of data make up a database, the savings achieved by using an index can be very significant.

Two types of indexes can be built in DB2, Type 1 and Type 2. Type 1 was the only type available in older versions of the database and should not (and, beginning with version 6, cannot) be used on newer applications. Among the advantages of Type 2 indexes are: ROW level locking is permitted and UNIQUE WHERE NOT NULL columns may be specified. Type UR isolation for an access path, processing of queries by multiple parallel tasks, and concurrent access to separate logical partitions all require type 2 indexes.

The usefulness of an index depends on its key. An index key can reference only one table, but that table can have many indexes each of which can have a one-column key or can be a composite key (with 2 to 64 columns). It is preferable, for performance reasons, to keep the key to the absolute minimum of columns needed. Usually, the smaller the index key, the more efficient the index because more index entries fit on each page, fewer I/Os are needed to read the index, and fewer storage areas (buffers) are required to store the index in memory. Columns that are used frequently in performing selection, join, grouping, and ordering operations are good candidates for use as keys. Columns with many duplicate values are often poor candidates for use as keys unless the index is clustered and retrieval is sequential.

Index Structure

Indexes can have a hierarchy of more than one level of pages. The lowest level, where index entries point directly to the data, are called leaf pages. When the index grows and fills more than one leaf page, a higher level nonleaf page is automatically added, containing entries that point to the leaf pages and an entry that indicates the maximum value of the keys in each of the leaf pages. When so many entries are included that more than one nonleaf page is needed, a higher level nonleaf page containing pointers to the leaf page and the highest value of each lower level nonleaf page is automatically added. The highest level will contain a single page called the root page.

What is Multiple Index Access?

When more than one index exists on a table, the optimizer may decide to use more than one index to access a table. Multiple Index Access might be a good access choice when no single index provides efficient access to the data and a combination of two or more index accesses does.

To use Multiple Index Access, the RDBMS searches each index to find the addresses of the rows that match a predicate (WHERE) condition. When the connection is via an AND keyword, all of the indexes in the Multiple Index Access must have the same RID for the condition to be satisfied. If the OR keyword is used, the row is used even when only one of the indexes has the key.

Utilities:

An important aspect of database usage is the efficiency and availability of utilities to more easily perform many of the required tasks. The DB2 utilities assist in loading a table, copying a table or tablespace, and recovering a database to a previous point in time. The DB2 utilities run as batch jobs under MVS. *Utility control statements* (JCL) may be prepared using the *DB2 interactive* (DB2I) feature under TSO.

Questions and Answers:

The following questions and answers are listed by category and should help you ace the technical interview.

DB2 Creation and Control

Q: *Which address spaces are used by the DB2 subsystem?*

A: DB2 uses the DBM1 address space for database services that manipulates the structures of user databases. DB2 also uses the *Internal Resource Lock Manager* (IRLM), which is used to control locking. The system services function occupies an address space (MSTR) as do the *stored procedures* (SPAS) at a DB2 server. There may also be an address space for the *distributed data facility* (DIST). There may also be several address spaces (WLM) for stored procedures and user defined functions and other address spaces for CICS, Batch, TSO, and so on.

Q: *What mechanism is used to acquire locks?*

A: The DB2 database manager (IRLM) records the locks that are acquired. The database manager releases all of the locks it has acquired, when the application ends. When the application fails, the rollback mechanism backs out all database modifications that are still locked and have not been completed (committed) and all of the locks are released. An application process may also explicitly request that the database changes be backed out (ROLLBACK).

Q: *Can the Internal Resource Lock Manager (IRLM) be shared between DB2 systems?*

A: No, each DB2 subsystem must have its own IRLM. The IRLM serializes the access to DB2 by controlling the locks placed on DB2 objects to ensure data integrity.

Q: *Can DB2 be controlled from a CICS terminal?*

A: A user with the appropriate DB2 authorization may access DB2 from CICS, by using the CICS attachment facility. The attachment facility is provided by CICS version 4 and later and provided by DB2 for versions prior to version 4. After DB2 is started (only from an MVS console), DB2 may be operated from a CICS terminal. Authorized operators may start and stop DB2 databases. The CICS attachment facility also allows CICS transactions to access DB2 databases. To perform DB2 online functions via CICS and to bind plans and packages, the TSO attachment facility and ISPF are required. The DSNC transaction is used to issue DB2 commands from a CICS terminal.

Q: *Does CICS support function shipping of SQL commands?*

A: At present, function shipping of SQL requests is not supported. A single CICS region may be connected to only one DB2 subsystem at a time.

Q: *How should DB2 be stopped?*

A: When the operator specifies: STOP DB2 MODE(QUIESCE), new applications are prevented from connecting to DB2 and the active threads are run to completion. New threads may be allocated to an application that is still running. Quiesce is the proper way to shutdown DB2 even though many operators do not have the patience to wait; therefore, they use: STOP DB2 MODE(FORCE). When FORCE is specified, no new threads are allocated and the work being done on existing threads is rolled back. The DISPLAY THREAD can be used to see the shutdown progress. It should be kept in mind that sometimes the rollback involved when STOP DB2 MODE(FORCE) is used will take as long as the completion of the in-progress threads. To immediately stop DB2 and defer the rollback to a later point (when DB2 is restarted), the IRLM can be stopped.

Q: *What happens when DB2 is stopped?*

A: DB2 stops accepting most commands, the connections end, the IRLM is disconnected, a checkpoint record is taken and the *Bootstrap dataset* (BSDS) is updated.

Q: *What happens when DB2 is restarted?*

A: The restart process applies or backs out the data on the log records that have completed or unresolved work. DB2 may be started or restarted from an MVS console that has been authorized to issue system control commands. When a specific DB2 object is causing problems, it is possible to defer the restart of that object. Certain portions of the log may also be skipped with a conditional restart. This process, however, may make some DB2 objects inconsistent, and the recovery to a prior point of consistency or the dropping of the object may be necessary.

Q: *Which functions of OS/390 does DB2 use?*

A: DB2 is a subsystem of OS/390 and uses the MVS SSI (Subsystem Interface) protocols. It uses SMF for statistics, performance and accounting information, Key 7 storage, synchronous cross-memory services, and various reliability and serviceability features. TCP/IP and VTAM are used for distributed data.

Q: *What is DSN?*

A: DSN is the DB2 command processor that executes under TSO. The DSN commands include:

- DCLGEN, which produces table and view declarations from the DB2 catalogs for inclusion in application programs.
- BIND and REBIND to build or rebuild a DB2 plan or package.
- RUN, which executes an application plan.
- SPUFI, the on-line SQL statement executor, which runs as a DSN command under ISPF.

Various DB2 commands may also be executed via a DSN session.

Q: *List some of the DB2 commands that may be issued via the MCS extended console feature?*

A: Many commands are used to control the DB2 databases and the subsystem environment. An archive command (-ARCHIVE LOG), for example, allows a current log to be closed and a new one opened. Processing on a thread may be cancelled (-CANCEL THREAD); database status may be displayed (-DISPLAY DATABASE); status information about the DB2 governor (resource limit facility) (-DISPLAY RLIMIT) may be displayed; traces, databases, and the governor may be started and stopped (-START xxxx / -STOP xxxx); and utilities may be terminated (-TERM UTILITY). Most of these functions are available only to the DBA staff.

Q: *What are some of the important aspects of planning for backup and recovery?*

A: The most important task is to create a backup where all of the data is at a point of consistency. This will enable the system to be restored to a point where all DB2 objects are consistent. Procedures need to be developed to take a point of consistency from time to time with a backup of the data, catalog, and directory and be able to restore the catalog, directory and data. Also, an alternate site for recovery in case of a disaster at the primary site is needed.

Q: *Aside from backup procedures, what other steps will improve the recovery capability?*

A: Production systems should use dual logging and the active log datasets, and the bootstrap dataset should not be placed on the same disk volumes. The DBA is responsible to either have procedures available to recreate the communication database (CDB), the application registration table, the object registration table and the governor-resource limit facility, or to periodically backup these tables.

Q: *When is a DB2 database defined?*

A: A DB2 database is defined when the DBA issues the CREATE DATABASE statement and includes the required parameters. A database is a logical structure containing a group of tables. One DB2 subsystem may contain many DB2 databases. Each database may be administered as a unit, although no inherent physical separation occurs, and a single SQL statement may access tables from different logical databases. Only one set of DB2 catalogs is included in a subsystem.

Q: *What are some of the structures (objects) of a DB2 database?*

A: The data (tables and indexes) is physically located in TABLESPACES or INDEXSPACES that consist of one or more VSAM files. These TABLESPACES and INDEXSPACES are defined to reside in a STORAGE GROUP, which consists of one or more DASD addresses.

Q: *Why would a schema be used to define DB2 objects?*

A: A schema is a named object collection that provides a logical classification of the objects in a database. The schema may include packages, tables, functions, triggers, views and other objects.

Q: *Where is all of the database structure information stored?*

A: The database structure information is stored in the DB2 catalog tables.

Q: *How does an operator or DBA control and maintain DB2?*

A: DB2 commands and utility jobs are used to maintain and control DB2. Commands may be submitted from a terminal, an APF authorized program, or the MVS console. Utilities jobs are MVS batch jobs.

Q: *How is data in DB2 tables accessed?*

A: The data is accessed by statements that refer to the content of the column rather than to the location or organization of the column.

Q: *What are Savepoints?*

A: This is a version 6 enhancement that allows the programmer to set points in an application that can be undone without affecting the overall outcome of a transaction.

Q: *What are temporary SQL tables used for?*

A: When a table, for example, is needed only during the time that an application is executing for SORT or for queries of intermediate results, a temporary table may be used. The SQL statements may execute faster because these temporary tables do not get logged or locked. Another good usage for temporary tables is to put non-relational data into them for joining to other DB2 tables. An IMS or IDMS database on the mainframe, for example, might be read, and the data stored to a temporary table. The temporary table then can be joined in the same program to DB2 tables, thereby joining a non-relational data source with a relational (DB2) data source.

Q: *How do "declare" temporary tables differ from "global" temporary tables?*

A: Declared tables do not have descriptions in the catalog tables. The columns may be implicitly defined. They support indexes, UPDATE statements and positioned DELETE statements.

Q: *How is a Global temporary table defined?*

A: A global temporary table is defined with a CREATE GLOBAL TEMPORARY TABLE statement. An instance of this table will be created each time an application issues an OPEN, SELECT, INSERT or DELETE to this table. The instance will be deleted when the application ends or when a ROLLBACK statement is executed. It will also be deleted when a COMMIT is issued, unless an open temporary table cursor was defined WITH HOLD to access the temporary table.

Q: *What is data shearing?*

A: Data sharing is a feature that allows the user to access data stored in one location from two or more separate DB2 subsystems.

Q: *Can DB2 take advantage of a Parallel Sysplex?*

A: Yes. Parallel Sysplex allows two or more processors to share the same data thereby maximizing application performance, improving system concurrency and availability, and providing greater capacity and flexibility. Data sharing allows several DB2 subsystems to concurrently read from or write to one set of data tables.

Q: *What are some of the elements of the new DB2 Management Tools package?*

A: There is a stored procedure builder, a UDB control center, Visual Explain, and a DB2 estimator. All of these tools come with the DB2 system.

Q: *Can a user migrate from DB2 version 4 to version 6?*

A: No. Migration to version 6 may only be from version 5. Migration to version 7 is possible from both version 5 and 6. It is also possible, of course, to simply install a new version 6 without migrating. Several incompatibilities exist between versions 5 and 6. The major incompatibility is that type 1 indexes are no longer supported in version 6. In addition, there is no support for RECOVER INDEX or for shared read-only data.

Q: *What is the maximum table size for a DB2 table?*

A: The maximum table size has been increased to 16 terabytes in order to increase the capacity of partitioned tables or tables holding LOBs and BLOBs.

Performance and Indexes:

Q: *What is usually the most effective way to improve performance for data access?*

A: While not the solution in every case, most performance problems can be handled with the addition of the proper index or indexes. When a table contains a large number of rows and DB2 can utilize an index to access a row, the access is much faster than if a table scan were utilized.

Q: *How does an index enforce uniqueness?*

A: Duplicate values are permitted in a key column unless UNIQUE is specified. When the index is created, the DB2 system checks to ensure that no duplicate value exists or is entered in the key. As data is inserted or updated, DB2 continues to ensure that the combination of columns for the unique key remains unique in the table.

Q: *Why is it more efficient to scan an index rather than the data itself?*

A: The index has a direct "pointer" to the data. The number of index pages is usually significantly less than the number of data pages, and the index may be searched using a binary search. The index is in sequence, whereas the data may be distributed randomly in the file.

Q: *What is the size of an index entry?*

A: The size of an index entry is four bytes for the RID plus the sum of the number of bytes in the column or columns that make up the key. One extra byte per entry is required for each column that can contain a null value. When there are duplicate key values, only one key value (depending upon the number of duplicates) is stored and all the RIDS of the duplicate value keys are chained in sequence to the key.

Q: *What is the cost of an index?*

A: Each index requires storage space and must be modified each time a new row is inserted or deleted and each time a column value in the key is updated. Index creation also takes time during LOAD, REORG and during RECOVERY. Conventional wisdom suggests that a table should have up to three indexes. This is pure nonsense. Every table should have as many indexes (10, 20 or 30) as can be justified. The performance benefit should be weighed and considered, rather than the cost in space and batch utility time. This in no way should limit the number of indexes created on a table. Every index should be justified, and every justified index should be created. Do not use any rule of thumb to determine how many indexes to create. Create EVERY index that is needed and justified. Only when excessive INSERTs or updating of key value occurs, should fewer indexes even be considered. Note that if no indexes are justified, it is ok to have no indexes on a table.

Q: *Are all of the columns in a multicolumn (Composite) index always used directly?*

A: No. A composite index is an index on more than one column. It is important to understand when more than one column of a multicolumn (composite) index may be used. If the first column in a three column index is checked via an inequality (< >, <, >, BETWEEN, and so on), the other two columns are not used directly (are not INDEX MATCHING) but may be used via index screening. Note that the larger the number of columns in an index, the fewer index entries that fit on each page (thereby increasing the I/O required to check the index).

To be more efficient than three separate indexes, each element of a query condition (WHERE clause), except the last condition, that uses a composite index must be compared for equality (=). If the predicates are

```
WHERE ACCTNO > :HACCT AND ACCNTYPE = :HV2 AND SEX = :HSEX
```

only ACCNTNO is index matching and used directly, when the index is ACCTNO, ACCNTYPE, SEX. The other two predicates are used, after all of the index entries with the ACCNTNOs greater than the value in :HACCT are retrieved via index screening. An index ACCNTYPE, SEX, ACCTNO or three separate indexes might be more efficient.

Q: *Why would DB2 decide to use multiple indexes to decide which rows should be retrieved?*

A: When a table consists of more than one index, and the WHERE clause has more than one predicate that may use an index, DB2 has the task of determining which index would best filter the rows. Let us assume, for example, that one index is on CITY and another index is on AGE in the EMPLOYEE table, and the query asks for all of the employees living in New York City who are between 18 and 30 years of age. The optimizer might estimate that the result of this query would return only 60 rows. We may also assume that there are 5,000 employees spread across 2,500 data pages, 2,100 of whom live in New York City and 1,900 of whom are between 18 and 30 years of age. It might be worthwhile for the optimizer to use the AGE index to find the RIDs of all employees between 18 and to 30 and to use the CITY index to find the RIDs of all employees from New York City. The RIDS would then be sorted, and only when both satisfy the criteria (e.g., there are two matching RIDs) would the data row actually be retrieved.

Q: *What is index screening?*

A: When a column in an index cannot be used for the binary search (see previous answer), it may still be used by the stage 1 processor to further filter the number of rows to be retrieved before the data pages will actually be accessed. When, for example, there are five conditions in the SELECT clause and three conditions refer to the index but only one is index matching and can be used in the binary search of the index, many index entries may match the first condition. Prior to retrieving the rows, however, the processor will check the other two conditions and thereby limit the number of physical rows that have to be retrieved.

Q: *Does DB2 use an index when equal predicates in a join are unequal in length?*

A: It is only in later versions (6 or 7) of DB2 that a performance enhancement was added to allow the use of an index when predicates in a join are unequal in length. Care should be taken to ensure that the lengtyh of values to be compared are equal.

Q: *During the process of creating and loading of tables, when should indexes be created?*

A: Indexes should usually be created before the tables are initially loaded. The CREATE INDEX statement is used to create an index. If the table being indexed is not empty, DB2 can build the index right away or can defer the building of the index until later when the REBUILD INDEX utility is used. A reason to defer the building of the index on a loaded table is if several indexes were being created. Each

CREATE without DEFER accesses all of the table rows to create each index. The REBUILD INDEX utility accesses the rows only once and builds all of the indexes.

Q: *What is a clustering index?*

A: When the data and the index keys are in the same sequence, the index is clustered. When an index is used to retrieve large quantities of data in sequence, the query executes much faster if the data on the data pages is in the same sequence as the index keys. This is true because the data to be retrieved is in sequence on the same physical data pages, fewer I/O requests are required, and a sequential prefetch may be performed. It is fairly obvious that only one index can be fully clustered on a table.

Q: *How is a clustering index designated?*

A: To specify a clustering index, use the CLUSTER clause in the CREATE INDEX statement, as per the following example:

```
CREATE INDEX XNEWDATE
ON DOV01. TRANSTAB (NEW_DATE) CLUSTER;
```

Q: *How can an index retain its CLUSTER when new rows are inserted?*

A: To ensure that any new data rows inserted into the table remain in the same clustered sequence as the existing rows, an index may be designated when created as the (one and only) clustering index on the table. If a clustering index exists, the DBMS attempts to insert a new row on the same (or nearby) page, as nearly as possible, in the order of their index values. Note that if a clustering index is created on existing data, the data may not be clustered (until the table is reorganized). When newly inserted rows are added, however, the DBMS still attempts to store a new row on the same or nearby page (even though the rest of the table is not clustered) as a row with a similar key value.

Q: *Are clustered indexes always useful?*

A: No, they are only useful when they provide significant performance advantage. Operations that involve the retrieval of many sequential records, such as non-equal comparisons (For example: WHERE new_date BETWEEN '12/12/2000' and CURRENT DATE), grouping (GROUP BY ACNTTYPE), and ordering (ORDER BY AMOUNT) are the logical candidates for clustering. These are fields that usually have many duplicate values, and when many sequential retrieval queries are used, clustering may be useful. A foreign key is often a good candidate for clustering, when the data is accessed as a group. In general, there is absolutely no reason to cluster an index by a unique identifier (such as a social security number, employee number, userid, and so on). A population table clustered by a unique social security number, for example, may not serve any purpose. The application may never request all of the rows with a social security number greater than some value. An application usually orders by social security number but usually only requests a small cross-section of the population, and the optimizer does not choose to scan the entire index and table in order to save a relatively small sort. Too many tables have a unique clustering index because the purpose of a clustered index is not carefully considered.

Q: *How does List Prefetch affect performance?*

A: As explained earlier, the index is made up of a key and a RID (pointer to the data consisting of a page address and a slot address). List Prefetch is the process used when the DB2 optimizer determines that the index and the data are not in the same sequence (the index is not clustered). When the data is read in the sequence of the index, many data pages may have to be retrieved multiple times. The optimizer may decide that it would be more efficient to sort the addresses (RIDs) of the rows to be retrieved (List Prefetch) in the data page address sequence, so that each data page would only have to be read once. The negative aspect of List Prefetch is that if the final output is required in the sequence of the index, the data rows retrieved have to be resorted in the correct sequence. The optimizer estimates whether or not the List Prefetch is more efficient despite the extra data sort.

Q: *Why is index-only access efficient?*

A: With index-only access, the data pages need not be accessed because all of the needed information is available in the index. The index is almost always significantly smaller than the table itself, and less processing and I/O will be required.

Q: *Would adding columns to an index to allow the query to use index-only access be worthwhile?*

A: The reason for preferring an index access is because the index usually requires significantly fewer pages than the data. If too many columns are added to an index, not only does the index require a great deal of additional DASD space, but the size advantage is reduced. If DASD overhead is unimportant and the size will not be significantly increased, index-only access definitely has advantages.

Q: *What is a partitioning index?*

A: When a table is stored in a partitioned table space, the system must know how to divide the data among the partitions. The division of the data is defined by using the PART clause in the CREATE INDEX statement. The index that divides the data is a partitioned index. It is also a clustering index because the data is clustered by the index key values.

Q: *Can a non-partitioned index be defined on a table in a partitioned tablespace?*

A: Yes, but when a non-partitioned index and a partitioned index are defined on the same table, some of the benefits of partition-level independence for utility operations are lost.

Q: *May an index be defined that is unique when the key is not null?*

A: If any column of the key allows null values and UNIQUE WHERE NOT NULL is specified, the uniqueness constraint does not apply to a key value where any component is null. The UNIQUE WHERE NOT NULL clause is a constraint on the index key, which prevents the table from containing rows that have duplicate keys unless the value is null. If only UNIQUE is specified, null values are treated like any other values and the index could contain no more than one row with a null value key.

Q: *Can an index be used to avoid a sort?*

A: An index not only provides selective access to data, but when the index is in the sequence of the ORDER BY parameter, or the GROUP BY, or join, or DISTINCT, the index may be used to order the data and eliminate the need for a sort. To ensure that the output is in sequence, the developer must specify ORDER BY.

Q: *What are identity columns used for?*

A: This is a version 6 enhancement where DB2 automatically generates a unique numeric value for each row inserted into the table. It may usually be used to generate primary key column values.

Q: *What is the function of the optimizer?*

A: The optimizer determines the access path that is used to access the data. The optimizer bases its decision upon the conditions in the WHERE clause, upon the available indexes and upon the statistics or defaults. The user has little direct control over the decisions of the optimizer. The user may be able to influence the access path if the user knows how the optimizer decides, but cannot choose the path.

Q: *If the user may be able to influence the access path but cannot choose the path, what is the purpose of the OPT-HINT column in the EXPLAIN table?*

A: Beginning with version 6 of DB2, a new capability is available to allow the user to SUGGEST to the optimizer that a specific index should be used. After running the EXPLAIN and finding that optimizer chooses the AGE index, for example, a user might update the PLAN_TABLE and place the CITY index name in the OP-HINT column. The optimizer then tries to use that index. Another scenario might be when a previous DB2 version uses an index, but a new version is no longer using the index and the query is running slower. The PLAN_TABLE data from the previous DB2 version might be used to influence the optimizer.

Q: *How is the system set up to allow the use of these hints by the optimizer?*

A: The first task is to set the subsystem parameter optimization HINTS(YES). The applications may be bound or rebound with a new option called OPTHINT('USESTATX'). Assuming 100 was the query number given to the updated PLAN_TABLE entry, the SELECT statement should contain a QUERYNO 100 as the last clause.

Q: *Will using the OPT-HINT column improve the performance of the query?*

A: Be aware that the optimizer is usually correct and that any "hints" given by the user may cause severe performance degradation. IBM provided the function that enables users to make small, simple changes on rare occasions where the absence of correct statistics and non-standard data might make the optimizer's decision incorrect. Realize, however, that it is very rare for the user or DBA to do a better job at estimating than the optimizer.

Stored Procedures:

Q: *What is a stored procedure?*

A: It is a compiled application program executed by DB2 in response to a single SQL CALL statement. It can contain logic and multiple SQL statements. It is stored at a remote or local server.

Q: *How does one build a stored procedure?*

A: One way to build a procedure is to use the Stored Procedure Builder, an element of the DB2 Management Tools package in version 6. Another option is to code the stored procedure program in a host language.

Q: *How do I set up a stored procedure?*

A: The CREATE PROCEDURE statement is used to contain the statements and list the parameters to be received from and passed to the calling application.

Q: *In which environment is a stored procedure most effective?*

A: They are most effective in a client-server environment. The stored procedure is invoked by one command of the client and executed in the server. This greatly reduces the network transmission of commands.

Q: *Under what circumstances is it worthwhile to use a stored procedure?*

A: When more than one SQL statement has to be remotely executed and some processing logic is required at the host. The stored procedure will reduce network transmission and will also limit the ability of the workstation user to modify sensitive SQL commands.

Q: *Are there security implications to the use of stored procedures?*

A: Security is improved because the procedure code is stored and controlled by the server, and the authority to access SQL tables need not be given to the client.

Q: *What authority is needed to run a stored procedure?*

A: The owner of the package or plan containing the CALL requires EXECUTE authority for the package associated with the stored procedure.

Q: *Can the stored procedure access only DB2 tables?*

A: The stored procedure can access any resource available to that address space (QSAM, VSAM, CICS transactions, and so on).

Q: *What are some of the SQL statements that should not be used in a stored procedure?*

A: The COMMIT (except starting in version 7), CONNECT, SET CURRENT SQLID, SET CONNECTION, RELEASE will all cause the thread to be placed in a "must rollback" state. These SQL statements should not be used.

Q: *Can a stored procedure run as a main program?*

A: The stored procedure can run as either a main program or as a subprogram.

Q: *What is the difference between running the stored procedure as a main program or as a subprogram?*

A: When run as a main program, the storage used by the procedure (and all program variables) will be reinitialized. When run as a subprogram, the storage is not reinitialized (but the developer should not assume that the program variables have not been reinitialized).

Q: *Can SQL stored procedures be written entirely with SQL statements?*

A: Yes. Stored procedures may be written entirely with SQL statements. This is a version 6 enhancement. You may use flow control, assignment statements, declarations of cursors, variable conditions and traditional SQL statements for defining and manipulating data. When the stored procedure is coded using the Stored Procedure Builder, the SQL statements are converted into a C program. The user can thereby code using easy-to-understand SQL statements, yet receive the performance benefit of a compiled, C program.

Q: *What option is required when a stored procedure is written in COBOL to be executed in MVS or OS/390?*

A: The compile option NODYNAM is required. If it runs in a WLM-established address space, AMODE(31) is required in the link-edit step.

Q: *Can REXX commands be used to write a stored procedure?*

A: Yes. This is a version 6 enhancement. The SQL interface to REXX now supports almost all SQL statements supported by DB2.

Q: *Can stored procedures for OS/390 be written in JAVA?*

A: Stored procedures may be written in C, C++, PL/I, Assembler and COBOL. Writing in JAVA is a version 7 enhancement.

Q: *Which language interface must be link-edited or loaded with a stored procedure?*

A: The language interface module DSNALI or DSNRLI, depending on whether the stored procedure will be run in a DB2 established address space (DSNALI) or in a WLM established address space.

Q: *Can a stored procedure reside on other systems?*

A: If DRDA access is used, a program can call stored procedures at other systems. The SQL statements do not have to be supported at the local server, but they do have to be supported at the remote server.

Q: *Does a COMMIT or a ROLLBACK in the application also cover the stored procedures processing?*

A: In newer DB2 versions, the COMMIT or ROLLBACK affects all SQL operations, whether executed in the stored procedure or in the application.

Q: *Under which DB2 thread is a stored procedure run?*

A: A stored procedure is run under the DB2 thread of the calling program and is part of the caller's unit of recovery.

Q: *What will help a user understand why the stored procedure failed?*

A: If a CEEDUMP dataset is allocated in the address space used to start the stored procedure, a diagnostic dump will be written to that dataset. The DBA can assist the user to understand the dump.

Some DB2 design considerations:

The following table will be used as an example in the following questions:

```
Columns: STOREADDRESS, DEPTNO, DEPTNAME, ITEMQUANTITY,
ITEMUSAGE
Key - ITEMNO, STORENO.
```

Q: *What is normalization?*

A: Normalization is the redesign process to remove multiple entity types from a table. The bundled multiple entity types that usually should be removed include repeating groups (employee fixed information and his children names variable information) or multi-value or other columns (a column, for example, with room for five children's names).

Q: *In the process of normalization, what is First Normal Form (1NF)?*

A: When the previously mentioned multi-valued columns are removed so that each column has "atomic" values, the table is in First Normal Form.

Q: *What is Second Normal Form (2NF)?*

A: When each column that is not in the key is dependent upon the entire key of the table, the table is in 2NF. If the multiple key of a table, for example, includes an ITEMNO and a STORENO, the column STOREADDRESS is not dependent upon the entire key but only upon part of the key. This violates the Second Normal Form. The columns ITEMQUANTITY, DEPTNO, DEPTNAME, ITEMUSAGE are in 2NF because they contain the number of items, the department name, department number and usage where the item was sold in that particular store and are thereby dependent upon the entire key.

Q: *What is the design problem when the table in the previous question is not in 2NF?*

A: The store address would be repeated for each item in the store. When the store address is modified, all item rows for that store must be modified. When a new store with no items is opened, no store addresses would be recorded. It is also possible that an element of inconsistency would be introduced when store addresses in individual records are updated and the address of one store would then be different in different rows.

Q: *How can the previous table be modified to not violate 2NF?*

A: Two tables should be created. One table has the ITEMNO, STORENO key and columns ITEMQUANTITY, DEPTNO, DEPTNAME, ITEMUSAGE. The other table would have STOREADDRESS and a key of only STORENO.

Q: *What is Third Normal Form (3NF)?*

A: Each non-key column is independent of all of the other non-key columns and dependent only upon the table key in 3NF. In the sample table above, DEPTNAME is also dependent upon the DEPTNO. If the DEPTNAME is updated for one item without also updating the DEPTNO, the table becomes inconsistent because one DEPTNO has the two different DEPTNAMEs. To conform to 3NF, a separate table with DEPTNO and DEPTNAME should be created.

Q: *What is Fourth Normal Form (4NF)?*

A: When a multi-valued dependency exists between two columns (for example - DEPTNO and ITEMUSAGE), the table is not in 4NF. The same hammer may be used for breaking wood, banging nails in the hardware department, and for cracking nutshells in the produce department. ITEMUSAGE should be moved to its own table with a key of ITEMNO.

Q: *What are some of the reasons for not normalizing a table or for denormalizing a table?*

A: In the current implementation of DB2, normalized tables often require JOINs every time data is selected. The overhead of the processing for JOINs sometimes becomes prohibitive and ways should be investigated to reduce this JOIN overhead. The value of the denormalization should be carefully investigated, because a tradeoff between performance, integrity, and purity in design is made when tables are denormalized.

Q: *What is a business model that should be developed as a first step in the design of a database?*

A: This business model is usually an informal identification of the entity types to be represented in the database, their attributes, cardinality estimates for the entities, and the logical relationships between the entities. This business model is often mapped to a formal data model. In DB2, the entities are the rows, the attributes are the columns, and the entity types refer to tables. Tables are the logical representation of entity types. If two employees, for example, have the same attributes (EMPNO, NAME, ADDRESS, HIREDATE), they are entities of the same type and would map to the same table.

Referential Integrity:

Q: *What is Referential Integrity?*

A: Referential Integrity refers to the need for the values in two or more tables to be synchronized. When more than one table contains a USERID, for example, the developer wants to be sure that a USERID exists in the USER table before it can be inserted into a SALARY table. The developer establishes a referential relationship utilizing a PRIMARY Key on USERID in the USER table and a FOREIGN key (also on USERID) in the SALARY table.

Q: *What is a PRIMARY key and how is it established?*

A: A PRIMARY key is a unique key used as a reference by other tables. It is defined in the CREATE TABLE statement or in the ALTER TABLE statement (or with the CREATE UNIQUE INDEX statement). DB2 tables do not require keys, and they definitely do not require PRIMARY keys. If a PRIMARY key is needed, a unique index must be created on the PRIMARY KEY columns.

Q: *What is the FOREIGN key used for?*

A: The FOREIGN key establishes the referential relationship between two tables. Each time a value is inserted or updated into a column that is part of the FOREIGN key in the dependent table, it forces DB2 to check the parent table index with the PRIMARY key to ensure that a matching value exists. If not, the non-matching value cannot be inserted or updated in the dependent table. It also is used to check whether a value in the PRIMARY key can be deleted.

Q: *What are the alternatives when a PRIMARY key is to be deleted?*

A: The FOREIGN key definition determines if a PRIMARY key can be deleted. If the ON DELETE clause of the FOREIGN key definition is RESTRICT, the PRIMARY key value in the parent table may not be deleted until all of the FOREIGN keys with the same value in the dependent table are deleted first. If the ON DELETE clause of the FOREIGN key definition is CASCADE, all of the rows in the dependent table with a matching FOREIGN key are also deleted. If the ON DELETE clause of the FOREIGN key definition is SET NULL, at least one of the columns with a matching FOREIGN key has to be nullable and it will be set to NULL.

Q: *What is the performance implication of ON DELETE CASCADE or SET NULL?*

A: If a PRIMARY key is deleted, it may result in the updating (SET NULL) or deletion (CASCADE) of hundreds or thousands of rows in other tables. This may tie up system and database resources considerably.

Applications:

Q: *Where can a programmer get the layouts for the tables he or she will work with?*

A: All of the definitions of existing DB2 tables may be found in the system catalogs. A SELECT of SYSIBM.SYSCOLUMNS, for example, provides the user with a description of the columns in the table. SYSVIEWS describes the views, SYSTABLES describes the tables and SYSINDEXES describes the indexes. Application programmers usually have access to these tables.

Q: *What are some of the reasons for using views?*

A: A view may be a partial representation of the data in a table. When a user is given authorization to access a view, part of the data may be hidden from his or her view. Only those columns and rows that the user is authorized to see are accessible. A view also provides a customized logical table with column names tailored for the user. (The SQL chapter has many more details.)

Q: *What method is used to move table data into a program?*

A: An application program uses program areas known as "host variables" to store the data to be received from, sent to, or compared with the data from the database. The "host variable" is defined in the application program as a standard work area field. In the SQL statement, it is written with a colon ':' as a prefix (such as :WORK1). Programmers often give the work areas the same name (label) as the column name in the table. DB2 can differentiate between the column name and the host variable name because of the colon (:) preceding the host variable.

Q: *Can REXX commands use SQL statements?*

A: Yes. This is a version 6 enhancement. In a REXX procedure, an SQL statement may be issued anywhere a REXX command is issued.

Q: *What is the difference between an alias and a synonym?*

A: An alias, like a synonym, represents a table or view name. A synonym, however, may only be used by its creator, while an alias may be used by any user. An alias is often preferable to a synonym, and it also allows a three-part-name which enables the access of remote tables.

Q: *What method would an application programmer use to create and load test tables?*

A: One of the easiest ways to create test tables, if the tables already exist in production, is to use an image copy (backup) of the data. The developer or the DBA can create test tables by using the load utility to load all or part of the production table into the test table. When the data in the test table will be acquired by combining data from several existing tables, the INSERT statement with an appropriate SELECT can be used to load the test table.

Q: *Will a non-correlated subquery for an IN condition be able to use an index?*

A: In the past, a SELECT * FROM tableA WHERE DEPT IN (SELECT NEWDEPT FROM tableB, would not be able to use an index. In version 6 (with the correct local fix), the IN may use an index.

Q: *Can a subselect be used in an UPDATE statement?*

A: Yes, this is a version 6 enhancement.

Q: *How does DB2 evaluate the predicate conditions in an SQL statement?*

A: The sequence of predicate evaluation by DB2 is explained by rules. The optimizer determines which index or indexes will be used and the index-matching predicates will be used first to find the index entries that satisfy the conditions. If additional stage 1 predicates have columns that could not be matching but are in the index, the predicates may be evaluated after the index matching values are evaluated. For example, if the first, second and fourth column of the index are in the condition, the first two are index matching and the fourth column is checked against the index values later. This later check is called index screening. The data page is then read from the table if needed. Any other stage 1 predicates are then applied to further filter the rows. If any additional (stage 2) predicates are in the condition, they are applied to further filter the rows before they are passed to the application.

Note that the SQL chapter has a great deal of additional application programming questions and answers and will explain STAGE 1 and STAGE 2 predicates.

Utilities:

Q: *What are the basic options of the load utility?*

A: The load utility can replace the existing table or add new records to the existing tables. If more than one table is loaded into the same tablespace, performance is enhanced if one LOAD statement is used to load all of the tables at the same time. The option of loading without logging the changes will usually speed up the load. After the load, however, the tablespace will be in COPY PENDING status and a backup should be performed.

Q: *What are the main utilities used for recovery?*

A: The QUIESCE utility provides a point of consistency, the COPY utility provides backup copies, the MERGECOPY utility allows the periodical backups to merge into one backup, the REPORT utility provides information needed to recover, and the RECOVER utility performs the actual recovery.

Q: *What is the difference between a REBUILD INDEX and a RECOVER INDEX?*

A: In previous versions of DB2, a backup image copy of an index could not be taken and the RECOVER INDEX was needed to restore the index. In DB2 version 6 & 7, REBUILD INDEX has replaced RECOVER INDEX. The REBUILD INDEX will reconstruct the index by accessing the table, extracting and sorting the keys, and recreating the index.

Q: *Where does the information needed for recovery reside?*

A: The main catalog table with backup information is SYSIBM. SYSCOPY. It contains the information about full and incremental image copies and the log RBA. It also contains information recorded by the various backup utilities (QUIESCE, REORG, REBUILD INDEX, RECOVER TOCOPY, LOAD and RECOVER TOLOGPOINT or TORBA). The SYSIBM.SYSLGRNX contains log RBA ranges and is a directory table.

8
Visual Basic 6

David McMahon

Visual Basic 6 is the latest incarnation of Microsoft's popular software development system. Since its inception in the early 1990s, VB has revolutionized the world of computer programming by combining a programming language that is easy to learn and use with a user-friendly GUI development system. This combination has allowed developers to shave weeks or even months of development time from complex projects, while at the same time giving users more of what they need.

While originally cast as a system for developing database front ends, VB has grown to be used for just about any type of software development. With each new release, the Basic programming language upon which VB is based has grown more sophisticated and therefore found a wider audience. From database programming to scientific programming to the Internet, you're likely to see VB in use. Since VB is used in such a wide variety of environments, you can make yourself more employable by having a broad knowledge of VB rather than just focusing on one area like database development.

Visual Basic is available in the three following editions:

- Learning Edition: This is a beginner's version of Visual Basic that is available for around $100. While it can be used to create distributable applications, the primary purpose of this edition is to learn the programming language or for hobby purposes. This edition lacks many of the features required by professional programmers.

- Professional Edition: The Professional Edition is available for about $549, or $279 for the upgrade version. With the professional edition, you will find all the advanced features you need for full-scale software development. This includes tools for Internet programming, ActiveX control development, and ActiveX DLL development.
- Enterprise Edition: Typically the Enterprise Edition will go for around $1300. The enterprise edition includes all of the features of the Professional edition, but is enhanced with features and products necessary to run VB in a multi-developer or team environment. This includes tools such as Visual Source Safe that enable multiple developers to work on the same projects.

A Visual Basic Job Interview

For any job, a prospective employee should have familiarity with at least the Professional Edition. The Learning Edition is not adequate for real world applications, so an applicant who only has experience with it would probably not be considered for most positions. While knowledge of the Enterprise Edition may not be specifically required, it may be helpful if you are applying for managerial or team leader positions.

Since Visual Basic can be used to develop almost any type of software, the specific focus of an interviewer's questions will vary from employer to employer. If you are applying for an MIS position in a corporate office, the focus may be on database applications. Another employer might focus on the Internet aspects of VB, or some combination of Internet programming and database applications. A scientific or engineering firm may focus on specific aspects of the language, the creation of ActiveX controls or object oriented programming. As such, it is difficult to frame a set of specific questions for a given skill level that can be tailored to any interview.

In any case, we can define a set of skills that every Visual Basic developer would be expected to have. This will include knowledge about the BASIC language as used by VB, the integrated development environment or IDE, and the various types of projects that can be created with VB. Beyond that, specific areas covered will depend on the type of employer and the type of projects you will be assigned. Generally, potential employees can be divided into three categories:

- Entry Level: A user at this level may be straight out of school or perhaps someone who is experienced with other programming languages but new to Visual Basic. A person at this level might be hired to develop a user interface or to do simple database development, for example. For an entry-level position, the developer will be expected to have a reasonable familiarity with the Visual Basic development environment. This will include knowledge of what types of projects can be created with VB and how they differ. It will be expected that you know how to create and save projects, and how to set project properties. You should be very familiar with the use of a Form as the basic user interface element, and know how to add controls to a form and set control properties. You will be expected to know how to respond to events and create code in Visual Basic modules. The use of third party controls will be important, and you will also be expected to know the basics of the Basic programming language, including declaration of variables and data types, using If-Then-Else statements, For and Do-While loops, and the use of subroutines and functions. Knowledge of areas such as database programming will probably be on a superficial level. For example you might be expected to know how to set the properties of a data control, how to bind controls to it and how to open a database. An entry level candidate will be expected to have familiarity with debugging software.

- Intermediate: An intermediate level programmer will be expected to have worked on projects of some complexity and go beyond simply building a GUI. This means that you will be expected to know how to use more advanced settings in the Development Environment, such as using the Tools Attributes dialog or creating ActiveX controls. Your knowledge of completing different tasks will be expected to be on a deeper level. For example, when it comes to database programming you will be expected to know not only how to use an ADO data control, but also how to program ADO in code and how to work in a multi-user environment. Knowledge of Jet and ODBC may be expected. When it comes to the programming language, you may be expected to know about classes and how to create and program objects in VB.
- Advanced: The advanced user will be expected to have a thorough and deep knowledge of Visual Basic. Chances are you will either be expected to work on complex projects or perhaps be a team leader. In this case, you should be able to demonstrate that you have knowledge of Source Safe and know VB so well that members of your team can come to you for help. You should have an excellent grasp of object oriented development and classes. You should know how to use the Windows *Application Program Interface* (API) and how to work with DLLs written in any programming language. Depending on the environment, you may need to know how to pass data between different programming languages. It

will be important to know about system performance and how to get the most out of memory management and compiler settings. If working with databases, you should have a good knowledge of database design, structure, and the use of SQL and stored procedures.

Questions and Answers

In this section, interview questions and answers have been grouped together by skill level. Keep in mind that developers in more advanced skill sets should be able to answer the entry level questions as well.

Beginner

Q: *What are the main components of a Visual Basic program?*

A: At a minimum, a normal Visual Basic program consists of forms, modules and controls.

Q: *What is the difference between an SDI application and an MDI application?*

A: With an SDI application, the user can only work within one active window at a time, whereas in an MDI application, a user can have many windows open and active.

Q: *What is the difference between a picture box and an image control?*

A: An image control uses fewer resources and repaints faster than a picture box. An image control can be stretched, while a picture box cannot. An image control can be placed in a container, but cannot be used as a container.

Q: *What is the difference between a function and a subroutine?*

A: Although both procedures allow you to pass parameters, only the function can return a value of a specific data type.

Q: *Explain how you would configure Visual Basic so that it will automatically save changes to your project each time you run it.*

A: This can be done with the Options dialog, which can be accessed from the Tools pull down menu. Once opened, select the Environment tab. Next, look for the *When a program starts* group and select *Save Changes.*

Q: *How do you bring up the Object Browser, and what is its function?*

A: The Object Browser can be opened by pressing the F2 key or by selecting Object Browser from the View pull down menu. The purpose of the Object Browser is to provide a reference where you can view all of the objects in your Visual Basic project and see the properties, methods and events associated with each object.

Q: *What is an ActiveX control?*

A: An ActiveX control is a custom control that can be used in a Visual Basic project. Usually it is a user interface component, such as a list box or graphics control. On your computer's hard drive, an ActiveX control is a file with an .OCX extension.

Q: *What is an Event,?*

A: An Event is an action that occurs in the system while your program is running. Events can be user driven or system driven. For example, a mouseclick or key press is an event generated by the user. The main task of a Visual Basic program is to write code to respond to events.

Q: *What key will open the properties window?*

A: The F4 key. You can also select Properties Window from the View pull down menu.

Q: *You are working in Visual Basic and a form is displayed in the middle of your screen. Describe how you can open the code window for that form, and talk about the basic elements and layout of the code window.*

A: The code window for a form can be opened in one of three ways. You can open the code window by double clicking on the form or any control placed on it. Alternatively, you can right click your mouse over the form and select View Code. The third way is to click the View Code button found in the Project Explorer window. A code window is displayed in the center of the Visual Basic IDE. Here you will find a text editor that can be used to enter and edit your Visual Basic code. In the upper left corner of the code window for a form, you will see a drop down list that can be used to select the object for which you want to enter code. This will include the form, the General Declarations section of the form, and any objects or controls that have been placed on the form. When you select an item from this drop down list you can choose a procedure associated with that object from the drop down list just to the right. For example, if you want to add code to the Form Load event procedure, you select Form from the left hand drop down list and then select Load on the right.

Q: *Briefly explain the difference between a standard EXE project and an ActiveX Exe project.*

A: A standard EXE project is nothing more than a standard Windows application. If you select this option when creating a new project, Visual Basic will load a single form into the IDE. An ActiveX Exe project, on the other hand, is an executable that can also act as an ActiveX server. This means that it can expose its objects for use by other applications.

Q: *You are tasked with updating an old project that has been compiled into p-code. You are told to change this to a true executable and optimize it for speed. Explain how you would do this.*

A: This can be done from the Compile tab of the Project Properties dialog box. By specifying that the project be changed to a true executable, this means the Compile to Native Code option should be selected. Under this option, several options are found that can be used to configure the compiler. To optimize for speed, select the Optimize for Fast Code option.

Q: *You are instructed to add a textbox control to a form and name it txtName. You are also told to limit the number of characters that can be entered in this textbox to 25 and to display the text "Enter Student Name" when the user rests the mouse pointer over the textbox. Describe how this task could be accomplished.*

A: First, double click on the textbox icon in the Toolbox and position and shape the control as instructed. Next, with the textbox control selected, press the F4 key to bring up the properties window for the textbox if it isn't open already. To set the name of the textbox, we select the (Name) property which can be found at the top of the properties list and type in *txtName.* To restrict the number of characters to 25, we select the MaxLength property and enter 25. To display the text "Enter Student Name" when the user rests the mouse pointer over the textbox, we add this text to the ToolTipText property of the control.

Q: *What is the difference between p-code and Native code and what are the advantages of each?*

A: P-code is a shorthand notation for pseudocode. A pseudocode program is not compiled into native instructions that the microprocessor can understand directly. Instead, the application is put into an intermediate form that can be translated by a Visual Basic interpreter at runtime. This can be useful if your application will run on different types of processors, such as Intel and Alpha machines. The translation process takes time, however, so your application will be slowed down if compiled to p-code.

Native code compiled applications have been written in the native instructions of the processor at compile time. A Native Code compiled project results in a faster application. If the program will not run on different families of processors, this is how you should compile your application to get the best performance possible. You can also tweak a Native Code compiled project to get the most out of it for your specific situation.

Q: *What is the purpose of the References dialog?*

A: The References dialog box enables you to set object references for your project. This dialog will display a set of object libraries that are available on your system, such as the Microsoft ActiveX Data Objects 2.1 library. In order to use the library in your code, you must set a reference to it with the References dialog first.

Q: *How would you specify the application title and program icon for a Visual Basic project?*

A: Click on the Project pull down menu and select Project...Properties. The Application Title and icon can be set on the Make tab. Click on this tab and under Application, type in the Title you want to use. To specify an icon, you must specify the icon for a form that is contained in the project. Click on the Icon drop down list and select the form you want to use.

Q: *You have just created a standard EXE project in Visual Basic. Describe the basic elements that you will find displayed in the design environment.*

A: When creating a standard EXE project, Visual Basic will add a single Form to the project and display this form in a window in the center of the screen. A caption in the upper left of the window will list the name of the project and the name of the form, which will be Form1 by default. A form is the basic user interface element of a Visual Basic project. It is a window that will permit the user to use and interact with the newly created program. Custom Controls such as buttons, textboxes, and listboxes can be added to a form to build a functional user interface.

To the left of the Form window is the Toolbox. The Toolbox contains a set of icons that permit the developer to add custom controls to a form. The Toolbox can contain both standard controls that are built into Visual Basic as well as ActiveX controls that are provided by Microsoft or third party companies. You can add a control to a form by double clicking on its icon.

On the upper right side of the screen you will see the Project Explorer. This window displays all of the files that are contained in your project, including forms, standard code modules and class modules. You can access each element of your project by selecting it in the Project Explorer. This includes access to code windows as well as the ability to view objects like forms.

Directly beneath the Project Explorer you will see the Properties window. This is where you can view or set the properties of any selected object in your project, such as the Name or Caption of a form. Properties are listed in either Alphabetic or Categorized order.

In the lower right corner of the screen, you will find the Form Layout window. This window allows you to set the startup position of a selected form graphically.

Q: *You are told to add a third party control named MyWidget to a VB project. What steps would you use to accomplish this and where would you find the MyWidget control?*

A: To add a third party control to a VB project, you need to open the Components dialog box. This is found under the Project pull down menu in the Visual Basic IDE. The Components dialog box has three tabs, Controls, Designers, and Insertable Objects. To add the MyWidgets control you are interested in the Controls tab. First, you will scan the listbox in the middle of the dialog that contains a listing of installed controls. If you find the MyWidget control in this list, check the box to the left of the name and click the OK button. If the control is not in the list, click Browse and search for the control, which will probably be installed as an .OCX file in the Windows/System directory. After the control has been selected in the Components dialog box, you will find it in the VB ToolBox.

Q: *You are working on a standard EXE Visual Basic project. The project is currently named with the default name given by VB: Project1. Explain how to change the project name to myprog and compile the project into an executable named myprog.exe.*

A: The project name can be changed from the Project Properties dialog box. This dialog can be opened by selecting Project1 Properties from the Project pull down menu. On the General tab of this dialog, there is a textbox labeled Project Name. Type myprog in this textbox and click the OK button. To compile the project, click on the File pull down menu and select Make myprog.exe.... A File Save dialog named Make Project will open that can be used to specify the location where the myprog.exe file will be created. To create the file, click the OK button. Visual Basic will then compile the program and proceed to write the executable if no errors are found.

Q: *Explain the difference between Step Over and Step Into while in debugging mode.*

A: Step Into enables you to execute a program one line at a time. If a call to a subroutine or function is encountered, control is passed inside the procedure where execution continues one line at a time. When using Step Over, the code is also executed one line at a time. However, when a call to a procedure is encountered, the procedure is executed in a single step without passing control inside the procedure. Execution then continues in single step mode.

Q: *What key allows you to single step through code when in debug mode?*

A: Step Into can be invoked with the F8 key. To use Step Over, press Shift + F8.

Q: *What is the effect of setting a breakpoint?*

A: When a Visual Basic program is executing, it will pause when it reaches a line of code that has been specified as a breakpoint. The debugger will then display that line of code. This will provide you with an opportunity to use any of the debugging tools, such as stepping through code or viewing the contents of program variables. When a break point is encountered, the line where the breakpoint has been set is the next line of code to be executed.

Q: *You are instructed to set a breakpoint on the first line of code in a sub procedure named MAX. The code looks like this:*

```
Sub MAX(GradeOne As Double, GradeTwo As Double)
Dim Sum As Double
Sum = 0
...
```

Where would you set the breakpoint and how would you do it? Also, how is a line of code with a breakpoint distinguished?

A: A breakpoint can only be set on a line of executable code, so breakpoints on variable declarations cannot be set. The breakpoint would be set on the line

```
Sum = 0
```

One way to set the breakpoint is to place the cursor on this line and then right click with the mouse. This will bring up a pop up menu where Toggle, Breakpoint is selected. When you set the breakpoint, that line will be highlighted and you will find a circle on the left side of the line.

Q: *You want to track a variable named anorm in a sub procedure. Your supervisor tells you to set a watch for this variable. She tells you to set the watch so that VB will pause if anorm exceeds 100. How would you do this?*

A: A Watch is an expression that can be used to display or monitor the value of a variable or expression in a VB program. You can add a Watch either at design time or at runtime while in debug mode. You can add a watch for the anorm variable by highlighting it in your code. Next, right click and select Add Watch. Enter the following text in the Expression input box:

```
anorm > 100
```

In the Watch Type frame at the bottom of the dialog, select Break When Value Is True. When the program is executed in the development environment, if anorm is greater than 100, VB will enter design mode and pause on the line where this occurred. This will enable you to track down the source of the error.

Q: *What is the purpose of Step Out when in debug mode?*

A: Step Out allows you to exit the currently executing procedure. In other words, if you are stepping through code one line at a time, Step Out will execute the remaining lines of code in the current procedure in a single step and pause execution on the line of code following the line that called that procedure.

Q: *What is the effect of using Run to Cursor, and what key combination will invoke it?*

A: Run to Cursor enables you to skip over a number of lines while single stepping through code during debug mode. To use Run to Cursor, select a line of code where you want VB to pause. Then press Ctrl + F8. Visual Basic will then execute all lines of code up to the line you selected. You can also invoke Run to Cursor from the Debug pull down menu.

Q: *You are told to setup a variable named Total_Students inside a procedure to track the number of students enrolled in a class. The maximum number of students that can enroll is 100. What is the most efficient data type to use for this variable?*

A: This variable should be declared as type Byte. A Byte has a range of 0 to 255, making it perfect to track this information. Since a Byte only requires a single byte of memory, it is a very efficient way to store numeric data.

Q: *Visual Basic does not require the explicit declaration of variables. How would you force it to do so, and how can this be done automatically for a project?*

A: If the keywords Option Explicit are included at the beginning of a code window, Visual Basic will require all variables in that code window to be declared before use. To setup a project so that Visual Basic will automatically include these keywords in every code window, open the Options dialog from the Tools pull down menu. On the Editor tab, check the Require Variable Declaration box. From this point forward, Visual Basic will include the keywords Option Explicit in the code window of every form or module you add to the project.

Q: *Describe the basic data types found in Visual Basic.*

A: Visual Basic includes the following basic types:

- Byte: A byte variable can be used to store numeric data in the range of 0 to 255. Like the name says, a byte requires a single byte of memory storage.
- Integer: An integer can store whole numbers in the range −32,768 to +32,767. An integer requires two bytes of memory storage.
- Long: A long can store whole numbers in the range −2,147,483,648 to +2,147,483,647. A Long requires four bytes of storage.
- Single: A single is used to store floating point numbers. The range for a Single is −3.402823E38 to −1.401298E-45 for negative values and 1.401298E-45 to 3.402823E38 for positive values. Singles require four bytes of memory storage.
- Double: A double is also used for floating point numbers. A double uses eight bytes of storage, giving it a much larger range of values. The values that can be stored in a double range from

−1.79769313486232E308 to −4.94065645841247E-324 for negative values and 4.94065645841247E-324 to 1.79769313486232E308 for positive values.

- Currency: Currency is used for financial data. It has four digits of precision. Requiring eight bytes of storage, the range for Currency is −922,337,203,685,477.5808 to 922,337,203,685,477.5807.
- Decimal: A variable of type Decimal is a number scaled to a power of ten. A Decimal can be used to represent whole numbers or numbers with a fractional part. For whole numbers, the range is +/−79,228,162,514,264,337,593,543,950,335. Decimals with a fractional part can store up to 28 decimal places. The range is +/−7.9228162514264337593543950335.
- Boolean: A Boolean is used to store True/False values. A Boolean requires two bytes of storage.
- Date: A variable of type Date can be used to store Date/Time information. The dates that can be represented fall between January 1, 100 to December 31, 9999. A Date requires eight bytes of storage space.
- String: Used to store text information. Strings can be variable length, in which case they require ten bytes plus one byte for each character. The range is up to 2 billion characters. A fixed length string has a range of up to 65,400 characters.
- Variant: A variant can hold any type of data. A variant requires excess overhead, however. For example, a number stored in a variant requires 16 bytes of storage while holding the range of a Double.
- Object: An Object variable is a reference to any object in Visual Basic. It requires 4 bytes of storage.

Q: *You are working on a program that tracks the hourly wage of an employee. The user types this information in a textbox named txtWage, and you want to store it in a variable of type currency. Describe how you would read in the data and convert it from a string to currency.*

A: The data can be converted to the appropriate data type by using one of the Visual Basic Data Conversion functions. In this case, we need to use the CCur function, which will convert the argument to type Currency. The following code will do the job:

```
Dim curWage As Currency
curWage = CCur(txtWage.Text)
```

Q: *Explain the difference between Public and Private variables. Describe how you would declare a variable of type integer named Temp as a Public variable, a Private variable, and inside a sub procedure named Min.*

A: If a variable is declared with the Public keyword, it will be accessible throughout the program, outside of the form or module where it has been declared. A Private variable, on the other hand, is only accessible to code in the form or module where it has been declared. The Public and Private keywords can only be used in the general declarations section of a form or module. To declare the Temp variable with Public access, write:

```
Public Temp As Integer
```

To restrict access to the form or module where it has been declared, use the Private keyword:

```
Private Temp As Integer
```

Inside the Min sub procedure, do not use the Public or Private keywords. Use the Dim keyword instead:

```
Dim Temp As Integer
```

Q: *You are working on a standard EXE project with a single form. You are told to create a Public constant of type integer named minTemp. You are to set this constant to the value 32. Explain the steps required to complete this task.*

A: A Public constant cannot be declared in a form module. As a result, to include the constant in your project will require a standard module. This can be done by clicking on the Project pull down menu and selecting Add Module. Select the Module icon in the Add Module dialog box and click Open. Next, add the following line of code to the General Declarations section of the new module:

```
Public Const minTemp As Integer = 32
```

Q: *What is an array? Describe how you would declare an array of type integer with 100 elements named TestScores inside a sub procedure.*

A: An array is a collection of elements that are all of the same data type. This collection of elements is identified by a variable name and an index that specifies the element you want to access. To declare the TestScores array, write:

```
Dim TestScores(100) As Integer
```

Q: *What is the default lower bound of an array? How can you change this value?*

A: In Visual Basic, the default lower bound of an array is 1. There are two ways that you can change the lower bound. The first is to use the Option Base statement. This statement is placed at the beginning of a form or code module and allows you to specify the default lower bound of all arrays declared in that module as 0 or 1. For example, to enable all arrays to start at 0, add this statement:

```
Option Base 0
```

An array declared with the statement:

```
Dim TestScores(100) As Integer
```

would be indexed from 0 to 99. If we omitted the Option Base 0 statement or used Option Base 1, the array would be indexed from 1 to 100. Another way to change the lower bound of an array is to specify the array bounds in the declaration. For example, for an array to be indexed from -50 to 50, declare it as:

```
Dim MyArray(-50 To 50) As Integer
```

Q: *How would you declare a two-dimensional array of type Long with 40 rows and 50 columns, and initialize each element to the value -1?*

A: Declare the array like this:

```
Dim MyArray(1 To 40, 1 To 50) As Long
```

To initialize the array, we need variables to loop through each row and column. Use a For Loop to fill in the array values:

```
Dim i As Integer, j As Integer
 For i = 1 To 40
  For j = 1 To 50
   MyArray(i , j) = -1
  Next j
 Next I
```

Q: *How can you use a With...End With statement to set the properties of a textbox control?*

A: A With...End With statement begins with the keyword With and is followed by a list of properties denoted with "dot" syntax. For example, set some properties of a textbox control named txtData this way:

```
With txtData
  .Text = "Data"
  .BackColor = vbRed
  .FontName = "Arial"
End With
```

Q: *What is a comment, and how do you specify comments in Visual Basic?*

A: A comment is a line of text in a program that is not an executable line of code, but is instead placed there as an instruction or reminder for the programmer. In short, the purpose of a comment is to document your code. Comments in Visual Basic are indicated with a single apostrophe character. Comments can be placed on their own separate lines or as a part of a line of code. Here's an example:

```
'This is a comment line
'The MAX variable should never exceed 100

Dim MAX As Byte 'Another comment here on same line as code
```

Q: *What is the final result in the following code (all variables type integer):*

```
a = 4
b = 7
c = 17
d = 5
r = 8
s = 12
t = 4
f = a + b * c -s/t + d^2
```

A: The variable f will be assigned the value 145. Remember the precedence rules that are used in Visual Basic. This means that multiplication and division will be computed before addition and subtraction. So in this case:

```
4 + (7)*(17) - (12)/(4) + 25 = 145
```

Q: *You want to express the following equation in Visual Basic:*

$$r = \frac{a + b + c*d}{14}$$

Q: *What would you do to get the proper answer?*

A: Using the Visual Basic rules of precedence, recall that multiplication and division will have precedence over addition and subtraction. This means that division by 14 will have precedence over the addition terms in the numerator. To get Visual Basic to perform the addition first, place the terms that have the highest precedence in the numerator within parentheses. The code looks like this:

```
r = (a + b + c*d)/14
```

Q: *Comparison operators are used to make decisions in If-Then-Else statements. How would you write a statement that would set the value of a variable sum based on the following conditions, assuming that another variable is named average:*

```
sum = { 0 if average less than or equal to 18
        20 if average greater than 18, but less than 100
        -1 otherwise
```

A: This can be done easily with an If-Then-Else If-Else statement:

```
If( average < = 18 ) Then
  sum = 0
Else If (average < 100) Then
  sum = 20
Else
  sum = -1
End If
```

Q: *You are tracking a variable named txtShirtColor that can be one of the following: "Red," "Blue," or "Green." Depending on the color, you are to activate the function respectively. If the color is not one of these values, display an error message.How would you do this using a Select Case statement?*

A: This can be done as follows:

```
Select Case txtShirtColor
 Case "Red"
  Call Red()
 Case "Blue"
  Call Blue()
 Case "Green"
  Call Green()
 Case Default
```

```
  MsgBox "Invalid color. Please try again."
End Select
```

Q: *You are asked to check if a variable named MAX is not equal to 100. If this is the case, you are to reset MAX to 0. How would you do this using an if statement?*

A: The Visual Basic comparison operator for not equal is < >. The code looks like this:

```
If ( MAX < > 100) Then
  MAX = 0
End If
```

Q: *How would you create a user defined type named Student that tracked the following information?*

```
Name as a string variable
Age as an integer
Grade as an enumerated type fresh, soph, junior or senior
SSN as a string with 12 characters
```

Specify where the type must be defined and give a simple example of how it could be used.

A:
```
Enum GradeLevel

  Fresh = 0
  Soph = 1
  Junior = 2
  Senior = 3
End Enum
Type Student
  Name As String
  Age As Integer
  Grade As GradeLevel
  SSN As String*12
End Type
```

This type of declaration must be placed in the general declarations section of a standard code module. Declare a variable of this user-defined type and access the elements of the type with the dot syntax:

```
Dim Bob As Student

Bob.Name = "Bob Smith"
Bob.Age = 16
```

```
Bob.Grade = Junior 'Notice we are using the enumerated
values

Bob.SSN = "555-55-5555"

MsgBox Bob.Name
MsgBox Bob.Grade
```

Q: *Name the basic loop structures that are available in Visual Basic and explain the difference between a Do-While loop and a Do-Until loop.*

A: Visual Basic includes the following loop structures:

- For-Next loop
- Do-While loop
- Do-Loop-While
- Do-Until-Loop
- Do-Loop-Until
- For-Each-Next Loop

The main difference between a Do-While loop and a Do-Until loop is that a Do-While loop will test the terminating condition at the top of the loop, while the Do-Until loop will execute at least once and tests the terminating condition at the bottom of the loop.

Q: *You have written the following code:*

```
Dim j As Integer, jj As Integer, sum As double

j = Cint(text1.Text)
jj = MAX
sum = 0

Call FixIt j, jj, sum
```

When you compile it, you get the error: "Expected: End of Statement." What is the problem?

A: The problem is on the line which calls the sub procedure FixIt. When using the Call keyword, any parameters passed to a procedure must be enclosed within parentheses. The correct way to write this line of code is the following:

```
Call FixIt (j, jj, sum)
```

If you omit the Call keyword, you can leave off the parentheses, and write the call as:

```
FixIt j, jj, sum
```

Q: *You are writing code that computes the average of the elements in a one dimensional array of doubles named InData. You are instructed to compute the average using a For loop, but the loop must terminate and display a message to the user if the sum of the elements exceeds 999. Explain how this could be done.*

A: This can be done by inserting an Exit For statement inside the loop:

```
For i = 1 to MAX

Sum = Sum + InData(i)
If ( Sum > 999 ) Then
  MsgBox "ERROR: Sum has exceeded Maximum allowed.
  Terminating average."
  Exit For
End If

Next I
```

Q: *You are instructed to loop through the controls on a form and if a control is a textbox, to set the Text property to "NONE." How could you do this?*

A: This can be done by declaring an object variable and using a For-Each-Next loop:

```
Dim objControl As Object
For Each objControl In Controls
    If TypeOf objControl Is TextBox Then
    objControl.Text = "NONE"
  End If
Next objControl
```

Notice that we used the TypeOf statement to determine the type of the control.

Q: *You are instructed to add an ADO Data Control to a form and connect it to the Biblio.mdb database using Jet 4. Explain how you would accomplish this.*

A: First, make sure the ADO Data Control is part of the project. If it is not found in the toolbox, open the components dialog and select Microsoft ADO Data Control 6.0 (OLE DB). Now add the ADO data control to the form. Right click on the control and select ADO DC

Properties. Under Source of Connection on the General tab, select Use Connection String and click Build. This will open the Data Link Properties dialog. OLE DB providers are listed on the first tab. Specify that the control use the Microsoft Jet 4.0 Provider. Click on this item once to select it. Next, click on the Connection tab to specify the database. Use an input box labeled Select or enter a database name with a command button labeled by an ellipsis (...) to the right. Click on this command button to browse the system for the desired database. Find Biblio.mdb with the File Open dialog box, select it, and then click OK to close the Data Link Properties dialog box.

Q: *You are working on a project that uses the Biblio.mdb database. This database contains four tables: Authors, Titles, Title Author, and Publishers. You already have an ADO data control on the form connected to this database. Explain how you would configure the control to open the Publishers table.*

A: Select the ADO data control and right click. Next, select ADO DC properties. Click the Record Source tab. On this tab, notice a drop down list labeled Command Type. The Command Type is used as information for specifying the type of record source that will be used for this connection. For example, Command Type can be text (an SQL statement), a table, or a stored procedure. In this case, open a single table. Click open the Command Type drop down list and select 2-adCmdTable. When you do this, a new drop down list labeled Table or Stored Procedure Name will appear. If you open this list, you will find a list of tables contained in the database. Select Publishers and click OK.

Q: *Working with an ADO data control, you are told to configure your form so that it will prompt the user before saving any changes made to a record. Describe a way to do this efficiently.*

A: This can be accomplished by using the Will Change Record event of the ADO data control. This event fires before the contents of a record are changed. Two important parameters pass to this event procedure. The first, adReason, can be tested to find out why the event has fired. For example, it can tell you if the user has added a new record, attempted to move to another record, or closed the recordset.

Another important parameter passed to this procedure is adStatus. You can set adStatus to the VB constant adStatusCancel and this will cancel any changes the user has made to the record. This is helpful for the task at hand. First, write code in the WillChangeRecord procedure to ask the user whether to save changes. If not, set adStatus to adStatusCancel. The ADO data control has been named adoBookTitles:

```
Private Sub adoBookTitles_WillChangeRecord(ByVal adReason
As ADODB.EventReasonEnum, ByVal cRecords As Long, adStatus
As ADODB.EventStatusEnum, ByVal pRecordset As
ADODB.Recordset)

Dim intResponse As Integer

intResponse = MsgBox("Save Changes?", vbYesNo)

If intResponse = vbNo Then

  adStatus = adStatusCancel

End If

End Sub
```

Q: *You are told to configure your ADO data control so that it will abort an attempt at making a connection after 30 seconds. Explain how you would do this.*

A: The Connection Timeout property of the ADO data control is used to specify the amount of time to wait for the connection before aborting. The default value is 15 seconds. To change this value to 30 seconds, select the ADO data control and press F4 to bring up the properties window. Select Connection Timeout and type 30.

Q: *How can you configure the ADO data control so that there is no limit on the number of records returned?*

A: The maximum number of records returned by the recordset associated with an ADO data control is specified by the MaxRecords property. If it is set to 0, there is no limit on the number of records returned.

Q: *You are working with a form that has two ADO data controls. The first, named adoBooks, is connected to a database you have designed. This database has a table named books and a text field named Publisher. The second ADO data control, named adoBiblio, is connected to the Publishers table in the Biblio.mdb database. You are told to use the Company Name field in this table as a lookup in a drop down list that will allow the user to select a value for the Publisher field in the books table. Explain what control you would use and how you would configure it to accomplish this.*

A: The best control to use in this situation is the Data Combo control. To work with the ADO data control, select the OLE DB version. To add the control to your project, select Microsoft Data List Controls 6.0 (OLE DB) from the Components dialog box. First, configure the control so that the lookup list comes from the Publishers table in Biblio.mdb. The first step is to set the Row Source property. Click on this property and select adoBiblio. Specify the field to use to populate the drop down list. This is done by specifying the value for the List Field property. After you specify the Row Source, click open this property and select Company Name from the list.

The next step is to tell Visual Basic to which field to bind the control. First, click open the Data Source drop down list and select adoBooks. Next, click open the Data Field drop down list and select Publisher. This will configure the control to work properly. When the user clicks open the drop down list, a list of Company Names stored in the Publishers table of the Biblio.mdb database will be displayed. The value the user selects, however, will be placed in the Publisher field of a record in the Books table of the database that you have designed.

Q: *You are told to bind a textbox on a form to the Company Name field in the Publishers table of the Biblio.mdb database. You are instructed to configure the form so that the textbox will not allow the user to edit the contents of that field. There is an ADO data control on the form named adoBiblio. Explain one way that you can do this.*

A: Select the textbox icon from the Toolbox and add it to the form. Next, click open the Data Source property of the textbox and select adoBiblio. Now, click open the Data Field property of the control and select Company Name. We can make the textbox read only by setting the Enabled property to False. When the program runs, the user will be able to view, but not edit, the contents of the textbox.

Intermediate

Q: *What is the DLL Base Address?*

A: DLL Base Address is specified from the Compile tab of the Project Properties dialog. This is used if your project is an ActiveX DLL. It will specify the base address where your DLL will load in memory. DLL Base Address must be between &H1000000 and &H80000000

(16,777,216 and 2,147,483,648 in decimal). The default set by Visual Basic is 0X100000000.

Q: *When setting options for the compiler, what does Assume No Aliasing mean?*

A: Visual Basic assigns a code called an alias to each variable that references the same memory location in your program. For example, a code is assigned to a global variable and a local variable that has the same name. If you select Assume No Aliasing, Visual Basic will leave variables that are not modified in the local scope unchanged. This will allow VB to optimize loop constructs and use registers to store variables, possibly resulting in a speed boost.

Q: *What is CallbyName?*

A: CallByName is a function in Visual Basic. It enables the properties or methods of an object to be accessed at runtime using a string variable. For example, name this procedure that sets the text property of a textbox control, txtData:

```
Dim strText As String
Dim strProperty As String

strProperty = "Text"

strText = "Hello"
CallByName txtData, strProperty, vbLet, strText
```

Q: *What is a lightweight control, and what advantage, if any, is there to creating one?*

A: A lightweight control is a VB control that does not have a windows handle. A lightweight control is less resource intensive, and therefore advantageous when building an application to run in an environment where smaller resources are a plus. For example, you might want to use lightweight controls for an Internet application.

Q: *What is the Procedure Attributes dialog?*

A: The Procedure Attributes dialog enables you to specify important information for a property or method in a class. This includes a text description of the procedure that will appear in the Object Browswer, a Help File that will be invoked along with Help Context ID for the procedure, and more advanced information such as data binding, Procedure ID, and Property Category.

Q: *Your project uses a DLL (Math.DLL) that was created in Visual Basic. The DLL contains a class, clsMath, that you will use to access a library of mathematics functions for use in your program. How can you set up the DLL to use in your program, and how would you access a function called Average(a() As Double, Num As Integer) As Double in your code?*

A: The first step is to set a reference to the DLL. Click open the Project Reference dialog and select the Math.DLL file. Next, declare an object of type clsMath in your program:

```
Private objMathFunctions As clsMath
```

The functions and sub procedures of the class are accessible using the standard dot syntax. To call the Average function, we write:

```
Dim ave As Double, MyData(100) As Double, NumVals As
Integer

...
ave = objMathFunctions.Average(MyData(), NumVals)
```

Q: *You are using the clsMath class in the Math DLL described previously. This time, you need to modify your program to use an event in the class. What needs to be changed?*

A: To use any events in a DLL, use the With Events keyword in variable declaration. It should look like this:

```
Private With Events objMathFunctions As clsMath
```

Q: *What is the Ambient object?*

A: The Ambient object can be used to obtain information about the environment of an ActiveX control. For example, you can determine information about the form where the control has been placed by the developer.

Q: *You have designed an ActiveX control. How can you determine if the user of your control is using your control in design mode or at runtime?*

A: Check the UserMode property of the Ambient object. If False, this indicates the control is in design mode.

Q: *How can you create a read-only property for a class or ActiveX control?*

A: Create the property with the Add Procedure dialog box, then delete the Property Let/Set procedure.

Q: *What are Extender properties?*

A: Every control in Visual Basic has a set of built in properties that provide information about the container where the control has been placed. These properties are Index, Left, Top, and TabIndex.

Q: *You have created an ActiveX control. When the user places the control on a form for the first time, the control should set each property to an initial default value. How do you do this when designing the control?*

A: This is done by setting property values in the InitProperties event procedure of the User Control object.

Q: *Describe two ways to include a property in a VB object.*

A: Create a property by adding a Public variable to the object or by creating Property Let/Get/Set procedures.

Q: *How can you identify a thread in a multithreaded application?*

A: This can be done by checking the ThreadID property of the App object, as in the following example.

```
Dim lngThisThread As Long

lngThisThread = App.ThreadID
```

Q: *Explain the difference between an in-process and out-of-process server.*

A: The first obvious difference is that an out-of-process server is an executable file with a .EXE file extension, while an in-process server is a DLL file. An in-process server shares the address space of the client application that is using it, which gives it a speed advantage. An out-of-process server, however, runs in its own memory space. While this may cut down on performance as compared to an in-process server, an out-of-process server can run on its own as an application.

Q: *What is a PublicNotCreatable class?*

A: A class that has its Instancing property set to PublicNotCreatable is one that cannot be created in a client application. However, it can be passed to the client by the server. This can be done by creating an externally creatable collection class that uses the PublicNotCreatable class as a member. It creates objects of this class and passes a reference back to the client.

Q: *How do you create a method for an ActiveX control?*

A: This is done by adding a public Sub or Function procedure.

Q: *You are instructed to use Property Let/Get procedures to create a property. How will you store the property value internally?*

A: Create a Private member variable. The Property procedures then read from and write to this variable. For example, to return the value of the property, use the Property Get procedure:

```
'General Declarations section
Private mCount As Integer
...

Public Property Get Count() As Integer

  Count = mCount

End Property
```

Q: *You are creating an ActiveX server that will have a class with events. Where is the code for each event located?*

A: The user of the ActiveX server needs to write the code for each event. As the developer of the server, all you do is provide the events for the client and raise them when the appropriate conditions have been met.

Q: *You are told to develop an ActiveX control. It must be invisible at runtime. Explain how this can be accomplished.*

A: To make a control invisible at runtime, set the InvisibleAtRunTime property of the User Control object to True.

Q: *You have created an ActiveX control. When a developer is using the control, when is an instance of this control created and destroyed during the development process?*

A: The control will be created and destroyed at several points during design time and runtime. Some instances when this will happen are the following:

- The user opens the form where the control is situated by selecting it in the Project Explorer.
- The user closes the form while in design mode.
- The user is in design mode and presses F5 to run the program.
- The user shuts down a running program and returns to design mode.

Q: *When creating an ActiveX control, what object can you use to save property values?*

A: This is done with the Property Bag. The Property Bag has two methods, ReadProperty and WriteProperty. The ReadProperty method takes two arguments, a string representing the name of the property and a default value to store if the user has not changed the property. For example, you can read a property named *FocalLength* with the following code.

```
mFocalLength = PropBag.ReadProperty("FocalLength", 1.2)
```

where mFocalLength is the private member variable representing the property. To save a property value, call WriteProperty, again passing the name of the property and a default value. In addition, pass the private member variable for the property:

```
PropBag.WriteProperty("FocalLength", mFocalLength, 1.2)
```

Q: *What events can be used to read and write property values?*

A: To read and write property values for an ActiveX control, use the ReadProperties and WriteProperties events of the User Control object. Each event procedure takes a single argument: PropBag As Property Bag. You read and write all of the properties that you want to save in these two procedures.

Q: *You have created an ActiveX control with Visual Basic. Does Visual Basic automatically save property values?*

A: No, it does not. You must let Visual Basic know that the value of a property has changed so it will save it. This is done by calling the PropertyChanged method, passing the name of the property as a string. You can do this in the Property Let procedure. To do this for a property named FocalLength:

```
Public Property Let FocalLength (dblNewValue As Double)
  mFocalLength = dlbNewValue
  PropertyChanged(“FocalLength”)
End Property
```

Q: *The Visual Basic properties window often includes an About property. If the user clicks on this property, an About box will open for the control. How can you implement this behavior for a control you are creating?*

A: Add a form to your ActiveX control project. When adding the form, select About Dialog. Configure the dialog to provide the information you want the user to see. Add a public Sub procedure to your project called ShowAbout, and add a line of code to open the form modally. Open the Procedure Attributes dialog for this procedure and set ProcedureID to AboutBox. Set Attributes to Hide this member.

Q: *What is the main component of an ActiveX document project?*

A: The main element in an ActiveX document project is the UserDocument object. At design time, the UserDocument resembles a form and you can place controls on it and write code. It cannot run stand alone at runtime; instead, it is wrapped into a Web page and opened in the user's Internet browser.

Q: *What event fires when an ActiveX Document loads into an Internet browswer?*

A: The InitProperties event. This event fires every time your ActiveX document gets loaded into memory. This event can be used to initialize any code or controls on the document. For example, you could initialize the elements of a list box.

Q: *You have a Public sub in your ActiveX control project. You want to prevent the user of your control from having direct access to this method. How can you prevent the user from calling it, even though it is public?*

A: Open the Procedure Attributes dialog and click the Hide this member checkbox under Attributes.

Q: *How could you design your ActiveX document to visit the Microsoft.com Web page when the user clicks on a command button?*

A: This can be done by using the Hyperlink object of the ActiveX document. To visit the Web page, use the NavigateTo method:

```
UserDocument.Hyperlink.NavigateTo
"http://www.microsoft.com"
```

Q: *What is the function of the Viewport in an ActiveX document?*

A: The Viewport represents the area that the container application in which our document has been situated has given to the document. The container application may be an Internet browser such as Microsoft Internet Explorer. Four properties are available to determine the area allotted to the document:

- ViewportHeight
- ViewportLeft

- ViewportTop
- ViewportWidth

Q: *To work with ADO in code, what reference must be set?*

A: You must set a reference to the Microsoft ActiveX Data Objects 2.x library.

Q: *Name the seven objects contained within ADO.*

A: ADO contains the following objects: Connection, Recordset, Field, Command, Error, Parameter, and Property.

Q: *Prior to opening a recordset, what step must be taken?*

A: You must establish a connection with the data source.

Q: *Give an example of opening a recordset.*

A:
```
Dim myconnection As New ADODB.Connection
Dim strSQL As String
Dim myrecordset As New ADODB.Recordset
  myconnection.Provider = "SQLOLEDB"
  myconnection.ConnectionString = "User ID=Master;
Password=WXUser; Data Source=Sales;"
  myconnection.open
strSQL = "Select * From Sales Where ID = '9883'"
Set myrecordset.ActiveConnection = myconnection
myrecordset.Open strSQL
```

Q: *What is the Cursor Location property of a recordset?*

A: Cursor location specifies where the resources used to hold the data in the recordset are located. This can be on the client computer, in which case the CursorLocation property of the recordset is set to adUseClient, or it can be on the server, in which case CursorLocation would be set to adUseServer.

Q: *Name the four cursor types available for an ADO recordset.*

A: Cursor type can be Forward-Only, Static, Dynamic, or Keyset.

Q: *What is the difference between pessimistic and optimistic locking?*

A: Pessimistic locking locks the record when an edit has been initiated. Locking is done on a record by record basis. When optimistic locking is used, locking is also done on a record by record basis, but each record is not locked until a call to the Update method has been issued.

Q: *How can you add a new record in code, reference the Name, Address and Phone properties by name while assigning new values and save the record?*

A: Assuming we are using a recordset object named myrecordset:

```
Myrecordset.AddNew
Myrecordset("Name") = "John Smith"
Myrecordset("Address") = "555 Main St"
Myrecordset("Phone") = "555-5555"
Myrecordset.Update
```

Q: *How can you delete all of the records contained in a recordset object variable named rsData?*

A: This can be done with a Do While loop. Remember that we need to issue a call to the MoveNext method after deleting each record, otherwise the cursor will be positioned on the record that has just been deleted.

```
Do While rsData.EOF = False
  rsData.Delete
  rsData.MoveNext
Loop
```

Q: *How can you search a recordset for a particular record?*

A: This can be done with the Find method. This method takes the following arguments:

- *Criteria* A string representing the search criteria.
- Sk*ipRecords* A long that can be used to specify how many records to skip before searching
- *SearchDirection* Can be adSearchForward or adSearchBackward
- *Start* The starting position in the recordset for the search. If not specified, begins the search at the current record.

Q: *What is wrong with the following code?*

```
Dim MyRecordset As ADODB.Recordset
Dim MyConnection As ADODB.Connection

MyConnection.Provider = "Microsoft Jet.OLEDB.3.51"
MyConnection.Open "Data Source
=C:\Programs\Data\Biblio.MDB"
```

```
Set MyRecordset.ActiveConnection = MyConnection
MyRecordset.Open "Select * From Authors"
```

A: Like any VB object, a connection or recordset must be instantiated prior to use. This is done with the New keyword. You can do this when declaring the variable:

```
Dim MyConnection As New ADODB.Connection
```

Or later using the Set...New keyword combination:

```
Set MyRecordset = New ADODB.Recordset
```

Q: *Your program needs to access Web pages. What modification of your standard EXE project is necessary to do this simply?*

A: Open the Components dialog box. Select Microsoft Internet Controls. This will add a Web Browser and Shell Folder View controls to your project. The Web Browser control can be used to access the Web pages.

Q: *How can you configure a Web browser control to navigate to a Web page for which the user has typed in the URL in a textbox? Assume the Web browser is named Web1 and the URL is typed in a textbox named txtURL.*

A: A command button can be added to the form and named cmdGo:

```
Private Sub cmdGo_Click()

  Web1.Navigate txtURL.Text

End Sub
```

Q: *How can you use a Web browser control to return to the page the user looked at previously?*

A: This is done with the GoBack method:

```
WebBrowser1.GoBack
```

Q: *What are the properties of the Error object that can be used in standard VB error handling?*

A: The error object has the following properties:

- *Description* A text description of the error that occurred
- *HelpContext* A Help Context ID for the error
- *HelpFile* The path and filename of the help file for the error
- *LastDLLError* System error code if a call to a DLL has failed

- *Number* An integer representing the error code
- *Source* The name of the object that generated the error

Q: *Name the three ways you can resume execution after an error occurs.*

A: The three ways are:

- Resume Next : Resumes execution on the statement following the one that caused the error.
- Resume : Attempts to execute the line of code which generated the error again.
- Resume Label : Passes execution to the statement specified by Label.

Q: *If you want to ignore errors in a sub procedure, but prevent VB from crashing if an error occurs, what is a simple way you can do this?*

A: Use the following line of code as the first line in the procedure:

```
On Error Resume Next
```

Q: *How can you print to the immediate window during debugging what is the Assert method?*

A: You can print to the immediate window by using the Print method of the Debug object. To print the value of a variable named myData, write:

```
Debug.Print myData
```

The Assert method can be used to pause execution if a certain condition is met. For example, if your program crashes when an integer variable exceeds 100, you might add the line:

```
Debug.Assert myvar = 100
```

If this statement is reached and the variable myvar is equal to 100, execution will pause. All debug statements are ignored when your application is compiled.

Q: *How do you turn on error handling?*

A: With the On Error statement. Error handling in a procedure is not enabled until execution has reached this statement.

Q: *How can you design a VB application that uses HTML rather than forms?*

A: Create a DHTML application that uses the DHTML page designer.

Advanced

Q: *How do you grant a user access to applications that are integrated into Visual Source Safe?*

A: To grant access to Visual Source Safe, an account must be created for each user. This is done with the Admin utility, which can be opened by selecting *Visual Source Safe 6.0 Admin* from the Visual SourceSafe icon on the Windows Start Menu. To create an account for a user, select Add User from the Users pull down menu. Enter a name and a password for the user.

Q: *How do you bring up the Visual SourceSafe Explorer from Visual Basic? Briefly describe Visual SourceSafe Explorer.*

A: Click on the Tools menu and select SourceSafe, then Run SourceSafe. Visual SourceSafe Explorer is a graphical type interface that allows you to browse the projects and files in SourceSafe and check out a file if desired. The interface is built around three window panes. The All Projects window pane displays a listing of the project files in the SourceSafe database in a folder format similar to that found in the Windows Explorer. When you select a particular project, the files contained in that project will be displayed to the right in the Contents window pane. If the file has been checked out, the user who is currently working on the file will be displayed along with other information such as the Date/Time the file was checked out. The lower pane is called the Results pane and will display the results of any action you take in SourceSafe, such as checking out a file.

Q: *If you start a new project in Visual Basic, how can you add it to Source Safe?*

A: Once SourceSafe has been installed and integrated into Visual Basic, you will be prompted each time you start a new project and asked if you want to add the project to Source Safe. If you select Yes, each time you close the project you will be asked if you want to save the changes to SourceSafe.

Q: *Generally speaking, what is the purpose of Visual SourceSafe and when would you want to use it?*

A: The purpose of Visual SourceSafe is to manage projects in a team environment where multiple developers will be working with the same files. Visual SourceSafe gives you a means to protect a file when someone is working on it. The user can check it out and work on it, and while it is checked out, other users will not have access to it. This will prevent two programmers from making modifications the file of which the other is not aware. In short, Visual Source Safe maintains the integrity of your files in a team environment.

Q: *Describe the Version Compatibility Options that you can use when creating components in Visual Basic.*

A: Version Compatibility enables you to produce new versions of a component that will let users of older versions migrate successfully to your new release. Three types of version compatibility are:

- *No Compatibility* When you select this option, Visual Basic will generate new Class IDs and new interface IDs for the component. This creates a new component that has no relation to the old one. No backward compatibility exists in this case.
- *Project Compatibility* This type of compatibility will maintain the Class IDs each time you compile the component. The main purpose of this option is to provide an aid in debugging components. It allows interface IDs to be changed for classes that are no longer binary compatible with previous versions.
- *Binary Compatibility* This option provides true backward compatibility. Clients that used a previous version of the component will be able to use the new one if it is compiled with this option.

Q: *How do you set Version Compatibility in a VB ActiveX control project?*

A: Open the Project...Properties dialog box. Click on the Component tab and select No Compatibility, Project Compatibility, or Binary Compatibility from the Version Compatibility option list. Project Compatibility is the default option.

Q: *Explain the difference between registering an in-process or an out-of-process component.*

A: An in-process component, which is a DLL or an OCX file, can be registered with the Regsvr32 utility. For example, the following command line, entered in the Run dialog of the Windows start menu will register an ActiveX control named MyBox.OCX:

```
Regsvr32 MyBox.ocx
```

To register an out-of-process component, which is an executable file, the program just needs to be run. It will then register itself.

Q: *What is the Visual Component Manager, and how do you publish a component to the Repository?*

A: The Visual Component Manager is a tool in Visual Basic 6.0 that keeps track of the components that you have created on a development machine. An explorer type interface enables you to manage components based on development platform, such as Visual Basic and Visual C++. The Visual Component Manager can be opened from the View menu in Visual Basic. To publish a component, open the local database folder and select the appropriate subfolder, such as Visual Basic. Next, click the Publish a New Component button. This will open the Publisher Wizard, which will step you through the process of publishing the component.

Q: *Briefly describe how you can configure DCOM on a client machine.*

A: When a DCOM component is run on a client computer, it needs to know where to find the server application. This can be done by using the Distributed COM Configuration Properties dialog box. This can be opened from the Run dialog of the Widndows Start menu. The command line is dcomcnfg. Once the dialog box opens, select the appropriate application from the list found on the Applications tab. Once selected, click the Properties button. Next, click the Location tab and select where the application should run.

Q: *When using DCOM, what important information needs to be specified on the Server prior to running the application?*

A: The client application will need to have security information such as a user account and user permissions specified. This is done by opening the DCOM configuration Properties dialog box on the Server computer. These properties can be set from the Security tab.

Q: *What is three tiered development? Describe the three tiers used in such a development scheme.*

A: Software projects based on a three tiered model are divided into three layers: the UI layer, the Business Logic layer, and the Data layer. The UI layer is generally considered the first tier and consists of a client application to which the end user has access. This will be a Standard executable with forms and ActiveX controls that permit the user to manipulate data. The next layer, the Business Logic layer, involves the development of classes that model the data and business rules that underlie the application. This layer is built on business objects that model the real world and the interface for each object. This layer can be built as an ActiveX in-process server, such as a DLL file. The Data layer is the final piece of the three tiered model. This consists of the database itself on the server computer. Information is passed from this layer to the Business Logic layer. The client application has no direct link to the Data layer, and can only get to the data through the Business Logic layer.

Q: *Explain the difference between unit testing and integration testing.*

A: Unit testing involves testing an individual unit or component in a project, such as a form, module, or ActiveX control. Once the individual unit has been tested thoroughly, it can be moved onto integration testing. This phase of testing involves the process of determining how well the different components of a project work together.

Q: *How can you alias a field name in an SQL statement?*

A: You can rename or alias a field that has been returned from a query. This is done by using the As keyword. For example:

```
Select Empl As Employee, Division From Company
```

Q: *What is wrong with the following code?*

```
Dim strSQL As String
Dim rs As ADODB.Recordset
Dim con As ADODB.Connection

Set con = New ADODB.Connection
Set rs = New ADODB.Recordset

con.Open "Provider=Microsoft.Jet.OLEDB.3.51; Data
Source=C:\MyData.MDB"

rs.Open "Select * From Employees Where ID = AJ749", con
```

A: Text comparisons in SQL statements must be delimited with single quote marks. The correct way to open the recordset is:

```
rs.Open "Select * From Employees Where ID = 'AJ749'", con
```

Q: *Briefly describe the steps required to create an OLE DB provider.*

A: An OLE DB provider enables you to create a program that exposes OLE DB objects. You must set a reference to the Microsoft OLE DB Simple Provider 1.5 library to do this. Next, you need to add two classes to the project. In the first class, set the DataSourceBehavior property to None. In the second class, set the DataSourceBehavior property to OLEDBProvider and add the following line to the general declarations section:

```
Implements OLEDBSimpleProvider
```

Q: *You are working on a VB 6 Data Source project. What function is used to return references to ADO data objects?*

A: The GetDataMember function. This function accepts two parameters, DataMember As String and Data As Object. The name of the object the user wants a reference to is passed via Data Member. Inside the GetDataMember function, you set a reference to the object using the Data parameter (which can be a recordset, for example). Here is how this could be done:

```
Private mEmployees As ADODB.Recordset
Private mCompany As ADODB.Recordset
...
Private Sub Class_GetDataMember(DataMember As String, Data
As Object)
If DataMember = "Employees" Then
Set Data = mEmployees
Else
Set Data = mCompany
End If
End Sub
```

Q: *What is a Callback?*

A: A *callback* is a function that is used when Windows calls a function periodically in the background. This is best understood by example. Consider the EnumWindows API function, that locates all child windows that are currently open on your system. To work with EnumWindows, you must write your own function that will act as the Callback function. Each time EnumWindows locates a window, it will call the Callback function you have provided.

Q: *Describe the purpose of having a dependent class and a dependent collection class in a project.*

A: A dependent class functions as a regular class. In other words, it simply defines the object with which you are working. The dependent collection class provides wrapper functions for the class. These wrapper functions implement the methods of a collection such as Add or Delete.

Q: *What is the interface of a class?*

A: The interface of a class includes the properties and methods of the class.

Q: *What is the function of the VB keyword Implements?*

A: The Implements keyword provides a primitive form of inheritance among classes. It enables you to define a class and use it as the basis for creating new classes that will include the methods and properties of that class. The new class will be able to add its own properties and methods, and must supply its own code for the methods of the parent class, which is known as the interface class. For example, you can have an interface class to define a solid geometric object. Assume you name the class ISolid and it includes a function named Volume:

```
Public Function Volume() As Double

End Function
```

In the interface class, function and sub procedures do not contain any code. Now create a new class called Sphere that will implement the ISolid class. Add the following line to the general declarations section of the Sphere class:

```
Implements ISolid
```

Visual Basic will automatically add the functions from the interface class. For example, you will find the Volume function:

```
Public Function ISolid_Volume() As Double
```

Now put in the specific code required to calculate the volume of a sphere. The advantage is that you can use the interface to create classes that have similar properties, yet differ in the details. For example, you could create Sphere, Cube, and Cone classes, each behaving the same way in code, but all having unique definitions for the Volume method.

Q: *What is a Session object?*

A: A Session object is a Web class object that maintains information about the current user session. Sessions are created for a user when an ASP page is requested.

Q: *You are working on an Internet application that includes features for specific Internet browsers. How can you make sure the user will be able to use your Web page?*

A: You can use the BrowserType WebClass object.

Q: *A user has filled in a request form on your Web site. What object can you use to display a thank you note to the user?*

A: You can use the Response object. The Response object can be used to display HTML in the users browser, direct the user to a specific Web address, or set cookie values. For example, we can thank the user with the following header:

```
Response.Write "<HTML>"
Response.Write "<HEAD>"
Response.Write "<TITLE>Thank You For Taking Our
Survey.</TITLE>"
```

Q: *What event used in Web class programming corresponds to the Form Load event?*

A: The WebClass Start event. This event takes no parameters and is used to do any initialization your application needs. For example, you may use it to direct the user to a specific page. If we had a template page named Survey, the event would look like this:

```
Private Sub WebClass_Start()

  Set NextItem = Survey

End Sub
```

Q: *Describe how Visual Basic, ASP, IIS and a Web class interact.*

A: Each Web class that you create in your application will have an ASP page that corresponds to it. This ASP page is generated by Visual Basic. Your application is an *Internet Information Server* (IIS), and the user invokes it by calling the ASP page that corresponds to a Web class in your project.

Q: *You are working on a Windows NT 4.0 platform. What components need to be installed on your system to create an IIS application?*

A: You need to install Internet Information Server 3.0 or later. The Active Server Pages component must also be installed. If you are running NT Workstation, you need to install Peer Web Server 3.0 or later with the Active Server Pages component. Windows 95/98 uses the Personal Web Server 3.0 or later.

Q: *You have created a DHTML application. When it is in use by the customer, where will it be located?*

A: A DHTML application is placed on the browser's machine.

Q: *What is the Visual Basic object model?*

A: The Visual Basic object model provides objects that you can use to interact with the Visual Basic IDE. The purpose of this is to enable you to create an Add-In, which is basically an extension to the IDE. The Visual Basic object model is arranged in a hierarchical fashion, with the VBE or Visual Basic Environment at the top. The VBE represents the current copy of Visual Basic that is running. You can access the elements of the IDE by setting references to the VBE object.

Q: *How can you close Visual Basic with an Add-In that you have created?*

A: This can be done by making a call to the Quit method of the VBE object.

Q: *Your Add-In is looping through the code windows in a VB project. How can you determine if a member of a code module is a procedure?*

A: This can be done by testing the Type property of a member object. For example, Type can be vbext_mt_Event or vbext_mt_Method if you have encountered an event procedure or method. For example, if you wanted to access all event procedures you could write:

```
Dim c As CodePane
Dim m As Member
....
For Each c In VBInstance.CodePanes
  For Each m In c.CodeModule.Members
    If m.Type = vbext_mt_Event Then
...
```

Q: *When creating a VB Add-In, how do you access the actual code that has been typed into a code window?*

A: This is done by accessing the CodeModule object that belongs to a Code Pane. The elements of a CodeModule are accessed via the Members collection.

Q: *Your Add-In is required to add the line "Copyright ABC Company" as a comment to a procedure. How can this be done?*

A: You can add a line of text with the InsertLines method of the CodeModule object. For example, if the cCodePane variable is a CodePane object, we can insert the comment as the last line in a procedure with the following code:

```
'Get the number of lines in the procedure
lngNumLines = cCodePane.CodeModule.ProcCountLines(strName,
vbext_pk_Proc)

'determine next to last line position. LngLocation has
position of 'procedure in code window
lngLast = lngNumLines + lngLocation - 1
'Insert the comment
Call cCodePane.InsertLines(lngLast , "'Copyright ABC
Company")
```

Q: *Describe the different package types available with the Package and Deployment wizard.*

A: There are three options:

- *Standard Setup Package* This creates the usual setup.exe program that can be used to install an application on an end users machine.
- *Internet Package* This type of package is used to create CAB files. A CAB file contains INF files, OCX files, and any dependencies for an application.
- *Dependency File* This will create a file containing the dependencies of your application.

Q: *How can you use the Package and Deployment wizard to deploy an application in a single file on a CD-ROM versus using several floppy disks?*

A: This is done by setting Cab Options to Single Cab or Multiple Cabs. If you select Multiple Cabs, several cab files will be created that will be mapped to floppy disks.

Q: *When deploying an application over a network, what is the best way to structure the Cab files?*

A: When deploying an application over a network, typically the setup program will be available in a folder on a server computer. In this situation, specify a single CAB file from the Cab options screen.

Q: *You are asked to draw up commenting standards for your organization. What elements should be specified at the beginning of every procedure?*

A: The comments at the beginning of a procedure should include the procedure name, the author, the date the procedure was created, a brief description of what the procedure does, a list of expected input parameters, and a dated revision history.

Q: *What are some of the difficulties that can arise when meeting deadlines set by management for a software project?*

A: Often when writing code, unexpected problems crop up. The time required to write code is usually underestimated by management, and this can result in unrealistic goal setting. Other problems that can cause problems with deadlines include unforeseen technical difficulties, new customer demands, and bad or ineffective communication among team members.

Q: *What is a major drawback when using arrays of type variant?*

A: The variant data type provides a great deal of flexibility, but this must be paid for with a huge amount of memory overhead. Even a numeric value stored in a variant adds 16 bytes of overhead. It is better and more efficient to stick to a single data type.

Q: *How can you redimension an array and keep the data it contains?*

A: This is done with the Preserve keyword. For example:

```
Dim TestData(1 To Max) As Double
...
ReDim Preserve TestData(1 To MAX + 5)
```

This adds 5 elements to the TestData array without erasing any data the array already contains.

Q: *What is the difference between a standard SQL statement and a stored procedure?*

A: Executing stored procedures in code is done with a recordset object and appears similar to executing SQL statements. However, a stored procedure is a part of the database you are using. It exists inside the database and remains there during and after execution. A stored procedure can be used to execute complicated queries, and in general, will run much faster than an SQL statement because the stored procedure is a compiled part of the database.

Q: *How can you use an ADODB connection and recordset to execute a stored procedure named CountRecords?*

A: The following code will do it:

```
Dim Conn As New ADODB.Connection
Dim Rs As New ADODB.Recordset
'code to open connection
...
'The stored procedure is executed with a call to the Execute
method of the connection.

'A recordset is returned

Rs = Conn.Execute "call CountRecords", , adCmdStoredProc
```

Q: *What is concurrency?*

A: Concurrency problems arise in a multiuser database application when several users attempt to access the same record or records at the same time. You can manage concurrency problems by adopting an appropriate locking strategy.

Q: *What is the Call Stack window?*

A: The call stack window is used in debug mode. It will display a list of functions that are currently on the call stack. This is a list of functions that have not completed execution, and it will include functions that were interrupted by a call to another function. The function which is currently active is found at the top of the call stack.

Q: *Describe how you would debug an ActiveX control.*

A: This can be done by adding a standard Exe test application to the project group for your ActiveX control. You can add an instance of your control to a form in the test project and run the test project to debug the control.

Q: *What is a DECommand object, and what is the DEExtDesigner?*

A: A DECommand object is an object that contains the design time properties of ADO command objects. The DEExtDesigner is the top level container of the Data Environment.

Q: *Define Apartment threading.*

A: Apartment threading is a model used to create multi-threaded applications. In this model, each object that is created during runtime gets its own thread and runs in a separate space called an Apartment. Each object is unaware of the objects in other apartments. Each Apartment has its own local copy of global data, so the model maintains thread safety by eliminating global data conflicts.

Q: *You are creating a Data Consumer. Explain the difference between SimpleBound and ComplexBound.*

A: These are two options that can be set for the DataBindingBehavior of the class that will function as the data consumer. If the class is SimpleBound, an object created from this class will bind to a single data field. A ComplexBound object can bind to an entire row in a data source.

Q: *What is the SetAbort method in the Active Server Page object model?*

A: SetAbort declares that the transaction initiated by the script has not completed and the resources should not be updated.

Q: *What is CacheControl, and what object in the ASP object model does it belong to?*

A: CacheControl determines whether or not proxy servers are able to cache the output generated by ASP. CacheControl is a property of the Response object.

Q: *When programming with ASP, how can you determine the values stored in the client certificate?*

A: This can be done by accessing the ClientCertificate collection of the Request object.

9
C and C++

Marc Temkin

C++ is a general purpose programming language that supports procedural, object-based, and object-oriented coding methods. C is considered a subset of C++. Dennis Ritchie created C in 1971-73 to help develop the Unix operating system. Bjarne Stroustrop designed C++ in 1979 through 1985 to write efficient object-oriented systems programs. Both Ritchie and Stroustrup have created Web sites dedicated to the history and concepts of C and C++. Ritchie's site is located at http://cm.bell-labs.com/cm/cs/who/dmr/chist.html and Stroustrup's site is at www.research.att.com/~bs/C++.html.

C and C++ are certified by the *American National Standards Institute* (ANSI)/*International Organization for Standardization* (ISO) committees. Certification ensures portability of the language across all compilers and operating systems. A compiler that adheres to the ANSI standard includes the core language, *Standard C++ Library* (STL), and *C Run-time Library* (CRT). *Integrated Development Environments* (IDEs), such as Microsoft Visual C++, may include proprietary or "foundation" libraries.

Extensive libraries from numerous vendors are available for a variety of applications ranging from audio, graphics, numerical calculations, and gaming to office applications.

Requirements for a Successful Candidate

Experienced programmers can teach themselves C++, while novice programmers should consider courses in C++, Data Structures, and *Object-Oriented Programming* (OOP). An academic study in C++ will cover the use of core languages and the run-time library. Data Structures works with classic algorithms that are commonly found in C programs and are essential to understanding the Standard Template Library. OOP covers the concepts of data abstraction, inheritance, and encapsulation that programmers need to understand in order to successfully use and create class libraries.

A C++ programmer needs to be willing to explore the use and foundations of the language and libraries. Good research skills can be a help in finding solutions in an efficient manner. The skillful use of existing code is a hallmark of a valuable programmer. Various journals, Web sites, and books are available to help you stay current on the topics of C++ and computing.

A novice programmer knows the rudiments of C++ and can write properly scoped procedural programs. The intermediate programmer should be capable of writing OOP programs and know the common system library functions. The advanced programmer should have a thorough knowledge of the language and the system libraries, as well as an understanding of object-oriented design.

A candidate with experience in large projects that covered any language or applications package should have the persistence to work in a production environment. Knowledge of scripting languages such as Visual Basic or JavaScript can prepare you to work with users and other programmers. Also, a familiarity with relational databases and the *Structured Query Language* (SQL) is essential in most application programming.

Advantages/Disadvantages of C++

Managers commonly question the value of using C++ when productive *Rapid Application Development* (RAD) tools promise productivity with a simpler learning curve.

Advantages

A C++ programmer using OOP can reuse and specialize existing class libraries. Reusing them can make a C++ programmer more productive than a RAD programmer.

C++ programs can perform in-memory data manipulations to perform searches, sorts, and mathematical operations. A RAD programmer would need to use disk-based operations to perform the same tasks.

C++ can fine-tune performance by choosing when to use static, efficient memory and when to use dynamic, flexible memory. The RAD programmer has no comparable control.

A C++ compiler, written to produce system-level programs, can produce extremely fast programs. Most real-time, graphics, and audio applications, as well as operating systems, are written largely in C/C++ along with some assembly language.

Disadvantages

C/C++ requires a period of six to 18 months of programming experience before one can write industrial-strength programs. A novice can write somewhat robust programs in a RAD environment within a few months.

RAD tools have more accessible high-level language constructs and user-interface tools than the C++ programmer does. The novice C++ programmer may have to write more code at a lower level to accomplish the same task as the RAD programmer, but advancements in modern C++ compilers and IDEs have given programmers most of the same "power tools" as their RAD associates.

Two standard attacks on C++ programmers are that they create programs rife with memory leaks, and that they delight in coding highly efficient but barely decipherable and difficult-to-maintain code. Responsible programmers that code in a clear and maintainable manner refute this argument.

Interview Types

Technical non-programmer managers will try to determine whether you can be a productive team member. They prefer to hire a candidate who possesses good communication and research skills and who is open to new approaches and tools. They avoid candidates who prefer to "go it alone."

A programmer/developer will ask you specific questions about ANSI/ISO C++ and proprietary libraries. This interviewer may try to determine your approach to problem solving.

You should assess the potential job and its effect on your career. Investing your time in work that uses current tools or projects such as distributed computing that may complement your specialized knowledge will be more worthwhile than maintaining legacy code with archaic tools.

An Illustration of Experience in Coding

The following demonstrates examples of how beginning, intermediate, and advanced programmers might code a procedure to test for a palindrome, a word or phrase that is spelled the same backward and forward.

The beginning programmer would attempt to write a function entirely from language primitives. The algorithm he or she creates would be difficult to describe to a non-C programmer, let alone a non-programmer.

Both the intermediate and advanced programmers would write a program that actually determines if a phrase is a palindrome. A non-programmer, unlike a computer, would not care about the case of the letters.

An intermediate or advanced programmer should be able to solve problems largely with the functions available in the CRT or in the C++ STL.

Here is the beginning or low-level approach:

```
inline bool IsPalindrome (const char* s){
   int i = 0, j = strlen(s) - 1;
   bool flag = true;
   /* Compare each pair of characters from the outside in to
test for equality. */
  while (flag && i != j)
         flag = tolower(s[i++])== tolower(s[j--]);
   return flag;
}
```

Using routines from the C Runtime Library.

```
inline bool IsPalindrome(const char* s) // version A
{
char *p = strdup(s); // Copy
strrev(p);      // Reverse the copy
// Test for match
return   (stricmp(s, p) == 0);     }
```

Here is an example using routines from the C++ STL:

```
#include <algorithm>
      inline bool IsPalindrome(const std::string& s)
      {
      using namespace std;
      string x(s), y(s);    // Make two copies of the string
      reverse(x.begin(), x.end());// reverse x copy
      // transform each copy to lower case
```

```
        transform(x.begin(), x.end(), x.begin(), tolower);
        transform(y.begin(), y.end(), y.begin(), tolower);
        return (x.compare(y) == 0); // Test for match
}
```

Beginner Questions

Q: Define the minimum C++ program.

A: int main() {return 0;}

Q: Will the following program compile?

```
#include <stdio.h>
int main() {
printf("%s, %s\n", "Hello#", 1);
return 0; }
```

A: Yes.

Q: Find the run-time error in the previous program.

A: The type field of the second placeholder,%s, in the format specification is wrong for the numeric argument, 1. The correct statement is

```
printf("%s, %d\n", "Hello#", 1);
```

Q: Without fixing the printf error, how could you prevent the run-time error from terminating the previous incorrect program?

A: Use a try, catch construct to capture the error:

```
#include <stdio.h>
int main() {
try { printf("%s, %s\n", "Hello#", 1); }
catch (...){printf("Error in printf specification\n"); }
return 0; }
```

Q: Rewrite the Hello, 1 program using the iostream library.

A:
```
#include <iostream>
        using namespace std;
               int main()
               { cout << "Hello#" << 1 << endl;
               return 0; };
```

Q: Printf requires type specifiers to convert the arguments. Why does cout not need any type specifiers?

A: The iostream library has overloaded operators for all built-in data types of C++.

Q: Describe the standard parameters to main, "int argc, char argv[]" and their purpose.*

A: The parameters to main are the command-line parameters that can be specified at program invocation. Argc is the count of separate character strings in the command line. Argv is an array of character strings. These strings are delimited by spaces in the command line.

Q: Which command-line argument is "Two" in the following invocation: Test 1 Two 3? Test.exe is a C++ program.

A: Two is the third argument. The first argument is the fully qualified path to the program. Argv[2] accesses the third argument.

Q: In a new development, should you use the functions of the CRT or the corresponding functions in the C++ STL?

A: The C++ STL is the better choice for new development. Competence with the CRT is necessary in order to maintain existing programs.

Q: Should you use both printf and cout in the same program?

A: You can do this, but it would be confusing to other programmers. Instead, use either the stdio functions or the iostreams functions, but not both.

Q: Which CRT functions are used to allocate and deallocate dynamic memory?

A: Use Malloc() to allocate memory and Free() to deallocate memory.

Q: Which keywords are used to allocate and deallocate dynamic memory keywords in C++?

A: Use New to allocate and Delete to deallocate.

Q: Should you mix Malloc/Free with New/Delete in the same program?

A: You should use New/Delete with C++. Malloc/Free must be used in a strict ANSI C compilation. Never mix these pairs of dynamic memory allocators when referring to the same object. Using Free() to release an object instantiated with New can lead to unpredictable results.

Q: What advantages does New/Delete have over Malloc/Free?

A: New and Delete are operator functions, while Malloc and Free are CRT functions. Also, classes can contain overloaded New and Delete operators.

Q: What are the rules for a function declaration?

A: Functions must be declared to the program before it is called. Functions with the same name at the same scope level must have distinct parameter lists.

Q: What is the difference between a function declaration and a function definition?

A: A function declaration is the function's name, return type, and parameter list. A function definition contains the declaration information along with a list of statements within curly braces known as the function body.

Q: Describe the visibility of a global variable.

A: It is visible within the file where it has been defined.

Q: Define header files. What is their purpose?

A: Header files contain object and function declarations. The header file is inserted by the #include directive into any file that needs the declarations.

Q: What is meant by the definition of an object?

A: An object definition declares and allocates storage for an object.

Q: What is the purpose of the extern keyword?

A: Extern enables a programmer to declare an object without allocating storage. A statement such as extern int i indicates to the compiler that the object int i will be defined somewhere in the program. Any file that includes that statement can access the object.

Q: How many times can a global object or a function be defined within a program?

A: An object can only be defined once at the global scope. A function definition has only one true definition, but the same definition can be repeated in other parts of the program. This is known as the one definition rule.

Q: A program has two implementation files, first.cpp and second.cpp. Each cpp file contains the directive "#includes globals.h." Globals.h contains the definition of an integer object xx (int xx). A build will not be complete due to a linker error stating that int xx is already defined in first.obj. What is the cause of this linker error? Resolve this without any special knowledge of the linker.

A: A separate definition of int xx is inserted into every file that contains the #include globals.h statement. Under the one definition rule of C++, it is illegal to define an object more than once within a program. The solution is to use an object declaration, extern int xx, in globals.h and to define int xx in any single implementation file. The global value then can be used in any file that includes globals.h.

Q: *Explain the difference in syntax for #include directives. Some #include directives surround the filename with double quotes, while others use angle brackets.*

A: Using the angle brackets indicates that the header is one of the standard header files supplied by your compiler. The compiler searches for these files along predefined paths that are established by the compiler. Using the double quotes, the file is a user-defined header file that is assumed to exist in the local directory.

Q: *An #include directive shows a standard header filename, as in <map>, that does not have a file extension. What does the lack of a file extension tell the programmer?*

A: The header file belongs to the C++ STL.

Q: *In order to use cout, you must prefix the namespace std along with the scope operator in front of each reference to cout, cin, cerr, and endl. Which alternative makes the use of these keywords simpler?*

A: Include the statement "using namespace std" prior to these statements either at the global or function scope.

Q: *How do you identify a preprocessor directive?*

A: The pound sign, #, is the leftmost character of the preprocessor directive line.

Q: *What is the purpose of preprocessor directives?*

A: Preprocessor directives are typically used for conditional compilations and to insert text into a file.

Q: *Should #define directives be used to create macros and constants?*

A: Do not use #define directives for macros and constants unless you must work with strict ANSI C compilation. C++ programs should use inline functions and constant definitions rather than preprocessor alternatives.

Q: *Create a const definition for WIDTH and an inline function for MAX with integer arguments that returns an integer result.*

A:
```
        const int WIDTH = 80;
        inline int MAX( int x, int y) { return x > y ? x :
y; }
```

Q: *Use the template facility to allow MAX to compare any data type.*

A:
```
template <class T> inline TMAX (T& x, T& y)
        { return x > y ? x : y; }
```

Q: *Why use templates, as macros seem to have a simpler syntax?*

A: Macros do not use typesafe parameters, and each parameter to a macro is evaluated twice, which can be a problem with post-incremented parameters. Also, compiler error messages refer to the expanded macro rather than to the symbol. Templates can also take advantage of specialization and datatype promotions.

Q: *A program has a function that takes one double parameter. Your program calls that function with an argument of type int, rather than double. Explain how the compiler enables this call, being that C++ is a typesafe language, which is particular about datatypes.*

A: C++ has a set of implicit or automatic type conversions that promote a smaller type to a larger type. In this case, the int argument is promoted to a double in the call to the function.

Q: *Is goto a C++ keyword?*

A: Goto, a C++ keyword, provides unconditional branching, which makes program control flow difficult to understand. You should avoid using goto.

Q: *The continue statement has what effect on control flow?*

A: Continue bypasses any remaining statements in the smallest enclosing do, while, or for statement and resumes with an evaluation of the condition.

Q: *The break statement has what effect on control flow?*

A: Break bypasses any remaining statements in the smallest enclosing do, while, for, or switch statement and resumes at the statement following the statement.

Q: *Why is the break statement used at the end of each case in a switch statement?*

A: A switch matches the switch expression with each case label. The execution of statements begins with a match and continues until the end of the switch statement, unless the break is used, which terminates the switch. The expression is not reevaluated with each successive case label.

Q: *Can you use a switch based on floats?*

A: No, the switch expression must be an integral value and the case labels must be constant integral values.

Q: *Which method of parameter passing is used by a swap function?*

A: Pass by reference.

Q: *Name the data types that are referred to as the built-in types.*

A: These are the char types; the integer types such as int, long, and short; the floating point types double and float; and the bool types.

Q: *When should a parameter be passed to a function by value rather than by reference?*

A: A parameter should be passed by value when it is a built-in data type and that value does not need to be modified.

Q: *When should a parameter be passed by reference?*

A: Any large object should be passed by reference rather than by value. Passing by reference avoids the copy constructor of class objects.

Q: *Can an array be passed by value as a parameter to a function?*

A: Arrays are always passed by reference as only the address of the initial element of an array is passed to the function.

Q: *How do you tell the compiler that a parameter to a function, when passed by reference, cannot be changed by that function?*

A: The formal argument for that parameter should have the modifier const preceding its declaration, as in strcmp(const char* a, const char* b). This tells the function that neither a nor b can be modified by the function itself.

Q: *What does pass by value and pass by reference mean?*

A: Pass by value means that a copy of the argument is placed on the run-time stack. Pass by reference means that the address of the argument is placed on the stack.

Q: What run-time error is caused by the following statement?

```
for (int i = 100; i > 0; i++)
std::cout << "Hello" << i << std::endl;
```

A: The for statement contains an infinite loop. In this case the error is that the conditional test will not fail until i is zero. This will never happen since the loop-expression is incrementing the value of i, rather than decrementing it.

Q: What is the pseudo-code for a function, IsPalindrome, which returns true if a phrase is spelled the same backwards and forwards?

A: Copy the phrase and reverse the copy. Convert both the original and the copy to lower-case characters. Then compare the strings for equality.

Q: Which CRT functions are used to reverse a string and to compare a string without regard for case?

A: Strrev() is used to reverse a string. Stricmp() is used to compare two strings without regard for case.

```
string comparison.
```

Q: Find the common run-time error in the following code:

```
int i = 2;
while ( i = 2 )     if (!(i % 2)) i *= 4;
```

A: The expression, "while (i = 2)," is an assignment rather than a test for equality. Substituting the single equals for the double equals is one of the most common run-time errors of C++ programmers.

Q: How can you write conditional equality tests in order to make the above run-time error into a compile-time error?

A: The compile will fail if a const variable is used for the left-hand side of an assignment. A const variable can succeed in an equality test.

Q: Which shorthand techniques are available for assignments?

A: C++ has increment and decrement operators, as well as compound assignments and subexpressions. Subexpressions enable an assignment to be made within a conditional statement.

Q: How does scope affect the visibility of objects?

A: Global objects are visible throughout the program. A function-level object having the same name as a global object hides that global object. An object at the level of a compound statement or local block within the function sharing a function-level or higher name hides that higher level object. An object within a namespace having the same name as a global object hides that global object.

Intermediate Questions

Q: *Define a pointer.*

A: Pointers hold the address of an object. The data type and the object addressed have the same data type. The value of the address can be null and can change during the lifetime of the pointer.

Q: *What are the uses of pointers?*

A: Pointers are used for linked data structures, the management of dynamic memory, and as parameter types for functions. Pointers are often used to store the address of an array.

Q: *Define a reference.*

A: A reference is like a pointer except that it must be initialized at the time of definition. A reference cannot be reinitialized during its lifetime. References are typically used as formal parameters to a function.

Q: *Explain the relationship of pointers and arrays.*

A: An array identifier is a synonym for an address. As pointers hold addresses of a given type, it is convenient to assign an array address to the pointer. Using an array with array syntax is usually more clear than the corresponding pointer syntax.

Q: *A program tracks the number of radios sold within each month of a 12-month period. Should the program use dynamic memory or an array to store these values?*

A: Arrays are preferred when the size of a memory structure is known in advance. The program needs an array of 12 integer objects.

Q: *A program requires a count of each model of radios sold within each month of a 12-month period. Which type of data structure can best hold this information?*

A: The data can be stored in an array of linked lists to a user-defined struct. Each element in the list holds the model name and monthly sales count for that model.

Q: Does the C++ STL make dynamic storage requirements, such as arrays of linked lists, as described in the previous question, simpler to implement?

A: Using STL, the radio count program could be coded as a vector of lists of radios. The programmer does not need to create linked list routines, such as insert and delete, or maintain any dynamic memory.

Q: Describe the general facilities of the C++ STL.

A: STL has facilities for coding various collection types such as arrays, lists, queues, and strings. Each STL type has functions that complement the particular collection. Generic algorithms complement these collections in order to provide solutions to problems that once could only be solved with a dynamic memory allocation via pointers.

Q: Can a programmer forget about pointers and dynamic memory given the capabilities of STL?

A: Programmers still need to understand pointers and dynamic memory for at least two reasons. 1) Large amounts of code, existing and current, use dynamic structures as implemented through linked lists, maps, and trees. 2) The Interface Definition Language (IDL), used by COM and CORBA for distributed computing, can only transfer the traditional C data types and structs, as well as pointers and arrays.

Q: Which loop control statement guarantees that the statement(s) are executed at least once?

A: The do while loop. The do keyword precedes the statement or compound statement block. The while (expression) statement follows these statements. Even if the conditional expression evaluates to false, the preceding statements have been executed once prior to this test.

Q: Should a programmer rely on the rules of order of precedence when processing a complex statement?

A: No, parentheses should be used to clarify the order of precedence in a complex expression. Programmers cannot be expected to remember the orders of precedence. Using parentheses can specify or clarify the following expression:

```
int i = x + b * c / n + a;
int i = (x + (( b * c ) / n )) + a; // equivalent statement
using parentheses
```

Q: The order of precedence specifies that the increment operator is higher in precedence than the relational operators. Is the following statement a safe use of the language rules?

```
int nums[10]; int index = 0;
if (nums[index++] < nums[index])
;      // do something
```

A: In general, you should not modify the value of an object that is referred to within the same statement, as is the case with the index object. In this statement, we have no assurance that the left operand, nums[index++], will be evaluated first as expected.

Q: Can the conditional operator call functions as the result of the evaluation of the conditional expression?

```
int i = (a > 10) ? processA() : processB();
```

A: The previous statement is legal but not advisable when calling functions that do more than return a value. You should use the if-else construct to control program flow.

Q: Explain how C++ enables math operations on objects of different data types without any special expressions or functions, as in

```
int i = 0; i = 6.67 + 3; // i would equal 9.
```

A: C++ defines standard conversions between objects of the built-in data types. A smaller type is converted to the larger type in an arithmetic expression, which would be converted to 6.67 + 3.0, yielding 9.67. The right-hand side of an assignment is converted to the left-hand side data type. In this case, 9.67 is truncated to the value 9.

Q: When should an explicit conversion be used?

A: An explicit conversion, also known as a cast, is used to override the type-checking facility. Typical uses of casting are to convert a pointer of some non-const type to a void* pointer, to override the implicit conversions, or to clarify the conversion of one type to another. Explicit casting is often used for converting a base class to a derived class. All conversions should be used carefully, as they are a potential source of bugs.

Q: Describe recursion and an appropriate application.

A: Recursion is a function that calls itself, perhaps using another function. Typical recursive functions call themselves until they encounter a stopping condition. Failure to include a stopping condition results in infinite recursion. Recursion can help create smaller, simpler functions than a similar non-recursive implementation. Note that non-recursive functions tend to perform better as they do not continually invoke function calls as a recursive solution does. A typical application is to traverse some tree-like structure such as a menu system, a directory system of a hard drive, or the various parts of an XML document. Understanding recursion is helpful in debugging and stopping recursive behavior in event-driven *graphical user interfaces* (GUIs).

Q: Describe the purpose of a debugger.

A: A debugger is useful to monitor the logic of a program and to review the state of memory during the running of the application. A programmer can step through individual lines of code and set breakpoints to pause execution at specified points in the code. The skillful use of a debugger along with the testing of a running application can help you resolve logic or run-time bugs.

Q: What identifies a C program written with K&R syntax?

A: K&R programs have function definitions that list the parameter names within the parentheses following the function name. The function body is preceded by the definitions of the parameters. K&R programs do not require function prototypes, as does ANSI C.

Q: Store the address of the third element of the nums array in this excerpt:

```
int *p, nums[] = { 0, 1, 2, 3, 4, 5, 6, 7, 8, 9 };
```

A: p = &nums[2];

Q: The removal of which character from a character string will cause unpredictable behavior?

A: Most string functions rely on the null terminator to inform them of the end of the string. Removing or replacing the null character at the end of a string will trigger a run-time error.

*Q: Given this function prototype, void sort(char *lines[], int n), describe the two parameters to the function.*

A: This function sorts an array of n pointers to char.

Q: Describe how to safely display to the standard output the final character string in an array of n pointers to char.

A: Initialize a char pointer p to the address of the n - 1 element of the array. If p is not a null pointer, then display p using either printf or cout.

Q: *What happens if a program dereferences a null pointer?*

A: Dereferencing a null pointer causes a run-time error.

Q: *What is the purpose of the C++ namespace mechanism?*

A: Namespaces add a qualification to global objects so that the same name objects can coexist without name collision. Access notation enables the compiler to distinguish between namespaceA::some Method() and namespaceB::someMethod().

Q: *A header file, Radios.h, contains the RADIO struct along with several function prototypes named: insert(RADIO* n), display(), remove(RADIO* n), count(RADIO* root), and an object of type RADIO* name root. What do you think the programmers had in mind considering the interfaces contained within this file?*

A: Radios.h describes a linked list and some of its supporting functions. A linked list begins with a user-defined struct, in this case RADIO, which contains a pointer to another RADIO object. Each RADIO object continues to point to another RADIO until the last item points to a null value. Linked lists need functions to insert a new RADIO object, or node, into the list following the current node or at the front or end of the list. Remove, display, and count are useful operations for the list.

Q: *Which methods are used to traverse the series of nodes in a linked list?*

A: Linked lists must have an external pointer to the first node of the list. Using the previous description, a RADIO* root contains the address of the first node in the linked list. A second RADIO* temp initially points at root and then is continuously reinitialized to temp->next as long as temp->next is not null. A typical implementation of this concept is

```
temp = root; // root points at the first RADIO in the list
while (temp.)
temp = temp->next;
```

Q: *A single pointer holds the address of a linked list. The pointer is used to traverse the linked list. Unfortunately, the list has no means of backtracking to the origin. How should the program be changed so that the beginning of the list is preserved?*

A: The address of the beginning of the list is lost once the single pointer is reinitialized to point to the next node in the linked list. Traversing a list requires one pointer to maintain the address of the beginning of the list and another to traverse the list.

Q: *What is the return value of the new expression?*

A: New returns a pointer to a newly allocated object:

```
int *i = new int[10];
```

In this case, new returns a pointer to an array of 10 int objects.

Q: *A program has two pointers to int, i and j, each of which are assigned their own dynamic array of 10 ints. At some point, i is assigned the value of j. The program deletes the array pointed at by i and then deletes the array pointed to by j. Describe the error in this program.*

A: A memory leak occurs when i is assigned the value of j. The memory that i pointed to is now lost and both i and j point to the same memory. The first deletion of i will succeed, but the second deletion of memory pointed to by both i and j will cause a run-time error.

Q: *Can the compiler prevent a programmer from losing the address of dynamic memory?*

A: Using a const pointer to dynamic memory will ensure that the compile will fail when any statement attempts to reassign the values of a const pointer.

Q: *A program has an array class with operations named push and pop. What is the name of the data structure being described by this code?*

A: A stack.

Q: *What are default arguments?*

A: Default arguments are parameters initialized to a default value in the absence of a call-specified value. Trailing arguments may not follow default arguments.

Q: *What are default arguments useful for?*

A: Programmers use default arguments in order to simplify the calling of functions that have long parameter lists. Default arguments are often used in conjunction with overloaded functions.

Q: *What are the available alternatives to "pass by value" when returning a value from a function?*

A: Functions normally return values "by value." A function can return a pointer or reference to an object "by reference." References and pointers should be used to pass large class objects. This approach should not return references to local objects, as these objects will terminate at the end of the function call.

Q: Describe the prototype of a function that returns the sum of an array of doubles of n elements.

A: inline double sum(double aDbls[], int n)

Q: Sum an array of doubles using the Standard Template Library.

A:
```
#include <numeric>

double d = std::accumulate(aDbls, aDbls + n, 0.0);
```

Q: What is pointer arithmetic?

A: Pointer arithmetic enables the programmer to use addition and subtraction operations on pointers in order to reposition the pointer, to find the differences in size between pointers, and compare pointers for address equality.

Q: Can pointer arithmetic be used to traverse linked structures?

A: No, pointer arithmetic is used to traverse contiguous memory structures, which limits its use to arrays. No guarantee exists that dynamically obtained memory has a contiguous layout. Dynamic memory that appears to be allocated like an array should be considered an implementation of a particular compiler and not be relied upon as a feature of the language.

Q: A copy of a struct can be made through the assignment operator. Assume that this instance of the struct has pointers to other objects. What happens when this instance of the struct, RADIO, is copied to another instance of RADIO?

```
RADIO rdo, rdo2;
rdo.next = new RADIO;
rdo.prev = new RADIO;
rdo2 = rdo;
```

A: The values of the member fields of the source struct are copied to their corresponding fields in the target struct. The two objects share the same dynamic memory since the pointers in the target instance point to the same objects as the pointers in the source instance.

Q: Using the CRT, describe how to open an existing file as input in text mode.

A: The fopen command attempts to open a file under one of the various modes, such as read or write mode. If successful, fopen returns a handle, an address to the file; otherwise, it returns null:

```
char* fname = "readme.txt";
  if( (stream = fopen( fname, "rt" )) == NULL )
```

```
    printf( "The file '%s' was not opened\n", fname );
else
    printf( "The file '%s' was opened\n", fname );
```

Q: What is required of a program that uses a file?

A: The program needs to check that a file can be opened or created. The program needs to close a file once it is no longer required.

Q: How does a program read lines from a text file?

A: It reads a line of text using fgets() as long as the End of File marker has not been found, which is detected with feof().

```
const int maxline = 100;
  char line[maxline];
  while (!feof(stream))
  {
 if (fgets( line, maxline, stream ) == NULL)
      printf( "fgets error\n" );
  else
      printf( "%s", line);
  }
```

Q: Your program needs to read a number of text memos that are each 1,024 bytes in length from a file. Each memo is used once after the retrieval. How would you effectively retrieve these memos using the CRT?

A: Each item to be read needs to be stored in a character buffer. The fread function is used to retrieve the memo. After each use, the character buffer is cleared prior to retrieving the next memo. The key difference to the code in the previous example is the use of the fread function rather than the call to fgets.

```
int numread = 0;
const int maxbuf = 1024;
char *line[maxbuf];
numread = fread(reinterpret_cast<void*>(&line), maxbuf, 1, stream);
```

Q: A program reads a file containing a number of text memos of unknown lengths. Each memo is terminated by the string "<END_OF_MEMO>." Although limited to using a single dynamic character buffer for each memo, explain how you could read through the series of memos.

A: A file consisting of memos of unknown lengths can be read in a single pass with the lines of text being stored in a linked list of char pointers. Alternatively, the program can determine the size of each memo on a first partial pass through the file and then initialize the single buffer on the second pass. Using the second approach, a solution might resemble the following steps:

1. Record the current file position.
2. Read a line of text until the End of File or END_OF_MEMO token is found.
3. Record the end of memo position and reset the file to the start of the memo.
4. Allocate and clear a buffer to accommodate the text.
5. Reread this portion of the file and copy the text to the buffer until the process reaches the end of memo position.
6. Process the buffer and then clear it prior to reading the next memo.

Q: *What advantages does the iostreams library offer in coding the previous problem?*

A: Using iostreams offers an object-oriented class library within the STL that duplicates the functionality of the CRT and enables overloaded input and output operators. These overloads enable a higher level use of output from user-defined classes. iostreams also offers special iterators that can load input directly into containers such as vectors.

Q: *What advantages do the string functions of the STL have over the string functions of the CRT?*

A: The STL string functions duplicate the functionality of their CRT counterparts. A major advantage is that an STL string is an object and offers superior and simpler memory management. STL makes it easy to transfer from CRT strings to STL string objects in either direction. The STL string object is an accessible way of learning the STL.

Q: *How does using the STL for simpler coding in the above described program that reads text memos of unknown length?*

A: Being that iostreams and string objects are both part of the STL, using them together makes a natural fit. Attempting to use the STL string object with CRT file functions involves an additional step of transferring from a CRT or C-style string to a string object. Combining the paradigms might confuse programmers on either side of the STL/CRT fence. The following is an implementation of #91 in the CRT, followed by its counterpart in STL:

```
void readDynMemos()        // CRT ("C" Runtime Library func-
tions)
```

```
{
 char* fname = "d:\\temp\\item.txt"; // Open the file
 if ( (stream = fopen( fname, "rt" )) == NULL )
 printf( "The file '%s' was not opened\n", fname );
const int maxline = 100; // Create a fixed-size buffer for
input
char line[maxline];
char *buf, *pdest; // Char pointers
fpos_t pos, endpos;      // file position markers
bool sentinel = false;   // flag set when memo is done
int success = 0, buflen;
while (!feof(stream)) {  // Read until end of file
 sentinel = false;
      // Record the current file position
 if ( fgetpos( stream, &pos ) != 0 ) break;
      // Read until no more input of END_OF_MEMO token is
found.
while (!sentinel) {
 if (fgets( line, maxline, stream ) == NULL) break;
 sentinel = (pdest = strstr( line, "<END_OF_MEMO>" )) !=
NULL;
 }
 if (!sentinel) break;
 // Record the end of memo position. Reset the file to the
start of the memo.
 // various error checks
 if (fgetpos( stream, &endpos ) != 0) break;
 if ((buflen = endpos - pos) <= 0) break;
 if (fsetpos(stream, &pos) != 0) break;
 // Allocate and clear a buffer to accommodate the text
 buf = new char[buflen];
*buf = NULL;
// Reread this portion of the file until program reaches
// the end of memo position.
// Concatenate the current line to the buffer.
 while ( (fgetpos( stream, &pos) == 0) && pos != endpos) {
  fgets( line, maxline, stream );
  strcat(buf, line);
 }
 // Process buf... and then clear for next run.
printf("%s", buf);
```

```
    delete [] buf;
  }
  if (stream) fclose(stream);
}
#include <fstream> // STL or C++ Standard Library
#include <string>
void readDynMemosIOS()
{
  using namespace std;
  string fname("d:\\temp\\item.txt"); // Open the file
  ifstream infile(fname.c_str());
  if (!infile) {
        cerr << "error: unable to open input file: " <<
              infile << endl;
  }
  string line, memo;   // string objects take care of memory
  while (getline(infile, line, '\n')) {       // Read a line
of text until eof
        // append to memo string while marker not found
        if (line != "<END_OF_MEMO>")
        {     memo.append(line).append("\n"); continue; }
        memo.append(line); // add the end of memo marker
        cout << memo;      // output
         memo.erase();     // clear memory for memo
  }
  if (infile) infile.close();
}
```

Q: *Given that STL iostreams and string objects in the previous example make the programs smaller and apparently simpler, is it advisable to encourage junior programmers to exclusively code in the STL?*

A: No, C++ programmers need to be familiar with the CRT string and file functions for a number of reasons. A great deal of existing code depends on the CRT. Programmers need to be fluent in the most common CRT functions in order to maintain or translate to the STL. Additionally, some of the STL classes are simply wrappers around the CRT functions (such as ctype.h). C++ programmers inevitably trace into systems and other libraries when trying to determine bugs in their programs. Much of the CRT code is available as C source and is not hard to understand. On the other hand, the underlying STL code can be rather forbidding until you are fluent in object-orientation and templates.

Q: #define macros can be found in C programs and can still be found in current programs. Given the following MAX macro, explain why the output of a text comparison is different in the two sets of similar code:

```
#define MAX(x, y) (x > y ? x : y)
Version 1: Output is "bass"
 const char* sstr = "bass";
 const char* fstr = "ace";
 std::cout << "Max(ace, bass) is:" << MAX(fstr, sstr) <<
 std::endl;
Version 2: Output is "ace"
 const char* fstr = "ace";
 const char* sstr = "bass";
 std::cout << "Max(ace, bass) is:" << MAX(fstr, sstr) <<
 std::endl;
```

A: The MAX function is not comparing the strings as in the function strcmp, but comparing the addresses of the const char pointers. Macros do not always produce the answer that you expect. Unless they are writing for strict ANSI C compilation, programmers should always use inline functions rather than macros.

Q: When should you use pass-by-value for parameters to functions? What are the advantages of using this method?

A: Built-in types and small class objects that are not to be modified by the function are suitable for pass-by-value. Pass-by-value is easy to understand and the function does not alter any of the calling functions' values.

Q: When should you use pass-by-reference for passing parameters to functions? What are the rules for using this approach?

A: Parameters can be converted via passed-by-reference to functions using either references or pointers. Both types are used for passing large objects that can be modified. The const modifier can be used to prevent any modification by the function. The key differences between using references and pointers are that references are bound to an object when the call to the function is invoked. Pointers do not have to be initialized and can be reinitialized to point to other objects during the course of the function. References offer easy syntax in that the caller writes a function with the same syntax as a pass-by-value. References, unlike pointers, do not need to be checked for a null state as they are guaranteed to be bound to an object.

Q: Can arrays be passed by value or be passed by reference?

A: Arrays are always passed by reference as a pointer to the first element of the array. A function does not know the number of elements in an array unless the caller passes an additional integral parameter specifying the length of the array. The function can declare that the array parameter is const.

Advanced Questions

Q: What are the rules for writing overloaded functions? What is their purpose?

A: Overloaded functions are functions at the global or class level that have the same name. The return type, name, and parameter list of a function is known as the signature of the function. Overloaded functions must be differentiated by the parameter list. The compiler does not accept an overloaded function that only differs by a return type. Overloaded functions are primarily used to offer an alternative to calling the same function with a varying number of required parameters. A Print function is a good example; numerous functions enable the user to invoke the Print function with more or less specific versions of the same command. As an example, a Print function may have a no-argument version, a version that specifies a printer, and another that specifies the printer and special formatting information. The common element is that all of the overloaded print functions are asking the program to perform a print job. Overloaded functions are often used in conjunction with default parameters. In the end, similar functions are available that are easier to use by the programmer.

Q: Describe template functions.

A: Template functions enable the programmer to write generic functions that offer strong type-checking as an alternative to macros. Templates automatically generate instances of a function varying by type, as they are required by the program. This generation is done at compile-time. Any errors would be reported as a compile-time error. Template functions are useful when a program needs generic handling of an algorithm, regardless of parameter data type.

A max function would be written as

```
template <class Type> Type max (Type a, Type b)
{ return a < b ? a : b; }
```

The compiler would generate max functions for ints, floats, chars, and char pointers based on the calls made in the following main():

```
int main()
{
        int i = max( 1, 2);
        float f = max(3.0f, 6.1f);
        char a = max('e', 'E');
        char* s = max("Space", "Ace");
s = max("Ace", "Space");
}
```

Q: *In the previous main(), all the max functions work as expected, except for the max comparison of strings. The max function in this case is not making a string comparison, but a comparison of the addresses of the const char pointers. How can you customize the max template so that comparisons required for strings and other pointer objects can be performed?*

A: C++ offers an explicit specialization definition where the template specifies a return type as well as parameter types. This characteristic of the language enables the programmer to create exceptions to the template generation based on the parameter arguments to the template function. In order to create a strcmp comparison for max, the following code is added to the header file:

```
template <class Type> Type max (Type a, Type b)    //
Original
{ return a > b ? a : b; }
template <> char* max< char* >(char* s1, char* s2) // char*
override
{ return strcmp( reinterpret_cast<const char*>(s1),
        reinterpret_cast<const char*>(s2)) > 0 ? s1 : s2 ; }
```

Q: *C++ has various named casts, such as reinterpret_cast, that perform an explicit conversion similar to old-style casts. Why and when should programmers use the named casts over the older general cast notation?*

A: All casts need to be used carefully, as the programmer will disable or weaken the C++ type-checking facility. Old-style casts should only be used under pure C compilers. One clear advantage of using the named casts is the ease of finding them within the source code. Attempting to find named casts within source code is easy. Trying to distinguish (char*) as a cast from (char*) as part of a prototype takes more time.

Q: When using relational databases, should your program communicate directly with a proprietary database library?

A: The speed of execution may be an advantage in making native calls to a database; however, most C++ programmers use a middle-tier database driver such as ODBC. A key advantage of using ODBC is the flexibility in being able to change from one database product to another with few changes to your program code. A database-oriented program typically will send SQL statements to the server or call precompiled parameterized SQL procedures.

Q: What are the general steps in calling a SQL statement using ODBC?

A: 1. Make a connection to the data source.
2. Create a statement handle.
3. Execute the SQL statement.
4. Get results, if any.

Q: Should a C++ program send SQL statements or call stored procedures?

A: Sending SQL statements from your program allows for great flexibility and portability at the expense of server execution. Calling a stored procedure dramatically improves the performance of the SQL statements, as they are compiled when created. Executing a SQL statement requires compiling that statement with each use. The security of data access logic and the data itself are compelling reasons to use stored procedures that encapsulate SQL logic on the server. Data security is high, as users can be given rights to the procedures for accessing underlying data without simply giving the users rights to access that same data.

Q: Should database requests, whether as statements or as calls to stored procedures, be embedded within an application program or placed in separate modules or tiers?

A: Separating data requests into component libraries allows for a division of labor between database specialists and component and application programmers. Programmers, regardless of the language, and database administrators can successfully code stored procedures. Component developers can then create the interfaces to these procedures. Thus, application programmers can use the interfaces made available by the component libraries.

Q: What is the purpose of typedef names?

A: The typedef definition serves to give a synonym for a built-in or user-defined data type. Typedefs can serve to identify the purposes of datatypes. Typedefs simplify the use of complex declarations such as pointers to functions, template declarations, and pointers to class member functions.

Q: *Define object-based programming and its purpose.*

A: Object-based programming concerns the use of C++ classes to define new datatypes. Classes describe objects such as automobiles, pets, or bank accounts. These classes can be used to model the interaction of objects within an application. Key to successful use of objects is the separation between the public interface and the private implementation. The separation of the interface and implementation can minimize the amount of work required to maintain and modify these objects during the lifecycle of the application.

Q: *Describe encapsulation.*

A: Encapsulation, or information hiding, is the concept of preventing outside access to the private members and functions of the class. Clients of a class can call the functions that make up the public interface of the class. The functions of the public interface have the rights to direct access to the non-public members of the class.

Q: *How does a programmer identify the public and private members of a class?*

A: The programmer uses the access specifier keywords public, private, and protected. Public members are available to any client or to members of the class. Private members are only available to members of the class. A protected status makes data members and member functions available to classes that are derived from the current class. The term members refers to the functions and data within the class. They can also be called data members and member functions or methods.

Q: *What is the difference between a class and a struct?*

A: User-defined types known as structs have been a feature since the original implementation of C. In C++, structs are the same as a class, except that all of a struct's members are public by default. Structs are generally used as pass-by-reference parameters to operating system and CRT functions. Although structs with functions can perform just as a class can, it is not something that is done in normal practice.

Q: *How do you design a useful class?*

A: Successful classes can be used for an unlimited variety of purposes. A good design will package related data and the related processes along with a clear programmable interface. Programmers generally break down the problem into a number of data entities and relationships. Classes are created to implement those data entities. The interaction of instances of the classes implements the relationships.

Q: What is meant by the instance of a class?

A: An instance is an automatic or dynamic allocation of some built-in or user-defined datatype. By this definition, all objects are an instance of something whether they are an instance of an integer object or an instance of your latest hubcab class. In common use, the term instance is typically used when referring to class objects.

Q: How would you design a checking account class?

A: An experienced class designer should be able to verbally describe such a class in an interview. A basic design for this class might have data members for the current balance, the last statement date, the balance at the last statement, and a collection of the recent transactions as private data. The public interface would enable the user to retrieve the balances, dates, and a method to iterate through the transactions.

Q: What is object-oriented programming (OOP)?

A: *Object-oriented programming* (OOP) is an extension of the object-based model that enables type/subtype relationships. Through the concept of inheritance, a derived class can inherit the data and processes from its base class in addition to specifying its own member data and processes.

Q: How does a programmer and designer use OOP to create better programs?

A: Programmers can create hierarchies of inherited classes that benefit the design of related objects. Objects can reuse the functionality and data of base classes to introduce specialized variations as needed. These hierarchies enable a more efficient design compared to an object-based system where variations would have to be coded for conditional use or as separate objects that could have a great deal of overlap with similar classes.

Q: What is polymorphism?

A: This is the capability of pointers or references to a base class type to manipulate any class derived from the base type. The base and derived classes must share the same public interface in order for polymorphism to be effective. At run-time, the actual type of the polymorphic pointer or reference is resolved through virtual functions or the appropriate class function.

Q: *What does the modifier "virtual" signify when used in the declaration of a class function?*

A: The use of virtual, as in virtual void printReport(), indicates that the particular function can be overridden in a derived class. print Report from a derived class will be called by a base class function if the derived class has defined an overload of the virtual base class function print Report.

Q: *In a simple class hierarchy such as the zoological hierarchy of cats, describe how a eat function can take advantage of polymorphism and virtual functions.*

A: The reader can answer this question with some creativity. A typical response could follow this line of explanation. The cat hierarchy includes such subspecies as tiger, lion, and domestic cat. A basic cat class would have as data members fields like age, weight, height, length, and eye color, among other attributes. Likely member functions would include sleep, play, and eat. An Eat() implementation for a lion could consist of { MakeLionessHunt(), EatYourShare(), and GoBackToGuardDuty() }, while the corresponding function for a domestic cat might be { GetOwnersAttention(), EatContentsOfBowl Partially(), and DoSomethingElse() }. The client application initializes a pointer, MyCat, of the class cat to an object of class DomesticCat. MyCat->Eat()invokes the Eat function for the DomesticCat.

Q: *Can you create objects of an abstract class?*

A: An abstract class is typically the base class of a hierarchy. A program uses a pointer of the abstract class to point to the derived types. An abstract class is never instantiated as an independent object, as is one of the derived types.

Q: *Which keyword is used to distinguish an abstract class type from a non-abstract class type?*

A: "Keyword" is meant as a trick, as abstract is not a keyword used in the definition or declaration of a class. What distinguishes an abstract class is the declaration of one or more pure virtual functions. A pure virtual function is always declared as virtual [return type] [function-name] ({arguments}] = 0. In the previous cats example, the declaration reads virtual void eat() = 0.

Q: *A new class is derived from an abstract class without adding any additional definitions. Why does the compiler give the error*

"cannot instantiate abstract class due to following members void __thiscall somefunc(void)' : pure virtual function was not defined"

when attempting to instantiate an object of the derived class:

```
class A {   int a;   virtual void somefunc() = 0;   };
class B: public A {};
```

A: A class derived from an abstract class must implement any pure virtual function in order to instantiate an object of the derived class. Class B must at least define somefunc in order to compile a program including an instance of B.

Q: *Is it required to define a constructor and a virtual destructor for each class?*

A: A class does not need to implement these two functions, as the compiler will create an implicit default constructor and destructor. Most real-world applications will implement these functions and optional overloaded constructors.

Q: *When is a virtual destructor required? Can a virtual destructor be overloaded?*

A: A virtual destructor should be implemented whenever a class allocates dynamic memory. The virtual destructor typically deallocates any dynamic memory. A virtual destructor takes no parameters; consequentially, it is not possible to have overloaded destructors, as no parameter list differentiates any possible variations.

Q: *Can a constructor be declared as virtual?*

A: The declaration of a constructor does not return a type or accept any modifiers except for inline.

Q: *How does a non-default constructor of a derived class initialize members of the base class?*

A: Class members are typically initialized in the member initialization list that follows the arguments to the constructor and the semi-colon separator. The list consists of the member names with the implicit form of initialization, as in member (parameter for member). If some or all of the arguments are to initialize the base-class constructor, then the name of the base class with those arguments is one of the member/name argument pairs.

```
DomesticCat() : Cat(1, hazel, 10, 1, 1) {}
Cat::Cat(int m_age, coloreyes m_eye, int m_weight, int
m_length, int m_height) :
```

Q: Is it necessary to specify a no-argument or default constructor?

A: A default constructor, implicit or explicit, is required if your program needs to instantiate arrays of the class. Arrays, static or dynamic, accept no arguments. If your class has a constructor that accepts arguments, then the class must also supply an overloaded no-argument class, as the compiler only creates the implicit default argument in the absence of any constructors.

Q: What is required for a derived class to access the non-public members of the base class?

A: Inheritance enables access to the public but not private members of a base class. The access modifier "protected" is used to identify the member and data functions that are to be accessible to any derived class. Note that a derived class of a derived class still has access to the protected members of the top-level base class.

Q: What is inheritance?

A: Inheritance is the relationship between a base class and classes called derived that build upon that base. A derived class can use the member functions and data of the base class in addition to defining its own member data and functions. Member functions of the derived class can override the base class implementation by using the same function signature as the base class.

Q: What are the advantages of using inheritance?

A: Inheritance enables you to transport the core data requirements and functionality to the base class while adding specialized enhancements to each derived class. A derived class can further serve as the base for another derived class. Client usage of inherited classes can be made simple by maintaining a common public interface to all levels of the inheritance hierarchy. Having a consistent public interface allows for easy maintenance and a modification of code as the calls to the object only need to be changed when the interface has been modified. Good OOP design specifies that a public interface is a contract with the user and that the interface should not be changed so that it breaks the client.

Q: *An existing class currently has a Print function that enables the users to interactively control the print job. The clients additionally want to print directly to a default printer without user intervention. How should the class design be modified to accommodate this change?*

A: A key concept of designing an interface for object-based programming or OOP is to not break an existing contract with its clients. By changing the parameter signature of a function, the clients of the program need to update all calls to the Print() function in order to recompile the existing client program. A successful alteration of an interface should add a new public function. By using an overloaded function such as Print (bool ToPrinter = true), the function retains the meaning of the Print action, yet does not interfere with the original Print function.

Q: *What is the purpose of namespaces?*

A: Namespaces are used to avoid name clashing within the global space. Although names of objects are unique within the various scoping levels of C++, situations will occur when a name may not be unique at the global level. Typically, this happens when the names of your objects conflict with the same name of a newly added library. Object definitions and declarations can be hidden from the global namespace by placing these statements within the namespace construct. Namespaces are distinguished by a unique name within the scope where it is defined. Namespaces can be nested within a namespace as a local procedure block is nested within a function definition.

Q: *How does the client access the objects within a namespace?*

A: Clients can access the objects within namespaces by using fully qualified names along with a number of mechanisms to simplify the required syntax. The using directive strikes a balance between a fully qualified path and using declarations, which reveal all the namespace definitions in the current scope. The using directive enables you to specify the names within a namespace that are exposed to the current scope. Once names are in the space, they can be used without further qualification.

Q: *What is the purpose of class static members and static functions?*

A: The purpose of static members is to have a single object for the use of all instances of a class. Rather than use a global object outside of the class, the static member provides that requirement of the shared object. The private and protected modifiers can control access to the static members. Although member functions can access static members, typically you will use static member functions for that purpose. Since static functions cannot reference nonstatic members, a user can invoke the static function regardless of any instantiations of the class. This is helpful when initializing a key value such as an interest rate for a class of bank accounts prior to the creation of any bank account objects.

Q: *Many books on object methodology refer to Is-A and Has-A relationships. Explain these concepts.*

A: Is-A refers to an object derived from some base type. For example, a checking account (Is-A) is a type of bank account (the base type). Has-A refers to an object that is contained in or is part of a larger object. For example, a car class has or contains an engine object and a transmission object.

Q: *A car class contains an instance of an engine class that contains many data members that the car class needs to access for display and modification. The designer of the engine object is unwilling to remove encapsulation yet does not want to create a series of public Get/Set functions for each data member. Given these constraints, what is an available solution so that the car class can easily access the data members of the engine class?*

A: The engine class can include the statement "friend class car" within its class definition. This enables full access to the engine instance only to the car instance. Friend status makes it simple for the car class to retrieve and initialize the various data members of the engine class. An example would be car.engine.cylinders = 6.

Q: *A* user interface *(UI) retrieves and initializes the data members of the car object. The UI does not inherit the friend status of engine, and engine is not a public member of the car class. How can the UI class access the engine with similar ease as the car class accesses the engine?*

A: The car class adds a public method, returning a reference to the engine object. The UI class can access the engine members by a qualified path such as car.GetEngine().cylinders = 6. If a number of members are to be used, then the UI class could declare a reference pointer to the engine object in order to have a shorthand means of accessing the data members:

```
Engine& eng = car.GetEngine();
eng.cylinders = 6;
eng.belts     = 2;
```

Q: Describe overloaded operators.

A: Overloaded operators enable us to specialize the default action of the typical assignment and arithmetic operators. Overloaded operators can only be defined for operands of a class type or enumeration type. Although they can be defined at the class or namespace level, at least one parameter must be of the class or enumeration type.

Q: How can you ensure that an overloaded operator is called regardless of the order of data types in an expression?

A: An overloaded operator as a class member is only called when the left operand of an expression is a class member. In situations where the left operand is not a class member, then an overloaded operator must be defined at the global scope. Some operators, particularly assignment operators, can only be defined at the class level.

Q: An instance of a car class serves as the model for the manufacturing of a number of cars. The model may have an optional radio that requires the dynamic allocation of a CarRadio object from the free store. How can an overloaded assignment operator help in initializing each element in the car array?

A: Each Car object needs to allocate a CarRadio if the model car has a radio. The Car object thus needs an overloaded assignment operator in order to allocate a new CarRadio object. If you have not supplied the overload and depend on the default memberwise initialization, then the address of the model's CarRadio would be copied to the current Car object. Every car would then be sharing the same CarRadio through the same object in memory. Your system would crash upon destruction of the second Car object due to the attempt to delete the radio object that is now a dangling pointer.

Q: A Cat class has the protected data members: age, weight, eye color, and name. Describe the object-oriented solution that enables the client to call for output in this manner:

```
Cat MyCat( 1, "Felix")    // Assume age and name are parame-
ters
cout << MyCat;       // Prints "Name: Felix, Age: 1"
```

A: Use an overloaded output operator to output the non-public members of a class. An output operator is a namespace function and does not belong to the class. In order to access the non-public members of the class, the output operator is declared a friend to the class. For Cat, the syntax would be

```
friend ostream& operator<<(ostream&, const Cat&).
```

Q: *What is the purpose of pointers to functions? What is the common use of this facility?*

A: Pointers to functions enable a programmer to specify alternative functions as an argument to a function. A programmer might supply a numeric, date, or string comparison function as a pointer to a function for sort capabilities. Placing pointers to functions in an array could allow a series of functions to be run or to create a menu-driven application of those functions. A notable application of pointers to functions includes assigning a pointer to a function as the callback used in multi-threaded applications. Microsoft Windows uses a callback in order to direct messages to a Windows procedure.

Q: *How can pointers to functions enable a user-defined sequence of global functions? Think of an application where this might be useful.*

A: An array of global functions of a particular return-type and parameter list could store the addresses of the functions. The user-specified order determines which array element is referenced, thereby calling the associated function. This situation could be useful for simulations, animations, and a macro-like playback.

Q: *What is a dangling pointer?*

A: A dangling pointer is a pointer that does not reference valid memory. This occurs when a pointer references memory that has been deleted or when it references memory local to a function that no longer exists. A fix for the dangling pointer problem is to reinitialize a pointer to NULL and to test for NULL prior to any use of the pointer.

Q: *In the interview, you may be asked, Which books on C++ have you read?*

A: A number of books on C++ are available, including the C++ Primer by Lippmann, The C++ Programming Language by Stroustrup, and others. An intermediate or advanced programmer should have read parts or all of a current edition of this type of book, if not several books on C++. In your interview, you should distinguish these books from material on specific class libraries, such as the *Microsoft Foundation Library* (MFC), which may be required by the position.

Knowledge of a class library or application combined with a vague knowledge of the C++ language may work against you if a programmer interviews you.

Q: *What computer journals do you read?*

A: A good programmer needs to stay current on developments in programming as well as other areas in computing. Read a variety of magazines that include titles specific to C++ as well as mainstream computing and the information technology business. Not reading any journals or focusing on a specific area may not be a good sign to the interviewer.

Q: *Which software products do you use?*

A: A programmer needs to use professionally developed software. You should be a knowledgeable user of at least one mainstream desktop product. Not only will this skill be useful to you and others, but also those products may serve as useful models for your particular development. An interviewer will be wary of any programmer who has no interest in any software other than what he or she develops.

Q: *Which Web sites do you visit?*

A: The skillful use of a Web site is equivalent to the expert use of a desktop software product. Being familiar with the current standard of Web layout and functionality will help you, as you may eventually contribute to the construction of a Web site. Ignoring or having little interest in the Internet and Web sites would be a negative sign to an interviewer.

Q: *What other languages do you know?*

A: It is a mistake for a C++ programmer to be only skilled in C and C++. A C++ programmer works with other staff members with different backgrounds, including scripting languages. A C++ programmer is more likely to understand the needs of others if he can converse in their common language. A C++ programmer who has an attitude of "I only speak C++" will not be a popular choice as a team member.

Q: *How do you use research to solve an immediate programming problem?*

A: A key indication of a programmer's value is how effectively he or she can search for a solution to a programming problem. Having a thorough knowledge of books on the C++ language and on your class library is essential. Programmers should be familiar with the online documentation for your primary class libraries and the C++ languages. Online journals and specific language Web sites are also helpful. Intensive reliance on discussion groups and desperate searches through the indices of unread books are signs of an ineffective programmer.

Q: *How do you learn a new application area in programming?*

A: A good programmer learns by a combination of reading, attending seminars, computer-based training, and first-hand experimentation. Although expanding on a simple example may initially yield successful results, most programmers need to combine the expert knowledge of others with their own experience in order to attain a high level of expertise.

Q: *What is IDL, COM, and CORBA?*

A: IDL is the Interface Definition Language. It is derived from C and specifies procedures, the parameters to those procedures, and the supporting datatypes. Because IDL is a standard, it can be used to describe the interfaces for binary components created in any language that supports IDL. Two popular ways of creating distributed components are the *Component Object Model* (COM), which was created by Microsoft and is largely used on Windows, and the *Common Object Request Broker Architecture* (CORBA), which was created by the Object Management Group and is used on many platforms. CORBA and COM components both use a unique identifier that makes it possible for the client application to call the objects as interfaces.

Q: *How do binary components differ from classes?*

A: Binary components can be written in any language and can be used by any language that supports IDL. Such diverse clients as a C++ application, a Perl script, or a Web site application can use an individual component on a given operating system. Components can run within the client's memory space or as a local or remote server process. A client app remotely manipulates the methods and properties of a component from an instance of the component's interface. A C++ class library can only be used by a C++ application and must have its source code or precompiled files available for compilation into the host application. Unlike binary components, C++ library classes can be extended via inheritance.

Q: *What practical advantages does object orientation offer a C++ programmer?*

A: The object-oriented method enables the significant reuse and specialization of existing code. A programmer skilled in OOP can quickly create a derived class and take advantage of base-class virtual functions and the ability to override them in order to create specializations of the existing functionality of a class.

Q: *What advantages does a knowledge of templates and the* Standard Library *(STL) offer a C++ programmer?*

A: An understanding of templates is essential to the modern C++ programmer. The STL has many useful classes, such as strings, lists, and vectors that simplify the work of a C++ programmer. Having experience in programming your own templates gives you the background to exploit the STL and other libraries, such as the Microsoft *Active Template Library* (ATL) that depends upon templates.

10

PL/SQL

Raghu K. Vullaganti

Procedural Language/Structured Query Language (PL/SQL) is one of the integrated sets of Oracle development tools that support the core database. PL/SQL, Oracle's procedural language, extends the capabilities of traditional *Structured Query Language* (SQL). PL/SQL is the main development tool and can be incorporated into many of the other Oracle development tools such as Oracle forms, Oracle reports, Oracle graphs, *Oracle Call Interface* (OCI), Oracle precompilers (Pro*C, Pro*Cobol, and so on), Enterprise Manager, Oracle Data Browser, and SQL*PLUS.

Oracle 8.0 contains the PL/SQL engine version 8.0. Oracle Developer version 6.0 supports PL/SQL version 8.0. This chapter covers the topics of the most recent PL/SQL version 8.0, as well as Oracle 8.0. You can also see the new features of Oracle 8i later in this section.

You can run your PL/SQL code on the server side through the creation of database triggers, stored procedures, and packages. It can also be used on the client side by incorporating PL/SQL code into the Oracle's front-end development tools, such as Oracle forms and Oracle reports.

PL/SQL, a block structured language, contains three main sections: the variable declaration section, the program code section, and the error-handling section. The following is a listing of a typical PL/SQL block structure:

```
DECLARE
  <Declaration Section>
BEGIN
  <Program Code Section>
```

```
EXCEPTION
  <Error Handling Section>
END;
```

Though PL/SQL is not case-sensitive, it is always good practice to specify keywords in upper case in the programming code. In the previous listing, DECLARE, BEGIN, EXCEPTION, and END are PL/SQL reserved words. The declaration section consists of variable and cursor definitions. The program code section contains all the executable commands and is followed by the error-handling section where exceptions are handled.

The following code snippet is an example in which you can see the declaration section, the executable code section, and the error-handling section.

```
DECLARE
  i    constant integer := 10;
  j    integer;
  sum  integer;
  diff integer;
  div  number(7,2);

BEGIN
  j := 0;
  loop
   sum := i + j;
   diff := i - j;
   div := i / j;
   exit when j > 10;
end loop;
EXCEPTION
  When ZERO_DIVIDE then
     INSERT INTO computations VALUES (0,0,0);
END;
/
```

In the previous example, variables and constants have been defined in the declaration section. Between the BEGIN and EXCEPTION block are executable commands. You can have as many statements as you want in this block. You can also see the initialization statement (j := 0) and the many assignment statements within this block. When j becomes zero, it raises the exception handler, and program control goes to the error-handling block.

PL/SQL contains the following elements for usage:

- *Operators* PL/SQL expressions hold various types of operators. These are arithmetic operators, comparison operators, logical operators, and string operators. The details of these operators are beyond the scope of this book.

- *Control statements* You can use conditional statements to control the flow of executable statements in the program code section. In PL/SQL, you can use IF, ELSE, ELSIF, and END IF commands for conditional logic. The following listing depicts the syntax of the conditional logic:

```
IF <condition true> THEN
   <execute statements>
ELSIF <condition true> THEN
   <execute statements>
ELSE
   <execute statements>
END IF;
```

- *Iterative Statements* Loops can be used to process multiple data rows within a block. PL/SQL supports various types of loops, such as FOR loops, WHILE loops, and LOOP...END LOOP. The EXIT clause is used to terminate an infinite loop. Cursor loops can be used to fetch multiple data rows for an explicitly defined cursor.
- *Exceptions* When an error is encountered, the program control automatically goes to the error-handling section. This section always starts with EXCEPTION reserved word and terminates with the END command.
- *Cursors* A cursor is a temporary work area in memory where the database holds the current SQL statement. Two types of cursors are available in PL/SQL: implicit cursors and explicit cursors. Implicit cursors are defined by the Oracle database. The user defines explicit cursors, which must be defined in a four-step process: Declare the cursor, open the cursor, fetch the cursor, and close the cursor. To reduce the number of steps, Oracle introduced the CURSOR..FOR..LOOP functionality. CURSOR..FOR..LOOPs only require two steps to access data.
- *Procedures and functions* The structure of procedures and functions in PL/SQL is similar, except for a few differences. Functions return a value, while procedures cannot. The function value is returned through the use of the RETURN command. Functions can also be used as part of an expression. Stored procedures and functions are compiled and stored in the database.
- *Packages* A package is a collection of objects. These objects include variables, procedures, functions, cursors, and exceptions. A package usually consists of two components: a specification and a body. The

specification component has the declaration of variables, cursors, procedures, functions, and exceptions. The body component has the definition of the declared elements and it implements the specification component. Packages must be recompiled after you make any changes to it. Package recompilation neither changes the package definition nor any of its objects. A benefit of using packages, as opposed to procedures and functions, is the capability to use global variables. Also, when you access any part of the package for the first time, the entire package is stored in memory, that is, Oracle's shared pool. Going forward, the source code is pinned in memory and the package body code is executed more efficiently.

- *Triggers* Database triggers, stored at the database level, can be fired when some database-related events occur. Triggers can be fired by the database when insert, update, and delete actions take place. Various types of triggers are available in PL/SQL. These triggers include row-level triggers, statement-level triggers, BEFORE and AFTER triggers, and INSTEAD OF triggers. The data load performance can be improved dramatically by disabling the triggers during the loading time.
- *I/O operations* In PL/SQL, *input/output* (I/O) operations can be performed using the following packages: the UTL_FILE package, the TEXT_IO package, and the DBMS_OUTPUT package. The UTL_FILE package is a powerful package, and it enables users to work with files on both the client and server sides. It is the most widely used package for file I/O operations. The DBMS_OUTPUT package is mainly used for debugging purposes.
- *Web-related* PL/SQL 8.0 and 8i play an important role in the development of Web-based applications. It is evident that recent versions of PL/SQL have become part of the Oracle application server technology. Two techniques are available in PL/SQL to connect Java programs with the Oracle 8i database: *Java Database Connectivity* (JDBC) and the *Java/Structured Query Language* (SQLJ). In SQLJ, you can embed SQL statements inside a Java program. It is somewhat similar to precompilers such as Pro*C and Pro*Cobol, which embed SQL statements inside the native language.

New Features of Oracle 8i

Several new features for PL/SQL are available in Oracle 8i. Significant new features include autonomous PL/SQL blocks, invoker rights, PL/SQL bulk binds, parameter passing by reference, improved dynamic SQL, the capability to call a Java program through PL/SQL, and the capability to call a PL/SQL program through Java.

Autonomous PL/SQL blocks enable you to run a transaction within a transaction. This new feature allows you to jump outside of the current transaction and commit records in another transaction without committing the records of the original transaction. If the original transaction fails, only that transaction's records are rolled back. This is significant for applications that require logging information as a large transaction progresses. Also, it helps out tremendously in writing a more robust error-trapping mechanism.

Invoker rights enable programs to be executed with the invoker's privileges. When creating PL/SQL programs in the past, the default was the designer's privileges, which were used for whoever ran the program. This new feature enables you to right truly generic PL/SQL code to be used by all users of the database referencing their own database objects.

PL/SQL bulk binds is a new feature that will enable you to send a collection or bulk bind of variables in one call. This significantly improves performance when assigning variable information from a table in bulk. Previously, for each record queried, that record would be assigned to the variable array. Thus, you would have a SELECT-SQL call for each record. Now you can assign the variable array with one call.

Oracle PL/SQL now enables you to pass parameters by reference with the use of the keyword NOCOPY. This means that PL/SQL no longer needs to copy the parameter variable from one area in memory to another. The variable location is simply referenced by the called program. This delivers a significant performance gain for programs that call other programs and pass parameters inside a long running loop. Also, performance is increased when passing large data structures as parameters.

Dynamic SQL has also been significantly enhanced. Implementing dynamic SQL requires much less coding and is integrated into PL/SQL. You no longer need to open a cursor, parse the statement, execute the statement, and finally close the cursor. These four steps have been reduced to one step with the EXECUTE IMMEDIATE *sql_string* command, which is native to the PL/SQL engine. You no longer need to use the DBMS_SQL package. This allows for more readable and more efficient program code.

In conclusion, the details of all the previous topics are beyond the scope of this book. This book is intended for those who already have some knowledge and/or working experience in PL/SQL. The next section, "Questions and Answers," covers a variety of important topics in PL/SQL.

It has two subsections, Beginners and Advanced. The Beginners section covers the questions and answers from the common topics of PL/SQL. The Advanced section covers the questions and answers from the advanced object-oriented and Web-related topics.

Some of the questions you see in this chapter might also appear in the SQL chapter. As PL/SQL and SQL are tightly integrated, it is a difficult task to draw a line between these two areas. Some of the repetitive questions, however, might help you brush up on your skills.

Questions and Answers

Beginners

Q: *What is PL/SQL?*

A: *Procedural Language/Structured Query Language* (PL/SQL) is a procedural language. It is the native database programming language within Oracle utilized by several Oracle development tools.

Q: *What is the difference between SQL and PL/SQL?*

A: SQL is a structured query language. It contains SELECT, INSERT, UPDATE, and DELETE statements. SQL is an ANSI standard tool and is widely used by relational databases such as Oracle, Informix, DB2, and so on. PL/SQL is a block-structured programming language, and the use of this tool is limited to the Oracle database and Oracle development tools.

In SQL, statements are processed by the database one at a time, whereas in PL/SQL, multiple SQL statements can be included in a single block and processed together in the database at the same time. This reduces the frequency of database calls. By doing so, PL/SQL obviously improves its performance. PL/SQL also has additional features such as control statements, iterative statements, error handling, procedures, functions, and so on.

Q: *What is DDL?*

A: DDL stands for *Data Definition Language*. You can create or drop the objects using DDL. Examples include CREATE TABLE, DROP TABLE, RENAME TABLE, CREATE VIEW, and DROP VIEW.

Q: *What is DML?*

A: DML stands for *Data Manipulation Language*. You can manipulate the object's data. Examples include INSERT, SELECT, UPDATE, and DELETE.

Q: *What is DCL?*

A: DCL stands for *Data Control Language*. You can control access to the data or to the database. Examples include GRANT and REVOKE.

Q: *What is ROWID?*

A: ROWID, an Oracle-defined column, contains the data block address. It can be used to directly point to where the data physically resides on the disk. It can also improve the performance of SQL transactions when referenced in the SQL statement.

Q: *How do you execute a host operating system command from SQL*PLUS?*

A: From the SQL*PLUS command prompt, you can use the HOST command to perform the operating system level tasks. Use the following example to list all SQL extension files in Unix:

```
SQL> HOST ls *.sql
```

Q: *Can PL/SQL be integrated with any other Oracle development tools?*

A: Yes, PL/SQL is already integrated with Oracle forms, Oracle reports, Oracle graphs, SQL*PLUS, Pro*C, Pro*Cobol, Oracle Call Interface (OCI), and Enterprise Manager.

Q: *Does PL/SQL code run at the server side or on the client machine?*

A: Both. If you run PL/SQL code in SQL*PLUS, it usually runs at the server side. Front-end tools, such as Oracle forms and reports, run PL/SQL on the client machine.

Q: *Is PL/SQL code case-sensitive?*

A: No. For code readability, it is always recommended to type reserved words in upper case.

Q: *What does a PL/SQL block contain?*

A: A PL/SQL block contains three sections: the declaration section, the program code section, and the error-handling section. The following is a listing of the typical PL/SQL block structure:

```
DECLARE
  <Declaration Section>
BEGIN
  <Program Code Section>
EXCEPTION
```

```
  <Error Handling Section>
END;
```

Here's another example:

```
DECLARE
  hours integer;
  rate number(10,2);
  amount number(10,2);
BEGIN
  amount := hours * rate;
EXCEPTION
   WHEN OTHERS THEN
      DBMS_OUTPUT.PUT_LINE('Error') ;
END;
/
```

Q: *What are the main data types available in PL/SQL?*

A: Though so many data types are available in PL/SQL, the following are the commonly used data types: NUMBER, INTEGER, DATE, CHAR, VARCHAR2, and BOOLEAN.

Q: *What is the difference between CHAR and VARCHAR2?*

A: CHAR is a fixed-length character string, while VARCHAR2 is a variable length. In other words, the CHAR data type will add spaces to data to make sure the populated data is the exact length of the defined width. VARCHAR2 holds up to the maximum length of a string, rather than the defined length.

Q: *What is the size limitation for VARCHAR2 in Oracle 8?*

A: The VARCHAR2 data type can have up to a maximum of 4,000 characters (bytes).

Q: *What is an anonymous block in PL/SQL?*

A: An anonymous block is a PL/SQL block with no name assigned. The following listing is an example of an anonymous block:

```
BEGIN
  DBMS_OUTPUT.PUT_LINE('Print this line.');
```

```
END;
/
```

Q: *How many categories of operators does PL/SQL support?*

A: PL/SQL supports four different categories of operators:

- Arithmetic operators: +, -, *, /
- Comparison operators: =, < >, !=, >, >=, <, <=, BETWEEN, IN, IS NULL, LIKE
- Logical operators: AND, OR, NOT
- String operators: concatenation operators such as ||

Q: *What is NULL? How can you substitute the NULL values in PL/SQL?*

A: NULL represents an unknown value. You can use an NVL function to take care of the NULL values.

Q: *What are the main data conversion functions?*

A: Three widely used conversion functions in PL/SQL convert information from one data type to another, as follows:

1. TO_CHAR transforms a number or date to a character string, such as

```
SELECT TO_CHAR(SYSDATE,'HH:MI:SS')
FROM DUAL;
```

2. TO_DATE transforms a character string to a date, such as

```
SELECT TO_DATE('29-JUN-99', 'DD-MON-YY')
FROM DUAL;
```

3. TO_NUMBER transforms a character string to a number, such as

```
SELECT TO_NUMBER('6.9')
FROM DUAL;
```

Q: *What is the control statement in PL/SQL?*

A: The IF...THEN...ELSE statement can be used to evaluate more than one condition. Here's an example:

```
IF (x > 10) THEN
  Y := TRUE;
```

```
ELSE
  Y := FALSE;
END IF;
```

Q: *Does SQL support any control statements?*

A: Although we cannot directly use IF...THEN...ELSE statements in SQL, we can achieve the same results by using the DECODE function. Here's an example:

```
DECODE(variable,if1,val1,if2,val2,........,else)
```

Q: *Can you use BETWEEN, LIKE, and IN operands in an assignment statement?*

A: Yes, PL/SQL extends the operand capabilities. Here's an example:

```
DECLARE
  found BOOLEAN;
  dept_id NUMBER;
  dept_name VARCHAR2(20);
BEGIN
  found := dept_id BETWEEN 1 and 5;
  found := dept_name LIKE '%eng%';
  found := dept_name IN ('Engineering', 'Procurement',
  'Sales');
END;
```

Q: *What is a loop? How many types of loops are available in PL/SQL?*

A: A loop is an iterative statement and can be used to process the code within a block repeatedly until it satisfies the condition. A FOR loop repeats a specified number of times. Here's an example of a FOR loop syntax:

```
FOR index IN low_num....high_num LOOP
  <execute statements>
END LOOP;
```

A WHILE loop evaluates the condition prior to entering the body of the loop. Here's an example of a WHILE loop syntax:

```
WHILE <condition true> LOOP
      <execute statements>
END LOOP;
```

LOOP...END LOOP is a simple loop. It becomes an infinite loop if you do not have EXIT or EXIT WHEN statements within the loop body. Here's an example of a LOOP...END LOOP syntax:

```
LOOP
  <execute statements>
  EXIT WHEN <condition true>
END LOOP;
```

A REPEAT...UNTIL loop executes the statements at least once before it evaluates the condition. Here's an example of its syntax:

```
REPEAT
  <execute statements>
UNTIL <condition true>
```

Q: *What is a cursor?*

A: A cursor is a temporary work area (a context area) in memory where a database holds the current SQL statement.

Q: *What is the difference between implicit cursors and explicit cursors?*

A: Implicit cursors are defined by the Oracle database, while users define the explicit cursors that are used to process queries that return multiple data records. By declaring explicit cursors, you obviously get an improved performance.

Q: *How do you define an explicit cursor?*

A: It must be defined in a four-step process: declare the cursor, open the cursor, fetch the cursor, and close the cursor. Here's an example:

```
DECLARE
  CURSOR dept_cur IS
    SELECT dept_no, dept_name
    FROM department
    WHERE dept_no IS NOT NULL;
  dept_number INTEGER;
  dept_names VARCHAR2(30);
BEGIN
  OPEN dept_cur;
  LOOP
    FETCH dept_cur INTO dept_number, dept_names;
    EXIT WHEN dept_cur%NOTFOUND;
  END LOOP;
 CLOSE dept_cur;
END;
/
```

Q: *Assuming that the cursor is defined, how would you retrieve multiple sets of data?*

A: A FETCH statement must be placed inside the loop to retrieve more than one record of information.

Q: *Can any alternate approach be used to define the explicit cursors?*

A: Yes, it can be used with a CURSOR FOR LOOP construct. It reduces the coding efforts and minimizes the human errors. In the following example, you do not need to use OPEN, FETCH, and CLOSE statements.

```
DECLARE
  CURSOR dept_cur IS
    SELECT dept_no, dept_name
    FROM department
    WHERE dept_no IS NOT NULL;
  dept_var dept_cur%ROWTYPE;
BEGIN
  FOR dept_var IN dept_cur
  LOOP
    INSERT INTO dept VALUES(dept_var.dept_no,
    dept_var.dept_name);
  END LOOP;
END;
/
```

Q: *What is the advantage of using cursor parameters?*

A: First, cursor parameters can be used to limit the local variables in a block. Next, the same cursor definition can be used for different parameter values, avoiding the code repetition.

Q: *Can you reference the same parameters in more than one cursor definition?*

A: No, the scope of the cursor parameters is limited to only one cursor definition.

Q: *What is a cursor variable? What are the advantages?*

A: A cursor variable is defined like a PL/SQL variable with a few exceptions. First, you have to define a cursor type declaration. Here is its syntax:

```
TYPE <cursor_type_name> IS REF CURSOR RETURN <return_type>;
```

Here's an actual example:

```
TYPE dept_cur_type IS REF CURSOR RETURN dept_cur%ROWTYPE;
```

Then you can declare the cursor variable. Its syntax is as follows: Here's an example:

```
dept_cur_type_var dept_cur_type;
```

This can be used to make the code more generic and reusable. It can also be used to pass variables from precompilers to a PL/SQL block and back.

Q: *What tells SQL*PLUS to display the DBMS_OUTPUT?*

A: Two steps are involved here. First, you need to type the following command at SQL prompt in SQL*PLUS.

```
SQL> SET SERVEROUTPUT ON
```

Next, you need to use a DBMS_OUTPUT package within the PL/SQL script. Here's an example:

```
DECLARE
  i char(1);
BEGIN
  i := 'A';
  DBMS_OUTPUT.PUT_LINE('Value of I is: ' || i );
END;
/
```

Q: *What is the difference between procedures and functions?*

A: Functions can return a value, whereas procedures cannot. The function value is returned through the use of the RETURN command. Functions can be used as part of an expression.

Q: *Explain stored procedures and stored functions.*

A: The format of stored procedures or stored functions is similar to regular procedures and functions, except that it is stored in the database. Here's an example:

```
CREATE OR REPLACE PROCEDURE dept_task_proc(dept_id number,
task_id number) AS
BEGIN
  IF (dept_id > 5) AND (task_id < 3) THEN
    UPDATE dept_task_tbl
    SET task_hours := task_hours + 8
    WHERE dept_no = dept_id
  AND task_no = task_id;
END;
/
```

Q: *What are the advantages of stored procedures and functions?*

A: It provides consistency, security, easy maintenance, and better performance. It is centrally located in the database, views the source code through the data dictionary, and reduces network traffic.

Q: *How do you invoke a procedure?*

A: You can call a procedure in SQL*PLUS by using the execute command. Its syntax is as follows:

```
SQL> execute procedure_name(parameter1,...., ...);
```

Here's an example:

```
SQL> execute dept_task_proc(dept_id, task_id);
```

Q: *How do you recompile a stored procedure?*

A: You can use the CREATE OR REPLACE PROCEDURE command. You can also use the ALTER PROCEDURE procedure_name COMPILE command.

Q: *How do you recompile a stored function?*

A: You can use the CREATE OR REPLACE FUNCTION command. You can also use the ALTER FUNCTION function_name COMPILE command.

Q: *If a compilation fails, how can you see the errors?*

A: You can see the errors using the SHOW ERRORS command. You can also use the USER_ERRORS table to display the errors.

Q: *How do you view the source code of the stored procedure or function?*

A: You can use the USER_SOURCE table to view the source code of all stored objects. Here's an example:

```
SELECT text
FROM user_source
WHERE name = object_name
```

Q: *What are the argument qualifiers in procedures or functions?*

A: Three argument qualifiers are used for procedures and functions.

- *IN* When calling a procedure, the procedure takes in the value of the IN argument.
- *OUT* It sends the value back to the caller through the OUT argument.
- *IN OUT* It does both.

Q: *What is overloading?*

A: Overloading is an object-oriented technique. You can have the same procedure name but with different arguments that have different data types:

```
dept_task_proc(task_rate number);
dept_task_proc(10.75);

dept_task_proc(task_hours integer);
dept_task_proc(8);
```

In this example, you can see the same procedure names with different data types of different parameters.

Q: *What is a package?*

A: A package is a group of objects, such as procedures, functions, variables, cursors, and exceptions. A package usually consists of two components: a specification and a body. The specification component has the declaration of variables, cursors, procedures, functions, and exceptions. The body component has the definition of the declared elements and it implements the specification component. An example of an package specification is as follows:

```
CREATE OR REPLACE PACKAGE dept_pkg_spec AS
dept_min NUMBER;
dept_max NUMBER;
CURSOR dept_cur IS
    SELECT dept_no, dept_name
    FROM department
    WHERE dept_no IS NOT NULL;
  dept_var dept_cur%ROWTYPE;

PROCEDURE dept_task_proc(dept_id number, task_id number);
END dept_pkg_spec;
```

Here's an example of a package body:

```
CREATE OR REPLACE PACKAGE BODY dept_pkg IS
PROCEDURE dept_task_proc(dept_id number, task_id number);
BEGIN
  IF (dept_id > 5) AND (task_id < 3) THEN
  UPDATE dept_task_tbl
  SET task_hours := task_hours + 8
```

```
  WHERE dept_no = dept_id
  AND task_no = task_id;
END;
END dept_pkg;
```

Q: *How do you recompile a package?*

A: Packages must be recompiled after you make any changes. Package recompilation neither changes the package definition nor any of its objects. You can use the ALTER PACKAGE package_name COMPILE command. If you make an edit within the package body, you only need to recompile the package body and not the package header. If you make an edit within the package header, you need to recompile both the package header and body.

If you want to compile the package body only, then you can type in the following command:

```
ALTER PACKAGE package_name COMPILE BODY;
```

If you want to compile both a package body and specification, you can type in the following command:

```
ALTER PACKAGE package_name COMPILE PACKAGE;
```

Q: *How do you invoke an object in a package?*

A: You can invoke a procedure or function within a package. Here is its syntax:

```
Package_name.object_name
```

Here's an example:

```
dept_pkg.dept_task_proc(dept_id, task_id);
```

Q: *What does the %ROWCOUNT attribute do?*

A: The %ROWCOUNT attribute can be used to find out the number of rows processed when performing a DML transaction load. It can be used for insert, update, and delete statements. Here's an example:

```
DELETE FROM dept WHERE dept_id = 10;
DBMS_OUTPUT.PUT_LINE('Number of rows deleted: || SQL%ROW-
COUNT);
```

Q: *What is the difference between %TYPE and %ROWTYPE?*

A: The %TYPE attribute can be used for a variable to inherit the definition of a table column data type. Its syntax is as follows:

```
<variable_name > <table_name>.<column_name>%TYPE;
```

Here's an example:

```
dept_number dept.dept_no%TYPE;
```

%ROWTYPE can be used for a variable to inherit the definition of the entire table record:

```
dept_rec dept%ROWTYPE;
```

Q: *What is a PL/SQL record?*

A: A PL/SQL record is a group of fields representing a logical structure (a table row) and of the type RECORD. Here's an example:

```
TYPE dept_rec IS RECORD
(dept_id INTEGER,
dept_name VARCHAR2(20));
```

Q: *What is a PL/SQL table? What is the difference between a database table and a PL/SQL table?*

A: A PL/SQL table is a composite data type and an object of the type TABLE. PL/SQL table has at least one column and one binary integer key. It can have any number of records. It works like an array variable in third-generation languages. A PL/SQL table is not like a database table. The structure and data are all held in memory. Its syntax is as follows:

```
TYPE <type_name> IS TABLE OF
<table_name>.<column_name>%TYPE
INDEX BY BINARY_INTEGER;
```

Q: *How do you insert and update a row in a PL/SQL table?*

A: It's simple. You have to use an array-like syntax to reference a row in a PL/SQL table. The following example shows how to insert or update a row numbered 45 in PL/SQL:

```
dept_name(45) := 'Procurement';
```

Q: *How do you delete a row in a PL/SQL table?*

A: The following example can be used to delete a row numbered 45 in PL/SQL:

```
dept_name(45);
```

Q: *What is a database trigger?*

A: A database trigger, stored in a table, can be fired when some DML event occurs to that table. A trigger can be fired by the database when insert, update, and delete actions take place. Twelve types of triggers are available in PL/SQL:

```
BEFORE INSERT ROW
AFTER INSERT ROW
BEFORE INSERT STATEMENT
AFTER INSERT STATEMENT

BEFORE UPDATE ROW
AFTER UPDATE ROW
BEFORE UPDATE STATEMENT
AFTER UPDATE STATEMENT

BEFORE DELETE ROW
AFTER DELETE ROW
BEFORE DELETE STATEMENT
AFTER DELETE STATEMENT
```

Here is its syntax:

```
CREATE OR REPLACE TRIGGER <trigger_name>
{ BEFORE | AFTER | INSTEAD OF }
{ DELETE | UPDATE | INSERT [ of column list ]} ON
<table_name>
FOR EACH ROW [ WHEN <condition true>]
<PL/SQL block>
```

Q: *What is the difference between a row-level trigger and a statement-level trigger?*

A: A row-level trigger executes once for each row in a transaction, whereas a statement-level trigger executes once for each transaction.

Q: *What is a mutating table error?*

A: A mutating table error occurs when a trigger modifies the contents of the same table where the trigger is defined on.

Q: *How can you view the source code of database triggers?*

A: No direct command in PL/SQL enables the viewing of the database triggers' source code, but you can view the information by querying the USER_TRIGGERS table. You can view the information from these three columns: DESCRIPTION, WHEN_CLAUSE, and TRIGGER_BODY, based on TRIGGER_NAME.

Q: *Can you disable the trigger? If you can, when do you disable the trigger?*

A: Yes, triggers can be enabled or disabled based on the context. You can use the following syntax to enable or disable a trigger.

```
ALTER TRIGGER <trigger_name> {ENABLED | DISABLED}
```

It can be useful to disable the triggers when loading the data.

Q: *What is an exception?*

A: An exception is an error that occurs during run time. When an error is encountered, the program control automatically goes to an error-handling section. This section always starts with an EXCEPTION reserved word and terminates with the END command.

Q: *What are the Oracle predefined exception errors?*

A: The commonly used predefined exception errors are as follows:

- TOO_MANY_ROWS returns more than one row, rather than a single row.
- NO_DATA_FOUND returns no data.
- ZERO_DIVIDE tries to divide by zero.
- INVALID_NUMBER is used when a number-to-string conversion fails.
- INVALID_CURSOR is an illegal cursor operation.
- VALUE_ERROR is when a truncation, conversion, or arithmetic error occurred.
- DUP_VAL_ON_INDEX tries to insert duplicate information on the unique columns.

Q: *Which exception traps all the errors?*

A: You can use an OTHERS clause to trap all the exception errors other than the defined ones.

Q: *What is a pragma?*

A: A pragma is a compiler directive and is used to handle the undefined oracle errors. Its syntax is as follows:

```
PRAGMA exception_init (exception_name, error_no);
```

You must define the pragmas in the declaration section of a PL/SQL block.

Q: *What is a transaction?*

A: A transaction is a logical unit of work. In Oracle, two types of transactions exist: commit and rollback. Commit submits the transaction to the database, while rollback works like an undo command.

Q: *What are the main transaction statements?*

A: As stated earlier, these consist of COMMIT, which submits a transaction, and ROLLBACK, which cancels a transaction.

Q: *What is SAVEPOINT?*

A: SAVEPOINT is an intermediate point within a transaction to which you can rollback.

Q: *How do you perform row-level locking?*

A: Row-level locking can be performed using the FOR UPDATE clause in a select statement. Here's an example:

```
SELECT dept_no, dept_name
FROM dept
WHERE dept_no = 10
FOR UPDATE;
```

Q: *How do you perform table-level locking?*

A: Table locks can be performed using the following five different modes: exclusive, share lock, row share, row exclusive, and share row exclusive.

Questions and Answers

Advanced

Q: *How do you tune the PL/SQL statements?*

A: You can tune the SQL or PL/SQL statements with the following checklist:

- Examine the indexes.
- Examine the optimization rules. Cost-based optimization is best.
- Set the SQL TRACE session to display the statistics.
- Use the EXPLAIN PLAN mechanism.
- Use the SET AUTOTRACE function in SQL*Plus to automatically see the EXPLAIN PLANS.
- Use ROWID to speed up the query processing.
- Tune subqueries, if necessary.

- Use explicit cursors as much as you can.
- Specify the driving table.
- Use hints wherever needed.
- Use PL/SQL tables to improve performance.
- Monitor the shared pool usage.

Q: *Which PL/SQL packages support I/O processes?*

A: The following are widely used packages for I/O processes:

- The DBMS_OUTPUT package
- The TEXT_IO package
- The UTL_FILE package

Q: *What is the difference between the DBMS_OUTPUT package and the UTL_FILE package?*

A: DBMS_OUTPUT can be used for standard output, which means writing it to a screen, whereas the UTIL_FILE package can be used to handle the file I/O processing.

Q: *What are the steps for defining a process for file reading?*

A: Reading the input from a file consists of four main steps. File I/O processing in PL/SQL is similar to the one in C language:

- Declare a file handler using the UTIL_FILE package.
- Open a file with FOPEN.
- Read a line from the file using the GET_LINE function.
- Close the file using FCLOSE.
  The syntax is as follows:

```
DECLARE
  <file_handler_variable> UTIL_FILE.FILE_TYPE;
BEGIN
    <file_handler_variable> := UTL_FILE.FOPEN(file_
    location, file_name, access_mode);
  GET_LINE(file_handler_variable, buffer_text);
  FCLOSE(file_handler_variable);
END;
```

Access mode should be "r" for file input.

Q: *What are the steps for defining a process for file writing?*

A: Writing the output to a file consists of four main steps. File I/O processing in PL/SQL is similar to the one in C:

- Declare a file handler using the UTIL_FILE package.
- Open a file with FOPEN.
- Read a line from the file using the PUT_LINE function.
- Close the file using FCLOSE.

Its syntax is as follows:

```
DECLARE
  <file_handler_variable> UTIL_FILE.FILE_TYPE;
BEGIN
    <file_handler_variable> := UTL_FILE.FOPEN(file_
    location, file_name, access_mode);
  PUT_LINE(file_handler_variable, buffer_text);
  FCLOSE(file_handler_variable);
END;
```

Access modes should be either "w" for write or "a" for append.

Q: *Which function do you use to clear the buffer and flush the data to the OS file?*

A: A FFLUSH function can be used to clear the buffer text and write to the OS file.

Q: *What is the difference between PUT, PUTF, and PUTLINE?*

A: The PUT function just writes the output to a file. The PUTLINE function adds the newline character at the end of the line. The PUTF function is used for formatted output.

Q: *What is the maximum buffer size for I/O operations using the UTL_FILE package?*

A: For input, the maximum size is 1,022 bytes. For output, the maximum size is 1,023 bytes.

Q: *What is an abstract data type?*

A: An abstract data type supports object-based programming. It is a new technique introduced in Oracle 8. It is a type of object with a class definition at the database level. It is also referred to as an object type.

Here's an example:

```
CREATE TYPE cust_addr_type AS OBJECT
(addr1   VARCHAR2(30),
addr2    VARCHAR2(30),
```

```
city      VARCHAR2(20),
state     VARCHAR2(2),
zip       VARCHAR2(5));
```

Let's look at the abstract data type in the following object table's creation script:

```
CREATE TABLE customer(
Customer_no NUMBER;
Customer_name VARCHAR2(30);
Address cust_addr_type);
```

Q: *What is the difference between database tables and object tables?*

A: A database table is a collection of common tables and is defined based on the relational management. Object tables are similar to database tables, except they store objects as table columns. Object types are defined based on the object-oriented techniques.

Q: *What is a method?*

A: A method is a collection of operations that affect the objects.

Q: *How many methods does an object have in Oracle 8?*

A: Three main methods are widely used in Oracle 8:

- The *accessor method* is used to get an object's attributes.
- The *constructor method* is used to create instance of that type.
- The *mutator method* is used to set the attribute values.

Q: *In object types, which method is defined automatically by Oracle 8?*

A: Constructor Method.

Q: *Can you define object types within PL/SQL procedures or functions?*

A: No, it can only be defined at the database level.

Q: *What are collectors?*

A: Collectors are data element sets that are considered to be part of a single record. Two types of collectors are available in Oracle 8: *varying arrays* (VARRAYs) and *nested tables.*

Q: What is a varying array (VARRAY)?

A: VARRAYs are data element sets referenced with the same data type. VARRAYs can be defined based on only one column.

Let's take an example. One order can have multiple products, and one product can have multiple orders. In a conventional relational fashion, you can join these two tables to retrieve the relevant information. You can also store the same relevant information at one place using VARRAYS. It can improve the performance while avoiding the conventional approach. The following statement creates a VARRAY called products_va:

```
CREATE OR REPLACE TYPE products_va AS VARRAY(10) OF NUMBER;
```

Now you can reference a VARRAY for a data element in a table:

```
Create table orders
(order_no NUMBER,
products products_va);
```

Q: *When you describe VARRAY tables, how are the VARRAY elements defined?*

A: You can see VARRAY elements defined as a RAW data type. Here is an example:

```
SQL> DESC ORDERS
Name          TYPE
________________________
ORDER_NO NUMBER
PRODUCTS      RAW
```

Q: *How would you identify the exact data type of a VARRAY?*

A: You can use USER_TAB_COLUMNS.DATA_TYPE to identify it. You can further identify the exact data type using USER_TYPES.TYPECODE based on the TYPE_NAME.

Q: *What is a nested table?*

A: A nested table, like a nested query, is a table within a table.

Q: *What is the difference between a VARRAY and a nested table?*

A: Both VARRAYs and nested tables function in the same manner with few differences. VARRAYs have a limitation on the number of entries per record, whereas nested tables have no limitations. Nested tables support a greater flexibility when querying, whereas varying arrays do not.

Q: *What is a LOB?*

A: A LOB, a large object, is used to store huge volumes of data such as audio, video, and so on. It can store data up to four GB. The available four LOB data types are BLOB, CLOB, NCLOB, and BFILE:

BLOB	The Binary Large Object holds binary data and is stored internally.
CLOB	The Character Large Object holds character data and is stored internally.
NCLOB	The National Character Large Object holds multi-byte character sets and is stored internally.
BFILE	The Binary File is a pointer to external file. It is located externally on the operating system directories.

Q: *Can you write to external files using BFILE?*

A: No, you can only read from the external files.

Q: *Which function do you use for ConText queries?*

A: The CONTAINS function is used to retrieve ConText queries.

Q: *Which package do you use to send event-based notifications?*

A: The DBMS_ALERT package.

Q: *Which package do you use for scheduling PL/SQL jobs?*

A: The DBMS_JOB package.

Q: *Which package do you use to send messages between sessions?*

A: The DBMS_PIPE package.

Q: *Which package do you use to create dynamic SQL or PL/SQL scripts?*

A: The DBMS_SQL package.

Q: *Which package do you use for various utilities?*

A: The DBMS_UTILITY package.

Q: *Which package do you use for system utilities?*

A: The DBMS_SYSTEM package.

Q: *Which package do you use for file I/O?*

A: The UTL_FILE package.

Q: *What is a PL/SQL cartridge?*

A: A PL/SQL cartridge is a process that can be used to run in the Oracle application server and in the Oracle database. You can run PL/SQL code through the Web URL.

Q: *What is a PL/SQL Web toolkit?*

A: The PL/SQL Web toolkit, a group of PL/SQL packages, is used to implement the PL/SQL cartridges in the application server. Three components are available in the Web toolkit:

- *Hypertext Procedures* (HTTP) sends HTML code to the Web browser.
- *Hypertext Functions* (HTF) returns HTML code as a function return value.
- The *Oracle Web Agent* (OWA) works as a common gateway interface.

Q: *Do you need to write HTML code within the PL/SQL code?*

A: No, you cannot directly write the HTML code within the PL/SQL. This can be achieved in two ways:

1. You can write HTML tags using the PL/SQL Web toolkit. Knowledge of HTML helps you understand the format of the Web toolkit easily.
2. Use the HTP.PRINT procedure to embed your own HTML code.

Q: *How do you pass parameters from the Web browser to the PL/SQL cartridges?*

A: You can use GET or POST methods to pass the parameters from the Web browser to the PL/SQL cartridges.

Q: *What are the main techniques used to connect Java programs to an Oracle 8i database?*

A: Two techniques are available: *Java Database Connectivity* (JDBC) and SQLJ.

Q: *What is SQLJ?*

A: SQLJ is an Oracle preprocessor like Pro*C that can be used to embed SQL statements within the Java code.

Q: *Which file extension is used for SQLJ source code?*

A: You have to use the *.sqlj* file extension for SQLJ source code.

Q: *What is SQLJ Translator?*

A: SQLJ Translator is a preprocessor that converts SQLJ source code into Java code.

Q: *Which command do you use to compile SQLJ code?*

A: You can use the following example command to translate SQLJ code.

Its syntax is as follows:

```
Sqlj -user username/password filename.sqlj
```

Q: *How do I use autonomous PL/SQL blocks?*

A: You must create a new procedure that is called from the original procedure. In the define section of this new procedure, you must place the keyword PRAGMA AUTONOMOUS_TRANSACTION. Thus, this new PL/SQL block runs in its own transaction without interfering with the transaction from the calling program.

Q: *How do I implement invoker right procedures?*

A: In the CREATE PROCEDURE | FUNCTION | PACKAGE command, you include the keywords AUTHID CURRENT_USER. Here's an example:

```
CREATE PROCEDURE my_proc ( param1 VARCHAR2, param2 VARCHAR2 )
                    AUTHID CURRENT_USER
                    AS
BEGIN
  INSERT INTO log_table VALUES (param1,param2);
  COMMIT;
END;
```

11
Unix

Val Carciu

The Unix system has a strange and perhaps unique history. Like many great ideas, it started as a space travel game developed by Ken Thompson and Dennis Ritchie for the DEC PDP at the beginning of 1970. Following this, they created a new file system structure, similar in concept to the file system currently in use. A processing environment with scheduling was added and the rest, of what today would be considered a rudimentary operating system, followed. Beginning in 1971, this original version was written in assembly language. At the same time, the "C" programming language was being developed. C then became the language used in the development of the Unix system. The kernel (memory resident part of the operating system) was recoded in C in 1973. Today, with very few exceptions, the entire Unix operating system is coded in the C language. C's portability is widely regarded as a major reason for the popularity of the Unix system.

The new operating system, Unix, captured the imagination of the computer scientists at AT&T Bell Laboratories. After three years, about a dozen Unix systems were running on different machines. By the mid-1970s, however, Unix became a functional operating system running on the DEC PDP-11. At the same time, AT&T released copies of the Unix system to universities around the world, which is how the BSD Unix (Berkeley Software Distribution) from the University of California at Berkeley came into being. Today's BSD implementation can be found in many universities and engineering communities, and the current BSD "splinter" operating systems include BSDI (commercially-supported BSD), FreeBSD (ostensibly focused on the i386 architecture), NetBSD (with a stress on portability between architectures), and OpenBSD (with a focus on security). AT&T also has moved to optimize the Unix system for the business community by rolling in some of the early BSD innovations and including many of their own. After a period of transition and changes, they came up with a standardized release—Unix System V. Today, Unix System V represents a majority of the commercial Unix market.

The Unix Job Interview

Over the years, several computer manufacturers have developed their own versions of Unix System V: SCO Unix System V Release 3 and UnixWare, IBM, AIX, HP-UX, and Solaris.

An interviewer will normally target specific areas of knowledge. The level of expertise expected is as follows:

- A "novice" Unix user should have knowledge about how to log in and out, what a password is and how to change it, the structure of directories and files, most of the commands related to directories and files, the vi editor, basic access to the development tools, and probably the most important of all, how to get help using Unix's on-line help facilities.
- An intermediate user, in addition to all of the above, should have knowledge about permissions and the related commands, pipes and redirection, processes, writing small scripts, different types of shells and environment, the structure of filesystems, print services, and related commands.
- An expert (usually the Unix system administrator) should know how to start and stop the system (including customization), use the audit subsystem, administer user accounts, and also manage and back up filesystems. In addition, he or she should know how to upgrade the hardware configuration, maintain system security, administer terminals, utilize modems (that is, remote logins), build a network using TCP/IP, "tune" system performance, and probably most important of all, troubleshoot the system.

It is dangerous to try to address "Unix development." Development on Unix is done with a variety of tools (the Bourne shell, C, C++, perl, awk, sed, Python, TCL, Java, and so on), and all of these tools have been ported to other operating systems and platforms. No single development language can really be considered Unix-centric, existing solely for Unix. The only thing that really marks Unix development is the system call interface to the Unix kernel, as laid down in the POSIX standards for the C programming language. In any case, the temptation to include a bit of the C interface to the kernel cannot be resisted, and it is included at the end of the chapter.

Questions and Answers

Q: *Describe the steps the system goes through, at boot time, before the users may sign on.*

A: When a Unix system is turned on, regardless of the architecture, a bootstrap program allows the administrator to boot the default Unix kernel or specify the name of an old kernel if an older version is desired. The system will display information, among which the hardware recognition (when you can see if your parallel port is recognized) is the most important. Next, it verifies if the root filesystem needs checking (is "dirty" or was cleanly unmounted at shutdown). If the root filesystem needs checking, you will be prompted to allow the checking and repair (fsck utility) of the root filesystem. When the cleaning is complete, various scripts continue bringing up Unix into either single or multiuser mode depending upon the configuration and options passed to the boot manager. Single-user mode is chosen mostly when system maintenance is needed. Once multiuser mode is chosen (or if it is the default boot level), a prompt is presented to enter the system time or take the default. The system then executes commands found in the /etc/rc* directories, generating startup messages for the various system services, such as the printer or network services. Finally, the system displays the login prompt.

Q: *When, and depending on what, are the other filesystems checked and mounted?*

A: The other filesystems are mounted after the root filesystem mount is complete. They are checked and mounted depending on the entries found by the system in a mount table file at boot time (the name, location, and structure of this table vary between the Unix vendors).

Q: *Name two ways to bring the system down. (Do not even think about turning the power off.)*

A: The most commonly used, and the recommended way, is shutdown. This will warn the user that the system is coming down and unless otherwise specified, will have a one-minute grace period (may be different from one implementation to another). Simply turning the power off will not properly unmount the filesystem; instead, it could possibly force a lengthy check upon boot.

The second way is the haltsys (or halt for BSD) command. This command halts the system immediately. It should not be used unless in single-user mode. The users are logged out (their work will be lost) and network servers and other programs are terminated abnormally. It is also a defined behavior that the system can be brought down by killing the init process with the default SIGINT signal, although this is rarely done in practice.

Q: *What are the files checked or scripts executed when a user logs in?*

A: The order is: /etc/passwd, /etc/profile, $HOME/.profile, and in case the Korn shell is used, $HOME/.kshrc. If the C shell is used, .profile is replaced by .login and .kshrc by .cshrc (although the C shell and its derivatives are rapidly losing popularity).

Q: *When an account, for various reasons, is not used anymore, how can the system administrator disable it?*

A: This can be accomplished in several ways. Assuming normal Unix authentication, the administrator can change the password with the *passwd* command, alternately edit the /etc/passwd file and replace the second field of the users password entry with an asterix (*), or remove the entry from /etc/passwd entirely. If this is done, the entries should be removed from /etc/group and /etc/shadow as well, the home directory and mail spool of the user should be removed, and all files owned by the user should be deleted or assigned to other users. The administrator should run the *find* utility to ensure that no files remain on the system that are owned by the user. If something other than standard Unix authentication is in use, such as NIS, DCE, Hesiod Bind, or a PAM-based authentication mechanism, this process will be different.

Q: *How can a user ensure that certain sensitive files cannot be read by others?*

A: Use GnuPG (available at http://www.gnupg.org). To encrypt a plain text file with Gnupg, enter "gpg -c textfile" where "textfile" is the name of the file that you want to encrypt. Enter the password twice as requested, and "textfile.gpg" will appear in the same location as the original file. Delete the original file (if desired), and when the time comes to decrypt, simply enter "gpg textfile.gpg" and provide the valid passphrase. The original file should appear. The old Unix crypt command should no longer be used. The contents of the files can be verified with cksum or md5sum if they are available on your Unix implementation and the checksums were previously computed.

Q: *How can a user remind another user about an important meeting taking place on a certain date, at a certain hour?*

A: A very good way is to use the at command as it follows:

```
$ at 9:30am Mar 29
echo "Meeting at 10" | mail frank
<Ctrl-d>
```

Q: *How can a user execute a long command and still have the terminal available for work?*

A: The user may execute the long command in the background using the & command as follows:

```
$ wc -c hugefil > wordcount &
```

Q: *Once the background command has been started, can it be aborted like any other foreground command?*

A: If the shell has job control, the command "fg" will bring the background process to the foreground, where the interrupt key (Control-C) will kill it (unless a signal handler is installed). Otherwise, background commands cannot be aborted with the interrupt key; instead, you have to use the kill command. The shell will print a number when launching a background process. This number is the Process ID (PID) of the background process and would be supplied to the kill command to terminate the process. For example, kill 123 would send the default kill signal (SIGINT). It is possible that the program has configured itself to ignore SIGINT, in which case signal level 9 (SIGKILL) could be used to forcibly terminate the process, as in kill -9 123.

Q: *What is a filesystem?*

A: A filesystem is a distinct division of the operating system consisting of files, directories, and the information needed to locate them. A filesystem can be thought of as a structure upon which directories and files are constructed.

Q: *What happens if you have a directory such as /tmp, and you mount a filesystem such as /dev/u, on this directory?*

A: If any files existed in the /tmp directory before the filesystem was mounted, they will disappear and then reappear when the filesystem is unmounted.

Q: *Can the system administrator enable users to mount a filesystem?*

A: Normally, only the super user can mount or unmount filesystems. Some vendors offer proprietary Unix extensions to grant this ability to non-root users, but a method to accomplish this that is largely portable across different Unix versions is the use of the sudo package. A non-root user might need these permissions in order to mount a CD-ROM or a floppy.

Q: *Does it make sense for a directory to have the execute permission on it?*

A: Yes, it does. If a directory does not have the execute permission on it, you cannot do a cd command to it.

Q: *By default, the GID (group identifier) of a newly created file is set to the GID of the creating process or user. How can this behavior be changed?*

A: This behavior can be changed by setting the SGID bit on that directory which results in a new file having the GID of the directory.

Q: *What is a link between files, and what is the command you would use to link files?*

A: A link is a directory entry referring to an inode. The same inode (file) can have several links. Any changes made to the file are effectively independent of the name by which the file is known. A file is not deleted until its last link is removed. The command to create links is ln.

Q: *What are the two types of links?*

A: Hard links, which increase the link count for a file and cannot span filesystem boundaries, and soft links, which can span filesystems but do not increase the link count.

Q: *Which type of link consumes an inode, and which type does not?*

A: A soft link will always consume an inode, but secondary hard links will not. Each physical file in a filesystem consumes a single inode, regardless of the number of hard links. A soft link, which cannot contain inode information since it may be on a separate filesystem, must consume an inode.

Q: *What is the most common way of locating files?*

A: The most common way is by using the find command, which enables you to locate all files with a specified name, permissions setting, size, type, owner, or last access or modification date. The locate and whereis commands are also prevalent on many versions of Unix, and might be useful.

Q: *How can you search a file for occurrences of a word or phrase?*

A: The grep command displays all lines in a file that contain the key word or phrase. It is a good practice to enclose the search pattern in single quotes in order to protect it from command substitution in the shell.

Q: *How can you list the names of all files in all subdirectories in which there is a certain pattern?*

A: You can use a combination of two commands:

```
find . -exec grep -1 "pattern" {} \;
```

Q: *Assuming you have a big file and you want to clear it (empty it), but you want to keep the file and its permissions, what could you do?*

A: You may use the following commands:

```
$ > filename #(for the Bourne family of shells)
```

or

```
$ cat /dev/null > filename #(for C shell)
```

Q: *Assuming that a directory becomes too large (has too many entries) and you decide to make two directories out of it (one of which has the same name), how would you proceed?*

A: On some Unix filesystem implementations, a directory, even if you remove all files it contains, never shrinks. Therefore, you should make two new directories, move all files into them, remove the old directory, and then rename one of the new directories using the name of the old one.

Q: *What is the purpose of the lost+found directory in a filesystem?*

A: During fsck (filesystem check) command, any files that are unreferenced but valid are placed in this special directory called lost+found. Depending upon the filesystem implementation, the fsck command does not create or extend this directory; therefore, it has to contain a sufficient number of empty slots for fsck to use when reconnecting files.

Q: *List three commands most often used for archive or data transfer between devices.*

A: The three most common are: tar, cpio, and dd.

Q: *If you were to make a script to back up your system, how would you make it?*

A: The script would look something like:

```
            cd /
find . -follow -print | cpio -ovaBL > /dev/rmt0h 2>
/u/list
```

where in the file /u/list a list of the backed-up files would be obtained. Otherwise, you could use an alternate approach of:

```
tar cvf /dev/rct02 .
```

If you are using GNU tar, you can use the "cvzf" option to enable compression (but cpio has better ability to recover from faulty tape). These scripts should have root's permissions.

Q: *Once you obtain a stable system, that is, a good kernel, what are some of the first things the system administrator should do?*

A: First, a backup of the entire system should be made. Then, depending upon directions for the specific Unix implementation, the administrator should make a bootable diskette and then a root filesystem diskette. This way, if the root filesystem gets corrupted beyond repair, you can boot the system and restore the system from tapes.

Q: *What steps should be followed when you find you have an unusable root filesystem?*

A: In case of an unusable root filesystem, the administrator can either reinstall the OS, or, if good backups exist, run fsck on the root filesystem until it passes (or reformat it), then follow these steps:

1. Boot from the diskette.
2. Insert the root filesystem diskette, when prompted.
3. mount /dev/hd0root /mnt
4. cd /mnt
5. ./usr/bin/tar xvf ./dev/rct0
6. umount /dev/hd0root
7. Reboot.

Q: *Can you copy files to a DOS floppy on a Unix system?*

A: Yes, the command to use is mcopy which is part of the "mtools" (available from http://www.tux.org/pub/tux/knaff/mtools/index.html). This command permits copying in both directions. An example is

```
mcopy /john/send a:
```

Q: *How can you find out the baud rate, the parity scheme, and other information about a serial line?*

A: By using the following command:

```
$ stty < /dev/ttyS0
```

Intermediate Questions

Q: *How do you set the terminal type?*

A: The preferable method for setting the terminal type is to assign the type to the TERM variable. This is usually done in .profile or .login sign-on scripts.

Q: *What performance tools can you use to diagnose system inefficiency?*

A: Depending upon what tools are available in your Unix version, top, sar, prof, time, timex, and also ps commands may be used. The top, ps, and sar commands view a "snapshot" image of system utilization. The time and timex commands gather detailed information on elapsed time and processor consumption over the life of a process. The prof tools enable the user to access detailed data on execution times for the individual functions within a program.

Q: *How can the time command be used?*

A: This command reports the time and resources consumed during the execution of a command.

Q: *What is swapping (paging)?*

A: As processes request more memory in order to run, the paging daemon is responsible for freeing up memory by writing pages of memory from other (hopefully inactive) processes to the disk swap area.

Q: *What should you do in the case of an intense swapping/paging activity?*

A: This activity is a sign that not enough memory is available for applications. The best thing to do is to increase the memory size. A temporary solution might be to decrease the buffer cache size, although this might decrease disk performance.

Q: *How can you check the status of processes?*

A: You can check the status of your task using ps command. This command lists all the active processes that are running, both in the foreground and background. The most useful options for ps under System V are **ps -ef**, while under BSD-style it is **ps aux**.

Q: *How can you stop a runaway process?*

A: To stop a process, use the kill command followed by an optional signal level and the required process ID. Signal names, their levels, and their normal behavior differ between Unix distributions. Omitting the optional signal level normally passes signal 2 (SIGINT) to the process.

Q: *Assuming that you have to start the execution of a long command and you want to log out and go home, how do you go about it?*

A: You can start the command in background, using the nohup command. The command would look like this: nohup command &. This traps the HUP signal that is sent when you exit the shell. You can now log out, and the process continues in background.

Q: *How can you prioritize processes?*

A: Assuming you do not need the results of your command immediately, use the nice command, for example, nice -15 latecommand. The command will execute with the priority of 35, instead of the default of 20. Only the root user can increase the priority of a process; other users can only affect a decrease. The root user, and only the root user, is allowed to raise the priority of a process which can be accomplished with a command of the form nice +5 earlycommand. Some versions of Unix also include the renice command, which can be used to adjust the priority of a process already running.

Q: *How can you schedule programs to run at specific times?*

A: Unix systems enable you to run programs automatically at specified times by using the cron or at programs. For cron, first create a crontab file, and then submit it to cron by using the crontab command.

Q: *What is a shell?*

A: A shell is a command interpreter. The shell gives the user a high-level language in which to communicate with the operating system.

Q: *How does the shell execute the commands?*

A: For the shell to execute a command, it has to be executable (to have the execute permission). If the command is a compiled program, the shell, as parent, creates a child process that immediately executes that program. If the command is a shell procedure (file containing shell commands), the shell forks a child to read the file and execute the commands inside.

Q: *How does the shell locate commands that the user wishes to execute?*

A: The sequence of directories that are searched is given by the shell PATH variable. Directory pathnames are separated by colons.

Q: *Which are the characters you could use to form regular expressions to match other characters?*

A: Some of these special characters are: the asterisk (*), which matches any string, including the null string; the question mark (?), which matches any one character; and any sequence of characters enclosed within brackets ([and]), which matches any one of the enclosed characters. Extended regular expressions and regular expressions unique to the perl scripting language add much more flexibility to these simple wildcard functions.

Q: *How can you redirect the output of a command?*

A: To redirect the output of a command, use > or >> redirection arguments. When > argument is used, a file will be created (or replaced if it exists) as standard output. When >> argument is used, the standard output is appended to the end of the file. The error output can also be redirected, but the semantics of doing so differ depending upon the shell family in use.

Q: *How can a command take the input from a file?*

A: Make a file the input for a command by using the < argument. For instance: sort < infile.

Q: *What is command substitution?*

A: Any command line can be placed within back quotation marks (`) so that the output of the command replaces the quoted command itself. This concept is known as command substitution.

Q: *What are positional parameters (arguments)?*

A: When a shell procedure is invoked, the shell implicitly creates positional parameters (arguments). The name of the shell procedure itself in position zero on the command line is assigned to the positional parameter $0. The first command argument is called $1, and so on.

Q: *What is a pipeline for a shell script?*

A: A pipeline is a sequence of one or more commands separated by vertical bars (|). In a pipeline, the standard output of each command (except the last) is connected (by a pipe) to the standard input of the next command. Each command in a pipeline is run separately; the shell waits for the last command to finish. A simple example of a pipeline is

```
cat /etc/passwd | grep luser | awk -F: '{print $3}' | more
```

Q: *How can you use parentheses or braces at the command line or in a shell procedure?*

A: A simple command in a pipeline can be replaced by a command list enclosed in either parentheses or braces. The output of all the enclosed commands is combined into one stream that becomes the input to the next command in the pipeline.

Q: *What is the difference between using parentheses and using braces?*

A: When parentheses are used, the shell forks a subshell that reads and executes the enclosed commands. Unlike parentheses, no subshell is forked for braces; the enclosed commands are simply read and executed by the shell.

Q: *What are functions from the shell's standpoint?*

A: Functions are like separate shell scripts, except they reside in memory and are executed by the shell process, not by a separate process.

Q: *What is a command's environment?*

A: All variables and their associated values that are known to a command at the beginning of its execution make up its environment. This environment includes variables that the command inherits from its parent process and variables specified as keyword parameters on the command line that invoke the command. The variables that a shell passes to its child processes are those that have been named as arguments to the export command (or the setenv command for the C shell).

Q: *How can you initialize new variables in a shell script and use them later in the sign-on shell?*

A: In the Bourne shell family, use the dot (.) command, which causes the shell to read commands from the script without spawning a new subshell. In the C shell, the source command is used instead. Changes made to variables in the script are in effect after the dot command finishes. The command would look like this: . procedure (Bourne shell) or source procedure (C shell).

Q: *How can you solve the following situation: You want the users, once signed on, to be put in the application program; once they quit the application, you want them signed off the system?*

A: A very efficient way is to put in their .profile or .login script, as the last command, the exec command, with the name of the application as an argument. In this way, once the users quit the application, they are signed off the system. Another way is to set the application program as the login shell in /etc/passwd.

Q: *How can you make sure that the work file created during the execution of a script will be removed even if the script was interrupted?*

A: Within a shell script, you can still take action (in this case remove files) when an interrupt signal is received by using the trap command. An example of a trap command is

```
trap 'rm -f tempfile; exit' 0 2 3 15
```

Q: *Assuming you have to run backups during the night, and there is no night operator and the backup utility prompts you for answers before it starts, how would you solve this problem?*

A: Create a shell script and put it in the crontabs directory, to be run by the cron process. The script would use a "here" document: it would have the interactive command (command which requires answers) followed by << eoi, where eoi is an arbitrary string, signaling the end of input. If the command uses the curses library, a more complicated solution would be required, possibly involving the expect utility. An example is

```
                command <<- eoi
0
1
2
3
eoi
```

Q: *How can you write the standard output and the standard error for a command to the same file?*

A: You can do this by using the file descriptors. A file descriptor is a handle to an open file. The C programming language defines default file pointers STDIN, STDOUT, and STDERR (standard input, output, and error). Pipelines and simple redirection alter STDIN and STDOUT, but STDERR can be explicitly directed in the Bourne family with the "2>" notation (this feature is not available in the C shell, which is one of its great failings). If necessary, STDOUT can be explicitly referred to as "1>" if desired. Furthermore, STDOUT and STDERR can be merged into the same file with the "2>&1" notation. An example command looks like this:

```
command 1>file name 2>&1
```

Q: *In a command list, how can you arrange the commands, so if one of them fails, the execution of the list stops?*

A: The list would look something like this:

```
command1 && command2 && command3 &&...&& commandn
```

Advanced Questions

Q: *In a command list, how can you arrange the commands so that, the second one is executed only if the first one fails?*

A: The list would look something like this:

```
command1 || command2
```

The first command is executed, its exit status is examined and only if it has a nonzero value, the second command is executed.

Q: *What can you do to fix the problem if one of your filesystems runs out of inodes?*

A: You can back up the filesystem, unmount the filesystem, rerun mkfs and specify more inodes for the filesystem, mount the filesystem, and restore the backups.

Q: *How can you check the amount of free space on filesystems?*

A: You can use the df command. On some systems, this utility reports sizes in 512 byte blocks.

Q: *What does it mean if a user has write permissions on a directory but is unable to remove files from that directory?*

A: It means that the sticky bit has been set for that directory. The sticky bit is a directory protection setting that allows only the owner of the file (or superuser) to remove files from that directory.

Q: *What command can be used to compare two text files?*

A: The diff command can be used to find out what lines must be changed in two files to bring them into agreement. This is especially useful for finding the differences between two versions of the same source program. The diff3 command is useful for comparing three separate files and merging the changes between them.

Q: *How can you convert a text file from Unix format to MS-DOS format?*

A: DOS text files differ from Unix text files in that they contain a carriage return ("\r") in addition to a line feed ("\n") at the end of each line. While most Unix vendors include proprietary utilities for accomplishing these conversions, modern versions of the Unix awk utility can strip the carriage return if called with the following syntax: awk '{sub(/\r/,""); print;}' dos.txt > unix.txt. A file could be converted back with awk using a reverse syntax: awk '{sub(/$/,"\r"); print;}' unix.txt > dos.txt.

Q: *What is umask?*

A: Umask is a three-digit octal number used by the system to establish the permissions for a newly created file. The system subtracts this number from octal 777, and the results are the permissions for the new file. Plain files will never be created with the execute bit set (using an implicit mask), but directories allow the execute bit (directory scan privilege) to pass through.

Q: *How can you find out what variables are currently assigned?*

A: By typing the command env, with no arguments, you can get a list of the variables currently assigned. The list can be lengthy, so it might be wise to pipe the output of env to a greater number.

Q: *What command can you use to archive a raw device?*

A: You can use the dd command, which allows you to specify the input and output block size, among other options.

Q: *What are device drivers?*

A: Device drivers are software routines, part of the kernel, which interface with the hardware. Unix represents most devices as block- or character-special files located in the /dev directory. Each has a major and a minor device number.

Q: *What are Unix daemons?*

A: The Unix daemons are a collection of processes that each perform a particular system task. Two examples are init and crond daemons.

Q: *Assuming you want to start the database engine every time you boot the system, how would you do it?*

A: Add the necessary commands in /etc/rc* scripts, (scripts executed when the system is booting).

Q: *When the system is coming down, how would you bring down the database engine?*

A: Locate the /etc/rc* scripts that perform system shutdown and add the entry there. If such entries cannot be found, add the necessary commands in the shutdown script (the path to the script varies among Unix distributions), which is an old pathname for the shutdown command.

Q: *What can you do if a scrambled terminal responds to keyboard input but the display is incorrect?*

A: First, check the TERM variable by entering env at the command line. If the terminal type is incorrect, reset it by entering at the command line TERM=wy60; export TERM (or setenv TERM wy60 for csh), if the terminal is a Wyse60. After resetting the terminal type, reinitialize the terminal by entering tset with no arguments.

Q: *What can you do if a terminal that responds to keyboard input does not display the characters entered at the keyboard?*

A: Sometimes, when a program stops prematurely as a result of an error, or when the user presses the <Break> key, the terminal stops echoing. To restore the terminal to normal operation, enter the following: <Ctrl>q<Ctrl>j stty sane <Ctrl>j. The <Ctrl>q unlocks any previous <Ctrl>s (which suspends output), and <Ctrl>j is the same as the enter/return key. The terminal should now display keyboard input.

Q: *How can all the files ending in ".foo" in a directory be renamed to end in ".bar"?*

A: Assuming Bourne shell syntax, here is one way:

```
for x in *.foo; do base=`basename $x .foo`; mv $x $base.bar; done
```

Q: *Why wouldn't the administrator be able to unmount a filesystem?*

A: No files can be open in the filesystem at unmount time. Additionally, all users must cd out of the filesystem. Until no processes are using data in the file system, it cannot be unmounted. The lsof (LiSt Open Files) can be helpful in such a situation, as can the kill command.

Q: *The following shells are installed on a Unix system:*

```
/bin/ash
/bin/bash
/bin/csh
/bin/ksh
/bin/pdksh
/bin/sash
/bin/sh
/bin/smrsh
/bin/tcsh
/bin/zsh
```

Which of these shells will natively run Bourne shell scripts?

A: ash, bash, ksh, pdksh, sh will run scripts written for the Bourne shell. zsh may run these scripts with modifications to its environment. It is rare to see all of these shells installed on a Unix system.

Q: *What function is used to delete a file within C?*

A: The unlink function, with the single argument of the pathname to be deleted, that is, unlink("/home/luser/deleteme");.

Q: *What is the basic function used to get information about a file (permissions, owner, size, etc.)?*

A: The stat() function and its derivatives return detailed information about a file in a stat structure. The stat structure contains the permissions, inode number, filesystem device number, device number for special files, number of links, uid of the owner, gid of the owner, size in bytes, times for last access, modification, file status change, best I/O block size, and the number of blocks allocated for the file.

Q: *What function is used to create a named pipe?*

A: The mkfifo() function can be used to create a named pipe. This is a file to which processes can be connected to exchange information, which the following shell commands demonstrate:

```
$ mkfifo /tmp/fifo
$ echo -e 'hello \n how are you \n goodbye' > /tmp/fifo &
[1] 123
$ $ grep h /tmp/fifo
hello
  how are you
```

In the above command, the "echo" was able to communicate with the "grep" through the named pipe (/tmp/fifo).

Q: *How can a C program set a timer to alert itself after a certain interval has passed?*

A: A timer can be set with the alarm() function. The number of seconds until the alarm is desired is passed as an argument. When the time expires, the process is sent the SIGALRM signal.

Q: *How can a C program catch a signal? How can a Bourne shell script catch a signal?*

A: The signal() function, which is part of ANSI C (not just Unix C), enables an arbitrary function to be called when a desired signal is received. The Bourne shell trap command serves a similar purpose.

Q: *What information does the size command report about a command object file?*

A: The size command reports the size of the text, data, and bss segments for a program.

Q: *When the fork() function splits one process into two, what is the return value for the parent, and what is the return value for the child?*

A: Assuming success, the child receives zero, and the parent receives the PID of the child.

Q: *What is the difference betweek fork() and vfork()?*

A: A call to fork() will make copies of the data, bss, stack, and heap segments of a program (the address space). If the child intends to replace itself with another process using an exec() function, the duplication of these data segments is both unnecessary and time-consuming. A call to vfork() puts the parent to sleep until the child has exited, and it causes the child to run in the same process space as the parent, negating the requirement to duplicate the address space.

Q: *What is a zombie process, and how is it avoided?*

A: When a process exits, it is the responsibility of the parent to call one of the wait() functions to read the process return value. The dying child process gives up all its memory, but the kernel must maintain at least the PID, the termination status, and the amount of CPU time that the process consumed. If the parent does not call wait(), the kernel is forced to retain this information, and reflects this with "zombie" or "defunct" processes in the process list.

Q: *Other than signals, pipes, and files of any sort, what mechanisms are available to Unix processes that enable them to exchange information?*

A: *Inter-Process Communication* (IPC) under Unix includes message queues, which allow small messages to be exchanged between processes; semaphores, which can be used to control access to a shared resource; and shared memory, which allow processes to exchange large blocks of data.

Q: *What is the difference between fopen() and open()?*

A: The fopen() function is defined in ANSI standard C as a portable method to read and write files. It returns a "file pointer" which is supported on all C platforms, and makes a variety of functions available for performing highly formatted input and output (printf() and scanf()). The open() function returns a "file descriptor," which is a much lower-level protocol that is accessed with the (unformatted) read() and write() system calls.

Q: *What is mmap(), and why is it better than read() or write()?*

A: The mmap() function maps a section of a file into memory, allowing the file to be accessed with pointer arithmetic (char *). Under certain derivatives of Unix, this allows much faster access to the file because the kernel is not forced to copy the file's contents between multiple buffers.

12
LINUX

Charles Fisher

The first the world heard about Linux came in 1991, in a Usenet post from Linus Torvalds containing the following embryonic statement:

```
Hello everybody out there using minix -
I'm doing a (free) operating system (just a hobby,
won't be big and professional like gnu) for
386 (486) AT clones
```

In the decade of gestation that has followed, this hobby has risen to become the server operating system with the second largest market share and the leading Web server operating system, bar none.

In truth, the story began long before the name Linux was ever uttered. In 1984, the Free Software Foundation (FSF) was founded at MIT with the goal of reproducing the Unix operating system with a new environment that they planned to call GNU. The Unix source and object code was copyrighted by AT&T and could not be freely shared, which annoyed the free thinkers at MIT. As a result, the GNU code was to be accompanied by a GNU license, which would guarantee the freedom and open nature of this great work.

The GNU environment began to grow with copies of Unix utilities that boasted many improvements over their progenitors. However, the one vital component that the GNU code lacked was a kernel—the core program that would control the computer and tie all of the other utilities together. The FSF had grand designs for their kernel, although implementation was lagging.

When Linus Torvalds released his quick-and-dirty, rough-and-ready kernel under the GNU license in 1991, he never imagined the enthusiasm with which computer science would grasp his work, the GNU environment along with it, and throw itself into producing equal amounts of code and freedom. That the resulting operating system is called "Linux" is perhaps a bit unfair, bearing in mind that the GNU contribution is so much larger than the kernel Linus Torvalds provided. However, in spite of occasional turbulence, the relationship between the Linux kernel and the GNU environment is both harmonious and symbiotic, and the dreams of creating a separate GNU kernel have floundered and largely been abandoned.

It is not surprising that this long association between independent thinkers has produced an environment that is stable, powerful, flexible, and mature. It is also becoming an area of keen interest for the modern business world, which leads us to the purpose of this chapter....

The Linux Job Interview

It is difficult to know what to expect when interviewing for a position involving Linux. The Linux environment is rather complicated, and those who are proficient in its operation are both valuable and mobile. The candidate might see a range of technical exposure in the interviewers, from novice to expert.

Caution is advised when neither the technical interviewers nor the organizations they represent have Linux exposure, but are running on Linux systems. Obviously, such an organization has given the individual with this skill set a reason to go elsewhere.

If the current technical staff is of much lower caliber than the candidate, decisions must be made. Should the organization possess sound judgement, the candidate will become a liaison to management and will probably rise to management itself in short order. If this is not what the candidate desires, it must be made clear that there is no interest in turning away from a technical focus, and steps must be taken to ensure that a technical path is possible. In spite of the most strenuous activity, project management is probably inevitable in this situation.

When the candidate is confronted with individuals of comparable technical skill, it is important to stress teamwork and a conservative hesitance to change established systems and procedures (Unix administrators in general are not thick-skinned, and might take such statements as a personal affront). Dedication to continued learning is also required; new systems and technologies continue to flood the industry.

When an interviewer of much greater skill conducts the technical interview, the candidate should earnestly try to see the experience as an opportunity for personal growth and not as an arena for intimidation or an opportunity for a display of hubris. In this case, it is extremely important to stress a desire to learn and study with a master, while resisting the urge to resort to flattery. Although it is always possible that such a relationship will not work out due to the territoriality or irascibility of the superior, the most that can be lost is a position that can easily be found elsewhere. The gains, on the other hand, could profoundly accelerate the learner's career.

Although every interview is a unique situation, with its own unique requirements, there are common threads to all types of interviews. You should be truthful about your skills (but not afraid to slightly embellish), should not hesitate to admit ignorance in a particular area, should know your own goals and state them, and should be succinct. Unfortunately, candidates do not in most cases receive an honest appraisal of their performance, and the art of interviewing and being interviewed is an imperfect one, improving only with time and experience.

Regarding the technical aspects of the interview, the questions that follow cover a broad range of areas that a Linux administrator might expect to see. It will be quite common for a particular interviewer to hone in on a specific subject and pursue it in greater depth; if possible, try to discern these areas of focus before the interview and study them, if necessary.

One final piece of advice: Approach the interview, and your life in general, with a sense of optimism and the right position will find you.

Questions and Answers

Assuming the following:

```
[root@localhost /root]# mount
        /dev/sda1 on / type ext2 (rw,noatime)
        none on /proc type proc (rw)
        /dev/hda1 on /fat type vfat (rw)
        /dev/hdc on /mnt/p0 type iso9660 (ro,nosuid,nodev)
        /dev/scd0 on /mnt/p1 type iso9660 (ro,nosuid,nodev)
```

Q: *Which of the previous are SCSI drives?*

A: /dev/sda1 is the first partition on the first SCSI drive.

Q: *Which are IDE drives?*

A: /dev/hda1 is the first partition on the first IDE drive.

Q: *Which are SCSI CD-ROMs?*

A: /dev/scd0 is the first SCSI CD-ROM drive.

Q: *Which are IDE CD-ROMs?*

A: /dev/hdc is an IDE CD-ROM drive.

Q: *Which are DOS filesystems?*

A: /dev/hda1 is a DOS FAT filesystem.

Q: *Which are Linux filesystems?*

A: /dev/sda1 is a Linux ext2 file system, and /proc is a synthetic kernel file system.

Q: *Which filesystems are on CD-ROM?*

A: /dev/scd0 and /dev/hdc are CD-ROMs.

Q: *What does the previous noatime directive do?*

A: Unix file systems maintain three separate timestamps for all files: the Access Time (atime), the Modification Time (mtime), and the Change Time (ctime). This behavior is further documented in the manual page for the "stat" system call. In the course of normal Unix and Linux behavior, the kernel will record the time of the read in the atime associated with the file when reading a file on the filesystem. The noatime mount directive prevents this behavior, which results in a faster filesystem, albeit one that provides less information. Noatime is particularly useful on busy Web servers, as the kernel is not required to write to every file that it reads.

Q: *Linux ext2 file systems are checked for errors at boot time when the maximum mount count or the mount interval are exceeded. How can these intervals be examined?*

A: The intervals can be examined with the dumpe2fs command.

Q: *How can the maximum mount count and/or the mount interval be changed for an ext2 filesystem?*

A: These intervals can be modified with the tune2fs command. The -c option can change the maximum mount count, and the -1 option will change the interval. It is critical that the file system be unmounted when the command is executed.

Q: *How can ext2 filesystems be checked for errors?*

A: Errors on ext2 filesystems can be detected and corrected by unmounting the filesystem (if it is mounted) and then running the e2fsck program on the filesystem's device file.

Q: *Why is it difficult to manually check the root filesystem of a Linux installation? How can it be done?*

A: It is difficult because the root filesystem cannot be unmounted in a running system. To check the root filesystem, the administrator could boot from a floppy that contained a kernel, a shell, and the e2fsck binary, or could physically remove the filesystem and install it in another Linux system that could check it. Under Red Hat Linux, if a file named /forcefsck exists in the root file system, then a check will be triggered at boot time, regardless of the mount count or interval. If filesystems that are not clean and/or have not been checked are mounted, a stern warning will be issued during the mount process.

Q: *A Linux administrator accidentally removes the /dev/hdc device file. What is the name of the command that can be used to recreate it?*

A: If the administrator had access to another Linux machine, he/she could list the device file:

```
$ ls -l /dev/hdc
brw-rw---- 1 root disk 22, 0 May 5 1998 /dev/hdc
```

It can be determined from the "b" in the first column previous that the file is a block special file. 22, 0 indicates the major and minor numbers that link to a kernel device driver. The administrator could then recreate the block special file with a call to mknod of the form **mknod hdc b 22 0**. It would be important to set appropriate permissions on the file after it was created to prevent unauthorized users from accessing and/or modifying the drive's contents. If access to another Linux system was not available, the administrator could use the /dev/MAKEDEV script to rebuild the device file, which is more complex.

Q: *An administrator adds a new hard drive to a Linux system. How is it formatted, and how should the administrator configure the drive to be mounted at boot-time?*

A: The drive is formatted with the mke2fs command. The drive can be mounted at boot time by adding an entry for it to /etc/fstab. For example, let us say that /etc/fstab contains the following:

```
/dev/hda5    /            ext2     defaults          1  1
/dev/hda6    /home        ext2     defaults          1  2
/dev/hda1    /dos         vfat     defaults          1  2
/dev/cdrom   /mnt/cdrom   iso9660  noauto,owner,ro   0  0
/dev/hda7    swap         swap     defaults          0  0
/dev/fd0     /mnt/floppy  ext2     noauto,owner      0  0
none         /proc        proc     defaults          0  0
none         /dev/pts     devpts   gid=5,mode=620    0  0
```

The administrator adds a slave drive on the primary channel, uses fdisk to create a single large partition covering the whole drive, and then formats this drive with the mke2fs utility. Assuming all of this, the new drive could be mounted at boot time with the line:

```
/dev/hdb1 /newdrive ext2 defaults 1 2
```

Here is a short description of each field:
/dev/hdb1 gives the device name of the filesystem.
/newdrive is the mount point of the filesystem and should be an empty directory.
Ext2 tells the type of filesystem.
Defaults indicate any special mount options for the filesystem.
1 is a value used by dump to control backups of the filesystem.
2 gives the fsck order of the filesystem; the root filesystem is 1, all others are 2.

Q: *An administrator compiles and installs a new kernel on a SCSI system. The administrator builds modular SCSI drivers, but fails to create an initrd. When the administrator selects his new kernel from LILO, the system will not boot. Why?*

A: IDE drivers are usually included directly in the kernel binary, but modular SCSI drivers are available only as modules loaded at run time. If the kernel is loaded without any special provisions, it has no drivers to access the filesystem on which the SCSI modules are stored. To solve this problem, the SCSI driver modules must be stored in a RAM-disk image called an initrd which is passed as an argument to LILO. The need for an initrd is obviated if the required SCSI driver is compiled directly into a custom kernel.

If the root filesystem of a Linux installation lies on a SCSI drive, upgrading the kernel without upgrading the initrd will result in a system that does not boot.

Q: *What kernel feature is required to create both an initrd and a boot disk?*

A: The loopback module (loop.o) or loopback device support is required to make these images. The loopback device allows files residing on a mounted filesystem to be mounted at a separate mount point; this has a variety of uses, but is mainly used to mount ISO CD-ROM images for verification prior to burning to a CD-R. This feature is also critical in creating boot disks and the initrd. Each command creates a small, empty file system, mounts it through loopback, then populates it with the required files (and, in the case of the boot disk, copies the image to the floppy). If the kernel is upgraded and this support is removed, these images cannot be created (when upgrading kernels through the rpm -Uvh method, it is *critical* to modprobe loop before initiating the upgrade).

Q: *What are the particular concerns associated with large hard drives in relation to LILO?*

A: For a stable system, the kernel and all its associated components must lie in a filesystem that is entirely contained within the first 1024 cylinders of the hard drive (with very old systems, within the first 512 megabytes). With newer systems that include Logical Block Addressing (LBA), this limit is raised somewhat (to approximately 9 gigabytes).

The Red Hat Linux operating system and its derivatives now place everything LILO needs in order to boot the system in a directory called /boot. This directory can be allocated as a separate filesystem, and this filesystem can be very small (32MB should be enough). It can be placed in such a way that it will meet the 1024 requirement, while allowing larger Linux partitions to be placed outside the 1024 boundary.

It is also important to be aware that the LBA mode can be disabled in the BIOS of most PCs, which will return a system to the 512-megabyte limit.

Q: *If the root password for a Linux system is lost, or if a new administrator must assume responsibility for a Linux system without any assistance from the previous administrator, and the password is not available, how can LILO be used to break in and reset it?*

A: Entering "linux single" at the LILO boot prompt will usually boot Linux into a root shell.

Q: *If LILO cannot be used, what are some other ways to boot a Linux system?*

A: An incomplete list of methods might include using:

1. a boot disk
2. the linload utility that is started from a DOS partition
3. the MILO utility, on a system with an Alpha processor
4. the SILO utility, on a system with a SPARC processor

Q: *What are some of the major Linux distributions that use RPM? What are some of the distributions that do not?*

A: Red Hat, Mandrake, Caldera, TurboLinux and Suse all use the Red Hat Package Manager (RPM). RPM packages may not be fully compatible between these distributions, and they are definitely incompatible between processor architectures. Debian and Slackware do not use RPM as the main packaging system, but do offer support for it, to some degree.

Q: *How are security errata RPM packages usually applied?*

A: They are applied with a command in the following form:

```
$rpm -Uvh packagename.arch.rpm
```

Please note that the -F option can be used instead of -U which only loads the RPM if a previous version was already installed. Actually, any RPM package can be installed or upgraded in this way.

Q: *How can you obtain a list of files in an RPM package? Assuming a configuration file for an installed package has been corrupted, how could the administrator extract the original file without reinstalling the package?*

A: The following command will list the files in a package:

```
$ rpm -qpl packagename.arch.rpm
```

Files can be extracted from a package with:

```
$ rpm2cpio packagename.arch.rpm | cpio -id
```

Intermediate Questions

Q: *What is the name of the new utility included in Red Hat Linux that scans a Linux system for packages that should be upgraded and which will perform the upgrades in an automated manner?*

A: The utility is named "up2date," and it was first made available in Red Hat Linux 6.1. Other packages that perform a similar function are available (the most notable is autorpm), but none of them are included in the distribution. Most distributions maintain websites and mailing lists dedicated to errata packages, should the administrator prefer manual maintenance.

Q: *What command should you use to examine the modules loaded in the running kernel?*

A: The command is lsmod. Here is an example run:

```
[root@localhost /root]# /sbin/lsmod
Module Size Used by
3c59x 19752 1 (autoclean)
st 25024 0
ncr53c8xx 52684 3
cpqarray 15328 1
```

Q: *The administrator needs to insert the ip_Masq_ftp module into the kernel of a Linux system to act as a firewall (which enables FTP). How is this accomplished? How is the module removed when the administrator wishes to shut the service down?*

A: The module is inserted with either:

```
$ modprobe ip_masq_ftp
```

or with:

```
$ insmod /lib/modules/2.2.16-3/ipv4/ip_masq_ftp.o
```

The module is removed with:

```
$ rmmod ip_masq_ftp
```

Q: *The system motherboard has multiple processors, but Linux detects only one. The board supports Symmetric Multi-Processing (SMP) under Linux. What is wrong?*

A: The Linux kernel was not prepared with SMP support. Either load an SMP-enabled kernel from the installation media (or errata site), or use the kernel sources to compile a custom kernel.

Q: *How can information on interrupt usage be determined under Linux?*

A: It can be determined by examining the /proc/interrputs file.

Q: *How can information on input-output ports be determined under Linux?*

A: Examining the /proc/ioports file will provide this information.

Q: *What packages encrypt file transfer and interactive shell sessions on Linux?*

A: The two preeminent packages are the Secure Shell (ssh) and kerberos. Kerberos is now included in Red Hat Linux version 6.2, and openSSH is included in Red Hat Linux 7.0. One source for ssh is http://openssh.com.

Q: *Is there a version of PGP for Linux? Can PGP be used for encrypted file transfers and interactive shell sessions?*

A: Red Hat Linux now includes the GnuPG package, which is compatible with PGP. PGP itself is available for Linux in both commercial and free versions. See http://web.mit.edu/network/pgp.html for the free version, and http://www.pgp.com for the commercial distribution. While GnuPG can use stdin/stdout with its encryption algorithms, it has no specific network functionality and is really more suited to the encryption of flat files.

Q: *What versions of ssh are available for Linux?*

A: Ssh version 1.2.27 is the last version from http://www.ssh.com that allows some commercial use with no charge. Ssh version 1.2.28 and above (including the entire 2.x series) require a license for any type of commercial use. Ssh versions 2.x use a different protocol specification than the 1.x series, and the two versions are largely incompatible. However, the OpenBSD organization has forked the 1.2.12 release into a new codebase named "openSSH," and this codebase integrates bugfixes, removes all patented algorithms, integrates support for ssh version 2.x, and preserves the "no-charge for commercial use" status of 1.2.27. Open SSH is available at http://openssh.com.

Q: *There are separate firewall configurations for the 2.0, 2.2, and the upcoming 2.4 series of Linux kernel. What are these utilities?*

A: In the 2.0 kernel, the utility was **ipfwadm;** in kernel 2.2, the utility changed to **ipchains;** and in the upcoming 2.4 kernel, the firewall configuration tool will change once again to **iptables.**

Q: *What is Network Address Translation (NAT) known as in the Linux kernel?*

A: It is known as IP Masquerade.

Q: *How is forwarding across the network interfaces enabled in the modern Linux kernels?*

A: It is enabled by writing a 1 to the file **/proc/sys/net/ipv4/ip_forward.** Startup scripts in Red Hat Linux will perform this operation if forwarding is enabled in **/etc/sysctl.conf** (Red Hat Linux 6.2) or **/etc/sysconfig/network** (all earlier releases). If a 0 is written to this file, all forwarding ceases instantly.

Q: *If forwarding between the network interfaces will not be allowed for security reasons, what tools remain available to build a firewall?*

A: Proxy tools, such as the TIS FireWall ToolKit (available at http://www.fwtk.org) or Squid (http://www.squid-cache.org) are available. SOCKS can also be used (http://www.socks.nec.com), if the client software supports this type of proxy.

Q: *If the expression "telnet localhost 25" works but telnet localhost smtp does not, what is the problem and how is it solved?*

A: The problem is that getservbyname() is not working for the smtp service, and the problem is solved by adding the entry smtp 25/tcp into **/etc/services**. One important utility that *requires* service names is inetd.

Q: *Where are the preferred DNS servers set for name resolution on a Linux system? What happens if this file doesn't exist?*

A: The servers are set in /etc/resolv.conf. If the file does not exist, a name server on the local host is consulted for all lookups requiring DNS.

Q: *What file controls the host resolution order (/etc/hosts, DNS, NIS) on a Linux system?*

A: The host resolution order is set in /etc/nsswitch.conf (similar to the method used in Solaris).

Q: *The Apache Web server recently consolidated the three main configuration files into a single server config file. What were the names of the three configuration files, and what is the name of the current unified file?*

A: The old file names were **httpd.conf, srm.conf,** and **access.conf.** The single file used in recent distributions is **httpd.conf.**

Q: *What is the key limiting factor in supporting a large number of virtual hosts with Apache under Linux?*

A: Linux has a per-process limit of 1024 file descriptors in the default kernel. Each virtual host server log will consume a file descriptor. When the limit is reached (and it will be on a busy Web server with hundreds of virtual hosts), either eliminate logs or build a custom kernel with a larger per-process file descriptor limit.

Q: *A CGI application won't execute under Apache. The permissions on the executable are 644 and the file is owned by user root group wheel. What is wrong?*

A: Execute permissions have not been set and the program cannot be executed without execute permissions. An appropriate set of permissions might be 755.

Q: *Where do daemons and other system processes record their status and alerts? Where does the Linux kernel log its status?*

A: Information on processes is logged by the syslog daemon and is usually sent to /var/log/messages (this default behavior is controlled via /etc/syslog.conf). The kernel logs go through the klogd logging daemon, which in turn calls syslogd (the kernel also keeps a logging buffer that can be examined with the dmesg command).

Q: *What command(s) can be used to display the contents of the mail queue when running sendmail?*

A: Either "mailq" or "sendmail -bp" can be used to display all messages that are awaiting delivery in the queue.

Q: *How often does sendmail attempt to deliver messages in the queue? When does sendmail give up and return the message as non-deliverable?*

A: The duration between runs through the queue is usually set as a command line argument when sendmail is started, as in "sendmail -bd -q1h," which will cause sendmail to process the queue once per hour (change -q1h to -q15m to trigger the queue every fifteen minutes). The expire times for messages in the queue are set in /etc/sendmail.cf.

Advanced Questions

Q: *How can a user trigger a single processing of the local queue? How can the administrator trigger the queue on a remote SMTP server?*

A: To trigger a processing of the local queue, any user can enter sendmail -q at a shell prompt. To trigger a remote queue, telnet to the remote SMTP server on port 25 and enter ETRN domainname.com (use the domain of the destination email address that you are awaiting from the remote queue). ETRN can be very useful in a situation where the administrator has had sendmail down for some time, has just brought it back up, is expecting important mail from a remote server, and does not want to wait for the remote's next scheduled run of the queue.

Q: *How can the location of the queue directory be determined?*

A: The /etc/sendmail.cf file contains an option line which controls the queue location; it is in /var/spool/mqueue on most systems.

Q: *NFS architecture changed substantially between the 2.0 and 2.2 Linux kernels. What was the nature of the change?*

A: Under the 2.0 kernel, the NFS server was implemented in user space as a single process. Under 2.2, NFS server functionality was moved into the kernel for much higher performance; the NFS server can handle much higher bandwidth under the new architecture.

Q: *What file controls the directories that other servers can access via NFS?*

A: The /etc/exports file controls the shared directories, the list of permitted servers, and the rights those servers have to the shared volumes.

Q: *What is root squash?*

A: If the root user on a client attempts to access an NFS volume, the root permissions will be given up and translated to an unprivileged user. This behavior can be disabled with the no_root_squash option in /etc/exports.

Q: *An NFS client cannot see the contents of a directory or any of its subdirectories, even though a parent of the directory is exported via NFS. The directory appears as a mount point in the df command on the server. What is wrong?*

A: Volumes exported over NFS do not cross filesystem boundaries. In order to make the directory visible, it must have a separate listing in /etc/exports, even though its parent is already exported.

Q: *The NFS server cannot start and complains that "connection is refused" and that it "cannot register service." What is wrong?*

A: The portmap daemon is not running. NFS is an ONC RPC service, and all such services must register with the portmap daemon before they can start.

Q: *How can the ONC RPC services supported by a particular server be determined?*

A: With rpcinfo, "rpcinfo -p remotehost.com" will print a list of all supported services on the remote host. The server should be configured to deny access to this information to all hosts excepting those that actually require it.

Q: *How can access to the portmapper be controlled?*

A: The portmapper can be instructed to permit or restrict access with the /etc/hosts.allow and /etc/hosts.deny files.

Q: *What is tcpd, what does it protect, how is it controlled, and why is it so rarely seen in the process list?*

A: The tcpd daemon is part of the tcp_wrappers package. The daemon is launched by inetd, and tcpd in turn launches many common internet services (such as FTP, Telnet, POP mail and IMAP mail, Finger, Talk, etc.). The tcpd daemon also uses the /etc/hosts.allow and /etc/hosts.deny files to restrict access to these services. It only runs a short time while checking its access lists (after which it denies service and shuts down, or allows access and overwrites its own memory image with the desired service).

Q: *The administrator wishes to reinitialize one of the common system daemons (that is, wishes to make the Web server, DNS server, or the inetd superserver restart and reexamine their configuration files); how is this accomplished?*

A: Passing a kill -HUP or kill -1 to the server process (or to the parent server process, when the parent spawns children) accomplishes this. Under distributions with a System-V style init, some of the startup scripts for these services have a reload option, which has the same effect.

Q: *What is the master file for all startup scripts and system services?*

A: /etc/inittab controls the init process, which is defined to be process number one and is the ultimate progenitor of all other processes under Unix.

Q: *How can the parent of a daemon process be determined with the ps command?*

A: Parent processes can be found by calling ps alx to see all processes (even those without controlling ttys) in long format (Linux uses the BSD nomenclature for ps). The pstree command can also be used to determine the parent PID if the -p option is used.

Q: *How can the CPU utilization of a process be determined?*

A: Per-process CPU utilization can be determined with ps aux or with the top utility.

Q: *How can information on the system CPUs be determined under Linux?*

A: They can be determined by examining the /proc/cpuinfo file.

Q: *If no external authentication is being used, and the password entries in the /etc/passwd file are a simple x rather than an encryption, what does this imply?*

A: The file /etc/shadow contains the true password encryptions for the accounts.

Q: *What encryption algorithms are used for authentication in the /etc/passwd or /etc/shadow files?*

A: The Data Encryption Standard (DES) and Message Digest 5 (MD5) are used.

Q: *What will happen if the root user executes the command chmod ug-s /usr/bin/passwd (assuming that the system password utility is in this location)?*

A: This command strips the setuid and setgroupid permissions from the password-changing program; the program will no longer work for non-root users.

Q: *A Samba installation can share files with Windows 95 and earlier versions of Windows NT but users of Windows 98, later versions of Windows NT, and Windows 2000 users can't log on. What is the problem?*

A: Encrypted passwords are not enabled in the Samba server; enable encrypted passwords in /etc/smb.conf, and then use a command of the form "smbpasswd -a luser" to add users to /etc/smbpasswd.

Q: *What production-quality office productivity software containing word processing, spreadsheets, and so on is available for Linux?*

A: The two leading packages are StarOffice and ApplixWare. StarOffice, made available by Sun, is available at http://openoffice.org. Applixware is available at http://www.vistasource.com.

Q: *What free and commercial SQL databases are available for Linux?*

A: Red Hat Linux ships with the PostgreSQL free database server (http://postgresql.org). Other vendors prefer the MySQL database (http://www.mysql.com). Inprise/Borland have opened the source to their Interbase database product (http://www.inprise.com), but the software has yet to be rolled into a major Linux distribution. Sybase has released a free binary-only copy of their Adaptive Server/Enterprise SQL server (http://linux.sybase.com) and they also have Linux ports for their current commercial products. Other major database vendors such as Oracle, Informix, and IBM DB2 all offer products that are available with free development licenses.

13
Client/Server Systems

David Dodge

In its earliest forms the term client/server referred to computer systems that consisted of the following elements:

- One or more intelligent workstations, personal computers, or portable devices that function as "clients" by requesting services from another system or system component
- One or more platforms such as personal computers, minicomputers, or mainframe hosts, that function as a "server" by providing processing, database, and communication services to clients
- The networking infrastructure and software that links them all

From an end-user viewpoint, client/server computing has typically meant being able to access a range of data, applications, computing power, printing, and other services from a single workstation—without having to know which machine or component of the system is actually providing the requested service. This capability or characteristic is referred to as *transparency* of location.

More recently, though, the definition of client/server has been expanded to recognize the evolution of the World Wide Web and its extension of client/server applications and middleware as part of the ultimate client/server system, the Internet. The Internet and the more conventional client/server systems are making use of newer technologies such as distributed objects and components, groupware, and web application servers.

Keeping Pace with Change

Designing, redesigning, and implementing client/server software applications require both discipline and tools. The discipline is typically provided by methodologies and techniques that capture the business requirements the system must support. Next, these methodologies and techniques help translate the requirements into system functions and features; then, they help direct how the system is to be developed and made operational.

The tools used by today's client/server professionals are many and varied. They range from programming languages to graphical development aids and from enterprisewide software packages to Enterprise JavaBeans. Change and improvement are the watchwords for this facet of client/server implementations. By keeping pace with the latest software innovations and the most current approaches to development on the Web, an individual can be a very valuable resource to any organization.

The Client/Server Environment: An Overview

The catalysts for the change to client/server computing have included market forces, increased competitiveness in many dimensions of business, an emphasis on business process reengineering, and new corporate attitudes about the value of information. No one can deny, however, the role of new technologies in producing the shift. Over the past few years, a vast array of enabling products and tools has been introduced at what continues to be a blistering pace. Different languages and development techniques have followed. In fact, it is the technologies, tools, and techniques that make client/server computing something new, not simply the architectural configuration or the role of any particular piece of hardware or software. Most people would agree that "client/server" and its latest technological incarnation, the internet, represent the computer architecture model of the next decade.

Networking Operating Systems

A *network operating system* (NOS) is the software program that makes it possible for computers to communicate with one another or with a network and to share resources. In other words, these NOSs permit client machines running on different operating systems such as Unix, Windows 9x, and DOS, to share computer files and network devices. The NOS enables a user to access a database, use a printer, or use another computer's applications as if they resided on his or her workstation. The most robust NOSs, such as Novell's NetWare and Microsoft's LAN Manager, were structured more like minicomputer or Unix operating systems from the outset. Since their server software mediates simultaneous requests for network resources and runs multiple programs at one time, they are considered to be multiuser, multitasking systems. Although a server can also function as an individual workstation with some NOSs or special versions, larger networks are usually not configured this way. Novell's NetWare actually requires a dedicated server.

NOSs help keep track of all the activity that occurs over the network, and they aid users in finding the application or services they want through the NOS directory service. A directory enables objects to be named and given attributes, and it allows searches over the network. The latest NOSs implement directory services as a distributed, object database. These NOS directories have user interfaces or *Application Programing Languages* (APIs) that permit users or other applications to locate objects on the network by asking for them by name or by their attributes.

Another advantage of the most robust, multitasking NOSs is that they usually offer additional features and tools for managing the network. System administrators also normally want software that provides enhanced security, print spooling, network administration capabilities, diagnostic support, improved memory management, and greater fault tolerance when purchasing these systems. The selection of a NOS is normally made based on these characteristics and on whether the organization wants to dedicate a workstation to the server role.

Database Management Systems

A *database management system* (DBMS) is a software program that is designed to collect, organize, store, and control data. In conjunction with a database application, it also permits the data to be updated, retrieved, and viewed.

Most client/server databases still use a relational database model. This model does not employ a parent/child concept to show the relationship between different data items. Instead, the data is organized into tables with columns and rows. Column names and indexing numbers or keys allow multiple relationships to be created among the data items. As a result, each table can be changed without changing the entire database structure. This gives the relational database model tremendous flexibility, and it provides the data through searches that do not rely on the position of the data in the database. These capabilities often make relational DBMSs particularly suited for client/server architectures because of the ease with which they handle queries and the high degree of data integrity they provide.

Many newer client/server database management systems are tending to use distributed object technologies and object-oriented languages. These *object DBMSs* (ODBMSs) use object classes and various constructs of object-oriented languages such as Smalltalk, C++, and Java to define and access data.

Methodologies and Design Techniques

Application design and development methodologies, including those for client/server applications, are most often described in terms of two basic approaches: the traditional waterfall approach and an interactive, spiral (or cyclone-like) approach.

The *waterfall approach* essentially entails a sequential set of phases, each one producing elements of the system design or function. One phase cascades into another phase. This approach generally has strong controls but lacks flexibility and often doesn't allow sufficient interaction with prospective application users. The *spiral* or *interactive approach* is more dependent on prototyping and piloting techniques that call for active user involvement and builds on previous steps.

Both the traditional waterfall and the spiral-type approaches used by professionals today have roughly the same phases such as requirements definition/refinement, analysis and design, application development/refinement, integration and testing, and implementation and deployment. However, these approaches tend to emphasize different phases and techniques.

The use of *Computer-Aided Software Engineering* (CASE) tools and data modeling techniques is frequently advocated today by both types of development approaches. CASE tools serve as analytic aids and as storage sites for application design characteristics and standards. Data modeling support is usually a key function of such tools. *Data modeling* is itself a set of procedures, graphic conventions, and techniques used to represent and organize data usage. When designing client/server applications, data modeling is a particularly valuable technique. Since client/server computing so often requires extensive data sharing and the distribution of data across multiple locations or servers, it becomes fundamentally important to understand how data needs to be organized and accessed for most efficient and accurate usage. Data modeling, with its depiction of data entities, their relationships, attributes, or characteristics, and its various levels or abstractions of the data, help application designers and developers cope with the complexity of client/server system data. Better data structures that take advantage of relational database technology are the result.

The newer object-oriented approaches to client/server application design and development involve techniques similar to data modeling and the spiral approach's emphasis on prototyping. Object-oriented approaches, however, take a somewhat different conceptual view of application software and the way it is used. In these approaches, an object is really a software "packet" that contains a set of characteristics and upon which a set of operations or access methods may be executed. The object is said to have a "state" (of value), and it exhibits a "behavior." By designing software applications around objects, professionals expect to achieve greater flexibility and responsiveness to changes in user requirements, as well as obtaining greater reuse of the application code.

Graphical Development and Data Access Tools

To many people, it is the front-end application software and graphical user interface environments that have made client/server computing so alluring. To discuss the topic with greater clarity, these tools can be divided into three major groups based on their primary uses and limitations: (1) desktop extension software, (2) application development tools, and (3) data access and query tools.

Desktop extension software products are essentially programs that add functionality to existing commercial database or application products such as Lotus 1-2-3 and dBase. The extension products make PC DBMSs and applications easier to use by providing access to servers and other databases, creating forms and reports, supporting development of ad hoc queries and data extracts, and populating spreadsheet packages with server-based data. The shortcomings of these tools: they are often tied to specific applications or DBMS products, and they can impose a performance penalty on the workstation because of the data translations they must make. These tools can also require additional workstation processing power and memory.

Application development tools are software products used to build customized, workstation-based, client/server applications. Some of these tools simply put a graphical front end on existing mainframe host applications without changing the "back-end logic," an activity referred to as *facelifting*. Facelifting is usually a measure that yields only a small subset of the benefits of true client/server computing.

Other development tools are intended to support construction of complete client/server applications. These products use proprietary procedural or object-oriented 4GL programming languages to develop applications that have a graphical user interface and that support *Structural Query Language* (SQL) queries to multiple back-end DBMSs. Professional developers with programming experience are the target users for most of these tools, although generally only a few days of training are needed before an individual can become competent with such a product. Most of the tools are designed to work in a Windows environment, and they enable the injection of multimedia, image, and other technologies into new applications.

Data access and query tools are most often intended for use by people who are not professional programmers. These tools support creation of database queries and the development of customized reports and forms. Some tools also support integration of data from multiple, disparate sources and are often characterized as *Executive Information System* (EIS) shells. Such tools are very good for users who need to retrieve data but do not need to change it.

Application Programming Languages

Over the last few years, various database access tools and user-query products have emerged. These tools tend to simplify aspects of using a DBMS, and they generally preclude the need to develop custom programs to retrieve limited sets of data from the database. Most complex information systems requirements, however, still mandate the development of custom application programs or the use of off-the-shelf software packages. These programs and packages are written in one or more programming languages. Typically, such languages can be grouped into three general classes: procedural languages, SQL-based languages, and object-oriented languages.

Most programming languages are considered to be procedural languages. This means the code is written as a series of procedures, with each procedure performing some task that contributes to the use of the application software. Procedures to update data and to re-sort the data are examples. The common *third-generation languages* (3GLs) such as COBOL, FORTRAN, Pascal, C, and BASIC are all procedural programming languages. In his guide to client/server databases, Joe Salemi also states that programming languages that are unique to particular products or DBMSs are often called *fourth-generation languages* (4GLs). Examples include Microsoft's Visual BASIC languages and the *Paradox Application Language* (PAL) used with Paradox. These procedural languages can be extended and linked to databases and other systems using APIs. An API is a set of precoded functions or procedural calls usually provided with a product or made available in a software library that can be coupled to an application or database.

SQL-based languages use the SQL as their foundation. SQL was designed as a language intended to provide access to relational DBMSs. However, there is no mandatory requirement that a relational database must understand SQL, and SQL can be used to access a nonrelational DBMS. While SQL is generally considered an important standard that helped foster the transition to client/server, no one should assume that all SQL-based languages are compatible with one another. A variety of SQL-based languages are in use today, each providing extensions or additional capabilities to the basic SQL specifications. Developers should therefore be cautious when selecting the languages and products they will use to build applications.

Object-Oriented Programming (OOP) languages are relatively new and require a very different approach to building application software. Rather than performing a series of procedures, OOP languages call for events or actions to be taken on objects such as a "customer," or a photographic image, or an "employee." Examples of such languages include C++, Java and SmallTalk. Several of the application development tools on the market today employ object-oriented languages and approaches. Other tools that up to now have used procedural or SQL-based languages have recently incorporated many of the object-oriented programming techniques and features. This blending can be expected to continue as vendors seek to optimize the strengths of the various languages and techniques.

Enterprise Client/Server Software Packages and Groupware

Over the last decade, many organizations have turned to a relatively small number of enterprise software package solutions designed to operate in a client/server architecture. These software packages generally support major functions performed by most businesses, such as accounting and finance, human resource management, order management, and production planning. Well-known examples are packages such as those offered by SAP, PeopleSoft, Baan, J. D. Edwards, and Oracle. Current releases of these software packages are already century-date compliant, and they facilitate the redesign of business processes, as well as the transition to client/server computing.

Selecting and implementing an enterprise software package can be a challenging endeavor. The analytic effort to pick a software package typically involves a comparison of functions and features versus a set of documented requirements. The performance and the technical environment in which the application operates can be important considerations, as well. Once a package has been selected, there is usually a phase of the implementation devoted to determining exactly what business processes the package will support completely, and how much the package might require customization. The next phase of package implementation often focuses on piloting the application and building interfaces to legacy systems with which the package must operate. Finally, package implementation calls for the software to be integrated, tested, and "rolled out" to other business locations.

Client/server groupware is a label claimed by several hundred products that are focused on helping groups of users work together. Although groupware typically involves multimedia document management, scheduling, e-mail, conferencing, and electronic imaging, it is considered a truly new form of computing by most industry commentators. Groupware products are different from other applications in that they support the development, workflow and coordination of non-structed information as part of collaborative group processes or activities. Novell's Groupware, Netscape's Suitespot, and applications such as Lotus Notes, Exchange, and Groupwise are some of the most widely used of these products.

Benefits of Client/Server Architectures

Properly architected and implemented client/server systems can yield tremendous benefits and advantages. One of their key advantages is the capability they provide to distribute data and processing to the places around the system and around the organization that make the most sense. Data, for example, can be managed centrally but distributed in servers among user departments or regional branches. This distribution scheme can put the data closer to users and improve system performance. Similarly, if processing tasks are properly shared among system components, that is, some on the server, some on a host, and some on the personal computer), the computing strength of each *central processing unit* (CPU) is likely to be the best utilized. Moreover, processing can be done at the place that will minimize data transfer requirements. If 50 customer records are to be retrieved, for example, it makes more sense for the sorting to be done at the site of the database rather than transferring a quarter of a million customer records over a network to do the sorting elsewhere.

Another key advantage of client/server computing is improved access to data. Not only can data be positioned for better access, client/server technologies can improve the retrieval process and integration of the data. When data from several systems or databases must be pulled to provide a required input, or when data from multiple sources must be viewed simultaneously, client/server system interfaces and server-based extracts can meet the need.

Well-designed client/server applications are also generally easier to use than are their conventional counterparts. The graphical user interfaces that typify new client/server applications employ point-and-click symbols, pull-down menus, and other graphical features that make them easier for users to understand. These applications can be structured to reflect a more natural, intuitive workflow, as well. As a result, less training and experience are usually required for end users to be competent with the system. These are significant benefits for organizations that contend with high employee turnover or small training budgets.

More efficient use of computer resources and the capability to add computing power incrementally are further benefits of client/server technology. Clearly, the opportunity to shift processing workload from mainframe computers to microcomputers is a cost-effective strategy when the smaller machine can support the business requirements. The substantially lower costs of microcomputer processing as measured in *millions of instructions per second* (MIPs) is well documented. Likewise, when requirements grow or additional capabilities are needed, the modular nature of client/server systems permits additional components to be linked to the network rather than pursuing a more expensive mainframe upgrade. The fact that client/server systems can be constructed in a modular fashion also contributes to system reliability and survivability. When one part of the system malfunctions, it can usually be isolated and not impact operation of the rest of the network. Alternatively, another network CPU might be called on to perform all or part of the processing a failed CPU was handling.

Client/server technologies can increase the probability that different information systems can interoperate, as well. Common interfaces, adoption of standards, and the use of operating systems and common query languages, such as Unix and SQL, have fostered more data exchange and application sharing. The opportunity to develop highly "portable" application software is raised significantly by the same technology elements. This means that applications developed to run on one type of computer platform can also run on other platforms with little or no modification. The application development languages, tools, and techniques that are part of client/server approaches, further enhance creation of this transferable or portable quality.

Implementation of client/server computing also provides opportunities for instituting standards and controls. With the proliferation of personal computers over the past few years, some organizations believe they have lost meaningful control of these resources. Many companies are plagued by a lack of data standards, redundancies among variant database products, and multiple suites of contending personal productivity software. Organizations that successfully pursue client/server application development tend to use this activity to reassert centralized authority over key shared resources, and, at the same time, increase end user autonomy with respect to unique needs and resources. In other words, end users in each functional department can be freed to address their unique requirements, but common needs and shared client/server resources are returned to the control of the Information Systems Department.

Client/server computing additionally represents the means by which many newer and emerging information technologies can be readily integrated with business applications. Multimedia, desktop imaging, pen-based computing, wireless local area networks, and speech recognition are just a few of the technologies that client/server is positioned to accept and leverage.

The technology benefits alone, however, are usually insufficient reasons to incur the costs of moving toward client/server. Any benefit or advantage of client/server computing should really be expressed in business terms and shown to be directly applicable to a company's business requirements. Improved data access, for example, should mean improved customer service, more rapid response to market conditions, or increased competitiveness. The predicted impact on the corporate bottom line, market share, and customer loyalty are other good yardsticks for determining if implementing client/server is justified for most companies.

Questions and Answers

The questions and answers in this chapter have been broken into major headings designed to classify subject material for easy access by the reader.

Entry Level

Q: *When referring to a client/server system, what is a client and what is a server?*

A: A client is a machine or device that uses a service or another network resource, and a server is a machine or device that supplies the service or resource to the client.

Q: *Explain what is meant by the terms* fat clients *and* fat servers.

A: Client/server applications can be characterized by how a distributed application is actually split between the client and the server machines. The fat client model places more functionality on the client, while the fat server model puts more of the processing or greater functionality on the server.

Q: *What is meant by the term* thin client*?*

A: A thin client is really just a low-end PC with minimal computing power. It is part of a larger client/server system, managed centrally by a server, and usually limited to requesting, downloading, and displaying information, rather than processing it.

Q: *What is middleware?*

A: Middleware is a term used to describe all of the software that supports distributed functions or interactions between clients and servers. Middleware usually includes the APIs on the client machine that permit it to invoke a service or make a request of the server, the software that sends the transmission over the network, and the software that enables the response to be sent back. Middleware does not include the user interface, the application logic software, or the database.

Q: *Explain the function of a firewall as it relates to the Internet.*

A: A firewall is software designed to protect an internal network from unwanted interference or intruders trying to access your network from an external point such as the Internet. A firewall helps protect the internal network by filtering message traffic to and from the Internet based on usage policies and rules that you define. The firewall helps you limit who can access the internal network and when they can do so.

Q: *What is the most often used database language in client/server application queries and commands?*

A: SQL is a powerful, database language that is used to manipulate tables of data. It has become an ISO standard and is the most commonly used database language today.

Q: *Name some examples of* Online Transaction Processing *(OLTP) systems.*

A: OLTP systems are usually mission-critical software applications that create and interact with large databases in a real-time mode.

Examples of these systems include point-of-sale, inventory control systems, reservation systems, stock exchange transaction systems, and banking systems.

Q: *How is a* Decision Support System *(DSS) used?*

A: A DSS is used to filter, analyze, and develop reports from data generated by OLTP systems or other software applications to answer "what if" questions, targeted queries regarding trends or patterns, and the need to represent data in different or more abstract formats.

Q: *Explain what is meant by the term Executive Information System.*

A: An *Executive Information System* (EIS) is a type of DSS usually employed by higher-level management personnel or executives. They use these systems with an eye toward making decisions using summaries of business data, graphical depictions of statistics, and answers to queries on data often already analyzed and pre-positioned by others in the organization.

Q: *What is the most widely used of the groupware products?*

A: IBM's Lotus Notes is the most widely used product of this type today.

Q: *Give a simple definition of the term* object.

A: An object is a capsule of information that includes programming code and data.

Q: *What are the current standards for developing components (objects) for the client side of client/server?*

A: The client or desktop standards from which developers can choose are primarily ActiveX and JavaBeans.

Q: *What is hypertext?*

A: Hypertext is a software tool that enables documents to be linked to other documents. The Internet uses the *Hypertext Transfer Protocol* (HTTP) to access and retrieve files.

Q: *For what is the Unified Resource Locator used?*

A: The *Unified Resource Locator* (URL) protocol is used to name and access Web resources on a global basis.

Q: *The commands used to structure Web documents and insert hyperlinks in them are written in what computer language?*

A: The *Hypertext Markup Language* (HTML) is used.

Q: *In Internet client/server parlance, what is a cookie?*

A: A cookie is a small data collection field or routine sent from a server to a client machine. It is used to store user identifications or other basic configuration information and then return this data to the originating server.

Q: *Name at least one popular Internet search engine that helps users locate information on the Internet client/server network.*

A: Search engines include Yahoo, Excite, and Alta Vista, among many others.

Q: *When a client/server vendor describes their product as being open, what do they mean?*

A: The vendor is generally referring to the fact that their product can interface and interoperate with other vendors' products without an extensive development of additional code or conversion methods.

Q: *When discussing object-oriented technology used in building client/server applications, what is meant by the term attribute?*

A: An attribute is simply a variable data element that describes or represents a property of an object.

Q: *What is an ERP system?*

A: An *Enterprise Resource Planning* (ERP) system is a client/server software package used to manage major business functions within an organization or enterprise.

Q: *What is meant by the term* cooperative processing*?*

A: Cooperative processing describes how a computer processing job is shared among two or more computing platforms. It implies that the processing workload is divided up in the most efficient fashion.

Q: *Explain the term* distributed processing.

A: Distributed processing refers to computer processing carried out in different locations (that is, geographically dispersed) on independent computer platforms connected by a network. The aim here is also the most efficient use of computing resources by dedicating each *central processing unit* (CPU) to the task for which it is best suited. This term and the term cooperative processing are frequently used as synonyms for client/server computing.

Q: *In the client/server technology arena, what is the term* downsizing *used to describe?*

A: Downsizing can imply full replacement of a mainframe host environment with networks and workstations. It definitely means offloading a significant processing workload or applications from the host, and deferring or avoiding altogether the purchase of additional host-based MIPS.

Q: *How would you explain what is meant by the concept of interoperability?*

A: Interoperability refers to the cooperative operation of software programs that reside on dissimilar computer systems. It implies the ready exchange of data and functionality.

Q: *What is a network topology?*

A: A topology is the layout or blueprint of a network. A logical topology describes how data and signals travel over the network to its stations, that is, sequentially or in a broadcast. A physical topology describes how the cables or wires are laid out to connect the nodes, such as a star or daisy chain.

Q: *Explain the purpose of a* network operating system *(NOS).*

A: A NOS is the software program that enables computers to communicate with one another or with a network. It also enables computers to share the other devices or resources on the network.

Q: *What does a* database management system *(DBMS) do in a client/server system?*

A: A database management system is a software program that is designed to collect, organize, store, and control data. It also permits a user to update, retrieve, and view the data.

Q: *What does the term* backward compatibility *mean?*

A: A system or product is said to be backward compatible if newer versions of the product continue to run the old software. For example, backward compatibility is normally provided by the vendors of computer operating systems.

Q: *How would you describe an applet?*

A: An applet is a Java program that has been built into a Web page. When a Web browser brings up that page, the applet downloads onto the system using the browser and is executed on that system.

Q: *On the Internet client/server system in the U.S., what is the presumed difference between a .com address and a .net address?*

A: A .com address is supposed to indicate that the Web site belongs to a commercial organization, while a .net address is supposed to be reserved for nonprofit net access groups or organizations.

Q: *Which net hardware provides the greater communication speed, an ISDN phone line or a T1 trunk line?*

A: The ISDN line is built to deliver 128K bits per second, but the T1 moves data along at the much greater speed of 1.544M bits per second.

Q: *What doe the acronym FDDI mean and what is it?*

A: The *Fiber Distributed Data Interface* (FDDI) is a standard for transmitting data on optical fiber cable.

Q: *What is a Web browser?*

A: A Web browser is a software application that provides a simple, user-friendly, Windows-like front end to Internet applications that retrieve things on the Web.

Q: *When using object-oriented programming techniques to build client/server applications, what is meant by the term* class?

A: Class is a term that means category or type. The programmer defines the class as a data type. Once a class has been defined, objects within that class can be designated. The class limits or defines the contents of the class.

Q: *What is an intranet?*

A: An intranet is the equivalent of a private Internet established inside a single organization. It employs the same technologies but is isolated for internal use by management and security tools.

Q: *What does an API provide to programmers or implementers?*

A: An *Application Programmer Interface* (API) provides a list of the programming libraries and system calls that a programmer can use. If the source of a program conforms to the specific parameters of an API, then that program will compile on any system that supports the API.

Q: *Identify some of the ways an application can be placed or distributed between a client workstation and a server.*

A: An application ordinarily has several components, including the user interface, its presentation management services, its business logic, and database logic. Any of these software components can reside on the client workstation, including a subset of the database management system services itself. The server generally provides the DBMS services and could house any of the other software components if required to improve the processing efficiency.

Q: *What are some of the network architecture issues you must address in the transition to client/server computing?*

A: The first issue is whether any existing network architecture exists. If so, is it sufficient to support the number of anticipated users and the amount of traffic or transactions that users need to send over the network? Additionally, it is important to determine if any corporate network protocols or standards must be adopted or adhered to in the move to client/server.

Q: *Describe the key advantages provided by a client/server database.*

A: A key advantage of a client/server database is the capability to locate the data in the most advantageous place for large numbers of users. Most of the important advantages of a client/server system result from splitting the computer processing between the client platform and the database server. One such advantage is that the workstation needs only the power and speed to be able to run the front-end software, thereby extending the life of less capable PCs that don't have the memory and processing horsepower required to operate a complex DBMS. Client/server databases also help reduce the amount of data transferred over the network, sending only the result sets rather than an entire file.

Q: *What is a* Remote Procedure Call *(RPC)?*

A: A remote procedure call is an element of an application program that transfers control and data to another part of the program across a network. When an RPC is executed, the calling program is temporarily suspended, while a set of parameters is transferred to another network node. It is there that the procedure is carried out. When the procedure is complete, the results are sent back to the original station where the calling program continues its operation. Remote procedure calls are important mechanisms in distributed transaction processing.

Q: *What is the purpose of a* network interface card *(NIC), sometimes called an adapter card?*

A: An NIC is a printed circuit board required by each computer on the LAN. These cards take the serial signals off the network cables and move them into a parallel data stream inside the PCs. The cards also change the data from parallel back to serial and amplify the signals so they can travel the required distance over the network. NICs also perform the media access control function.

Q: *What is TCP/IP?*

A: Protocols are essentially rules for exchanging and interpreting data transferred over a network. The elements of a protocol specify the format in which data is to be sent, the signal strength to be used, an information structure for handling the data, the sequence in which the data should be sent, and the proper speed for transmitting it. The *Transmission Control Protocol* (TCP) and the *Internet Protocol* (IP) are two U.S. Department of Defense-specified protocols that have been adopted by many companies worldwide. The TCP/IP software protocols provide a standard set of communication parameters that help facilitate a data exchange among dissimilar computer platforms.

Q: *What is meant by business process reengineering, and what is its relationship to client/server computing?*

A: Business process reengineering describes the effort associated with examining the current business activities and processes used within an organization to determine if better working methods can be adopted to meet the organization's objectives. It involves a review of the rationale behind the work, the logic of the information flow, the logic of who participates and in what sequence, and the consideration of alternatives for improvement. Business process reengineering often should precede or parallel the development of a client/server application because of the opportunities for improvement that are inherent in the architecture, the technology, and the integration capabilities that client/server computing provides.

Q: *In* graphical user interface *(GUI) terminology, what is a combo box and what is a radio button?*

A: A combo box is a combined data field and scrollable list box. The item that is currently selected in the list box automatically appears in the data field. The rest of the list box is displayed only upon demand by the user. This way it takes up less screen space. A radio button is a boolean switch used to provide settings where only one of a group of options can be selected at one time.

Q: *What is an API and how is it used?*

A: An *Application Programmer Interface* (API) is a set of program functions or a specification for them that provides the capability for applications to interact with network operating systems, DBMSs, or other application software. In other words, the API is used to link applications to other software or database management system services.

Intermediate Level

Q: *What does the term* scalability *mean in relation to client/server systems?*

A: Client/server systems can be horizontally scaled or vertically scaled. Horizontal scaling refers to the capability to add or delete workstations or users with a minimal impact on system performance. Vertical scaling refers to moving the workload to a faster or larger server or distributing the workload among a number of servers.

Q: *What does CORBA mean?*

A: CORBA is an acronym for *Common Object Request Broker Architecture*. Client/server applications built with distributed objects use this architectural approach to communicate by having the client object invoke a method or process on a remote server object using an *Object Request Broker* (ORB). The ORB locates the object or object class, invokes the method, and then sends the results back to the client object.

Q: *How is a two-tier architecture different from a three-tier architecture?*

A: With a two-tier client/server architecture, the processing or application logic is housed within the software residing on the client machine, within the database on a server, or on both machines. In a three-tier architecture, the application logic is positioned in a middle tier, separated from the client machine's user interface and the data that sits on a third-tier database server.

Q: *Why are three-tier architectures preferred in enterprise-wide systems and in Internet applications?*

A: A three-tier is considered easier to deploy and administer. It scales better, and it yields better performance because only the service requests from the client and the responses from the server are sent over the network. Better security is also usually achievable since the database and application servers can be in more tightly controlled environments.

Q: *Explain the concept of application threads.*

A: Some application programs or code residing on servers run most efficiently when tasks are given to various parts of the same program, rather than spreading them across multiple programs. These tasks are referred to as concurrent routines or threads of the same program.

Q: *How would you explain the difference between a simple* Graphical User Interface *(GUI) and an* Object-Oriented User Interface *(OOUI)?*

A: With a simple GUI, a user interacts with a menu bar, graphical text, scroll boxes, pull-down menus, pop-up lists, and so on to select objects or items. The user then designates the actions to be performed. With an OOUI, a user interacts with an icon that directly manipulates objects through drag-and-drop-type movements, rather than selecting actions from a list.

Q: *How are private keys and public keys used in client/server systems?*

A: A private key is a cypher used to encrypt and decrypt messages sent between two parties. Each pair of users agrees on and shares their private key to protect the information they send to one another. A public key is a cypher used primarily for authentication. Generally, a public key is used to encrypt shorter messages for transmission and to provide an electronic signature. These messages can be accompanied with a private key for decoding.

Q: *What is a digital certificate?*

A: A digital certificate is simply an authenticated, electronic container or file for a user's public key. It is a verified identity statement that has been attested to by a trusted, external authority that guarantees the authenticity of the certificate. This verification is often necessary so recipients of your public key can know it was really you who sent the key. Companies that provide this type of authentication of digital certificates are referred to as *Certificate Authorities*.

Q: *What do you get in a communication stack?*

A: Communication protocols for client/server networks are complex and are generally packaged into layers to reduce the complexity and make it easier for multiple protocols to work together. Vendors refer to these layers of protocols and their associated APIs as a stack.

Q: *Is* Secure-HTTP *(S-HTTP) different from HTTP?*

A: Yes, Secure-HTTP is a security-focused version of the standard Internet HTTP that offers many of the security features important to e-commerce. S-HTTP authenticates clients and servers, provides encryption using public key technology, and supports digital signatures and certificates.

Q: *What is a VPN?*

A: Client/server networks include *Local Area Networks* (LANs), the Internet, and intranets. An extranet extends the corporate backbone network to outside organizations using standard network operating system technology and the support of *Internet Service Providers* (ISPs). A *Virtual Private Network* (VPN) establishes a secure network across these other network types to connect a designated set of users by way of special VPN servers and security protocols.

Q: *Explain what is meant by the term* stored procedure.

A: A stored procedure is a designated set of SQL (or Java) statements or procedures that is compiled and stored in a server database for later use. A client workstation calls a stored procedure and passes it certain parameters that it requires to do a specific task. The stored procedures complete the task and ensure a set of results is sent back. One of the advantages of using stored procedures is that these procedures can accept different input data from multiple users without needing a new procedure each time.

Q: *What do you call the special actions automatically executed by a server based on pre-established, data-related events?*

A: These actions are referred to as *triggers*. A trigger enables an application or database to respond to certain events or errors as they occur.

Q: *What is* embedded *SQL (ESQL)?*

A: ESQL is a standard for planting SQL statements within other programming languages to facilitate their interaction with specific databases.

Q: *What is a data warehouse?*

A: A data warehouse is usually meant to be a separate database of aggregated information intended for decision support or EIS applications. It can also be a repository of data objects collected for specific business policies.

Q: *What does a* Transaction Processing *(TP) monitor do in a client/server system?*

A: A TP monitor can help manage computer system transactions move from their point of origin, across multiple servers, and back again to the client machine. A TP monitor helps ensure transactions don't break apart or get disrupted by other transactions. It can also help make certain that changes caused by transactions don't disappear if the system has a failure.

Q: *What is a nested transaction?*

A: A nested transaction is one where you have the ability to specify transactions inside of other transactions. This feat is achieved by developing hierarchies of transactions where an umbrella transaction contains subtransactions. The umbrella transaction starts the subordinate ones and is complete only when the subtransactions are finished. At least theoretically, nested transactions help track down or trap errors and failures more easily.

Q: *Explain workflow as it pertains to client/server systems.*

A: Workflow refers to the directing or routing of events or work items from one application program to another in a client/server environment.

Q: *How is a distributed object different from a traditional object?*

A: A traditional object is housed within a computer program and operates only within that program. A distributed object can be placed anywhere in a client/server network and can be accessed by remote users invoking methods or routines. Distributed objects can even call on other distributed objects. They should be viewed as software components because they are independent units of software not tied to particular languages, implementations, or programs.

Q: *What are the predominant standards for component (object) programming for the server?*

A: The developers can choose among COM+, CORBA Beans, and *Enterprise JavaBeans* (EJBS) for server-oriented, component standards.

Q: *What is persistence?*

A: Persistence is the capability of JavaBeans, inside a component infrastructure, to save the state and later restore it.

Q: *In the Internet client/server economy, by what name or term are companies that provide network bandwidth (UUNet or PSI Net) and companies that offer consumer online support services (America Online, Microsoft Network, or Prodigy) most frequently called?*

A: They are called *Internet Service Providers* (ISPs).

Q: *What is the term that describes the newer Internet broker markets being established where various businesses buy or sell products and/or services to other businesses rather than to consumers?*

A: This newer market is commonly called B2B, referring to the business-to-business transactions occurring over the Internet.

Q: *What is the most commonly used network management protocol?*

A: The *Simple Network Management Protocol* (SNMP) is used by network monitoring and management workstations to help define, track, and manage network resources.

Q: *Name some of the services or capabilities typically provided by a* database management system *(DBMS).*

A: A DBMS provides for data integrity (ensuring that the data is accurate or valid and does not inadvertently become corrupted), data manipulation (enabling an end user to create, update, modify, delete, and sort the data), data definition (allowing the data to be defined, structured, and indexed), data access (controlling and optimizing access to the data), data presentation (displaying the data), and data storage (providing the fields, records, or tables that hold the data).

Q: *What is a browser plug-in?*

A: A plug-in is a software program that can be loaded into a running browser to provide additional functionality that isn't in the basic browser.

Q: *Specify the differences between a bridge and a router.*

A: A bridge joins two physical networks into a single logical net, and a router moves data between two networks.

Q: *What is generally conceded to be Java's greatest advantage or breakthrough for client/server computing?*

A: The Java language is considered to be platform-independent. This means that the code can offer a "write once, run anywhere" capability, vastly reducing the costs of development and the deployment of client/server applications.

Q: *Which benefits normally result when an organization implements an intranet?*

A: When an organization creates an intranet capability for their users, at least three major benefits are derived from the initiative: information is distributed in paperless form, making it more reliable and faster; users can retrieve the latest information they need when they need it; and overall communication within the organization improves because it is easier to publish and disseminate information.

Q: *What is a network computer?*

A: A network computer is essentially another name for a thin client. A network computer is a device that costs less than a PC and depends on a server to deliver the services and system administration support often found on the PC. Palm computers, TV set-top machines, some kiosk devices, and even some portable telephone devices are examples of network computing technology.

Q: *What is OLE?*

A: *Object Linking and Embedding* (OLE) has been a Microsoft standard for some time. This feature enables various objects (such as files or spreadsheets) to be linked to other Windows objects or to be actually embedded within those objects. This capability is what enables a snapshot of spreadsheet data to be pulled into a word processing document, for example.

Q: *Define the term JSP.*

A: A *Java Server Page* (JSP) is a programming specification or technique created jointly by Sun and IBM to provide a standard approach to adding dynamic content to static HTML pages. The dynamic content is embedded within the HTML or accessed from other pages by using programming syntax (conventions) called tags. A Web server compiles the JSPs into servlets for easier component usage.

Q: *Explain what a use case is and its relevance to client/server application development.*

A: A use case is a relatively new term that refers to a method of documenting client/server application user requirements. A use case anticipates the important processes that a user will go through in employing the application, how the business rules will be applied for a particular transaction, which objects and functionality will be needed, and so on. A use case also helps to identify important system operating concepts and external system events. A series of use cases are developed as a prelude to the object-oriented design of client/server applications.

Q: *Explain the relationship between business process reengineering and a client/server architecture.*

A: Business process reengineering examines how an organization operates today versus how it could operate in the future. Business processes, work flows, task integration, and decision-making levels can all be redesigned for greater efficiency and speed. A client/server architecture often provides the enabling technology set to implement reengineered processes. Shared databases, networks, teleconferencing, and horizontally integrated application software that can be remotely accessed are just some of the architecture characteristics that can be important in achieving process reengineering.

Q: *How do you approach identifying the end users of a system and what do you need to know from them?*

A: You need to look for both the primary users of a system, such as a customer service representative or a salesperson, and any secondary users, such as a supervisor or an executive. An executive, of course, can be a primary user. Check an organization chart, understand where the information flows, and look outside the boundaries of the organization to identify potential users such as suppliers or customers. Each user will have his or her own expectations and needs. Ask about the types of data the user wants, the formatting and reporting requirements, how he or she wants to interact with the system (keyboard, mouse, light pen, or touch screen), whom the user communicates with, and the system speed and capacity the user must have. These are only a few examples of what you need to know from each type of end user.

Q: *If an organization says it wants to use groupware to improve communications, is there a need for a client/server architecture?*

A: Probably. The term groupware refers to a set of applications intended to provide electronic support to groups of people that usually work together. It can be loosely applied to applications such as e-mail and more accurately applied to structured workflow software and robust, multi-user software such as Lotus Notes. These types of software typically require significant group interaction and a client/server architecture that facilitates such electronic communication and collaboration.

Q: *How is peer-to-peer technology applied to client/server computing?*

A: Peer-to-peer usually refers to a communication link whose two sides use the same protocol to carry on a networked exchange of data. In client/server computing, the term describes communications between equal parts of the system. Normally, every computing platform can share information with every other platform on the network without having to be reliant on a server.

Q: *When migrating from a host-based environment to a client/server architecture, what are some of the issues that must be anticipated?*

A: The migration from a mainframe host environment to client/server computing can mean a big change in technology and in other areas. Some of these other issues or areas that need to be anticipated include the political shifts that might take place as more people have access to data, changes in training requirements, and changes in relationships with external organizations or customers. Workflow management, business processes, and internal organizational relationships could also be altered as client/server technology provides additional analytic capabilities, faster computing, and greater opportunity for productivity improvements.

Q: *Name some of the types of uses or special functions that servers support in a client/server system.*

A: Clients and servers communicate with each other over a network. Servers can perform general functions or they can be dedicated to special functions such as a database server, applications server, Web server, print server, facsimile/communications server, or image server.

Q: *Name the three standard protocols for LAN cabling and* media access control *(MAC).*

A: The three standard protocols for LAN cabling and MAC are Ethernet, ARC net, and Token Ring.

Q: *Explain how polling works in a LAN environment.*

A: Polling involves the sequential but extremely rapid inquiry of each device on a network to see if it wants to transmit a signal.

Q: *What is the* Simple Network Management Protocol *(SNMP)?*

A: The SNMP is a Department of Defense network-reporting and control framework that provides a structure for formatting, transmitting, and collecting information about devices operating on a network. SNMP works well and is used in many large networks today. The network management products that incorporate the SNMP structure are inexpensive and do not require a lot of CPU power or computer memory. However, variant configurations of the basic structure and a lack of good security features are considered SNMP weaknesses.

Q: *Why is it important to monitor LAN performance and analyze operating statistics?*

A: Performance measurements and LAN operating statistics can help managers and administrators detect early indicators of problems, plan for network growth, justify staff and budgets, and build a base of data for comparing LAN efficiency and performance.

Q: *What is meant by the acronym CUA?*

A: The *Common User Access* (CUA) interface standard is a derivative of IBM's System Application Architecture. It is intended to provide users with a consistent view of the applications he or she employs. The standard addresses how window layouts should appear on the user's screen, how action bars and pull-down menus operate, how push buttons work, how information is displayed within a window, how fields are formatted, how items are selected from the screen, how the cursor operates, and many other presentation techniques that users often take for granted.

Q: *What is a simple definition of the term* data domain*?*

A: A data domain is an allowable set of values for a specific data element in a particular field or table column.

Senior/Advanced Level

Q: *Define the term OLAP.*

A: *Online Analytical Processing* (OLAP) is a term that refers to automated, analytical tools that enable data to be viewed from various dimensions. OLAP's multi-dimensional capabilities enable more complex, sophisticated queries, making it easier to visualize data.

Q: *When should you use a three-tier architecture in a client/server application?*

A: A three-tiered approach is recommended when you will have multiple application programs written in different languages, when two or more different data source environments such as two different DBMSs are used, when the number of simultaneous users is anticipated to be in the hundreds, or when the transaction or query volume is expected to be several thousand per day.

Q: *Clarify the difference between asymmetric multiprocessing and symmetric multiprocessing.*

A: Asymmetric multiprocessing uses one master processor to run the operating system and control subordinate processors dedicated to specific functions. Symmetric multiprocessing employs all processors as equal entities, dividing applications into threads that are run concurrently on several processors and permitting any processor to run the operating system kernel. Symmetric multiprocessing improves application performance, but it requires multiprocessor hardware with shared memory and applications and databases that can really use multithreaded, parallel functions.

Q: *What does clustering provide?*

A: Clustering refers to interconnecting a group of servers to provide greater processing power. Potentially, you can increase system performance in symmetric multiprocessing environments and achieve greater availability and reliability in general because of the extra machines that can take over if any one server fails.

Q: *What is the advantage of LDAP?*

A: The *Lightweight Directory Access Protocol* (LDAP) is a simplified version of the X.500 DAP. It serves as a standard for universal directories that use distributed database and object technologies to keep track of distributed system resources. It is designed to facilitate access over TCP/IP networks and the Internet.

Q: *Explain the purpose of the e-commerce security feature called non-repudiation.*

A: Non-repudiation is a network operating system security feature that is designed to provide a sender proof that a delivery of information or a transaction took place and to provide a receiver with proof of a sender's identity. This feature is intended to protect against false claims that data was not sent or received or that it was tampered with before receipt.

Q: *What is meant by the acronym SQLJ?*

A: SQLJ is the embedded SQL standard for Java. It is the format by which you can insert SQL statements in Java programs.

Q: *What is JDBC?*

A: The JavaSoft *Java Database Connection* (JDBC) is an SQL Call Level Interface (a procedural interface) written in Java that permits a programmer to develop DBMS-independent Java code.

Q: *What are some of the kinds of external data often used by Executive Information Systems?*

A: Such data includes demographics, economic conditions, stock exchange news, information on competitors, information from customers or suppliers, statuses of relevant legislation, and studies by industry analysts.

Q: *When seeking to keep the information in a data warehouse current, what is the difference between updating and refreshing the data?*

A: If you refresh the data, you will generally replace the entire portion of the data you are interested in directly from the source. This technique is viable with smaller amounts of data. If you have to keep larger amounts of data current, you will probably want to update it, only sending the changed data to the data warehouse.

Q: *How would you explain the way an MDBMS functions?*

A: A *Multi-Dimensional DBMS* (MDBMS) works as if it were a multi-dimensional data cube. Data is stored in arrays along related dimensions, and it is accessed using indexing techniques. This type of data store yields higher speed access on pre-aggregated data in reasonable quantities.

Q: *What is data mining?*

A: Data mining is a form of data analysis that seeks out patterns and groupings that are not easily seen. The tools that facilitate data mining assist in evaluating information by looking for unexpected associations, sequences, and clusters that would not otherwise be apparent.

Q: *Would TP monitors be considered part of a two-tier client/server architecture or a three-tier architecture?*

A: TP monitors are representative of a three-tier architecture because they separate the GUI front-end on the client from the data resources on the back end. The TP monitors themselves tend to sit in the middle with the application logic.

Q: *What is meant when a JavaBean is described as introspective?*

A: Introspection refers to the fact that a JavaBean can reveal its characteristics or interfaces (its methods, properties, and events) through use of a BeanInfo class that specifies a bean's metadata or through a set of naming conventions that describe the same information.

Q: *Traditional second-tier Web servers on the Internet use which protocol to access the third-tier back-end servers that hold the documents and data being sought?*

A: They use the *Common Gateway Interface* (CGI) protocol.

Q: *How does a server determine who is authorized to use, retrieve, or view information the client is trying to access?*

A: A server will have an *Access Control List* (ACL) to control which clients and personnel can get access and which operations they are entitled to perform.

Q: *What does the T mean is the network hardware-designated 10baseT Ethernet?*

A: The T in this LAN technology indicates that the communications signal is carried on twisted pair wiring.

Q: *Why is* Dynamic HTML *(DHTML) significant?*

A: A shortcoming of traditional HTML is that a browser must download another Web page from a server to cause a change in what the end user is seeing on the computer screen. DHTML enables the appearance of a Web page (graphics, fonts, page location, and so on) to be modified dynamically based on input from the end user viewing the screen.

Q: *Why was the* eXtensible Markup language *(XML) created?*

A: XML was created as a follow-up to DHTML. It provides a syntax that enables programmers to add information (or to structure information a little differently on an HTML Web page). This is so that a user can manipulate the data on the screen more effectively and even query the Web page to present different fields, change data relationships, total the results, and so on.

Q: *How do the Microsoft* Component Object Model *(COM) and* Distributed Component Object Model *(DCOM) models apply to client/server computing?*

A: Microsoft's COM is the framework of standard protocols under which OLE works with various forms of data such as spreadsheets, audio files, calendar information, video clips, and so on. The DCOM extends this capability beyond a single desktop machine and permits remote Windows objects to be called.

Q: *Which Java technology is used to enable complex objects to be sent between the tiers in a distributed application?*

A: Java's *Remote Method Invocation* (RMI) is used to pass an object between the client and the server.

Q: *How do you provide business justification for transitioning to client/server computing?*

A: The best business justification can differ from organization to organization. Normally, though, the expense and effort associated with the transition to client/server computing is expressed in terms of

- Achieving better price/performance from computer platforms
- educing the costs of procuring computer hardware, or reducing training or maintenance costs over time
- Achieving greater interoperability and portability among applications
- Improving a company's competitive posture through productivity, reduced cycle time, faster responses to market changes, and so on

Q: *What are some of the rules of thumb that can be used to decide where to place the data in a client/server-based system?*

A: Data should normally be placed as close to the primary users as possible while still providing data security and data integrity. If important data is likely to be lost on individual workstations because of problems such as LAN instability or lack of user training, then it is better to keep the data on a server. Typically, data should be stored at the lowest point in the architecture that satisfies sharing requirements; timeliness/performance needs; capacity, update and access requirements; and issues of ownership/security. The requirements of the business rather than the needs of individual users should predominate if conflicting objectives occur.

Q: *How do technology training requirements change when an organization adopts a client/server strategy?*

A: Client/server computing demands new skills and different types of training for an organization's end users, system developers, and the information systems maintenance staff. These changes result from new design and development techniques such as data and object modeling, process redesign, prototyping, distributed design considerations, and Web development. New technology skills must also be cultivated in areas such as the use of application development tools, network design and management, system and application integration, and coding skills in languages such as SQL, C++, and Java.

Q: *What are some key changes that take place in the roles and responsibilities of a company's* Information Systems *(I/S) department when the company adopts client/server computing?*

A: Ordinarily, the I/S department has to become more a source of standards and system support than purely a development and maintenance organization. Users look to the I/S department to provide policies, technology recommendations, management of the network infrastructure, data management, and other aspects of systems management. The I/S department often needs to shift to responsibilities like system and software procurement, software distribution and updates, help desk operations, software licensing, and data archiving.

Q: *What are some of the key models or types of client/server architectures that companies frequently use?*

A: The several commonly encountered architecture models include the following:

- Distributed Presentation: here part of the presentation handling executes on the client and the rest executes on the server.
- Remote Presentation: here the presentation handling resides solely on the client workstation, while servers execute the business functions and data management.
- Distributed Function: here the presentation resides on the client, and the application or business functions execute on both the client and the server.
- Remote Data Management: here the presentation and business functions execute on the client, while data management resides remotely on the server.
- Distributed Database: here the data management functions and data reside on more than one client or server and can be accessed or updated from any system in the architecture.

Q: *Explain what is meant by the term* two-phase commit?

A: Two-phase commit refers to the two message-passing phases of a transaction-processing event. The first phase occurs when a coordinating node sends a message to subordinate nodes on a network to determine if all required work has been completed. If so, the transactional updates are temporarily recorded in nonvolatile storage. The second phase message is sent when the coordinating node determines whether to abort the transaction or permanently commit the update to stable storage.

Q: *What is the definition of* Distributed Computing Environment *(DCE)?*

A: The DCE is an open systems standard published by the Open Software Foundation. It describes an integrated set of technologies that are intended to promote interoperability (that is, make it easier to develop, use, and maintain applications in a heterogeneous distributed environment). DCE identifies specific technologies to support remote procedure calls, distributed naming services, distributed file services, time-stamping and synchronization, network security, and thread APIs.

Q: *How does disk mirroring provide database integrity?*

A: Disk mirroring provides database integrity by ensuring that data is automatically written to (or recorded on) two or more storage devices so that it can be recovered even if you suffer media failure in one copy or device. Sometimes disk mirroring is accomplished by writing to a duplicate database on another platform; sometimes it is done on another portion of the same hard disk.

Q: *What are the advantages offered by each of the two basic physical LAN topologies?*

A: Under the daisy chain topology, the cable is run along the shortest path between each network node. The result is that this topology uses far less cable. This topology also does not require special power or space for a wiring hub. The star topology has each node connected via a central wiring hub, usually located in a wiring closet. This topology's primary advantage is survivability. Even if the cable between the hub and any one station is lost, the rest of the network remains operating. With the star topology, it is easier to install, maintain, and change node locations.

Q: *When deciding which LAN cabling to use, how would you differentiate shielded twisted-pair, coaxial, and fiber-optic cable?*

A: Shielded twisted-pair cables provide protection against most electromagnetic interference, but they are relatively expensive. This type of cabling is also bulky and often requires custom installation. Coaxial cable costs less, is easier to install, and has similar resistance to electromagnetic noise. A caution with coaxial cable, though, is that you must be careful to select high-quality cable with the right impedance for the right protocol. Fiber-optic cable is more expensive than coaxial or shielded twisted-pair, but it permits signals to travel greater distances without repeaters. Fiber-optic cable is more secure and is much more reliable because it does not pick up electrical signals and impulses.

Q: *Describe the OSI model and its relevance to client/server computing.*

A: The *Open Systems Interconnection* (OSI) model has seven layers that describe standards by which computers can communicate with one another. These standards, ranging from physical cabling to presentation environments and application programs, provide the basis for integrating many of the client/server products available today. The OSI model also provides a reference framework for developing and evaluating communications protocols used in networks.

Q: *What is the NetBIOS interface?*

A: The *Network Basis Input/Output System* (NetBIOS) is a software program or protocol originally developed by IBM and Sytek to link a network operating system with a particular type of *network interface card* (NIC). This software program, now modified and used by many companies, operates at the OSI session and transport layers. It provides the interface between a computer and other resources on the network. In this regard, it functions much like the TCP/IP protocols. In fact, the *Internet protocol* (IP) portion of TCP/IP encompasses the NetBIOS interface.

Q: *Why is IEEE 802 important to a LAN design specialist?*

A: The *Institute of Electrical and Electronics Engineers* (IEEE) established a general committee to develop standards for network physical topology and cabling. These standards address the various protocols that are used in the physical and data-link layers of the OSI model. The two PC LAN standards of particular importance are 802.3 and 802.5. Standard 802.3 represents many Ethernet characteristics, while 802.5 describes the Token Ring architecture.

Q: *What is the purpose of a gateway?*

A: A gateway is a device that typically links PC networks to host machines, such as a minicomputer or mainframe, or larger packet-switching networks. A gateway provides linkage at the OSI session layer and permits different protocols to communicate with each other.

Q: *Identify some of the key functions or areas that network management addresses.*

A: Most commentators agree that network management includes the following:

- Fault Management: detecting and isolating system problems
- Configuration Management: monitoring and changing network connections, equipment, and software
- Asset Management: tracking the inventory of network components (cable, hardware, and software)
- Security Management: safeguarding against unauthorized access to network resources or components
- Performance Management: monitoring and controlling access to and/or the use of network resources to maintain adequate levels of responsiveness

Q: *What is the advantage of monitoring and controlling a network from the wiring hub?*

A: Since all LAN traffic goes through the wiring hub, it is easier to monitor and report on network activity from this point. The hub has a central view of every network node, allowing better data collection and more effective control of the devices at each node.

Q: *Explain why you should prototype an application or employ rapid application development techniques.*

A: Prototyping is a technique of interactively defining and refining end-user application requirements by building portions of a proposed application system. In parallel, the developers demonstrate their work to the users to determine if their needs are being satisfied by the (somewhat) superficial elements of the system that are taking shape. Rapid application development involves segmenting an application into smaller units or parts so that each one can be developed and put into operation much more quickly than conventional development techniques permit.

Q: *What are the characteristics of a good application design methodology?*

A: A good application design methodology is one that

- encompasses the entire development life cycle from the requirements definition through system maintenance.
- is modular so that it enables entry and exit at various points.
- enables the developers to select structured analysis, object-oriented,

information engineering, prototyping, or any other technique that is best for the task.

- addresses the unique challenges of building client/server systems and Web applications that have both distributed data and business logic.
- includes iterative planning and strategy refinement to deal with issues such as system management, documentation and training requirements, cultural and organizational implications, configuration management, software changes and upgrades, and support.

Q: *How does object-oriented design differ from more conventional techniques?*

A: Object-oriented design focuses on identifying discrete entities called objects that have a data structure and a behavior that involves operations of various types. In other words, software procedures are designed and built around objects. In a more conventional analysis and design, the emphasis is placed on identifying and decomposing the functions a system should perform and the data it should provide to a user. Object-oriented design is more complex, but the software built using this technique is considered to be more robust and less fragile. It is argued that if functions and requirements change, objects are easier to revise than software and a data design built around those functions.

Q: *What are BLOBs?*

A: *Binary Large Objects* (BLOBs) are large binary files of data ranging up to two gigabytes or so in size. A BLOB can be an image, a video, a voice track, a graphic, a document, or a database snapshot that is treated as a single object by the system or application.

Q: *What is referential integrity?*

A: Referential integrity refers to an operating principle of the relational database model. It is an aspect of data integrity that predetermines how the database management system should react when an end user attempts to delete a database record on which other records depend. Good referential integrity features do not permit a user to inadvertently orphan data records this way.

Q: *What is a multi-threaded application?*

A: The term thread describes a process within an application that performs a specific step or task. A single-threaded application does one thing at a time, whereas a multi-threaded application performs multiple tasks simultaneously. Multi-threaded applications, for example, can update a database, display a series of graphics, and print a report all at the same time.

Q: *What are some of the data management and control issues that you encounter when building a client/server system?*

A: The management and control of data is only one aspect of client/server system management, but a critical one. Some of the issues encountered in this area include

- Data security and copy control
- The ownership of data
- Read versus update rights
- Data definitions and key standardization
- Data archiving strategy and media
- Data distribution and synchronization
- Refreshment or update strategy
- Time-stamping techniques

Q: *Explain how a DLL is used.*

A: A *Dynamic Link Library* (DLL) is a group (or library) of software functions/procedures that are compiled and stored outside the main body of an application program. The DLL is accessed and executed at certain points in the application, either automatically or by the user's choice. A DLL is typically used to add special functions to software, such as providing imaging capabilities, performing special statistical procedures, or exporting data to graphics packages. Some application development tools are sold with DLLs to make it unnecessary to develop such code.

Bibliography

Derfler, Frank J. Jr., *Guide to Connectivity*, Ziff-Davis Press, Emeryville, Calif., 1991.

Guengerich, Steve, *Downsizing Information Systems*, Sams Publishing, Prentice-Hall, Englewood Cliffs, N.J., 1992.

Hopple, Gerald, *State of the Art in Decision Support Systems*, QED, Wellesley, Mass., 1989.

Salemi, Joe, *Guide to Client/Server Databases*, Ziff-Davis Press, Emeryville, Calif., 1993.

Schatt, Stan, *Understanding Local Area Networks*, 2nd ed., Howard W. Sams & Co., Carmel, Ind., 1990.

14
CISCO

Travis Niedens

"Are you ready? Cisco Systems routes almost 80 percent of Internet traffic today." This is Cisco's tagline in its most recent advertising campaign and is a metaphor for what we're trying to accomplish with this section: trying to get you ready for your technical interview.

Consider that Cisco sells in excess of $18 billion worth of networking products everyday and employs more than 21,000 people. This figure doesn't even include Cisco's *Value-Added Resellers* (VARs), training partners, or networking professionals working outside of Cisco. That's a lot of networking equipment that needs qualified people to operate it. Thus, the field of computer networking is still growing.

Networking is the science of connecting multiple computers and/or other devices such as printers so that they can communicate with each other. A basic network is typically in one location, such as a particular office building. A more complicated network could include over thousands of locations connecting thousands of computers around the world.

Internetworking is the process of connecting these individual networks together. One network located in Japan, another in Australia, and a third in New York City may well need to communicate with each other. The networks might also simply be on different floors of the same building. More often than not, the individual networks will have different physical and logical structures, adding to the complexity of the task.

What are routers and who uses them anyway? A router is a piece of computer hardware (or sometimes software) that provides a way for data from an originating host computer to reach a destination host computer on a different network or network segment. When a router receives data for a computer not on a local network, it forwards these data to the appropriate destination, which might be the target computer or another router.

Routers have the capability to filter data and to forward data to different locations, depending on how they are configured. They can connect networks that use different physical and logical topologies.

The Internet uses routers to make it possible for data to reach a destination. Corporations use routers to connect remote locations into a single large network or *Wide Area Network* (WAN). Even multiple networks within a single building use routers for efficient communication among network segments.

On the way to getting the technical job and obtaining the perks that are associated with a Cisco job, you may want to consider becoming Cisco certified. Cisco offers a wide range of certifications for networking professionals. Cisco-certified professionals are in demand and chances are you will increase your chances of getting a job working with Cisco products if you are certified. An excellent resource on Cisco certification is *Get Cisco Certified: Get Ahead* by Anne Martinez, published by McGraw-Hill (1999, ISBN 007-135258-9).

The preceding discussion is a brief, cursory overview of networking and Cisco systems, and it is not intended to be technical in nature. Our assumption is that our reader has a fairly extensive background and is using this book and this chapter as a refresher before entering the technical interview. Good luck!

General Networking Questions

Q: *How is a TCP session established?*

A: A TCP connection is created between two devices on an IP network using the following process:

- Host A sends Host B a TCP SYN packet.
- Host B sends Host A a TCP ACK SYN packet.
- Host A sends Host B a TCP ACK packet.

After this, the connection is established.

Q: *When a Novell client comes onto the network, what steps does it take to determine the services that are available on the network?*

A: The first thing that a Novell client does is issue a Get Nearest Server (GNS) request. Once this has been done and an answer has been received, the client keeps talking to this computer to learn which services are available on the network.

Q: *What are the classes of IP v4 addresses? Which classes are used by the public and what are the uses of the rest of the classes?*

A: Class A is used for public addressing: 1.0.0.0 - 126.255.255.254.
Class B is used for public addressing: 128.0.0.0 - 191.255.255.254.
Class C is used for public addressing: 192.0.0.0 - 223.255.255.254.
Class D is used for multicast: 224.0.0.0 - 247.255.255.254.
Class E is experimental: 248.0.0.0 - 255.255.255.254.

Q: *Which Ethernet port speeds does Cisco currently support with their products?*

A: The Cisco product line contains products that support 10-, 100-, and 1,000-Mbps Ethernet ports.

Q: *Which ATM port speeds does Cisco currently support with their products?*

A: The Cisco router line contains routers that support Asynchronous Transfer Mode (ATM) at OC3 (155 Mbps), OC12 (622 Mbps), and OC48 (2.4 Gbps). Some routers have interfaces that also support multiple ATM ports (that is, four-port OC3 line cards).

Q: *What are the following TCP/UDP ports used for?*

A: 25: Sendmail

23: Telnet

21: FTP

443: SSL/HTTPS

69: TFTP

Q: *Name all the layers of the OSI model and briefly describe them.*

A: The Application layer is the application interface with the user. The Presentation layer provides data encryption, compression, and management. The Session layer provides synchronization between applications. The Transport layer transports Network-layer data across a network in either a connection or connectionless fashion. The Network layer provides an addressing scheme to a network. The Data Link layer provides a mechanism to transmit data frames or cells across a network. The Physical layer contains the physical electrical transmission media used, such as Unshielded Twisted Pair (UTP), Signal Transfer Point (STP), and Fiber Optic.

Q: *What do ping and traceroute do and why would you use them?*

A: Ping is an Internet Control Message Protocol (ICMP) tool that sends a 56-byte packet (this can be changed) to a destination, expecting it to be returned. This is one of the elementary tools for checking network status.

Traceroute is an ICMP tool that functions like ping, but a data packet is sent back to the source every time a layer-3 device (such as a router) is encountered. This enables a network administrator to see the path a packet is taking through the network, the reliability of that path, and the time it takes at each point.

Q: *How does an AppleTalk client initialize its connection to a network?*

A: To communicate with a network device, the user selects a device type and a zone name. The client sends a Name Binding Protocol (NBP) request. The request asks for all specified devices in the zone. The router through which it normally receives packets forwards the request into the zone. The devices satisfying the request respond to the originating client.

Q: *What are the methods that Cisco supplies to provide network security?*

A: Cisco routers enable you to build access lists to manage how traffic is managed. Access lists can take most data found in the header of a packet to determine how to route the packet (source address, destination address, port, and protocol type). In addition to access lists, Cisco makes a device called the *PIX Firewall*. The PIX firewall not only can be used as a firewall, but it also can be used as a *Network Address Translation* (NAT) device to conserve on IP address space.

Q: *What are the three required configuration parameters to connect a device to a TCP/IP network?*

A: The IP address, default gateway, and subnet mask are the parameters that need to be configured for a device to correctly communicate on a TCP/IP network.

Cisco Troubleshooting Questions

Q: *If you have a Cisco 5507 switch connected to a Cisco 7513 in the following configuration, what issues could it cause? How would you fix it? The Cisco 5507's port 5/3 is running at 100 Mbps/full duplex. It is connected to a Cisco 7513 on interface e0/0 running at 10 Mbps/half duplex.*

A: For all Ethernet network connections, it is best that each side has the same speed and duplex configuration. If this is not done, you will have several collisions and runts generated due to the difference. To correct this specific issue, you would need to move the connection from the e0/0 interface to an interface that can support 100 Mbps/full-duplex Ethernet. In some instances, you may want to plug the connection into a 10/100 port on the switch and configure it for 10 Mpbs/Half Duplex. e equals 10-Mbps Ethernet, fa equals 100-Mbps Ethernet, and g equals 1-Gbps Ethernet.

Q: *If you are having problems with a specific computer on a network and you are given the IP address and MAC address of the computer, how would you be able to locate it? Assume that the network is using all Cisco routers and Catalyst switches.*

A: Follow these steps:

1. Traceroute to the end workstation.
2. Telnet into the last hop router listed before the destination address. This most likely will be the computer's default gateway.
3. Do "show ip arp X.X.X.X" where X.X.X.X is the IP address of the failing station. Notice the interface that is connected to it.
4. If you are running CDP on the network, type "show cdp nei int det," where int is the interface noted earlier. This gives you detailed information about the CDP neighbor, including its IP address. If CDP is not running, please confirm the address of the device that is connected to the port serving the failing station.
5. Telnet to the device (switch). At this point, type "show cam XX-XX-XX-XX-XX-XX," where XX-XX-XX-XX-XX-XX is the Media Access Control (MAC) address earlier recorded. Keep in mind that the router stores MACs as xxxx.xxxx.xxxx.
6. At this point, you should have displayed which switch port is serving the failed unit. To display the port, type "show port portnum," where portnum is the port number shown by the command listed in step 5.

Q: *How can you determine the status of a Frame Relay Permanent Virtual Circuit (PVC) on a Cisco router?*

A: The "show frame-relay pvc" command tells you the current status of all the PVCs that a router has connected to it as well as the statistics of those PVCs. If you type "show frame-relay pvc #," where # is the PVC number, it lists only the status and statistics for that specific PVC.

Q: *If you are having issues with frame loss on a Frame Relay link, which items would you look at and test?*

A: This frame loss can have several possible causes. The two main issues that could be causing this is that either you have a physical layer problem in your connection or you are exceeding your *Committed Information Rate* (CIR) and that frames are being marked as *discard-eligible* (DE). One could use the "show frame-relay pvc" command in conjunction with the "show interface serialint," where serialint is the serial port that your Frame Relay link uses to determine the Frame Relay link status. One other test that can be used is to send pings across the Frame Relay circuit that contains 0x0000 as data in the frame. Frame Relay switches see this as a test frame that can determine if the issue is a telco problem.

Q: *If you have an ATM link that is down, which commands would you use to determine the extent of the outage?*

A: Typing "show atm ilmi" shows the connection status to an ATM switch if you are using SVCs. You can also type "show atm traffic," which will show the amount of traffic that has been conveyed via ATM. As with any interface, "show interface atm intnum," where intnum is the interface number, displays most items to tell what has happened on the ATM link.

Q: *What is the proper procedure for upgrading the Internetworking Operating System (IOS) or firmware (FW) on a Cisco router or switch?*

A: Follow these steps:

1. Save the configuration of the device and reboot it. This clears out any possible memory issues that could cause a problem with upgrading. Note that the next steps must be done using enable privileges.
2. If space is available, copy the new IOS/FW to the device (usually bootlflash on switches and slot( ) on Cisco routers). However, this may vary.

3. Once the file has copied, it will be verified automatically. Just to be on the safe side, do this again manually by typing "verify device: flashfilename."
4. Update the boot statement for the router or switch. First, type "show boot" to see which flash file is being used to boot the device. Next, you need to clear out the old boot statement using the following commands:
   - Switch: clear boot system flash device:flashfilename
   - Router (in config mode): no boot system flash device:flashfilename

To add the new flash file into the boot statement, do the following:
  Switch: boot system flash device:flashfilename
  Router (in config mode): boot system flash device:flashfilename

5. At this point, you can either schedule a reload or reload the router or switch.
6. Set up a continuous ping to see when the router or switch comes back up. Once up, log into the device.
7. Once logged in, type "show version" to verify that the correct IOS/FW is being used.
8. You can either leave the old IOS/FW on the flash device or you can delete it. To delete it, run the following commands (depending on IOS/FW):
   erase device:flashfilename OR
   delete device:flashfilename THEN
   squeeze device:
9. To verify that everything is completed, type the "show flash" command. You should only see the IOS/FW files that you decided to leave on the device. Make sure you did not remove the IOS/FW you plan on running. The router or switch will enable you to do this and will cause the device not to boot on the next reboot.

Q: *How would you verify that Open Shortest Path First (OSPF) is running on a router? Through the Enhanced Interior Gateway Routing Protocol (EIGRP)?*

A: The command "show ip ospf interface" can be used to verify that OSPF is running on a router. In general, you can use the command "show ip routingprotocol interface," where routingprotocol is the routing protocol that you want to check. Taking this into consideration, for EIGRP, you would type "show ip eigrp interface."

Q: *Which commands would you use to view the route an IP packet is taking to get to its destination?*

A: The "show ip route X" command, where X.X.X.X represents the IP address or hostname of the destination, is used to display the current route(s).

Q: *How would you verify the utilization of a Cisco router interface? How would this help in troubleshooting an issue?*

A: The "show int inttype intnum," where inttype is the interface type (Ethernet) and intnum is the number, displays statistics about the interface in question, including utilization and availability. This helps if you are working on an issue where there is either slow connectivity or data loss.

Q: *If a Cisco switch is not configured with an IP address, will traffic still pass through it?*

A: Yes, it will. Layer-2 communication still can occur on a switch without an IP address. The IP address that is configured in a switch is for management purposes. However, if you are running more than one *Virtual Local Area Network* (VLAN) on the switch, you need an IP address for the switch so that each VLAN can talk to each other and the network.

Q: *Name the programs by Cisco and other vendors that can be used to monitor the status of a network and its connections.*

A: OpenView is a *Simple Network Management Protocol* (SNMP)/ICMP-based graphical monitoring tool created by Hewlett Packard. It is usually run on HPUX, but newer versions can run on Windows NT.

Netview is a proprietary version of OpenView created by IBM. NetView can take not only ICMP/SNMP data, but it can use *Systems Network Architecture* (SNA) and *Remote Network Monitoring* (RMON) data to determine the status of a network device. Usually, it is run on AIX.

Q: *Which Cisco proprietary layer-2 protocol can be used to verify network connectivity?*

A: The *Cisco Discovery Protocol* (CDP) must be running on both ends of a connection for CDP to be used. CDP is enabled on a router via the "cdp run" command, and the "show cdp neighbor" command shows the CDP neighbors that a router and/or switch has.

Q: *Which command is used to view the event log that a Cisco router stores or that a Cisco switch stores?*

A: The command "show log" shows the router's log of events and debug information for a router since the last reboot. On a Cisco switch, the command "show logging buff -X" shows the amount of most recent lines that you want to see of the log.

Routing Protocol Review

Q: *What is OSPF? What kind of routing protocol is it? What routed protocols does it support?*

A: *Open Shortest Path First* (OSPF) is a link-state routing protocol. OSPF only routes TCP/IP. Unlike most routing protocols, OSPF uses multicast in *Non-Broadcast Multi-Access* (NBMA) and point-to-multipoint networks to communicate network update information. Network update information is only sent out when a change occurs on a link. Updates are sent out to the network and, depending on the update, routes are changed after a *Designated Router* (DR) takes the update into its routing table, runs the SPF algorithm, and then retransmits the update to the rest of the network. In NBMA networks, a DR and a *Backup Designated Router* (BDR) are elected to maintain a hierarchical network setup. In point-to-point networks, DRs and BDRs are not elected and the updates are sent via unicast. OSPF supports *Variable Length Subnet Masking* (VLSM), route summarization, and discontinuous networks.

Q: *What is EIGRP? What kind of routing protocol is it? Which routed protocols does it support?*

A: *Enhanced Interior Gateway Routing Protocol* (EIGRP) is a Cisco proprietary routing protocol. It is a hybrid protocol, meaning that it is a combination of the best parts of distance-vector and link-state routing protocols. Like OSPF, EIGRP routing updates are sent out only when link states are changed, and it uses multicast to distribute these changes to its neighbors. EIGRP routers use the *Diffusing Update Algorithm* (DUAL) to determine the most efficient path (successor) and other paths (feasible successors). EIGRP supports routing for IP, IPX, and AppleTalk. EIGRP supports VLSM and route summarization as well.

Q: *What is RIPv1/RIPv2? What kind of routing protocol is it? Which routed protocols does it support?*

A: *Routing Information Protocol* (RIP) v1 and RIPv2 are both distance-vector protocols, meaning they rely purely on how many hops (routers) you must traverse to transport traffic from point A to point B. RIP only supports routing the IP protocol. RIPv1 has a 15-hop count limit and doesn't support VLSM or summarization. RIPv2 extends the hop count to 255 and adds support for VLSM, route summarization, and authentication. RIPv1 broadcasts updates every 30 seconds on UDP port 520, whereas RIPv2 sends its updates out via the multicast address of 224.0.0.9.

Q: *How do routing protocols exchange IP routing information, such as OSPF exchanging routes with EIGRP?*

A: Route redistribution is the mechanism that enables different routing protocols to exchange IP routing information. Use caution when doing this. Distribution lists can be used to control which routes are being distributed. These rely on IP access lists being configured first.

Q: *How can routes that are learned via a specific interface be filtered? Why would you want to do this?*

A: In configuring the routing protocol process and/or *autonomous system* (AS), you can specify that it should ignore updates with the passive-interface command. This can be used to avoid security holes and to make sure that less optimal routes are not being discovered or used. Another possibility is to apply an access list to the interface, but this has the downside of every packet being evaluated, thus using more *Central Processing Unit* (CPU) time.

Routed Protocol Review

Q: *What is the difference between the Transmission Control Protocol (TCP) and the User Datagram Protocol (UDP)? Why would you want to have this difference?*

A: TCP is a connection-oriented transport protocol and UDP is connectionless. UDP is designed for data streams that can handle data loss (voice, video, or updating for older routing protocols). TCP is designed to keep a constant connection between two hosts until all data has been transmitted. UDP relies on upper-layer protocols for transmission control and synchronization. In the IP packet header, the two are differentiated via the Protocol field, six being TCP, 17 being UDP.

Q: *What is the purpose of SAPs in an IPX network? How do these cause issues on most networks?*

A: SAPs are *Service Advertisement Protocol* packets. SAPs are usually sent out every 30 seconds on a network. If you have several devices on an IPX network, SAP broadcasts can cause a large amount of congestion. Using access lists, routing protocols and other methods can bring the amount of SAP traffic down to a reasonable amount on a network.

Q: *What is a broadcast storm? Which type of network protocols would you normally see cause this?*

A: A broadcast storm is when broadcast packets overwhelm a network in such a way that other traffic does not get onto the network. Due to the normal operation of protocols that broadcast such as the *Network Basic Input Output System* (NetBIOS) and IPX (SAPs), it is possible to have predictable broadcast storms. This is easily seen with a network sniffer.

Q: *How are non-routable protocols sent across a network?*

A: Non-routable protocols are encapsulated in protocols that can be routed across a network, or they can be bridged using technologies such as *Datalink Switching* (DLSw), *Source Route Bridging* (SRB), and *Remote Source Route Bridging* (RSRB).

Q: *What are the routing protocols that AppleTalk can use? When would you use them?*

A: AppleTalk is supported by three routing protocols: the *Routing Table Maintenance Protocol* (RTMP), the *AppleTalk Update-Based Routing Protocol* (AURP), and the *Enhanced Interior Gateway Routing Protocol* (EIGRP). RTMP should only be used on LAN segments due to the fact that updates are sent out every 10 seconds. AURP and EIGRP can be used on *Wide Area Network* (WAN) circuits since they only send updates when there has been a link change.

Q: *What is BGP? What kind of protocol is it?*

A: BGP is the *Border Gateway Protocol*. It is an *Exterior Gateway Protocol* (EGP) that is used to route between AS networks.

Traffic Management/Security

Q: *Which hardware/software products can be used to analyze the traffic on a LAN or WAN?*

A: Cisco has several products to do this, including:

- Cisco Switchprobe: This RMON v1/v2 device can send RMON data to collection stations. It can transparently monitor LAN/WAN links.
- CiscoWorks 2000: This contains programs that enable an administrator to monitor the performance of Cisco devices on the network and configure them.

Q: *What is the procedure that is used to determine what the average amount of traffic on a network is?*

A: The procedure that IT organizations use to determine the average amount of traffic on a given network is called *base lining*. This requires the use of network analyzation tools over a period of time to determine what kind of traffic and how much of it is on a network.

Q: *What are the traffic-queuing methods that Cisco routers support? What are their main characteristics?*

A: They are as follows:

- *FIFO queuing* is First in, First out.
- *Weighted Fair queuing* uses packet header data to determine data streams being sent and prioritizes them based on the weight they each have.
- *Priority queuing* enables a network administrator to configure queuing based on a protocol or interface. It uses four specific queues to determine how packets are treated. The higher queues must be empty for a lower queue to be serviced.
- *Custom queuing* enables a network administrator to create up to 16 queues based on packet header data. These queues are emptied out in a round-robin fashion.

Q: *What are access lists? What types of access lists do Cisco routers support?*

A: Access lists can be used to determine how many functions work within the Cisco IOS. Mainly, they are used to permit or deny the routing of specific packets from a given source and destination. Access lists can also be used to control traffic flow, routing updates, and the mapping of IP addresses to a destination. Cisco supports Standard (source node only) and Extended (source/destination addresses, masks, protocols, ports, and so on) for every protocol they support (IP, IPX, DEC, AppleTalk, and so on).

Q: *What does the following command do?*

access-list 101 ip deny 172.16.1.0 255.255.255.0 any

A: This command denies IP communications from this network, 172.16.1.0, to any other network.

Q: *What is traffic shaping?*

A: Traffic shaping is controlling the traffic in a given network so that the data flow is more predictable and that the network bandwidth is fully and efficiently utilized.

Q: *Name a few Cisco product features that can assist with traffic shaping.*

A: Cisco's queuing strategies can be used to effectively shape traffic that is being sent through an interface.

Quality of Service (QOS) can be used to prioritize all traffic on an interface using a bandwidth percentage allocation strategy similar to queuing. QOS can ultimately be controlled via upper layers to deliver better performance as needed.

Access lists can be used to keep traffic from traversing links that are overutilized.

LAN Switching

Q: *What is the purpose of a VLAN?*

A: The purpose of a *Virtual LAN* (VLAN) is to group computers on the same broadcast domain, even though they are located in geographically different areas. Usually, users with a common function/task are on the same VLAN in most companies. This enables added security and traffic control.

Q: *How can VLANs talk to each other?*

A: VLANs can talk to each other either through routers or with the *Virtual Trunking Protocol* (VTP).

Q: *What is Spanning Tree?*

A: Spanning Tree is an algorithm designed to avoid loops in a bridging environment.

Q: *What is trunking?*

A: Trunking enables you to connect multiple VLANs over a single link. It is mainly used for providing redundancy.

Q: *Which Cisco product line supports LAN switching?*

A: The Cisco Catalyst product line is designed for LAN Switching.

Q: *Which protocols can be used to transport NetBIOS or SNA traffic?*

A: NetBIOS can be run on top of IP or IPX to make it routable. The NetBIOS packets are encapsulated with IP and IPX. When using IP, UDP is used for broadcast messages and TCP is used for unicast messages. SNA can be transported using *Data Link Switching* (DLSw) or Source Route bridging over an IP router network.

WAN Connectivity

Q: *What are the common WAN connection protocols that Cisco supports?*

A: Cisco supports Frame Relay, X.25, ATM, the *point-to-point protocol* (PPP), and the *High-Level Data Link Control* (HDLC).

Q: *What is a NBMA network? How does this affect the configuration of routing protocols?*

A: NMBA stands for *Non-Broadcast Multi-Access* network. Depending on the routing protocol used, certain loop prevention protocols (poison reverse and split horizon) may cause routing update problems due to the nature of the NBMA network.

Q: *Which WAN protocols are considered Cisco-proprietary? What cautions should be used when deploying these?*

A: *High-Level Data Link Control* (HDLC) is a Cisco-proprietary WAN protocol. Even though other vendors offer HDLC solutions, they are not compatible with Cisco's. Any HDLC connection between a Cisco and a non-Cisco device may not operate correctly or at all.

Q: *How would you determine the amount of WAN links it would take to fully mesh a specific network?*

A: The equation n(n-1)/2 can be used to determine the amount of links needed to created a fully meshed network.

Q: *Which WAN protocols support native voice?*

A: In Cisco's voice implementations, voice can be run natively over Frame Relay and ATM. For other types of layer-2 protocols being used, *Voice over IP* (VoIP) must be used.

Network Design

Q: *How many backup routes does EIGRP store for a specific network?*

A: A router running the EIGRP routing protocol will store one main route (successor) and six backup (feasible successor) routes.

Q: *How many backup routes does OSPF store for a specific network?*

A: None, but OSPF can store up to four equal cost routes for load-balancing purposes.

Q: *What effect does configuring links in order to have an equal OSPF cause?*

A: If the links have a common destination, it causes OSPF to load balance traffic among the links.

Q: *Which Cisco proprietary routing protocol can be used to help maintain the availability of a network?*

A: The *Hot Standby Routing Protocol* (HSRP) was designed by Cisco to enable multiple routers to act as one in case of a failure. HSRP uses a Hello system between grouped routers to enable the routers to determine which router is the current router that is handling traffic. If these hellos stop, the backup router will become the active router and will start routing traffic.

Q: *What are the advantages and disadvantages of a fully meshed network?*

A: A fully meshed network is a network that is reliable due to the amount of routes it provides and also due to the load balancing it can provide. Due to the significant increase of links required to create a fully meshed network, the cost rises considerably. A partially meshed network uses generally about 75 percent of the links that a fully meshed network does, thus still providing multiple routes to a destination but doing it in a more cost-effective manner.

Q: *What type of servers would you deploy on a network to manage IP addresses on multiple networks?*

A: The *Domain Name Server* (DNS) enables IP network devices to be resolved to a specific IP address via a name.

The *Dynamic Host Configuration Protocol* (DHCP) enables network devices to be automatically configured by a server for connectivity to an IP network. In some implementations, DHCP can talk to other IP management types of servers, such as DNS and WINS, to give a computer more specific configuration information and also to update those servers for the new device on the network.

The *Windows Information Name Server* (WINS) is a Windows-specific server. It enables a NetBIOS name to be mapped to a specific IP address.

15
SAP R/3

Glynn Williams

SAP, a German company founded in 1972, has evolved into the world's leading inter-enterprise software company and the world's third-largest independent software supplier overall. In its most recent fiscal year, ending December 31, 1999, SAP AG reported revenues of EUR $5.11 billion.

SAP is an acronym for "Systeme, Anwendungen, Produkte in der Datenverarbeitung," which translates into English as "Systems, Applications and Products in Data Processing."

SAP R/3 is a complex integration of SAP modules and *Industry Solutions* (ISs), which represent different parts of the basic business process, and which are accessed through one user interface.

The modules used in most implementations are the *Sales and Distribution* (SD), *Financial Accounting* (FI), *Controlling* (CO), *Materials Management* (MM), *Production Planning* (PP), *Human Resources* (HR), and *Warehouse Management* (WM) modules.

IS is a specifically developed adaptation or modification that can be integrated into a SAP R/3 system for a given industry. An example of this is the SAP IS Retail. This solution provides additional functionality to the Sales and Distribution module, but it can also integrate with the various other modules used in the system.

These modules and solutions interact with each other to provide real-time data. It is this provision of real-time data that offers the business analyst complete control over the business, regardless of the company's size, number of locations, operating languages, or currencies.

SAP runs on a fourth-generation programming language called *Advanced Business Application Programming* (ABAP). As ABAP is a programming language, it is not covered in this section; however, we do cover the various tools used in conjunction with ABAP, which enable an analysis of the system and its data.

We will cover beginner, intermediate, and advanced questions and answers, discussing a combination of modules and tools as used in a SAP implementation or a SAP system.

Please note that all menu paths begin at the initial screen following logon at transaction code [S000], unless otherwise stated. All transaction codes are stated in closed square brackets, as follows: [xxxx].

Please also note that this chapter on SAP R/3 is intended as an overview, geared to interview-style question-and-answer sessions. Due to the nature of this book, it is not possible to insert screenshots. Should the reader want to learn more about SAP, numerous texts dedicated to the subject containing screenshots and explanations that expound on these subjects in greater detail are available.

Beginner

The more advanced a user's knowledge of SAP is, the more specialized in one or two modules a user is likely to be. As SAP is a very large and sophisticated business solution, it is difficult to master more than one or two modules and still remain effective in each of them.

Likewise, the converse is true. When introduced to SAP, it is important to grasp the structure of SAP in its entirety, including the various tools available to access and manipulate data. These tools are constant throughout SAP, whereas knowledge of a given module is unique to that module. Thus, this chapter will examine the basic structure of SAP as well as the basic tools needed for everyday usage.

Questions and Answers

Q: *What is the difference between a module and an IS?*

A: SAP is a system with many modules, where each module represents part of a business. A module is further broken down into various components. A module is the standard SAP solution for a business. For example, the SD module may be broken down into the component *Basic Functions*, and then even further into *Pricing*. An IS, on the other hand, may consist of R/3 core modules that cover, for example, administrative processes, industry-specific enhancements, and complementary software components from partners and customers as well.

Q: *Name the core modules.*

A: The core modules in SAP R/3 are *Financial Accounting* (FI)—often coupled with *Controlling* (CO) or *Treasury* (TR)—*Human Resources* (HR), and the logistics modules: *Sales and Distribution* (SD), *Materials Management* (MM), *Quality Management* (QM), *Plant Maintenance* (PM), and *Production Planning* (PP).

Q: *How many ISs are there? Give an example.*

A: More and more ISs are being added to SAP's powerful library of industry-specific enhancements. At the end of 1999, more than 19 such solutions existed. An example of such a solution would be IS-Oil, the industry solution for oil companies.

Q: *What is a component of a module? Give some examples.*

A: MM module one contains the component Consumption-Based Planning, which is abbreviated as MM-CBP. A general rule of thumb is that the *Implementation Guide* (IMG), accessed via transaction code [SPRO], is broken down into modules with the subnodes as components. Within a module, one has various components, which are broken down into various processes. For example in the Materials Management.

Q: *What is a client?*

A: A client is a SAP work environment in the highest organizational structure. Usually, several clients can be found in each system. QA and Development are the clients in the Training and Production system.

Q: *What is a user?*

A: A user is anyone that is given access to the SAP system by the system administrator.

Q: *What is an authorization?*

A: An authorization gives a user permission to perform a given set of transactions.

Q: *What is the IMG?*

A: IMG is an acronym for the term Implementation Guide, which system developers may use to customize the client they are working in.

Q: *What is master data?*

A: Master data is used in the system to represent the basic components of a procedure and to ensure data integrity throughout the process by ensuring that one common record is accessed for different procedures. For example, a customer master record may be referenced by more than one module. The FI module may access the customer master record to look at the payment terms of a customer, while the SD module may also look at these same payment terms for a sales document for this customer.

Q: *What types of master data are there?*

A: Master data exists in every module. For example, MM has master data for the material master record, a *bill of materials* (BOM), a routing, and so on. The SD module has the master data for the customer master record, pricing records, and so on.

Q: *What is an organizational structure?*

A: Organizational structures have different interpretations in the various modules. The *Personnel Management* (PA) module, for example, has an organizational structure that reflects the interrelationships and hierarchy between employees. However, the most commonly used interpretation of the organizational structure is that representing the business structure.

Q: *What is a sales area?*

A: A sales area is comprised of a specific combination of a sales organization, a distribution channel, and a division.

Q: *What is a financial management area?*

A: A financial management area is a central organizational unit for cash budget management and funds management. These areas subdivide an organization into units in which a user can carry out independent cash budget management and independent funds management. For the purpose of creating budgets, a user can group together, in a single financial management area, company codes with different currencies, operational charts of accounts, and fiscal years.

Q: *What is a controlling area?*

A: A controlling area may include one or more company codes that, in turn, may use different currencies. These company codes must use the same operative chart of accounts.

Q: *What is ABAP?*

A: *Advanced Business Application Programming* (ABAP) is a fourth-generation programming language that provides the source code, and thus the backbone, of SAP. Various ABAP tools can access data. ABAP also makes it possible to create additional reports or enhanced customer specific functionality.

Q: *What is a transaction?*

A: A transaction is a group of actions in the system, led by menu paths, used in order to perform a function.

Q: *What is a transaction code? Give some examples.*

A: A transaction code appears in closed square brackets and provides a shortcut to a specific function in SAP. This function may produce a screen from which to select further data or, alternatively, it may call a program. Transactions are generally grouped according to modules and components. For example, in the SD module, the transaction code [VA00] gives the sales order overview, [VL00] the sales delivery overview, and [VF00] the sales billing overview.

Q: *How would one find the transaction code of a specific screen?*

A: The user can identify the transaction code for a specific screen or for the transaction currently occurring by following the menu path from System to Status and then reading the transaction code.

Q: *How does one find the Help text for a specific field?*

A: The Help text can be located by placing the cursor over the name of the field where assistance is needed and then either pressing F1 or right-clicking on the field and selecting Help.

Q: *How does the user set the Help screen to open up in a modal dialog box instead of in an external viewer?*

A: Go to Help and select the Settings option from within any standard SAP front-end screen. Now select the In Modal dialog box.

Q: *How does the user find a list of possible entries for a specific field?*

A: A list of possible entries can be located by placing the cursor over the field for which assistance is needed and then either pressing F4 or right-clicking the field and selecting the Possible Entries option.

Q: *What is an ABAP Table? Give examples.*

A: Data can be stored in many ways in SAP R/3. The most common storage method is a table, which holds fields and their respective data elements. The sales tables include VBAK (sales document header), VBAP (sales document line item), and VBEP (sales document schedule line).

Q: *What is an ABAP field? Can you give examples?*

A: An ABAP field is used in tables, structures, queries, or databases. Each field holds data for the respective table, structure, query, or database. For example, in the table VBAK (refer to the previous question), there is a field named VBELN (sales document number). The combination of table and field permits the creation of ABAP programs.

Q: *How does the user discover the ABAP table and field names of a specific field?*

A: First, select the field, then press F1 for the Help screen, and finally press F9 for technical help to discover the table and field name of the selected field.

Q: *What is a data element?*

A: The data element of a field holds the data definition, data attributes, and data field labels. Field labels provide a description of the field wherever it is accessed in the system. This is beneficial when one has the description for an additional SAP field, such as the "Additional data A" field. Should one change the description for this field, the new description will be seen throughout the system.

Q: *What is a SAP GUI?*

A: GUI stands for Graphical User Interface and, as its name suggests, it is responsible for the graphical layout of the SAP software. GUIs in SAP R/3 may differ from version to version of SAP. For example, version 4.6 must run on the GUI appropriate for that version.

Q: *Are there different releases of SAP R/3?*

A: Yes, many releases of SAP R/3 are available. SAP released 74 versions as of July 2000, the latest being release SAP R/3 4.6D.

Q: *Is SAP modified in each new release?*

A: Certainly, the reason for a new release is to modify and update the software. Sometimes a new release may offer major changes to its predecessor. For example, Version 2.x used menu paths and transaction codes to navigate around the configuration screens, whereas version 3.x uses the IMG to guide one through the implementation process. Major graphical changes have taken place between releases as well. For example, the standard GUI for version 3.x does not integrate with the Internet as easily as the GUI for 4.6 does. Version 4.6 enables one to access suppliers' Web pages if necessary.

Q: *What is OSS?*

A: *Online Service System* (OSS) can be used to access information about a module in a given release. The OSS is a database of notes on known issues and their remedies. A user with a logon name and a password can access the information.

OSS can also be used to obtain quick responses from the SAP help desk representatives. The OSS provides other services as well, such as administration and registration of new users.

Q: *What is ASAP?*

A: *Accelerated SAP* (ASAP) is a project management software tool that is used on SAP implementations to guide the project through different phases. ASAP could, for example, take a project from the designing of the blueprint through to going live.

Q: *What is an OSS note?*

A: An OSS note is text about an issue and its associated solution that is available to the user through the online service system.

Q: *How does a user log on to OSS?*

A: To access OSS, users need to have a logon name and a password. The user types in the transaction code [S001] to reach the logon screen or, alternatively, follows the menu path beginning with System to Service to SAP Service.

Q: *What is a hot package?*

A: As with any software, especially software of this magnitude and complexity, users may find general operation errors. A hot package is a bundle of software and other source code changes applied to a given release in order to resolve any current malfunctions and to prevent the occurrence of other known malfunctions.

Q: *Can a SAP system operate in more than one country at the same time?*

A: Yes, it is possible to use a single system in more than one country at the same time. For example, a single platform can be used all across Europe.

Q: *Can a SAP system operate in more than one currency at the same time?*

A: Yes, a single system can operate in more than one currency at the same time. Each day the system downloads updated currency exchange rates.

Q: *Can a SAP system be used on more than one computer by the same user?*

A: Yes, it is possible to log in to the system on a different computer with the same user name.

Q: *Can a SAP system be operated by more than one user on the same computer?*

A: Yes, it is possible for a few users to log in on the same computer.

Q: *Can a single SAP system operate in more than one language at the same time?*

A: Yes, it is possible to operate a SAP system in more than one language. In a scenario where a single platform is being accessed by employees all across Europe, each user can log on in his or her own language. (However, languages that require a different typeface and structure, such as Chinese and Japanese, may not be compatible with a system operating in western languages, such as English and French, and so on.)

Q: *Define a material master record.*

A: A material master record contains all the necessary data required to manage a given material. This data may include a description of the material (giving size and weight, for example) and data with a control function (such as material type and industry sector). In addition to this data, which can be directly maintained by the user, the record contains data that is automatically updated by the system (such as the stock level).

Q: *Give an example of a material type.*

A: Material master records are controlled according to their material type. Many different material types exist, such as raw materials (ROH), semi-finished products (HALB), finished products (FERT), and trading goods (HAWA).

Q: *Define a customer master record.*

A: A customer master record contains all the data required to transact business with a customer. This data is grouped into three main areas: general data, company code data, and sales data.

Q: *Give an example of a customer account group.*

A: The customer master record is controlled via the customer account group. This account group defines many aspects of the customer master record and its behavior. For example, it defines whether a field requires input as well as what the acceptable number ranges are. Some examples of the standard account groups are Sold to party (0001), Ship to party (0002), Bill to party (0004), and Payer (0003).

Q: *What is a factory calendar?*

A: The factory calendar defines the working days of an object. This shows, for example, the working days of customers at a receiving point or the workdays of a given plant. This calendar is defined on the basis of a public holiday calendar.

Q: *What is a transport request?*

A: A transport request is used to order the transfer of customizations, programs, or repairs from one client (system) into another. For example, a transport request could be used to order the transfer of a repair made to the consolidation system to the production system.

Q: *What is a number range?*

A: A number range is an object assigned to particular master records or transactions in the system. A number range may have multiple intervals. For example, the number range (0001 to 1000) may have intervals (0001 to 0099) and (0100 to 0199). Each interval may be assigned to an individual object. Each object is allowed only one internal number range interval and one external number range interval.

Q: *What is an Area menu?*

A: An Area menu is a grouping of transaction codes that, when executed, open up different screens or execute programs. Area menus are configurable, which helps when a new Area menu is needed to represent selections tied to functions specific to a particular business.

Q: *What is the ABAP Workbench?*

A: The ABAP Workbench is SAP's graphical programming environment. It is used to write ABAP code, design screens, create user interfaces, obtain database information, and debug and test applications for efficiency.

Q: *How does the user discover the fields that make up a table?*

A: Users can see the fields that make up a table by using transaction code [SE12], entering the table name, and then selecting Display.

Q: *How does the user access the value of the fields in a particular table?*

A: The user can discover the values of certain fields in a table by using transaction code [SE16], the data browser. Care must be taken in using this transaction code, as it will access the entire database of entries for the specified table. Using all possible selection criteria when retrieving data will facilitate the process.

Q: *How can a user change the display settings in transaction [SE16] from the SAP name to a short description?*

A: The SAP name is the default entry in the SAP field. This name may be indecipherable should you be unfamiliar with SAP. Users can change the name to a short description by executing transaction [SE16], choosing Settings, selecting User parameters, and finally choosing Field text (in place of Field name).

Q: *Can I restrict the number of entries displayed in the data browser when searching for the contents of a table?*

A: Yes, you can restrict the number of entries displayed. However, by limiting the number of hits, you also limit access to the database. You can change this each time you use transaction [SE16] or you can set user parameters by selecting User parameters after you have clicked on Settings.

Q: *What is a selection option? Give an example.*

A: A selection option is useful when using a selection screen, such as you might see in transaction code [SE16] or in an *Logistics Information System* (LIS) structure. A user can double-click on a field that is available for an entry. Alternatively, a user can simply select the field and then choose Selection options. From there, users can access an advanced selection, where it is possible to select multiple values for a field or exclude values from a selection.

Q: *Give an example of a standard business document flow from quotation to invoice.*

A: This would be as follows:
quotation (document type QT), order (document type OR), delivery (document type LF), and invoice (document type F2). This flow may vary, depending on whether other modules or industry solutions have been included. For example, should you be using Warehouse management, you would create a transfer order and then confirm the transfer order after the creation of the delivery but before the goods issue of the delivery is carried out.

Q: *What is a customer material information record?*

A: The customer material information record is a master record that stores customer-specific data for a material master record in the SAP system. For example, the customer may order part number ABS0001; however, the customer may refer to this as part number ABS. The customer material information record would permit the customer to order a part using his own part number in the sales order.

Q: *What is order combination?*

A: Some customers require that each sales order be delivered in an individual delivery. Order combination is used in the opposite situation. It will, if activated in the customer master record, permit multiple sales orders requiring delivery to the same customer to be placed on one delivery document, as long as such specific master data as the ship-to party is identical.

Q: *What is the unloading point used for?*

A: The unloading point indicates the exact location where goods are received at the ship-to party location; it is defined on the customer master record. The unloading point might specify, for example, at which door of a plant a shipment should be unloaded.

Q: *What is the customer statistic group needed for?*

A: The customer statistic group is used in conjunction with the document statistics group, the material statistics group, and the sales area (sales organization, distribution channel, and division) to determine which update group must be used to update the data for the LIS (used for reporting and planning purposes). The customer statistic group is placed on the customer master record.

Intermediate

With a greater understanding of SAP, we can focus on specific areas of the various modules and intermediate usage of the ABAP tools.

Questions and Answers

Q: *What is a program?*

A: A program is a statement or set of statements designed to solve a particular problem. Programs consist of a sequence of commands that can be interpreted and executed by a computer. ABAP programs are the backbone of SAP.

Q: *What is a variant?*

A: When executing a program, one may use different selection parameters. These different selection parameters are stored as variants. This is beneficial, for example, when running the delivery due list program as a variant for different shipping points. This permits the specification of different shipping points in one plant or even of entirely different plants. The program will then process data solely for the relevant shipping point (as per the variant).

Q: *What is a program attribute?*

A: The attributes of an ABAP program define its basic characteristics so that the system can process it correctly. Program attributes include the following elements: the program title, program type, program status, the authorization group, and the development class.

Q: *What is a background job?*

A: A background job is a program or function executed in the background; it is not executed in a dialog session or online. Taking our example of the delivery due list, a user could either execute this delivery due list online in a dialog session or process it in background mode. The user could also execute this job in background mode at a scheduled time.

Q: *What is a user profile?*

A: A user profile is a set of authorizations that enable user access to certain parts of the system.

Q: *What is a user parameter?*

A: A user parameter is a setting in the user profile that enables faster processing in the system by allowing the user to set default data for specific fields. To verify whether a field in the system contains a given user parameter, press F1 and then press F9 to access the technical data of the field in question. Within this technical data, you may see "Parameter" followed by a value. Set this parameter and the requested default entry to agree with your profile. A user parameter also enables access to additional screens or functions. For example, the parameter MCL with value X permits users to view their update logs in transaction [MC30]. A user parameter may also be used as a mini-authorization to determine user access to data.

Q: *What is workflow?*

A: A workflow consists of a sequence of steps that are processed by people or automatically by the system.

Q: *What is EDI?*

A: EDI stands for Electronic Data Interchange. This is the electronic exchange of data, such as business documents, between business partners who may be using different hardware, software, and communication services.

Q: *What is an IDOC?*

A: *Information Documents* (IDOCs) can be subdivided into various types. Each IDOC can be translated into an EDI message, or vice versa, in order to cater to other systems (R/3, R/2, or third-party software).

Q: *Is it possible to debug an ABAP program?*

A: Yes, the transaction /h activates system debugging. Alternatively, one can select System and then choose Utilities. From there, select Debug ABAP to activate the debugging.

Q: *How do users debug programs?*

A: Once in the ABAP debugger, a number of tools are available. The objective of debugging a program is to discover why the program is behaving in a certain way. To locate the cause of an error, follow the standard process in the dialog (on the front end) until the error occurs. Activate the debugger at that point. Next, step through the source code and watch each step until the error occurs. You can also select tables and fields to determine what the values of the entries are. Another good diagnostic tool is to set a breakpoint automatically at a statement, subroutine, function module, or system exception. This is useful in a situation where the system is sending an error message, but you do not understand the cause. You can set a breakpoint at a statement (by pressing Shift + F5) and then type in the statement that one wants to stop on, such as the message.

Q: *What is a breakpoint?*

A: A user may want to scrutinize how the system behaves at a certain point in the ABAP code. To ensure that the system goes into debug mode at that point, one can set a breakpoint. This is extremely useful in investigating how routines and requirements function. By accessing the routine source code and setting a breakpoint at its execution point, a user can follow the routine through each step.

Q: *How are breakpoints set? Give an example.*

A: Dynamic breakpoints are only valid for the user that sets them and are automatically deleted when the user logs off. To set a breakpoint in the source code of a requirement, for example, use transaction [VOFM], which takes the user to the Requirements and Formulas screen. Now select a requirement such as goods issue by choosing Subsequent Functions from the Requirements menu and then selecting Goods Issue. Next, select the requirement 113, for example, and then click on the Requirement Maintenance button. This takes the user to a screen where the routine can be selected again. Now press F5 or click on the icon for source text, which takes the user to the source text (ABAP code). Placing the cursor on the position in the text that one wishes to analyze and selecting the Stop icon automatically sets the breakpoint in the program. Should this requirement be active, the next time the user attempts to post Goods Issue, the system will stop at that breakpoint. If it does not, the system is not entering that code.

Q: *How do I view the update error log?*

A: Transaction code [SM13] enables users to view the update error log.

Q: *How do you view the system dumps?*

A: Transaction code [ST22] enables the user to view the update of system dumps.

Q: *Is it possible to compare customizing across systems?*

A: Yes. The transaction code [OY19] enables users to compare customizing across various clients. This is beneficial in determining whether transports have gone through correctly or whether two configuration clients have equivalent data. Equal results may be expected from the execution of transactions.

Q: *How does one access user maintenance?*

A: To reach the user maintenance section, use transaction code [SU01] or begin with transaction code [S000] and then choose the Tools menu. Next, select Administration. Now choose User Maintenance, and finally select Users.

Q: *How do users access object names for which they do not have authorization?*

A: Should a user try to execute a transaction code and receive a message stating that he or she does not have the authorization for the object or transaction, using transaction code [SU53] will display the object that failed the authorization check.

Q: *How are locked entries viewed?*

A: Use the transaction code [SM12] to view locked table entries. Then use transaction [SU01] to display the user's details and inform the user of the lock. This will also unlock the user.

Q: *Is it possible to see a list of users on a system?*

A: Yes, by using the transaction code [SM04], or by beginning with transaction code [S000] and then choosing the Tools menu. Next, choose Administration. From there, select System Monitoring. Now choose User Overview and a list of users logged in to the system and the transactions they are currently in will appear.

Q: *In the FI module, where do users maintain the screen fields for a customer master record?*

A: In the IMG (reached via transaction [SPRO]), choose the Financial Accounting menu. Next, select Accounts Receivable and Accounts Payable. Choose Customer Accounts, then Master Records, and select "Preparations for creating customer master records." Finally, select "Define account groups with screen layouts." Alternatively, use transaction code [OBD2].

Q: *In* Controlling-Profitability Analysis *(CO-PA), what is an operating concern?*

A: An operating concern represents part of an organization for which the sales market is structured in a uniform manner. The individual segments of an operating concern are represented in the form of profitability segments.

Q: *What is variant configuration?*

A: Variant configuration describes complex products such as vehicles that are manufactured with a large number of variants. All these variants are defined as one variant product. The variant product has a bill of material, containing all the components that can be used in at least one variant of the product, and a routing, containing all the operations that can be used to manufacture at least one variant of the product. By allocating the variant product to a class, you assign characteristics to the variant product. You use these characteristics to describe an individual variant.

Q: *What is the condition technique? Give an example.*

A: The condition technique is used throughout SAP. It is the technique used to determine which instruction from a list of possible instructions must be used. Pricing offers a good example, as multiple prices may exist for one customer. Although there may be a standard price for all customers for a certain material, a customer may belong to a special group and thus be entitled to a special price. However, the customer may also be entitled to an even lower price should a material of a special group be purchased. All these different conditions specify price. The condition technique would be used here to sort these conditions into an access sequence and thus specify which one of these conditions must be accessed and used for the price. The access sequence is usually assigned to a condition type that is usually placed into a determination procedure. A pricing determination procedure, in this case, would contain the list of condition types and their associated access sequences.

Q: *In the MM module, under inventory management, you will find a movement type. How is it used? Can you give an example?*

A: The movement type enables the system to find predefined posting rules determining how the accounts of the financial accounting system (stock and consumption accounts) are to be posted and how the stock fields in the material master record are to be updated. The movement type is responsible for the systematic movement of stock from one location to another. For example, the movement of stock from our plant and storage location to the customer's site might be represented by goods issue movement type 601, goods issue for delivery (Shipping).

Q: *In* Production Planning *(PP), what is* Sales and Operations Planning *(SOP)?*

A: SOP is made up of both standard SOP and flexible planning. Flexible planning offers multiple options for customized configurations. Planning in standard SOP follows product group hierarchies and is always carried out level by level. Flexible planning follows hierarchies containing any chosen organizational levels, such as sales organization, distribution channel, material, and plant.

Q: *In the PP module, what is a* Bill of Materials *(BOM)?*

A: A BOM is a complete, formally structured list of the components that make up a product or assembly. The list contains the object number of each component, together with the quantity and unit of measure. These components are known as BOM items. You can create the following BOM categories in the R/3 System: material BOM, document BOM, equipment BOM, functional location BOM, and sales order BOM.

Q: *In the PP module, what is a routing?*

A: A routing contains sequences of operations. Each operation describes how a step or procedure is to be performed. Operations can be combined into sequences to show parallel or alternative processes. (A given operation can occur in several sequences.) Several similar routings and their operations can then be combined in one group. An operation can also be divided into suboperations to provide more detail. An operation can require a certain quantity of material components or production resources/tools.

Q: *What is a work center?*

A: A work center is the place where an operation or suboperation of a routing is performed.

Q: *In the SD module, what are the three levels of a sales document?*

A: Each sales document has three main levels and each level is represented by a table that holds the data for that level. Data for the header level is stored in table VBAK. Data for the item level is stored in table VBAP, and data for the schedule line level is stored in table VBEP.

Q: *In the SD module, what is the difference between material determination, material listing, and material exclusion?*

A: In material determination, the system allocates an alternative material on the basis of a material previously entered in the system. By contrast, material listing restricts a customer to parts allocated to him or her on a list. Material exclusion is similar to material listing, but it is used to prevent a customer from purchasing stock on a given list.

Q: *What happens at "Post goods issue" for a delivery?*

A: Post goods issue offers a good example of SAP R/3's integration. It transfers ownership of the materials to the carrier (who in turn relieves himself of the ownership once the customer signs for the materials) and causes the system to update data. The system updates the stock quantity, reducing the level of stock by the amount leaving the warehouse or plant. The system also updates the general ledger accounts by decreasing the value of the stock on hand and increasing the cost of goods sold. Next, it updates the stock requirements list transaction [MD04]. The materials have been shipped, and there is no need for the requirement to sit in the stock requirements list. The system then updates previous documents to indicate that delivery is complete and finally updates the delivery status to enable it to be found on the billing due list, should it be relevant for billing.

Q: *Is it possible to delete a delivery once it has been created?*

A: Yes, as long as goods issue has not been posted for the delivery, one may delete any packaging (shipping units) and delete the delivery. From version 4.0 onward, a user can delete the delivery after goods issue has been posted. To do this, first reverse the goods issue posting, delete the packing items, and finally delete the delivery.

Q: *In the WM module, what is a transfer order?*

A: A transfer order is an instruction to move materials from a source storage bin to a destination storage bin within a given warehouse at a specified point in time. The transfer order consists of items containing the quantity of the material to be moved and it specifies the source and destination storage bins. A transfer order can be created based on a customer delivery, a transfer requirement, or a posting change notice. Source and destination storage bins can be in different warehouses.

Q: *What is a storage bin in the WM module?*

A: A storage bin is the smallest addressable unit of space in a warehouse (often referred to as a slot).

Q: *How does one place stock into a plant and storage location?*

A: The transaction code [MB1C], used for Other goods receipts, allows the user to enter the material number, destination plant, and storage location, as well as the movement type. The movement type for entering initial stock balances into unrestricted use is movement type 561.

Q: *What is a customer hierarchy?*

A: A customer hierarchy defines a complex customer structure, such as a chain store. A user can create this hierarchy as master data, and assign special privileges (special pricing, for example) to certain parts of it. The customer hierarchy is comprised of customer master records and hierarchy nodes. The hierarchy nodes resemble an organizational or geographical element, such as customers in Europe. The node is created using customer account group 0012.

Q: *What is a product hierarchy?*

A: A product hierarchy is an alphanumeric character string, composed of a maximum of 18 characters, used for evaluation and pricing purposes. It defines a product family or the composition of a product. For example, in the product hierarchy 0001000200010001002, the first four characters, 0001, indicate that the product is a pump. The second four characters, 0002, specify cold liquid only; the third set of four characters, 0001, indicate the use of electric power only; the next four characters, 0001, specify voltage 250v; and the last three characters, 002, tell that the color of the pump is blue.

Q: *What is a sales area?*

A: A sales area combines the sales organization, the distribution channel, and the division and is used throughout the system.

Q: *What is the relationship between a sales office and a sales group?*

A: The sales office is assigned to a sales area. A sales group is a subdivision of the sales office. Employees may be assigned to a sales group. Sales offices and sales groups may be used for reporting purposes, as, for example, Key fields in the LIS.

Q: *Name the fields that can be grouped together, for pricing purposes, such as in a customer master record.*

A: Many valid fields in the customer master record can be used to group customers together for pricing purposes. An obvious example would be to base pricing on organizational elements, such as the Sales organization, the distribution channel, and the division. However, one may also use customer group, ABC classification, price group, price list type, industry, industry code, customer classification, the customer additional data fields 1 through 5, and the customer hierarchy.

Q: *What does the total replenishment lead time consist of?*

A: The total replenishment lead time gives the total time required for the in-house production or for the external procurement of a product. In the case of in-house production, the replenishment lead time is determined to cover all BOM levels. The total replenishment lead time is equal to the time stated on the MRP 2 screen. Should this field be empty, it is equal to the in-house production time plus the goods receipt processing time.

Q: *What fields are checked when determining pricing procedure?*

A: The pricing procedure is based on the sales organization and distribution channel, division, customer pricing procedure indicator (placed on the customer master record), and document pricing procedure indicator (placed on the document type).

Q: *What fields are checked in determining the shipping point?*

A: Shipping conditions that are placed on the customer master record or defaulted via the sales document type are checked. The sales document type default will override any shipping condition placed on the customer master record. The loading group (placed on the material master record) and delivering plant (found in the sales document) fields are also checked.

Q: *What fields are checked in route determination?*

A: Route determination is based on the departure zone (shipping point and shipping country), shipping conditions (from the customer master record), transportation group (from the material master record), destination zone (of the ship-to party), and the weight group.

Q: *How does the system determine which General Ledger accounts to post to in an invoice?*

A: In the pricing procedure, each condition type is allocated an account key. This account key is then accessed by the account determination. The account determination proposes a general ledger account based on the determination technique.

Q: *What are payment terms?*

A: Payment terms are the specified conditions for invoice payment. Payment terms may offer a discount for customers who pay in a timely manner.

Q: *What does MRP stand for?*

A: MRP stands for *material replenishment lead time*. It is the generic term used in requirements planning for procedures that take into account and plan for every future requirement (independent requirements, dependent requirements, and so on) during the creation of order proposals.

Q: *In* Quality Management *(QM), what is the usage decision?*

A: Users must make usage decisions in order to free an inspection lot and carry out stock processing.

Q: *In QM, what is an inspection plan?*

A: An inspection plan is defined by operations and characteristics. An operation could, for example, be a laboratory inspection; a characteristic might, for example, involve checking the hardness of a material.

Advanced

Advanced usage in SAP indicates thorough knowledge in the module, industry solution, or ABAP a user knows best. The ability to reply correctly and in depth to a question, as well as offer advice in issues such as integration with alternative modules of SAP, will demonstrate this expertise to an interviewer.

This section will cover advanced questions and answers pertaining to various modules as well as ABAP tools.

Questions and Answers

Q: *What is a logical database?*

A: A logical database is an ABAP program that combines the contents of database tables.

A logical database is linked to an ABAP report program as one of the program attributes. It supplies the report program with a set of hierarchically structured table entries derived from different database tables. This saves the developer from having to program the data retrieval. The logical database term covers both the program and the dataset.

Q: *Is it possible to see a list of all changed entries in customizing tables?*

A: Yes, by turning on table logging, one can view each changed entry to the customising table. Information is shown by system, date, time, user, the old entry, and the new entry; a list of all prior modified data is also supplied.

Q: *What is a* CATT*?*

A: CATT stands for *Computer Aided Test Tool*. It is SAP's tool for running transactions automatically. It is also useful in bringing in data, such as a mass maintenance of the material master in Excel, from an application to modify master data.

Q: *How does one create a CATT?*

A: To create a CATT, begin at screen S000. Next, select Tools. From there, choose ABAP Workbench. From that menu, select Test and then Test Workbench from that group. Finally, select CATT or CATT extended. One may also use the transaction code [SCEM] or [SCAT] respectively.

The user then assigns a name to the CATT and selects Execute. The user will then be prompted to follow through a transaction whereby the system will record the steps being carried out until he or she chooses to end the recording. The user can now execute this CATT, which will run through the steps automatically.

Q: *How does one close periods for inventory?*

A: Should one need to close a period for the material master records, one can use the transaction code [MMPV].

Q: *In the SD module, how is consignment processed?*

A: Consignment stock is stored locally at the customer's site and is dedicated for his use only. The standard transaction flow uses a fill-up document type KB, which follows the move of stock into the customer's site. Once the customer consumes the stock, he moves the stock via a document type KE, which moves the stock out of his storage, and an invoice may be issued to the consignment holder by the company. Should any of the stock be damaged, the customer can return the materials into his storage using document type KR. A credit note for returns may be issued by the company. At the completion of the consignment period, the company may pick up the unconsumed or damaged stock via document type KA.

Q: *How can users view inventory in the plant or at the customer's site?*

A: Users can pull down the Logistics menu and select Materials Management. Next, choose Inventory Management. From there, select Environment. Now select Stock and, finally, Stock Overview. Or use transaction code [MMBE]. This will give an overview of stock at the plant, the storage location, and the batch level. One has the option of viewing stock (for example, consignment stock or returnable packaging) at a customer's site by using transaction code [MB58].

Q: *How does a user access details of a spool?*

A: When using output (and thus spools), one can use the transaction code [SPAD], which is the Spool Administration Overview Screen. This screen allows the investigation of spools as well as of output devices and requests for output.

Q: *What is copy control?*

A: Copy control is a critical part of the document flow process. It is responsible for the transfer of data between sales documents, from quote to cash. The copy control governs the data at header and schedule-line level. The copy control is responsible for pricing, determines whether new pricing is carried out, and so on. It also determines which data is transferred. One can set a requirement at the copy control level to restrict the execution of the copying process, if required.

Q: *What is a user exit?*

A: A user exit is a point in an SAP program at which a customer's own program can be called. User exits allow developers to access program components and data objects in the standard system. Two types of user exits exist: user exits that use includes (customer enhancements that are called from the program) and user exits that use tables, which are used and managed directly via customizing.

Q: *Give an example of a user exit and define what is a formula.*

A: Many user exits are available in the system. An example of a user exit could be the USEREXIT_NUMBER_RANGE_INV_DATE (Module pool SAPLV60A, program RV60AFZC). Depending on the number range, table TVFKD is used to set the billing date for this user exit. (This is particularly helpful for country-specific requirements in Italy). USEREXIT_NUMBER_RANGE is automatically deactivated when this user exit is being applied. A formula is a mathematical algorithm. In SAP, a formula is a portion of source code that manipulates data. This portion of code, called a *routine*, can be maintained by the customer. Users can maintain formulas and requirements by using the transaction code [VOFM].

Q: *Give an example of a formula used in the system?*

A: An example of a formula being used in the system would be a pricing formula. For example, here's pricing formula (002 - Net Value):

```
* Betrag excl. Steuer
FORM FRM_KONDI_WERT_002.
 XKWERT = KOMP-NETWR.
ENDFORM.
```

Q: *What is a requirement?*

A: A requirement is a portion of code that is used to determine if a function or formula should be executed. For example, a requirement can specify that the item data of a document will only be transferred if the overall status of the document is equal to x. A requirement may be in the form of a pricing requirement or a copying requirement. The requirement can be maintained by the customer, who has access to maintain formulas and requirements by using the transaction code [VOFM].

Q: *Give an example of a requirement used in the system.*

A: An example of a requirement used in the system might be a pricing requirement determining whether an item is relevant for pricing (pricing routine - 2). This requirement would then be accessed by the pricing procedure:

```
* Pricing is turned on in item category configuration (TVAP)
FORM KOBED_002.
 SY-SUBRC = 4.
 IF KOMP-KPOSN NE 0.
  CHECK: KOMP-PRSFD CA 'BX'.
  CHECK: KOMP-KZNEP = SPACE.
```

```
  ENDIF.
  SY-SUBRC = 0.
ENDFORM.
* Prestep
FORM KOBEV_002.
  SY-SUBRC = 0.
ENDFORM
```

Q: *What is ATP?*

A: ATP stands for *Available-to-Promise.* It is the process of checking for available quantities of a material. The ATP quantity is equal to warehouse stock plus planned receipts (incoming stock) minus planned issues (outgoing stock). ATP takes into account all movements into and out of the warehouse. The stock examined for ATP could be safety stock, stock in transfer, stock in quality inspection, or blocked stock, while the planned receipts and planned issues of the stock associated with ATP could be purchase orders, purchase requisitions, planned orders, production orders, reservations, dependent reservations, dependent requirements, sales requirements, or delivery requirements. If the business produces special stock, such as made-to-order goods or consignment stock, the ATP check is done against the special stock.

Q: *How is an availability check determined?*

A: An availability check can be carried out in the sales document and or in the delivery document and can be configured specifically for a special process, such as a consignment. The availability check is used to determine whether there will be enough stock of a material to meet the requested quantities on a requested date. The control for an availability check is carried out based upon the checking group, which is assigned to the material master record of the product being sold or shipped, and the checking rule, which is pre-defined and assigned to the sales and distribution transaction, be it the sales order or the delivery. The control for an availability check is the place where the user selects the stock to be used, as well as the incoming receipts and outgoing issues, to determine the available quantity.

Q: *What prerequisites must exist before the ATP check can be used for a schedule line in a document?*

A: The availability check must be switched on at the requirements class level through transaction code [OVZG]. A requirements type, through which the requirements class can be found, must exist (use transaction code [OVZH]). To do the ATP check in the sales documents, the indicator must be set at the schedule-line category level through transaction code [OVZ8]. A plant must be defined in the sales order for the line item. It can either be automatically proposed by the system (from the customer, customer material information record, or the material master record) or it can be entered manually in the document. A checking group must be defined in the material master record on the MRP 3 screen in the Availability Check field. The checking rule must be assigned to the document type.

Q: *What is backwards scheduling?*

A: The time required to perform the business functions that must be completed before a delivery date can be met can be described as follows: the time taken to procure materials, that is, to obtain them from a supplier; the time taken to plan the transportation, such as obtaining space on a ship; the time taken to pick the items and pack the items; the time taken to load the materials; and the time taken to transport the materials to the customer. The process of scheduling the business process from the requested delivery date backwards to the specified delivery date is called backwards scheduling.

Q: *What is an inter-company sale transaction?*

A: An inter-company sale can be best described using the following example. The customer orders stock from sales organization A. Sales organization A belongs to a company code, such as company code 3000. Sales organization A then creates the sales order and indicates that the delivering plant is a plant that belongs to a different company code, such as company code 1000. The delivering plant then issues the stock to the customer. Sales organization A then invoices the customer for the stock purchased. Next, the system automatically creates an inter-company invoice at the same time as the customer's billing document is created. This inter-company invoice requires the selling sales organization A to reimburse the delivering sales organization and plant.

Q: *What is an inter-company stock transfer?*

A: When dealing with different company codes, one may need to transfer stock between them. Should the stock be transferred within the same company code, there would be no need for an inter-company transaction; however, should the stock be transferred between different company codes, there would be a transference of value, and thus an inter-company sale. For example, company code 3000, which has plant 3000, creates a purchase order to purchase stock from plant 1000, based in company code 1000. After the stock is delivered to plant 3000, company code 1000 creates an inter-company invoice and bills company code 3000 for the stock. This is referred to as an inter-company stock transfer.

Q: *What is legal control?*

A: Legal control supervises shipping materials to and/or conducting business with foreign countries. One can implement procedures specific to a given type of material, such as military equipment, or specific to the trade licenses required for a certain country. This enables, for example, a requirement to be placed that a trade license must be entered prior to a delivery being issued.

Q: *What is foreign trade?*

A: Foreign trade is the process of governing trade between countries. It includes the definition and usage of commodity codes, import codes, and customs tariffs.

Q: *What impact does an item category group have on material and sales documents?*

A: The item category group is used to determine the behavior of a material. The system uses a combination of the item category group placed on the material master record, the sales document type, and the usage of the item and the header-level item category, should they exist, to determine the sales document item category. An example of an item category group would be a NORM or LUMF. An item category group is placed on the Sales 2 screen of the material master record.

Q: *What reporting tools are available in SAP?*

A: SAP has many reporting tools. The most common are logistics information structures, ABAP reports (which are specific ABAP programs), and ABAP queries.

Q: *What is the LIS?*

A: LIS stands for Logistics Information System. The LIS is made up of the following information systems:

Sales Information System
Purchasing Information System

Inventory Controlling
Shop Floor Information System
Plant Maintenance Information System
Quality Management Information System

The information systems in LIS can be used to plan, control, and monitor business events at different stages in the decision-making process. They are flexible tools for collecting, aggregating, and analyzing data from the operative applications. The level of detail in which information is displayed is freely definable. Informative key figures enable users to continually control target criteria and to react in time to exceptional situations. Data can be analyzed using either standard analyses or flexible analyses. One can create a self-defined information system and tailor it to specific requirements for reporting purposes.

Q: *In an information structure, what is a key figure?*

A: The information structures that belong to the LIS are modular yet have a variety of techniques in common that enable one to analyze data. This type of structure also allows the individual information systems to retain their special features. Thus, all information structures have the same structure comprised of, among others, key figures and characteristics. A key figure is a value one can report on; key figures normally take the form of a number or a percentage and are expressed in a currency or unit of measure. Examples of possible key figures are invoiced sales, order quantity, and total net value. Two types of key figures exist: the simplest form of key figure is a numerical value field stored in a database table. This type is called a *basic key figure.*

You can also calculate key figures within a report or structure using formulas or rules for computing other values. This type is called a calculated key figure. Key figures may have a total value.

Q: *In an IS, what is a characteristic?*

A: A characteristic is a component of an information structure. Key figures can be summarized by a period for these characteristics. Some examples of the characteristics would be the sold-to party, material number, and sales organization.

Q: *Can you view the update of a transaction into LIS?*

A: Yes, by assigning user parameter MCL with a value X, the user can view the update. One can use the transaction code [MC30] to view the update log of a previous transaction, such as a sales order, into LIS. This will show the structures that were updated and the key figures with their values.

Q: *What is an ABAP Query?*

A: An ABAP query is a reporting tool that uses a logical database, individual table, or combined tables to form a report.

Q: *What is a user group?*

A: ABAP queries may be assigned to a user group. The group consists of users who have been assigned to that group and who thus have the required authorization to run the query.

Q: *What is a functional area?*

A: A functional area is assigned to the query. It is the representation of a logical database or tables with their respective table joins. This defines which tables and fields the query can reference.

Q: *What is the report tree?*

A: As there are many reports one can use to analyze data, it may be confusing to try to access these reports or structures. The report tree is used as a central repository in which one has access to standard SAP reports, queries, and structures. One may also add custom defined reports to this tree.

Q: *As of SAP version 4.6, the report tree has been changed; in what way was it altered?*

A: In release 4.6, the reporting tree is replaced by an area menu. This is done by assigning the reports a transaction code that, when used, transfers the user into the selection parameters for that report. This area menu may then be incorporated into the initial area menu S000.

Q: *What transaction code is used to migrate the report tree to an area menu?*

A: The transaction code needed to migrate the report tree to an area menu is [RTTREE_MIGRATION]. This will assign a transaction code to all reports, logistics information structures, and ABAP queries, so that they can be called up from the area menu.

Q: *Is it possible to create and change area menus?*

A: Yes, by using the transaction code [SE43], users can create and change area menus. Users can copy a SAP standard area menu and add elements to it; they can also add additional nodes, or subnodes. A transaction code is assigned to a node that requires execution. One can assemble the area menu according to a specific function a user requires. This newly created menu can be assigned to the users profile as his or her start menu, thus limiting their access or streamlining their available selections for ease of use.

Q: *What is an MRP type and what impact does it have on the material?*

A: The materials requirement procedure (MRP) type is the key that controls the MRP or reorder point to be used for planning a material. It contains additional control parameters used in forecasting materials planning, firming order proposals, and so on.

Q: *How do you change a data element and why would you do it?*

A: Users can create their own field descriptions for the fields in SAP screens. This is done without changing the SAP standard code, data dictionary, functions, or screens. Instead, users change the data element for a field. Use the transaction code [SE11], followed by selecting the button dictionary. When changing the data element, one will be required to enter an access key.

Q: *How does a user access an overview of logical databases in the system?*

A: A logical database is obtainable by using the transaction code [SE80] and clicking on the Other objects radio button, followed by clicking on the push button Edit. Then click on the radio button Logical database and use the match code to select the required logical database. In the match code, one can click on the push button Information system, followed by selecting Enter to obtain a list of logical databases.

Q: *What is a SQL trace?*

A: Often, when creating a sales order, for example, a user may want to know from where the system is obtaining information. This is especially true when trying to ascertain the cause of a problem. For this reason, SAP provides the use of a SQL trace. A SQL trace records all open, prepare, fetch, execute, and actual SQL statements, as well as the duration time for each step in a procedure. A SQL trace can be initiated by selecting the System menu, choosing Utilities, and then selecting SQL Trace. Transaction code [ST05] will also initiate the trace. Now select the button SQL trace and then click on the push button Trace On. (Traces are requested by a user.) One can then proceed to another session and carry out the process that requires recording.

After finishing the process, a user can proceed back to the SQL trace session, or back to transaction code [ST05], where the user can select the push button Trace Off. To view the trace, select the push button List Trace. Choosing the indicator Show SQL Trace and selecting Execute will reveal the results of the trace. All other entries required for selection should be present automatically by default.

Q: *What is a logical database?*

A: A logical database is linked to an ABAP report program as one of the program attributes. It supplies the report program with a set of hierarchically structured table entries derived from different database tables. This saves the developer from having to program the data retrieval.

Q: *How does the user access changes to the header and item levels of a sales document?*

A: Should the user want to see the changes made to documents, he or she can use the data browser [SE16] with tables CDHDR (for change header) and CDPOS (for change item). Should you use these, be very careful to enter as much selection criteria as possible to narrow down the selection, as these tables are very large and may sap resources.

Q: *What is a batch input?*

A: The batch input facility in SAP is a convenient tool for capturing data into SAP or updating large amounts of information in SAP transactions. For example, you may want to change the customer pricing procedure indicator on the customer master record for a list of customers. One could use batch input to make the changes. A batch input can be utilized in many ways; one of the simplest is as follows: first, record the batch input for the transaction used to enter the data in SAP and then export the batch input recording to a text file.

From the recording, you know what data is required. Create a spreadsheet or word processor document containing all the data to be captured or changed. Then mail merge the exported text file with the data in a word processing program. Then import the merged file, upload the file into SAP, and finally execute batch input in SAP.

Q: *How does the user add new fields to a pricing structure?*

A: To use a field in pricing, the user creates a condition table. This condition table is created using the allowed fields from the field catalog. Should the fields one requires not be included in the list of allowed fields, the user can add the fields from the list of available fields. However, a new field will not be in the list of available fields. For this reason, one has to create new fields for pricing.

The field catalog is a structure (KOMG) that consists of two tables (KOMK and KOMP). These tables contain the header and the item data for pricing, respectively. They are called KOMx because they are communications structures used to communicate the transaction data with the pricing procedure. Table KOMG contains the fields of tables KOMK and KOMP.

If you require a field that is not in KOMG, it means that it is not in KOMK or KOMP. This means that the field you require cannot be used in pricing because there is no communication of this field from the transaction to the pricing procedure via the communication structures. To use a field not defined in the field catalog, you need to add this field to the KOMK or KOMP structures and then write the ABAP code to transfer the data in the field from the transaction tables to the communication structure. Create the field in the KOMK (header data) and KOMP (item data) tables using the standard includes provided for this requirement. Write the code in the user exit to read the transaction data and transfer it to the KOMx structures.

Q: *How does one access a list of transaction codes in the system?*

A: Users can see a list of transaction codes and their descriptions by accessing the table contents of tableTSTC, using the data browser, transaction code [SE16].

Q: *In QM, what is a status profile?*

A: A status profile defines the location of the part number and supplier in the approval process. This is held on the quality information record and can be seen on the status tab, using transaction [Q102].

Q: *What is the difference between rescheduling and back order processing?*

A: Backorder processing is the processing of a backorder, which is a sales order that has not been confirmed in full or has not been confirmed at a certain delivery date. Rescheduling is a proposal for how confirmed quantities already assigned to sales orders might be reassigned to other orders with a higher priority due to an earlier delivery date, for example.

Q: *In QM, what is the inspection type?*

A: The inspection type is held on the material master record in the quality view in the inspection setup. The inspection type is the kind of inspection that will be carried out on the material; inspection type 01, for example, refers to a goods receipt inspection.

Q: *How does one run MRP for a material?*

A: One runs MRP in order to plan for a material. This is done by using the transaction code [MD02], should one want to plan for single item, multilevel planning for a material within a plant. This will create purchase requisitions, purchase orders, or planned orders for the material, based upon the settings selected in the transactions. For example, should the user want to create purchase requisitions for externally procured stock, the user can run MRP for the material in the respective plant to generate requirements from a sales document.

Q: *Is it possible to have a self-defined transaction code?*

A: Yes, generally self-defined reports or functions will need to be accessed by a large number of people on a frequent basis. For this reason, SAP has allowed the creation of user-defined transaction codes. Creating a transaction code allows the user to speed up access to specific reports/programs as the user no longer needs to use transaction code [SA38], for example, followed by entering the program name and pressing Execute in order to access a program. The user can then simply use a transaction code, which will automatically open the program. One can use transaction code [SE93] to create transaction codes.

16
Oracle Applications

Raghu K Vullaganti

Oracle Applications is a tightly integrated suite of application software for the following areas of business operations: manufacturing, process manufacturing, financial accounting, human resource management, supply-chain management, marketing, payroll, projects, professional services, sales force automation, travel management, treasury, and *Customer Relations Management* (CRM). Because it is difficult to cover all the topics in this chapter, the focus will be limited to certain areas in the *Enterprise Resource Planning* (ERP) applications suite, such as General Ledger, Accounts Payable, Accounts Receivables, Fixed Assets, Inventory, Purchasing, Sales Order Entry, Bills of Material, Work in Process, *Material Requirements Planning* (MRP), Human Resources, Oracle Alerts and System Administration.

This chapter discusses the basic features of Oracle Applications Release 11. Yet the details of these features are beyond the scope of this book. This book is intended for those who already have some knowledge and/or working experience in Oracle Applications. Figure 16-1 shows the business flow of Oracle financial and manufacturing applications.

When you invoke the Oracle Applications through the Web browser, the first screen you see is the login screen, shown in Figure 16-2. Once you enter the user name and password, you are taken to the List of Responsibilities window. In most cases, you can get your user name and password from the applications system administrator who sets up your account. Upon selecting a responsibility from the list, you can access the navigator window.

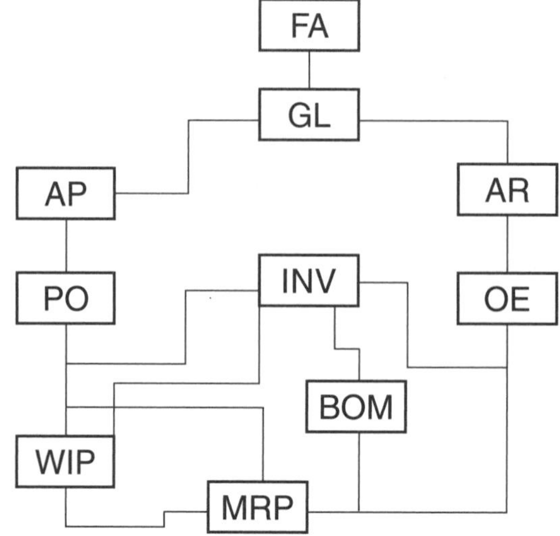

Figure 16-1 The business flow of Oracle financial and manufacturing applications (partial).

Figure 16-2 Oracle applications login screen

The following window depicts the navigation of a responsibility. The name of the responsibility (in this case, System Administrator) can be seen in the window title. You can see a list of functions and menus in the navigator list (left) window (in Figure 16-3).

The functions in the navigator window include forms, reports, batch jobs, and so on. All the functions in Oracle Applications are developed using Oracle development tools, such as Oracle Forms, Oracle Reports, SQL*PLUS, PL/SQL, and Pro*C. Various types of forms are available in Oracle Applications: setup screens, inquiry forms, data define forms, and transactional forms. You can use wild card characters (such as % or _) and placeholders (:variable) to specify the search criteria in Inquiry forms.

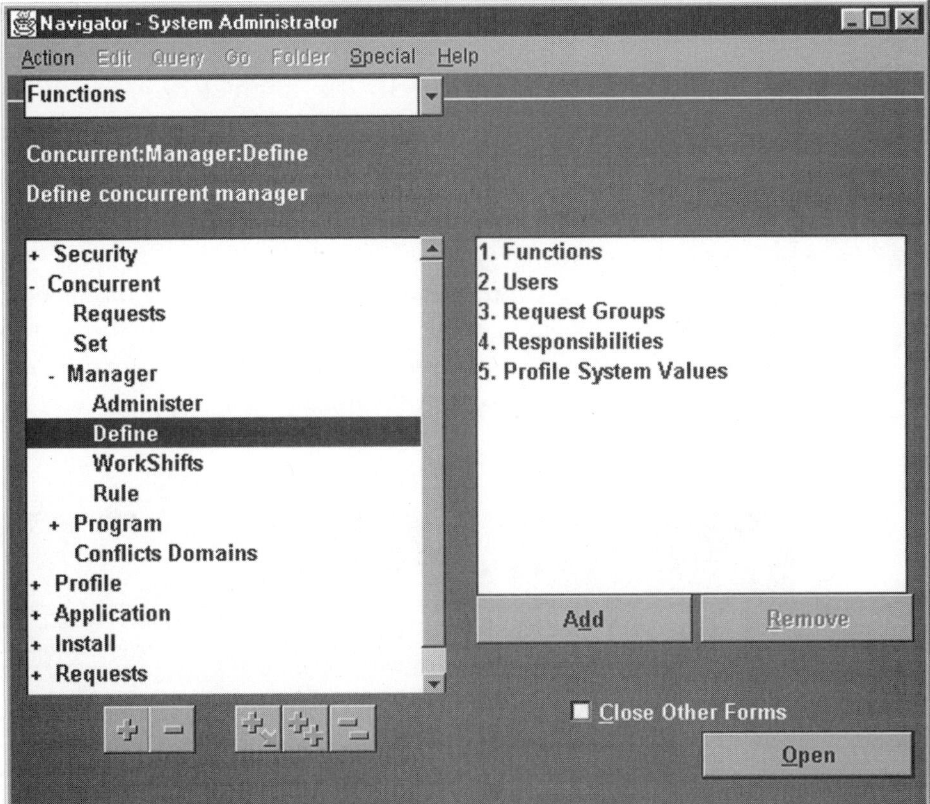

Figure 16-3 Oracle Applications navigator window

Oracle Applications Technical Environment

This section covers the basic features of Application Developer, System Administration, and Oracle Alerts.

Application Developer/AOL

Using the Application Developer responsibility, you can register the custom applications, tables, batch programs, and forms. The window in Figure 16-4 shows the registration of a new application. Application Developer is also known as *Application Object Library* (AOL).

The window in Figure 16-5 illustrates the registration of a custom form. If you have any custom tables for custom forms, you must register the custom tables first.

Custom Processes can be registered through Define Concurrent Program Executable forms. You must specify the parameters, associate them with a request group, and submit the concurrent program.

The main prerequisites for the creation of a custom application or responsibility are as follows: set up a directory structure for a custom application and define an environment variable that translates to your application base path.

In order to add a custom program to Oracle Applications, you must follow these steps: develop a program and report, identify what is executable, and register it with the application. Then create a concurrent program with parameters, and add a concurrent program to a request set.

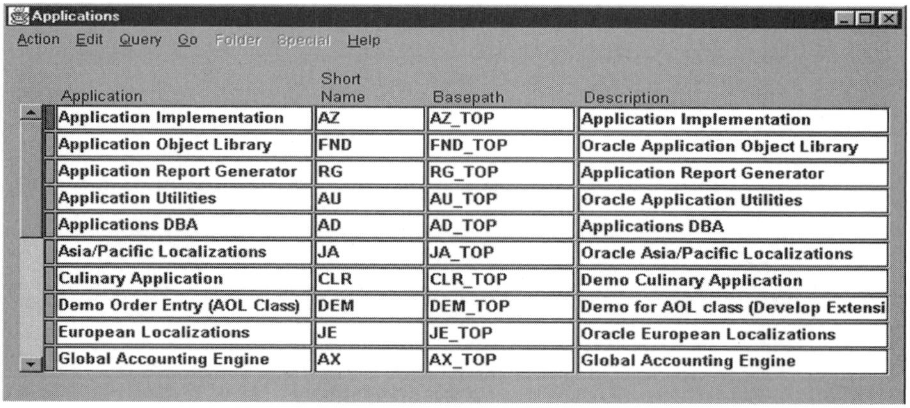

Applications

Action Edit Query Go Folder Special Help

Application	Short Name	Basepath	Description
Application Implementation	AZ	AZ_TOP	Application Implementation
Application Object Library	FND	FND_TOP	Oracle Application Object Library
Application Report Generator	RG	RG_TOP	Application Report Generator
Application Utilities	AU	AU_TOP	Oracle Application Utilities
Applications DBA	AD	AD_TOP	Applications DBA
Asia/Pacific Localizations	JA	JA_TOP	Oracle Asia/Pacific Localizations
Culinary Application	CLR	CLR_TOP	Demo Culinary Application
Demo Order Entry (AOL Class)	DEM	DEM_TOP	Demo for AOL class (Develop Extensi
European Localizations	JE	JE_TOP	Oracle European Localizations
Global Accounting Engine	AX	AX_TOP	Global Accounting Engine

Figure 16-4 Registering new applications

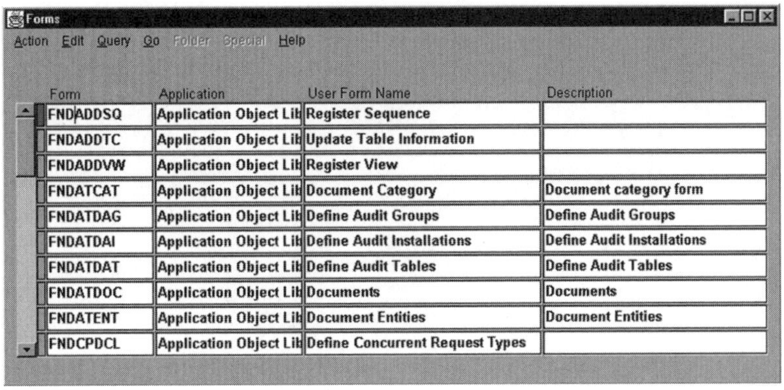

Forms

Action Edit Query Go Folder Special Help

Form	Application	User Form Name	Description
FNDADDSQ	Application Object Lib	Register Sequence	
FNDADDTC	Application Object Lib	Update Table Information	
FNDADDVW	Application Object Lib	Register View	
FNDATCAT	Application Object Lib	Document Category	Document category form
FNDATDAG	Application Object Lib	Define Audit Groups	Define Audit Groups
FNDATDAI	Application Object Lib	Define Audit Installations	Define Audit Installations
FNDATDAT	Application Object Lib	Define Audit Tables	Define Audit Tables
FNDATDOC	Application Object Lib	Documents	Documents
FNDATENT	Application Object Lib	Document Entities	Document Entities
FNDCPDCL	Application Object Lib	Define Concurrent Request Types	

Figure 16-5 Registering new forms

System Administration

System Administration in Oracle Applications does not take place at the operating system level. The term "System Administrator" causes confusion because it is used both in the Unix/Windows NT world as well as by Oracle Applications users. To minimize the confusion, it is best to use the term "Applications System Administrator." The responsibilities of the Oracle Applications System Administrator include managing applications security; administering concurrent managers; managing profiles, printers, concurrent programs; and auditing system resources. Figure 16-6 shows the status of previously submitted concurrent job requests.

Flexfields

Flexfields are segmented identifiers that provide many capabilities to Oracle applications. Two types of Flexfields exist: Key Flexfields and *Descriptive Flexfields* (DFFs). A key flexfield is defined as an identifier for each application entity and consists of multiple segments. Some examples would be the GL Accounting Flexfield and the Inventory Item Key Flexfield. DFFs are used to define custom fields into standard forms by avoiding form modifications. DFFs in forms are represented by the following symbol: [ ] (a single space field enclosed by brackets). This is called a "beer mug" field. A Value Set is a list of values validated against segments. Cross-validation rules can be applied to only some of the Key Flexfields. You can plan and define the Flexfield structures, assign the qualifiers to the Flexfields, define and implement the value sets, and define and implement the cross-validation and security rules.

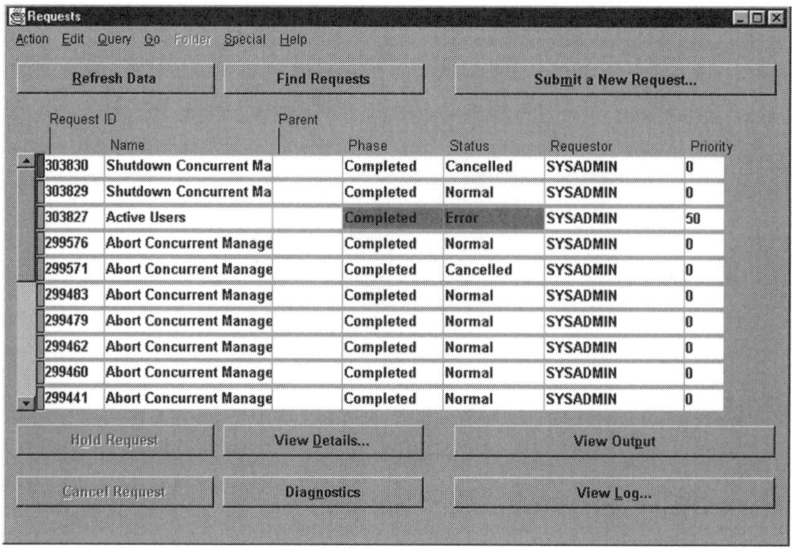

Figure 16-6 Concurrent job requests

Oracle Alerts

Oracle Alert is an exception-reporting system. It keeps you informed on an as-needed basis. It also sends exception messages to other users through e-mail. Two types of alerts exist: periodic and event. You can define and implement periodic and event alerts, maintain an event history, and manage the response processing. The following window, illustrated in Figure 16-7, can be used to define and maintain Oracle Alert, including defining alert names, alert types, alert frequencies, and associated SQL statements.

Oracle Applications Functional Environment

Next, we will discuss the basic concepts concerning the main functional areas of Oracle Applications.

General Ledger

General Ledger is the primary component of the financial accounting system. It is a comprehensive financial management solution that manages financial controls, data collection, information access, and financial reporting.

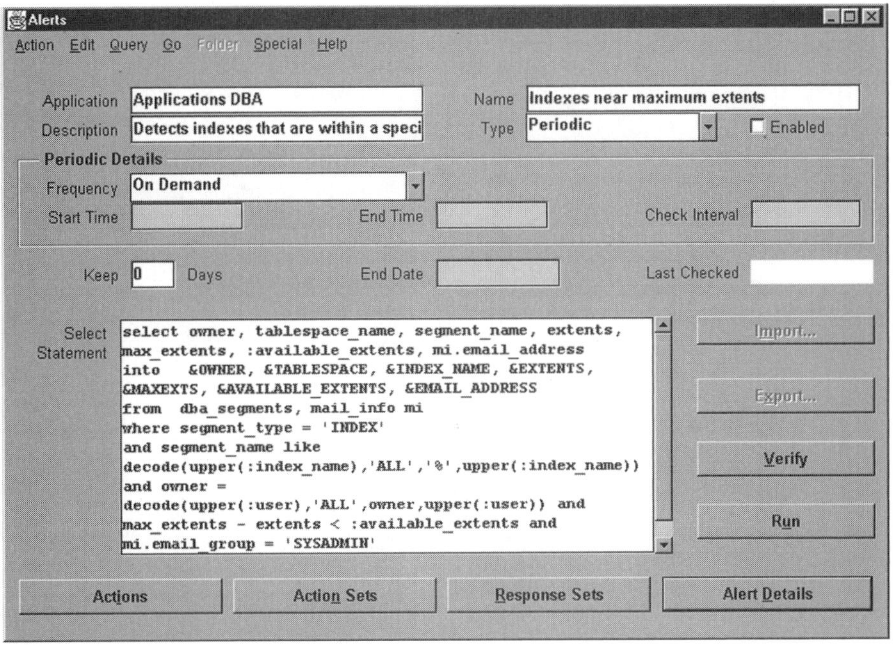

Figure 16-7 Define alerts window

A *set of books* (SOB) is comprised of the following: a chart of accounts structure, a calendar, and a currency. You can define one account structure for both journal entry and budgeting. The set of books determines how the accounting information is collected and categorized for reporting purposes. Figure 16-8 shows an example of a screen for a SOB.

An accounting period must be opened before you enter any journals. Journals can be entered manually or imported from external systems. Various types of journals can be used, including standard, reversal, and recurring. Once the journals are entered, they can be approved and posted. You have the ability to review the balances and make corrections if necessary. General Ledger will enable you to consolidate the balances into a parent set of books and close the accounting period. Custom reports can be created using the *Financial System Generator* (FSG). The *General Ledger Desktop Integrator* (GLDI), a powerful end-user desktop tool, can be used to integrate General Ledger information with Microsoft Excel. Mass allocations can be used to automate the process of cost and revenue allocations. *Multiple Reporting Currency* (MRC) functionality can be used if there is a need to report General Ledger daily transactions in more than one currency.

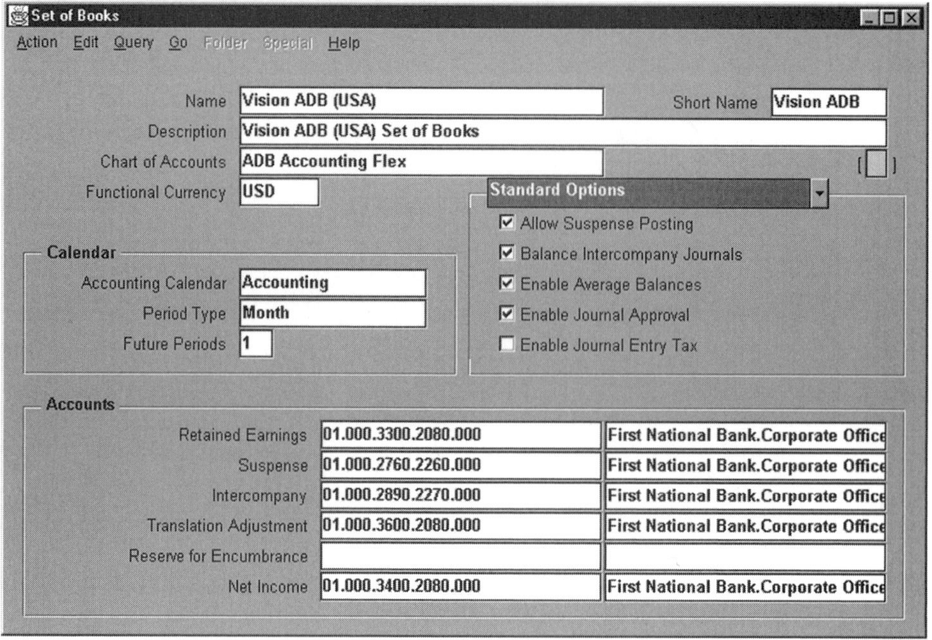

Figure 16-8 SOB window

Purchasing

Purchasing is the procurement process within an organization. It is the initial phase of supply-chain management. Suppliers, also known as vendors, must exist in the system before you begin the purchasing process. Its major features include sourcing, purchase requisitions, the requisition approval process, purchasing, and receiving. Two main types of purchase orders, standard and blanket, are widely used. Purchase orders can be created with or without requisitions. The screen shown in Figure 16-9 is an example of a purchase order.

A purchase order can have one or more line items. Each line item, in turn, can have one or more distribution lines and each line can have multiple line locations. Requisitions can also have headers, lines, and distributions and are defined in the system prior to the creation of purchase orders. Employees should exist in the Human Resource system before you set up the approval hierarchy, approval routing, and approval authorization control.

You need to set up the buyers, purchasing options, receiving options, approval groups, document types, and lookup codes. It is also important to control the purchasing periods.

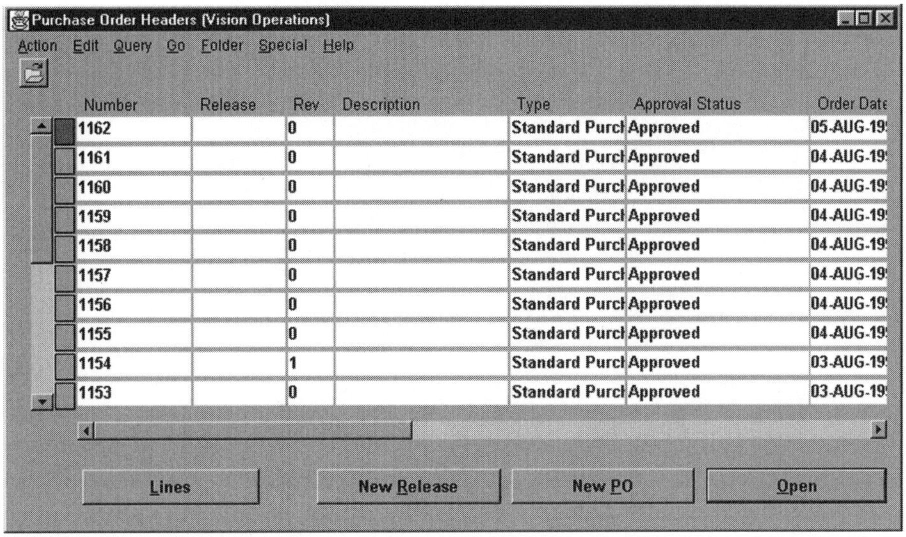

Figure 16-9 Purchase order headers window

Purchasing integrates with the Accounts Payable module. Once the purchase order is created and the item is received from the supplier, the order status will be changed to "closed" and a liability will be recorded in payables. Consequently, the sub-ledger transactions are posted to the General Ledger. Items received from the vendor arrive at the company's receiving dock and go through the inspection process. Once they pass quality control, they are placed in the inventory stock by incrementing the stock quantity. Rejected items are returned to the vendor.

Accounts Payable

Accounts Payable is the final phase of supply-chain management. The primary function of Accounts Payable is to manage the procurement cycle and cash flow. As noted earlier, suppliers' purchasing information integrates with accounts payable.

You can enter invoices through the Entering Invoice screen. Figure 16-10 illustrates the entry of a single invoice.

Payables have two workbenches: invoice and payment. The workbenches are used to create, adjust, and review the invoices or payments based on the workbench you select. In the payables cycle, all payments are processed as follows: establish the supplier information, match the invoices with the purchase orders, approve the invoices manually or through the

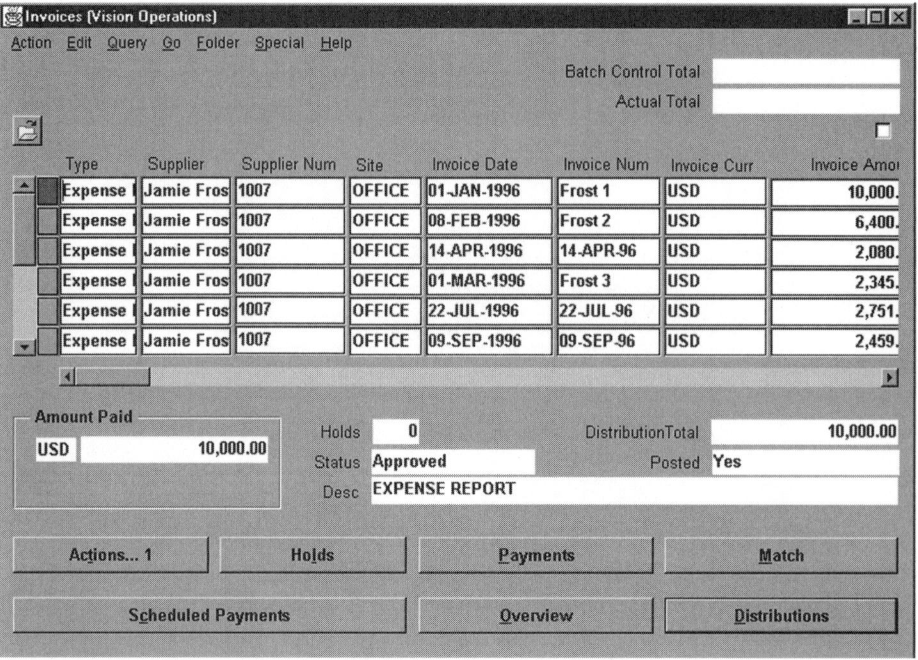

Figure 16-10 The Invoices window

auto approval process, pay the invoices through the payment workbench, post the journal entries to the Oracle General Ledger, and check the payment reconciliation in bank statements from the cash management system.

The invoice importing process can import invoices from an external system to Oracle. Invoice approval can be accomplished in one of two ways: through the online approval process or the batch approval process. The payment process consists of five steps: selecting the invoices, modifying the payment if required, formatting, printing, confirming, and delivering.

Order Entry

Order entry is a sales order process that brings customers to the point of placing an order. Order entry is tightly integrated with inventory, receivables, sales compensation, and service.

Order entry passes through a number of specific steps to complete its cycle. A customer profile must exist before the order is placed. Once the customer places an order, it goes through the orders workbench and then to the pick release process. Pick release matches the open order lines, checks the order quantity against the available inventory quantity, and prepares the shipment. Once the shipment is confirmed, it notifies Oracle Inventory to decrement its inventory balances. It also notifies Oracle Receivables to generate a customer invoice.

You can enter, modify, and view sales orders or customer returns through the sales order screen. Figure 16-11 shows an example of a sales order window.

The sales order screen contains features that enable you to do the following: adjust pricing, assign sales credits, record payment information, attach notes, schedule shipments, enter model options, query material availability, and make material reservations. Customer returns can be handled through the *Return Material Authorization* (RMA). Once the RMA receives the customer return items, it puts them back into the inventory and issues a credit to the customer.

Accounts Receivable

Accounts Receivable is a process that sends invoices to customers, sends dunning letters to inform customers of past-due obligations, and records

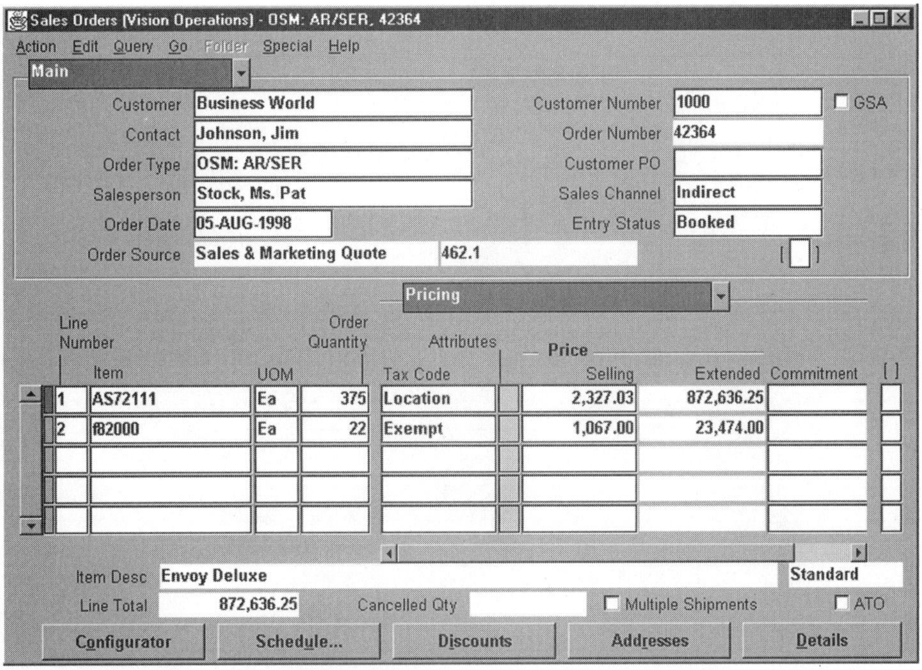

Figure 16-11 Sales order window

customer payments as receipts. Accounts Receivable is tightly integrated with Order Entry, General Ledger, and Inventory. Once it receives full payment from a customer, it closes the invoice transaction status and posts the journal entries to the General Ledger. You can enter, modify, and view the customer payment receipts through the Receipts screen (see Figure 16-12).

Accounts Receivable provides four standard open interfaces. Invoices can be imported into Oracle from external systems using the AutoInvoice open interface. AutoLockbox is another open interface in Accounts Receivable and can be used to load the bank receipts. The Sales Tax Rate interface lets you load the sales tax information into Oracle from a sales tax feeder system. The Customer interface enables you to load the new customer records and/or update the existing customer information into Oracle.

Accounts Receivable provides three workbenches that can be used to perform your day-to-day receivables operations: Receipts, Transactions and Collections. The Receipts workbench can be used to create customer payment receipts. The Transactions workbench can be used to process invoices, credit and debit memos, perform on-account credit chargebacks, and make adjustments. Finally, the Collections workbench can be used to

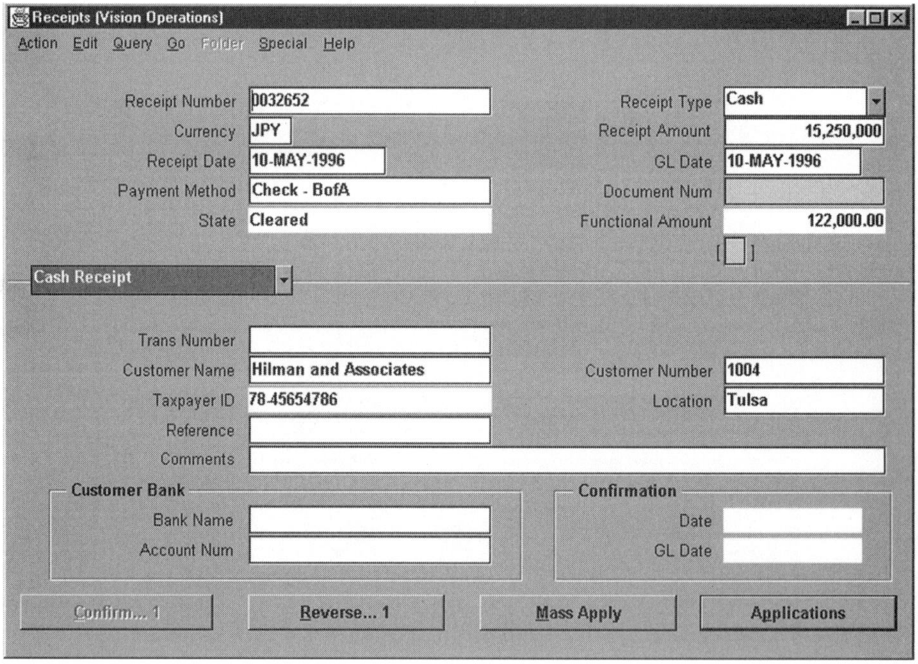

Figure 16-12 Receipts window screen

perform collection activities, such as recording customer calls, and sending dunning letters to customers.

Oracle Assets

Oracle Assets is a complete asset management solution that maintains an organization's property, plant, and equipment accurately. Asset management keeps track of the three primary activities: physical maintenance, asset tracking, and financial administration. With Oracle Assets, you can add, transfer, and retire assets. Assets can also be added from external sources. Oracle Assets supports the following functionalities: preparing capital budgets, projecting depreciation, managing tax books, submitting reporting, and reconciling and processing inventory.

Oracle Assets integrates with the General Ledger, Inventory, Human Resources, Purchasing, Payables, and Projects. You can view the asset information through the Asset Details screen, as shown in Figure 16-13.

Asset workbench is a flexible tool that can be used to view your assets based on asset details, assignments, invoices, or lease information. Oracle Assets has three key Flexfields: Asset Category Flexfield, Location Flexfield, and Asset Key Flexfield. Mass additions upload, a new feature in Release 11, is a part of the *Applications Desktop Integrator* (ADI).

ADI loads the data directly into Oracle tables.

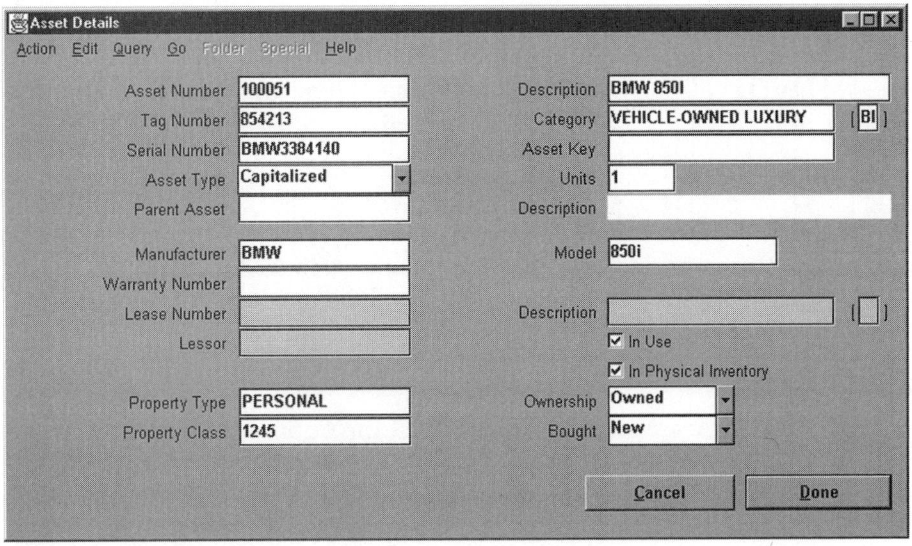

Figure 16-13 Asset details window

The SOB, Asset Category Flexfield, Location Flexfield, Asset Key Flexfield, system controls, fiscal years, calendars, book controls, pro-rate conventions, and asset categories are required steps to set up the Oracle Assets.

Oracle Assets automatically closes the period and runs the depreciation, calculates deprecation using a variety of depreciation methods, projects the depreciation expenses, and archives and purges the depreciation data.

Oracle Inventory

Oracle Inventory is the central repository for manufacturing, distribution, and financial accounting applications. The Inventory system manages various types of items until they are either depleted or sold. Make items and buy items are the two types based on the primary source of materials, such as purchasing and work in process. Order Entry and Work in Process act as primary sources of consumers to sell the items, to use it internally, and to put them into products. Order Entry decreases the inventory quantity, whereas purchasing increases the inventory quantity.

The item number consists of several segments. Oracle handles the item structure through its Key Flexfield feature. Items can be defined, maintained, and viewed through the Master Item and Organization Item Screens. Figure 16-14 shows an example of a Master Item screen.

You can identify one or more templates to set the item attributes. Items are stocked under *units of measure* (UOM). You can define UOM and the associated classes as well as set up the conversion. Categories and category sets are used to group the inventory items. A category is a group of items. A category set, usually defined at the application level, can be divided into multiple categories. Oracle defines physical storage in a hierarchical fashion. The first is Inventory Organization, then Subinventories, and finally Stock locators.

ABC Analysis and Cycle counting are the item-counting methods in physical inventory.

The stock replenishment process is handled through MIN-MAX logic, *Reorder-Point* (ROP), and *Material Requirements Planning* (MRP).

Bills of Material

Bills of Material is a listing of all the subassemblies, intermediates, parts, and raw materials that go into a parent assembly showing the quantity of each required to make an assembly. It is used in conjunction with the *Master Production Schedule* (MPS) to determine the items for which purchase requisitions and production orders must be released. Bills of

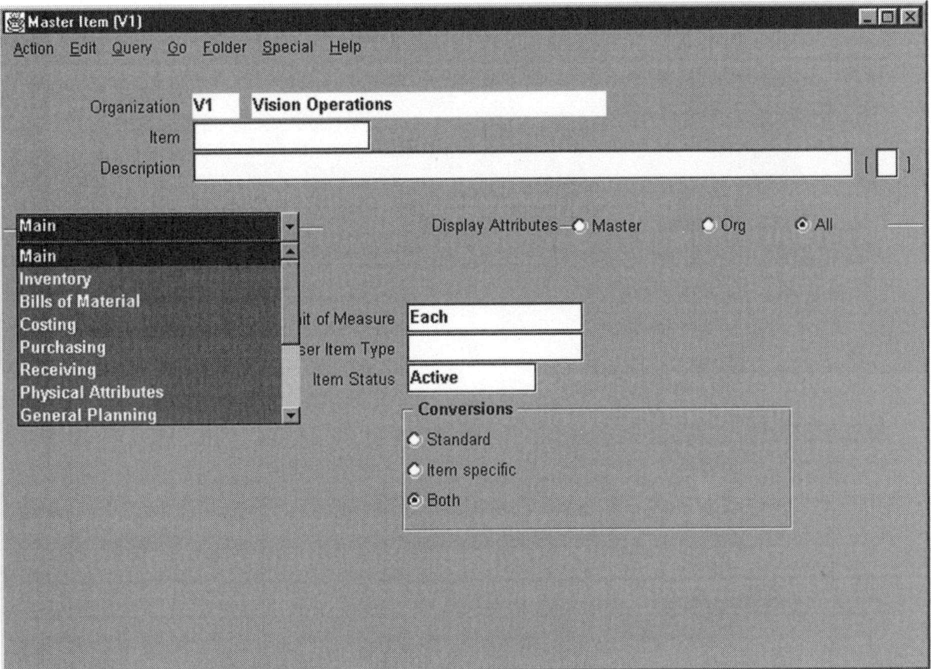

Figure 16-14 Master Item definition window

Material can be displayed in different formats: single-level, indented, and multiple-level. You can define, modify, and view the Bills of Material through the screen shown in Figure 16-15.

Many types of Bills of Material exist: Standard, Model, Option class, Planning and Engineering. A Phantom Bill of Material is used primarily for transient (non-stocked) subassemblies.

Routing is a body of information detailing the manufacturing instructions for a particular item. It includes the operations to be performed, the corresponding sequence, the various work centers to be involved, and the standards for setup and activation. You can copy the bill or routing information from your current organization rather than defining a new one. Bill and routing supports the following functionality: copying or referencing bill and routing information, creating reference designators, assigning substitute components, defining item revisions, mass changing bills of material, viewing indented bills of material, creating standard operations in routing, viewing resource usage in routing, creating routing revisions, assigning operation resources, rolling up costs, and assigning a completion subinventory and locator for routings.

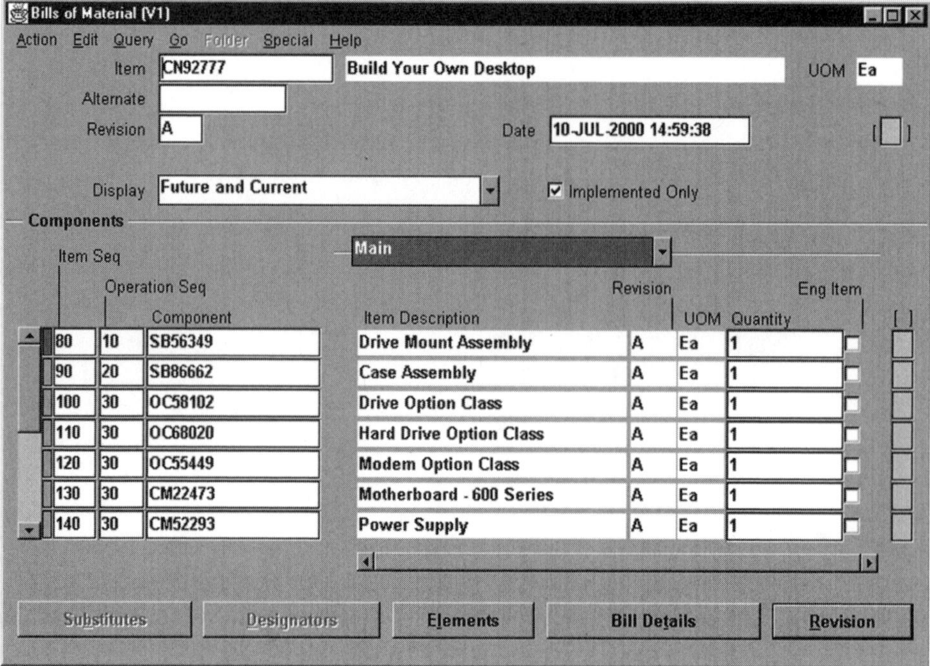

Figure 16-15 Bills of Material definition window

Work In Process (WIP):

Work In Process (WIP) is a complete production management system that uses one or more products in various stages of completion throughout the plant. The business process includes everything from raw materials that have been released for initial processing to completely processed material awaiting final inspection and acceptance as a finished product. WIP supports various manufacturing methods, such as discrete, repetitive, project, assemble-to-order, and work order less.

You can check the status of material transactions, resources, costs, and job and schedule progress information by viewing the inquiry screens or reports. Figure 16-16 shows a screen with WIP parameters.

You can set up WIP parameters, WIP accounting classes, shop floor statuses, labor rates, schedule groups, standard documents, production lines, and profile options prior to building the jobs. You can build discrete jobs, project jobs, or repetitive schedules for manufacturing support. You can also schedule the start and stop times or update the master production schedule automatically.

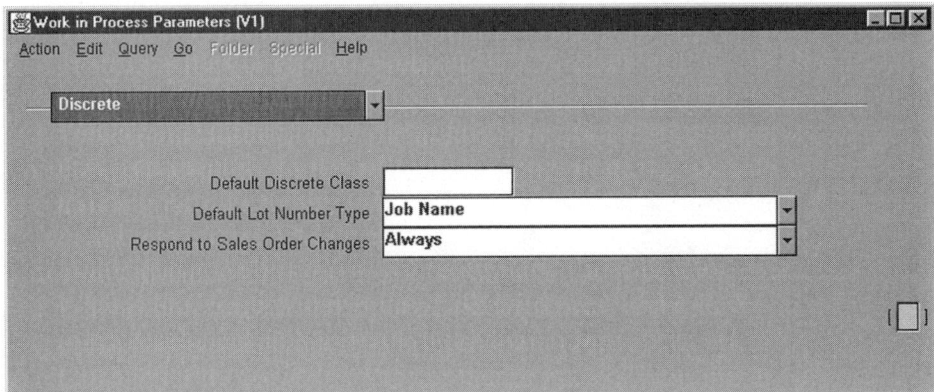

Figure 16-16 Define WIP parameters

You are also able to create, build, update, complete, and view the discrete jobs. You can also simulate the discrete jobs and save the simulated jobs. After the completion of the process, discrete jobs can be closed or purged.

Bills of Material and routing information can be fed into a budget to create a work order, while WIP gathers the actual data. The difference between budget and actual will be charged to variance accounts.

You can use shop floor control to manage the following activities: moving assemblies within operations or between operations, defining and assigning shop floor statuses, using dispatch reports to prioritize the work at specific operations, using WIP to create purchase requisitions automatically, and managing the rework operations.

Material Requirements Planning (MRP)

MRP is a set of techniques that uses Bill of Material, inventory data, and the master production schedule to calculate requirements for materials. The basic function of material control is to have enough of the right materials available to manufacture the company's products. It makes recommendations to release replenishment orders for material. Because it is time-phased, it makes recommendations to reschedule open orders when due dates and need dates are not in phase. MRP is primarily a priority planning and scheduling tool; it plans the company's manufacturing priorities by creating a schedule. With proper feedback from purchasing, inventory, and the shop floor, MRP controls those scheduled priorities. Figure 16-17 shows a plan status window.

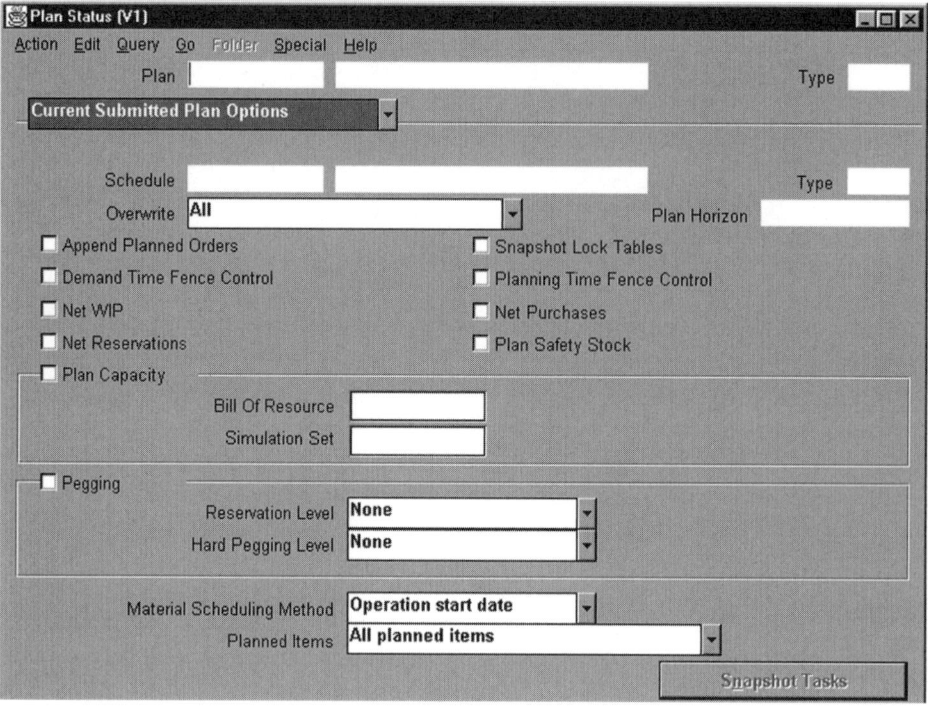

Figure 16-17 The MRP plan status window

When you define an item in Inventory, you can define one of the following methods for MRP planning: MRP planning and MPS planning. For supply-chain planning, you can select one of these methods: DRP planning, MRP and DRP planning, and MPS and DRP planning.

In MRP, the net requirements for a part or an assembly are derived as a result of applying gross requirements and allocations against inventory on hand, scheduled receipts, and safety stock. Net requirements, lot-sized and offset for the lead time, become planned orders.

Human Resources Management (HR)

Human Resources Management (HR) views employees as assets to the company and thus they can be managed in the same way as regular assets. HR does a thorough job of tracking the time dimension.

Several HR activities can be performed during the HR cycle: defining and maintaining organization structures, defining roles and managing the job evaluation process, defining the staffing plan and setting the head-

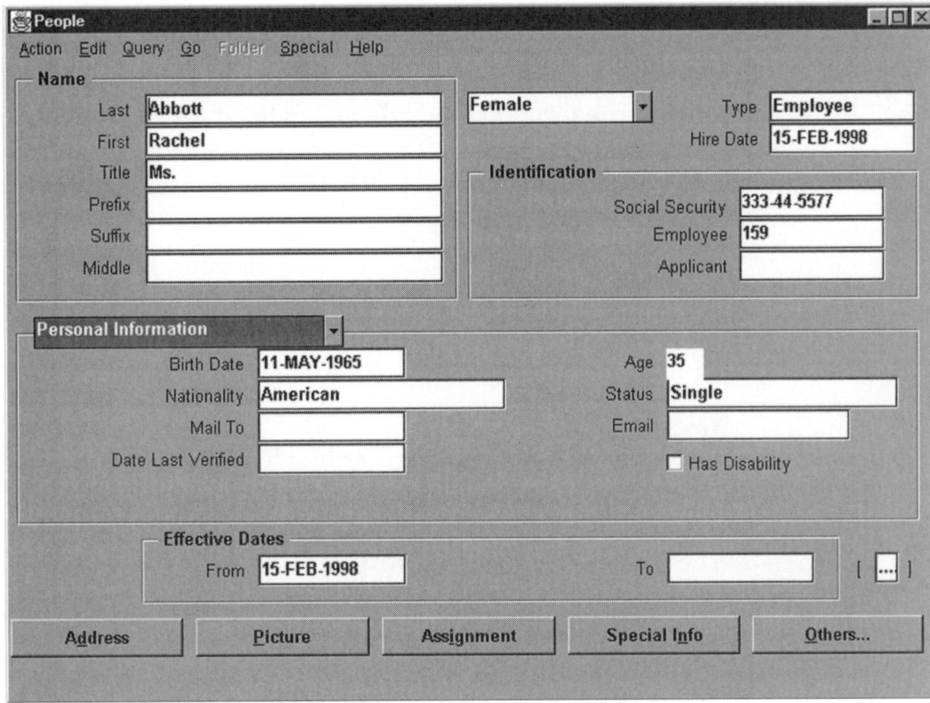

Figure 16-18 Define HR People window

count budget, defining compensation and benefits policies, identifying and managing vacancies, managing recruitment, maintaining employee records, maintaining absence records, and managing training records and employee development.

Employee information can be maintained through the People Screen as shown in Figure 16-18. With HR, you can store information about current and former employees, applicants, external contacts such as contractors, and employee contacts such as relatives and dependents.

New Features in Oracle Applications 11i

Oracle Applications 11i provides Internet-based solutions. The new features include, but are not limited to, changing Order Entry to Order Management, iProcurement, *Customer Relations Management* (CRM), Self-service applications in ERP, and electronic gateways.

The details of the previous topics are beyond the scope of this book. This book is intended for the people who already have some knowledge of and/or working experience in Oracle Applications. The next section, "Questions and Answers," covers a variety of important topics in Oracle Applications. It has two sections: Technical Environment and Functional Environment. The technical section covers the questions and answers from the system administration, AOL, and custom development environment. The functional section covers the questions and answers from the financial accounting and manufacturing areas.

Questions and Answers: Technical Environment

Q: *How do you make your own query when you are in forms query mode?*

A: You can use a placeholder to achieve this. If you enter a single colon (:) in one of your query fields during the Enter Query mode, Oracle Forms Run Query will prompt you to enter the text of SQL Where clause.

Q: *What is concurrent processing?*

A: Concurrent processing is a process that simultaneously runs programs in the background (usually on the server rather than your workstation) while you work online.

Q: *What is a Concurrent Manager?*

A: A Concurrent Manager is a component of concurrent processing that monitors and runs requests while you work online. Once the user submits a request to run the job, the information is stored in the request table. A concurrent manager gets the information from the request table and executes the specified concurrent job.

Q: *What is a request set?*

A: A request set is a collection of reports or programs grouped together. Once you submit a request set job, it executes all the programs in a report set sequentially or in a parallel manner as defined in the request set.

Q: *What are the four phases of a concurrent request?*

A: The four phases are as follows: inactive, pending, running, and completed.

Q: *How would you identify the results of the request in the Concurrent View Requests window?*

A: Whenever a concurrent job is submitted, Applications creates a Request ID. You can use this Request ID to view the results.

Q: *What are the profile options? How many levels of profile options are available?*

A: Profile options are set to determine how the applications look and feel. There are four levels of profile options available: site level, application level, responsibility level, and user level. You can have various categories of profile options, such as personal options, system options, auditing profile options, currency options, Flexfield options, online reporting options , personal output viewer options, and user profile options. Refer to Appendix B for more details.

Q: *What is a document sequence?*

A: A document sequence assigns unique numbers to the documents (transactions) generated by Oracle Applications. For example, each invoice has its own unique invoice number and each purchasing document has its own unique purchase order (PO) number.

Q: *What are the steps involved in adding a custom program to Oracle Applications?*

A: 1. Develop a concurrent program or report.
2. Identify the corresponding executable and register it with the application.
3. Create a concurrent program and its parameters.
4. Add a concurrent program to a request set.

Q: *How do you register a printer?*

A: To add a new printer, go to Install Printer Register.

Q: *What is a Flexfield? How many types of Flexfields exist?*

A: A Flexfield is a field made up of segments. Each segment has an assigned name and a list of valid values. Two types of Flexfields exist: Key Flexfields and *Descriptive Flexfields* (DFFs).

Q: *What is a Key Flexfield?*

A: A Key Flexfield is a unique identifier that is made up of meaningful segments to identify GL account numbers and item numbers. Key Flexfields are usually stored in SEGMENT1...SEGMENTn database columns. Some examples would be Item No 34H-AFR-223-112.G and GL Account No: 100-00-1000-324-11100.

For an example GL Account, segments could be identified as Organization, Cost Center, Account, Product, Product Line.

Q: *What are the Key Flexfields in Oracle Applications?*

A: The following table lists some of the Key Flexfields available in Oracle Applications.

Key Flexfields	Using Applications
Accounting	General Ledger
Asset Key	Fixed Assets
Location	Fixed Assets
Category	Fixed Assets
Account Aliases	Inventory
Item Catalogs	Inventory
Item Categories	Inventory
System Iitems	Inventory
Stock Locators	Inventory
Sales Orders	Inventory
Sales Tax Location	Receivables
Territory	Receivables
Job	Human Resources
Grade	Human Resources
Position	Human Resources
Soft Coded Key	Human Resources

Q: *What is a Descriptive Flex Field?*

A: A DFF lets you define the custom fields into Oracle Application forms without customizing the program code. DFFs in forms are represented by a "beer mug" field (a single space field enclosed by brackets) that looks like the following symbol: [ ]. They are usually stored in ATTRIBUTE1...ATTRIBUTEn database columns. DFFs can also be used to accept report parameters.

Q: *What types of segments can be set up for DFFs?*

A: Global or context-sensitive.

Q: *What is a value set?*

A: A value set is a list of values validated against segments. You can create a value set and assign it to a Flexfield segment.

Q: *How many validation types are there?*

A: Six validation types exist:none, dependent, independent, table, special, and pair.

Q: *What are the required and optional steps for setting up Flexfields?*

A: The required steps are as follows: define the value sets, define the structures, and define the values, if needed.

The optional steps are as follows: define the security rules, define the cross-validation rules, and define the shorthand aliases, if necessary.

Q: *Can you define cross-validation rules for DFFs?*

A: No, you cannot. You can only define them for Key Flexfields.

Q: *Can a value set be shared between Flexfields?*

A: Yes, value sets can be shared between Flexfields.

Q: *Can a value set be shared within a Flexfield structure?*

A: No, value sets cannot be shared between segments within a Flexfield as long as they do not carry the same type of information. For example, date information can be shared between segments within a Flexfield.

Q: *What are the advanced validation options?*

A: Three types of advanced validation options are available.

- $PROFILES$, which references the current value of a profile option. An example would be $PROFILES$.profile_option_name.
- :Block.field, which references the block field.
- $FLEX$, which refers to the current value of a previously used value set. An example would be $FLEX$.value_set_name (cascading dependencies).

Q: *What is the next step after defining the segments for Flexfields?*

A: Freezing and compiling the structure.

Q: *What are the steps required to set up value security rules?*

A: Make sure security is enabled, define rules for the value set, and assign rules to the user's responsibility.

Q: *What is Oracle Alert?*

A: Oracle Alert is an exception reporting system. It keeps you informed on an as-needed basis. It also communicates with other users through e-mail regarding exception messages.

Q: *How many types of alerts are there?*

A: Two types of alerts exist: Periodic Alerts and Event Alerts. Periodic Alerts fire at a time interval, and Event Alerts are fired by database table changes.

Q: *What are Quick Codes?*

A: Quick Codes, also known as Quickpicks, are standard sets of user-defined values.

Lookup is a combination of a code and a description. The lookup tables are generally populated by the scripts located in /install/odf directory. See Appendix A for a list of lookup tables.

Q: *What is an Open Interface in Oracle Applications?*

A: Open Interface, also known as the *Application Programmer Interface* (API), is a process whereby the Oracle Applications are linked with external or legacy systems. Open Interface works as a temporary staging area to load the external information into Oracle Applications tables. Once the data is validated, it sends the information to the permanent tables. Rejected transactions can be corrected and resubmitted. See Appendix C for the Open Interfaces list.

Q: *Which schema has complete access to the Oracle Applications data model?*

A: The APPS schema. AutoInstall automatically sets the FNDNAM environment variable to the name of the APPS schema.

Q: *What is the top directory in Oracle Applications?*

A: $APPL_TOP.

Q: *What is a product top directory?*

A: It starts with the product shortname and is suffixed with TOP, such as _TOP.

For example, General Ledger's top directory is GL_TOP.

Q: *What are the log and output directory names for a product group?*

A: The product group environment file sets the APPLLOG variable to log and APPLOUT to out. For example, the output directory for General Ledger is $GL_TOP/$APPLOUT. For log, it is $GL_TOP/$APPLLOG.

Q: *What data dictionary tables do you use to obtain detailed information regarding Oracle Applications database tables and columns?*

A: You can write a query by joining the FND_TABLE and FND_COLUMNS tables.

FND_INDEXES and FND_INDEX_COLUMNS tables are part of the data dictionary.

All the FND_ table names are self-explanatory.

Q: *What are the primary underlying tables for concurrent processing?*

A: FND_CONCURRENT_PROGRAMS, FND_CONCURRENT_REQUESTS, FND_CONCURRENT_PROCESSES, and FND_CONCURRENT_QUEUES tables.

Q: *What are the primary underlying tables for Flexfields?*

A: FND_DESCR_FLEX_CONTEXTS, FND_FLEX_VALIDATION_RULES, FND_FLEX_VALUE_SETS, FND_ID_FLEXS, FND_ID_FLEX_SEGMENTS, and FND_ID_FLEX_STRUCTURES tables.

Q: *What is the primary underlying table for AOL QuickCodes?*

A: FND_LOOKUPS table.

Q: *What is the application dummy table used by a form block?*

A: FND_DUAL table.

Q: *What is the main underlying table for Profile Options?*

A: FND_PROFILE_OPTIONS table.

Q: *What are the main prerequisites for creating a custom application or responsibility?*

A: Set up a directory structure for a custom application, and define an environment variable that translates to your application base path.

Q: *What are the WHO columns?*

A: WHO columns are used to track the changes to your data in the application tables. WHO columns exist in all Oracle Applications standard tables. The following five are considered WHO columns:

WHO Columns(5)

Column Name	Data Type	NULL?	Foreign Key?
CREATED_BY	NUMBER(15)	NOT NULL	FND_USER
CREATION_DATE	DATE	NOT NULL	
LAST_UPDATED_BY	NUMBER(15)	NOT NULL	FND_USER
LAST_UPDATE_DATE	DATE	NOT NULL	
LAST_UPDATE_LOGIN	NUMBER(15)		FND_LOGINS

Q: *Do I need to have WHO column information in custom forms?*

A: Yes. It is strongly recommended to add WHO columns to the custom tables and call standard API, FND_STANDARD.SET_WHO in PRE-INSERT, and PRE-UPDATE triggers in each block of the form. Also, specify these fields as hidden in each block of the form.

Q: *What are the additional WHO columns used for concurrent programs?*

A: Concurrent programs use all nine WHO columns including the following four.

Additional WHO Columns (4) for Concurrent Programs

Column Name	Data Type	NULL?	Foreign Key?
REQUEST_ID	NUMBER(15)		FND_CONCURRENT_REQUESTS
PROGRAM_APPLICATION_ID	NUMBER(15)		FND_CONCURRENT_PROGRAMS
PROGRAM_ID	NUMBER(15)		FND_CONCURRENT_PROGRAMS
PROGRAM_UPDATE_DATE	DATE		PROGRAM_UPDATE_DATE

Q: *Can you disable the WHO columns' information in a form block?*

A: Yes. You can disable HELP -> ABOUT THIS RECORD information within a block.

Call the following procedures in a block level WHEN-NEW-BLOCK-INSTANCE Trigger:

app_standard.event('WHEN-NEW-BLOCK-INSTANCE');
app_standard.enable('ABOUT','PROPERTY_OFF');

Q: *How do you register your custom tables in PL/SQL?*

A: You can use AD_DD package to register custom tables in PL/SQL.

Q: *How do you define the passing arguments in SQL/PLUS and PL/SQL concurrent programs?*

A: You must name your passing arguments as &1, &2, &3 and so on.

Q: *How do you call your custom reports from a form?*

A: You can call your custom Oracle reports in a form using the FND_REQUEST.SUBMIT_REQUEST procedure.

Q: *What is a template form?*

A: A template form is a starting point for the development of custom forms. Copy the Template.fmb file from $AU_TOP/forms/US directory to your local directory and rename it.

Q: *Which libraries are attached to the template form?*

A: The following main libraries are directly attached to the template form.

APPCORE contains packages and procedures for standard menus, toolbars, and so on.

APPDAYPK contains a calendar package.

FNDSQF contains packages and procedures for Flexfields, concurrent processing, profiles, and a message dictionary.

Q: *What is a calendar?*

A: A calendar is an object that lets you select the date and time. It is automatically included in the template form.

A Calendar package example would be calendar.show.

Q: *Which template form triggers require some modifications?*

A: The ACCEPT, FOLDER_RETURN_ACTION, KEY-DUPREC, KEY-MENU, KEY-CLRFRM, ON-ERROR, KEY-LISTVAL, POST-FORM, PRE-FORM, QUERY_FIND, WHEN-NEW-FORM-INSTANCE, WHEN-NEW-BLOCK-INSTANCE, WHEN-NEW-RECORD-INSTANCE, and WHEN-NEW-ITEM-INSTANCE triggers.

Q: *Which template form triggers cannot be modified?*

A: The CLOSE_WINDOW, EXPORT, FOLDER_ACTION, KEY-COMMIT, KEY-EDIT, KEY-EXIT, KEY-HELP, LASTRECORD, WHEN-WINDOW-CLOSED, WHEN-FORM-NAVIGATE, and ZOOM triggers.

Q: *What are the main template files for Pro*C concurrent programs?*

A: The main template files are EXMAIN.c and EXPROG.c .

Q: *What is the Oracle-recommended application short name for extensions?*

A: Oracle recommends an application short name begin with XX. As an example, extensions to Oracle Purchasing would be XXPO.

Q: *Where do you maintain the list of your custom programs?*

A: All custom programs should be listed in the applcust.txt file. This file is located in the $APPL_TOP/admin directory. When you apply the patches, Oracle Applications uses this file for informational purposes.

Q: *What are the steps involved in modifying an existing form?*

A: First, you identify the existing file and then you copy the file to a custom application directory, making sure to rename it. You then make the necessary modifications, generate the form, and document it in the custom program list using applcust.txt file.

Q: *Where do you maintain database customizations?*

A: You can maintain all your table changes by creating a new schema. You can use your custom application short name (such as XXPO) as your Oracle schema name for easy identification. The new schema must be registered in the Oracle AOL.

Q: *Can you create extensions to Oracle Applications without modifying the standard form code?*

A: Yes. This can be done using the CUSTOM library, which is an Oracle Forms PL/SQL library. You can integrate your custom code directly with Oracle Applications without making changes to your Oracle Applications forms code. The CUSTOM library is located in the $AU_TOP/res/plsql directory. Once you write the code, you compile and generate the CUSTOM procedures to make your changes.

Q: *When do you use the CUSTOM library?*

A: You can use the CUSTOM library in a variety of cases. You can use it to incorporate Zoom logic, logic for generic events, logic for product-specific events, and to add entries for the special menu.

Q: *What are the steps involved in implementing your own message dictionary?*

A: Create your own message directories and name it *mesg*, define your messages through a message window, create your own message files, code the logic using FND_MESSAGE package to setup, and display the messages.

Questions and Answers: Functional Environment

General Ledger and Fixed Assets

Q: *Explain the General Ledger business process.*

A: The General Ledger business process is as follows: open the accounting period, create and post the journal entries; verify, review, and correct the balances; consolidate the balances to a parent set of books; close the accounting period; and run the financial reports.

Q: *What is the standard open interface used in the General Ledger?*

A: Journal Import, Import budget, actual and encumbrance data from legacy systems.

GL_INTERFACE is the main interface table.

Q: *What is GLDI?*

A: *General Ledger Desktop Integrator* (GLDI), a spreadsheet end-user tool, is integrated with Oracle General Ledger and is used to create budgets, record transactions, and run financial statements. GLDI supports various wizards, such as Journal Wizard, Budget Wizard, Report Wizard and Analysis Wizard.

Q: *What is a set of books (SOB)?*

A: An SOB is a financial reporting entity comprised of the following: a chart of accounts structure, a calendar, and a currency. You can define one account structure for journal entry and budgeting. SOB determines how the accounting information is collected and categorized for reporting purposes.

Q: *What is the Oracle Financial Analyzer?*

A: The Oracle Financial Analyzer, an analytical reporting tool, is developed based on Online Analytical Processing (OLAP) technology. It enables users to easily identify, analyze, model, budget, forecast, and report on information stored in the General Ledger.

Q: *Briefly explain the Oracle Assets business process.*

A: Oracle Assets can add assets manually or import the information from external systems using the Mass Additions process, running depreciation, and posting it to GL.

Q: *What is the standard open interface used in Oracle Assets?*

A: The Mass Additions Interface. It imports the data into FA_MASS_ADDITIONS table.

Purchasing and Accounts Payables

Q: *Can you explain the Supplier role in purchasing?*

A: Supplier, also known as vendor, plays a major role in both purchasing and payables. Supplier information must exist in the system before you place a purchase order. A supplier can have multiple supplier sites (example: pay site, purchasing site, RFQ only site). Each supplier site can have multiple supplier contacts. PO_VENDORS, PO_VENDOR_SITES_ALL, and PO_VENDOR_CONTACTS are the main underlying tables to store the supplier information. VENDOR_ID is the unique key and is used to link these tables. You can get vendor number information from SEGMENT1 column.

Q: *What is the standard open interface used for vendors?*

A: There is no standard open interface available for Vendors in Oracle Applications. You can write your own interface to load the vendors from external systems. You can load the supplier information into PO_VENDORS, PO_VENDOR_CONTACTS, and PO_VENDOR_SITES_ALL tables.

Q: *What is a requisition? Explain the requisition business process.*

A: A requisition is an authorization process that identifies the item and quantity required prior to place a purchase order. Requisitions are the starting point in the purchasing process. They can be entered manually or loaded from external systems using open interface. Requisitions have to go through the approval process before the information will be fed to purchasing.

Q: *What are the underlying tables for requisitions?*

A: PO_REQUISITION_HEADERS_ALL stores requisition header information such as requisition number, status, and description. Requisition headers can have multiple requisition lines. Each requisition line can have multiple requisition distributions. The main underlying tables for requisitions are PO_REQUISITION_HEADERS_ALL, PO_REQUISITION_LINES_ALL, and PO_REQ_DISTRIBUTIONS_ALL. REQUISITION_HEADER_ID is the unique key to link these tables. You can get requisition number information from the SEGMENT1 column. PO_REQUISITIONS_INTEFACE_ALL table is used to load requisitions from the external systems into Oracle through standard open interface.

Q: *What is a Purchase Order (PO)?*

A: A Purchase Order or PO is a buyer's document used to formalize a purchase transaction with a vendor. A purchase order contains buyer, supplier, and terms and conditions information. Six types of purchasing documents are available: standard purchase orders, blanket purchase orders, planned purchase orders, contracts, RFQs, and quotations.

Q: *Briefly explain the data model for purchase orders.*

A: A PO header can have multiple PO lines. Each PO line in turn can have multiple PO line locations. And, each PO line location can have multiple PO distributions. The main underlying tables for a PO are PO_HEADERS_ALL, PO_LINES_ALL, PO_LINE_LOCATIONS_ALL and PO_DISTRIBUTIONS_ALL. PO_HEADER_ID is the unique key for linking these tables. You can get PO number information from the SEGMENT1 column. PO_HEADERS_INTERFACE, PO_LINES_INTERFACE, and PO_DISTRIBUTIONS_INTERFACE tables are used to load the external data into Oracle through the standard open interface. The PO_RELEASES table is used for blanket orders.

Q: *Explain the receiving business process.*

A: Items received from the vendor arrive at the company's receiving dock, and go through the inspection process. Once they pass quality control, they are placed in inventory stock and the stock quantity is incremented. Rejected items are returned to the vendor. Receiving can have three source types: Receiving from vendor (VENDOR), inter-organization transfer (INVENTORY), and internal order.

Q: *Briefly explain the data model for Receiving.*

A: RCV_SHIPMENT_HEADERS can have multiple RCV_SHIPMENT_LINES. RCV_TRANSACTIONS, RCV_LOT_TRANSACTIONS, and RCV_SERIAL_TRANSACTIONS tables are the primary underlying tables.

Q: *What is an RFQ?*

A: A Request for Quotation is a bid that is supplied by the vendor based on your inquiry. It is usually considered an offer to sell. Once the quotation is approved, it can be used as reference for the creation of purchase orders.

Q: *How can you match invoices to purchase orders?*

A: You can match invoices to purchase orders in three ways:

1. A two-way match confirms that an invoice matches a purchase order.
2. A three-way match confirms the matching of invoices, purchase orders and receipts.
3. A four-way match requires invoice, purchase order, receipt and inspection.

Q: *Briefly explain the payables business process.*

A: Payables help you to manage your procurement cycle. In a payables cycle, all payments proceed through the following steps: make sure the supplier information is established, match the invoices to purchase orders, make sure the invoices are approved either through the auto approval process or manual process, pay the invoices through payment workbench, post the journal entries to Oracle General Ledger, and check the payment reconciliation in bank statements from the cash management system.

Q: *What are the different invoice types in payables?*

A: The invoice types in payables are as follows: a standard invoices, credit memos, debit memos, expense reports, prepayments, quick matches, withholding taxes, and mixed, which includes more than one of these on the same invoice.

Q: *What are the steps involved in a pay run?*

A: 1. Select the invoices.
2. Modify the invoices, if necessary.
3. Format and print the selected invoices.
4. Confirm the payment.
5. Deliver the payment.

Q: *Explain the data model for payables (AP).*

A: AP batches can have multiple AP invoices. Each invoice can have multiple invoice distribution lines. The main underlying tables for payables are AP_BATCHES_ALL, AP_INVOICES_ALL, AP_INVOICE_DISTRIBUTIONS_ALL, AP_CHECKS_ALL, AP_PAYMENT_SCHEDULES_ALL and AP_INVOICE_PAYMENTS_ALL. AP_INVOICES_INTERFACE, and AP_INVOICE_LINES_INTERFACE tables are used to load the external data into Oracle through the standard open interface.

Order Entry & Accounts Receivable

Q: *Explain the customer role in Order Entry.*

A: The customer plays a major role in both order entry and receivables. Customer information must exist in the system before you place a sales order. A customer can have multiple addresses with multiple site uses, and multiple customer contacts. RA_CUSTOMERS,

RA_ADDRESSES_ALL, RA_SITE_USES_ALL and RA_CONRACTS are the main underlying tables for storing customer information. CUSTOMER_ID is the unique key and is used to link these tables.

Q: *Explain the business process of customer sales orders.*

A: Order Entry is a sales order process that brings customers to the point of placing an order. Order Entry is tightly integrated with Inventory, Receivables, Sales Compensation, and Service. Three types of orders exist: customer orders, RMAs, and internal orders.

Order Entry must pass through a number of steps to complete its cycle. A customer profile must exist prior to the order placement. Once the customer places an order, it goes through the Orders workbench and then to the Pick Release process. Pick Release matches the open order lines, checks the order quantity against the available inventory quantity, and prepares the shipment. Once the shipment is confirmed, it notifies Oracle Inventory to decrement its inventory balances and notifies Oracle Receivables to generate a customer invoice.

Q: *What is kitting?*

A: Kitting is a process of constructing and staging kits. Kits, the components of parent items that have been pulled from inventory, can be ready for shipment under a single part number.

Q: *What is a drop shipment?*

A: Orders can be placed, but the items do not have to be handled, stocked or delivered. You can have a supplier ship your order items directly to another supplier. You can also have a supplier ship your order items directly to your customer. The advantage of drop shipments is eliminating your stock maintenance costs incurred at a warehouse. It provides a direct automated link between your suppliers and customers.

Q: *What is a backorder?*

A: It is an unfilled customer order or commitment. If the inventory organization cannot satisfy the entire quantity ordered on a sales order, it may elect to ship what is available and backorder the remaining.

Q: *What is Pick Release?*

A: Pick Release is a process by which items are taken from inventory for a specific sales order and instructed to ship to a customer. SO_PICKING_HEADERS_ALL SO_PICKING_LINES_ALL, SO_PICKING_BATCHES_ALL and SO_PICKING_LINE_DETAILS, are the main underlying tables for picking process.

Q: *Explain the data model for sales orders.*

A: SO_HEADERS_ALL can have multiple SO_LINES_ALL. SO_HEADERS_ALL, SO_LINES_ALL, SO_LINE_DETAILS, SO_AGREEMENTS, SO_PRICE_LISTS, and SO_ORDER_TYPES_ALL are the main underlying tables. Order Cycle actions result information is stored in columns S1 through S30.

Q: *Explain the Receivables (AR) business process.*

A: The Accounts Receivables process sends invoices to customers, sends dunning letters to inform customers of past-due obligations, and records customer payments as receipts. Accounts Receivables is tightly integrated with Order Entry, General Ledger and Inventory. Once it receives a complete payment from a customer, it closes the invoice transaction status and posts the journal entries to General Ledger.

Q: *What is dunning?*

A: Dunning is a process of sending reminders to customers regarding overdue invoices.

Two dunning methods exist: days overdue, and staged.

Q: *What is AutoLockbox?*

A: AutoLockbox is an open interface that is used for loading bank receipts.

Q: *What are the debit and credit transactions in Receivables?*

A: Invoices, chargebacks, debit memos, and deposits are considered debit transactions; whereas receipts and credit memos are part of the credit transactions.

Q: *How do you reverse a receipt in Receivables?*

A: You can create either a standard reversal or a debit memo reversal to reverse a receipt.

With the standard reversal, Receivables automatically updates GL and reopens the closed invoices. With the debit memo reversal, the customer account is charged with another receivable.

Q: *Can you explain the Receivables data model in brief?*

A: RA_BATCHES_ALL, RA_CUSTOMER_TRX_ALL, RA_CUSTOMER_TRX_LINES_ALL, RA_CUST_TRX_LINE_GL_DIST_ALL, RA_CUST_TRX_LINE_SALESREPS_ALL are the main underlying tables for invoices, chargebacks, and debit memos. AR_BATCHES_ALL, AR_

CASH_RECEIPTS_ALL, and AR_DISTIBUTIONS_ALL are the main underlying tables for receipts.

Inventory

Q: *Describe the Inventory business process.*

A: Oracle Inventory is the central repository for manufacturing, distribution and financial accounting applications. The Inventory system manages various types of items until they are either used up or sold. Make items and buy items are two types based on the primary source of materials such as purchasing and WIPs. Order Entry and WIP act as primary source of consumers to sell the items, to use it internally, and to put them into products. Order Entry decrements the inventory quantity, while purchasing increments the stock quantity.

Q: *How are items laid out in physical storage?*

A: Items are usually stored in inventory in a hierarchical fashion. There are three types of hierarchical storage locations: Inventory organization, sub-inventory, and stock locators. Sub-inventories are a subset of inventory organizations. Stock locators are within the sub-inventory.

Q: *Briefly explain the physical inventory business process.*

A: Physical inventory determines inventory quantity by taking an actual count. Physical inventories can be taken on a continuous, periodic, or annual basis. Two methods are typically used: cycle counting and ABC analysis. Cycle counting can be done on a cyclic schedule rather than annually. An ABC analysis divides items into three categories based on volume, value or other criteria. Class A refers to high volume, Class B to middle, and Class C to low volume. In an ABC analysis, counting usually starts with class A items.

Q: *What is backflushing?*

A: Backflushing is a process of reducing the item balance in inventory for the parts taken from inventory and used in an assembly or subassembly. The quantities are determined by determining the quantities used in each unit based on the BOM and multiplied by the production count of assemblies produced.

Q: *What is Kanban?*

A: Kanban, which means "card," "billboard" or "sign" in Japanese, is a term applied to the Just-in-Time production method that uses standard containers or lot sizes with a single card attached to each. By using a card, work centers signal that they wish to withdraw the parts from feeding operations or suppliers. It is best suited for flow manufacturing.

Q: *Briefly outline the inventory data model.*

A: MTL_SYSTEM_ITEMS is an inventory master table that holds various item attributes and other characteristics. MTL_ITEM_LOCATIONS defines locations within an organization. MTL_SECONDARY_INVENTORIES, MTL_ITEM_SUB_INVENTORIES, and MTL_SECONDARY_LOCATORS tables are used to store items in a hierarchical storage fashion. MTL_CATEGORIES, and MTL_ITEM_CATEGORIES tables are used to categorize the items.

Q: *Provide a description of costing.*

A: Costing is a process by which various costs of production are applied to individual items or groups of items. There are numerous methods used to decide exactly which costs get assigned to which products. Two common types of costing are standard costing and average costing. Costs are usually set at two levels: buy and make. Setting up the costing of buy items is a straightforward process. For make items, you need to take five cost elements into consideration for calculating item costs: material cost, overhead cost, burden cost, outside processing, and resource. Five steps are involved in setting up standard costs: defining pending costs, rolling up pending costs, printing and reviewing pending costs, updating pending costs, and printing new standard costs.

CST_ITEM_COSTS and CST_ITEM_COST_DETAILS are the main underlying tables.

Q: *How do you handle the stock replenishment process?*

A: The stock replenishment process is handled through MIN-MAX logic, *Reorder-point* (ROP), and *Material Requirements Planning* (MRP).

Bills of Material, WIP, and MRP

Q: *Explain the Bills of Material (BOM) business process.*

A: Bills of material is a listing of all the sub assemblies, intermediates, parts and raw materials that go into a parent assembly showing the quantity of each required to make an assembly. It is used in conjunction with the *Master Production Schedule* (MPS) to determine the items for which purchase requisitions and production orders must be released.

Q: *How can you display the BOM data?*

A: Bills of material can be displayed in different formats: single-level bill of material, indented bill of material, multiple-level bill of material.

Q: *How many types does Oracle BOM support?*

A: Bill of material has various types: Standard bill of material, Model bill of material, Option class bill of material, Planning bill of material and Engineering bill of material. A phantom bill of material is used primarily for transient (non-stocked) subassemblies.

Q: *What is routing?*

A: Routing refers to a body of information detailing the manufacturing instructions of a particular item. It includes the operations to be performed, their sequence, the various work centers to be involved, and the standards for setup and run.

Q: *Briefly explain the BOM data model.*

A: BOM_BILL_OF_MATERIALS, BOM_INVENTORY_COMPONENTS, BOM_OPERATIONAL_ROUTINGS, BOM_OPERATION_RESOURCES, and BOM_OPERATION_SEQUENCES are the main underlying tables for bills of material and routings.

Q: *Briefly explain the Work in Process (WIP) business process.*

A: The WIP business process is a complete production management system that uses one or more products in various stages of completion throughout the plant. The business process includes everything from raw material that has been released for initial processing to completely processed finished products awaiting final inspection and acceptance. WIP supports various manufacturing methods, such as discrete, repetitive, project, assemble-to-order, and work order less.

Q: *Provide an explanation of the WIP data model.*

A: WIP_ENTITIES, WIP_OPERATIONS, WIP_OPERATION_RESOURCES, WIP_TRANSACTIONS and WIP_LINES are the main underlying tables for WIP.

Q: *What is MRP?*

A: Material Requirements Planning refers to a set of techniques that uses bills of material, inventory data, and the master production schedule to evaluate requirements for materials. The basic function of material control is to have enough of the correct materials available exactly when needed for manufacturing the company's products. Because it is time phased, MRP makes recommendations to reschedule open orders. MRP is primarily a priority planning and scheduling tool; it plans the company's manufacturing priorities by creating a schedule. With proper feedback from purchasing, inventory, and the shop floor, MRP controls those scheduled priorities.

Q: *Explain the activities of Human Resource Management.*

A: Several HR activities can be performed during the HR cycle: defining and maintaining organization structures, defining roles and managing the job evaluation process, creating a staffing plan and setting a headcount budget, devising a compensation and benefits policy, identifying and managing vacancies, managing recruitment, maintaining employee records, maintaining absence records, managing training records and employee development.

Appendix A: Lookup Tables

The following table lists the lookup tables for quick codes in Oracle Applications. The naming conventions of lookup tables are so easy that almost all tables are self-explanatory.

Lookup Tables	Used Application
AP_LOOKUP_CODES AP_LOOKUP_TYPES	Quick codes for Accounts Payables
AR_LOOKUPS AR_LOOKUP_TYPES	Quick codes for Accounts Receivable
FA_LOOKUPS FA_LOOKUP_TYPES	Quick codes for Fixed Assets
ALR_LOOKUPS	Quick codes for Alerts
FND_LOOKUP_TYPES	Quick codes for AOL
GL_LOOKUPS	Quick codes for General Ledger
MFG_LOOKUPS	Quick codes for Manufacturing
SO_LOOKUPS SO_LOOKUP_TYPES	Quick codes for Order Entry
PA_LOOKUPS PA_LOOKUP_TYPES	Quick codes for Project Accounting
PO_LOOKUP_CODES PO_LOOKUP_TYPES	Quick codes for Purchasing

Appendix B: Options Tables

The following tables store default, control, and option information that you provide to Oracle Applications.

Table name	Description
AP_SYSTEM_PARAMETERS_ALL	Payables system defaults and parameters
AR_SYSTEM_PARAMETERS_ALL	Receivables options, and defaults
BOM_PARAMETERS	Bills of Material options, and defaults
RG_REPORT_PARAMETERS	Budget, encumbrances report parameters
FND_FLEXBUILDER_PARAMETERS	Flexbuild parameters
GL_STORAGE_PARAMETERS	General Ledger options, and defaults
MTL_INTERORG_PARAMETERS	Inter- organization options, and defaults
MTL_PARAMETERS	Inventory options, and defaults
MTL_MOVEMENT_PARAMETERS	Material movement options, and defaults
MTL_INTERCOMPANY_PARAMETERS	Inter- company parameters
MRP_PARAMETERS	MRP options, and defaults
SO_REPORT_PARAMETERS	Order Entry options, and defaults
WIP_PARAMETERS	WIP options, and defaults
PO_SYSTEM_PARAMETERS_ALL	Purchasing options, and defaults
RCV_PARAMETERS	Receiving options, and defaults

Appendix C: Open Interfaces List (API)

The following list identifies the names of open interfaces in each application, its description, and data model. Most of the interface table names in Oracle Applications are suffixed with _INTERFACE. Once the data is loaded into the interface tables, it will go through the validation process. Accepted transactions are loaded into the permanent tables. Rejected transactions are written to the error tables.

Interface Name	Description	Underlying Interface Tables
Invoice Import	Loads payables invoices.	AP_INVOICES_INTERFACE AP_INVOICE_LINES_INTERFACE
Customer Interface	Loads all the customer information.	RA_CUSTOMERS_INTERFACE_ALL
Sales Tax Rate Interface	Loads sales tax info.	AR_TAX_INTERFACE
AutoLockbox	Loads bank receipts.	AR_PAYMENTS_INTERFACE_ALL
AutoInvoice	Imports invoice information into receivables.	RA_INTERFACE_LINES_ALL RA_INTERFACE_DISTRIBUTIONS_ALL RA_INTERFACE_SALESCREDITS_ALL

continues

Interface Name	Description	Underlying Interface Tables
Order Entry/ Shipping Open Interface	Integrating Order Entry/Shipping with Receivables.	RA_INTERFACE_LINES_ALL RA_INTERFACE_DISTRIBUTIONS_ALL RA_INTERFACE_SALESCREDITS_ALL
Open Routing Interface	You can Lloads the routing information into these tables.	BOM_OP_RESOURCES_INTERFACE BOM_OP_ROUTINGS_INTERFACE BOM_OP_SEQUENCES_INTERFACE
Open Bills of Material Interface	You can import Bills of material components into these tables.	BOM_BILL_OF_MTLS_INTERFACE BOM_INVENTORY_COMPS_INTERFACE
Budget Open Interface	Loads budget data.	FA_BUDGET_INTERFACE
Daily Rates Interface	Loads daily foreign currency rates.	GL_DAILY_RATES_INTERFACE
Journal Import	Loads GL journals.	GL_INTERFACE
Open Demand Interface	Loads the data into demand table.	MTL_DEMAND_INTERFACE
Open Item interface	Loads item attributes.	MTL_SYSTEM_ITEMS_INTERFACE
Open Transactions Interface	You can load inventory transactions into the transactions table. If the item is lot controlled, load the lines into lot controlled table. If it is serialized, load it into the serial table.	MTL_TRANSACTIONS_INTERFACE MTL_TRANSACTION_LOTS_ INTERFACE MTL_SERIAL_NUMBERS_INTERFACE
Open Forecast Interface	Loads forecast data.	MRP_FORECAST_INTERFACE
Order Import	Integratesing order entry/shipping using Order Import.	SO_HEADERS_INTERFACE_ALL SO_LINES_INTERFACE_ALL SO_LINE_DETAILS_INTERFACE SO_SALES_CREDITS_INTERFACE SO_PRICE_ADJUSTMENTS_INTERFACE SO_LINE_ATTRIBUTES_INTERFACE SO_HEADER_ATTRIBUTES_INTERFACE
Open Requisitions Interface	Loads requisitions into these tables.	PO_REQUISITIONS_INTERFACE_ALL PO_REQ_DIST_INTERFACE_ALL
Purchasing Documents Open Interface	Loads purchasing documents into these tables.	PO_HEADERS_INTERFACE PO_LINES_INTERFACE PO_DISTRIBUTIONS_INTERFACE
Receiving Open Interface	Loads receiving information into these tables.	RCV_HEADERS_INTERFACE RCV_TRANSACTIONS_INTERFACE

Interface Name	Description	Underlying Interface Tables
Open Job and Schedule Interface	Loads discrete jobs and create pending repetitive schedules	WIP_JOB_SCHEDULE_INTERFACE
Open Resource Transaction Interface	Loads resource transactions.	WIP_COST_TXN_INTERFACE
Open Move Transactions Interface	Loads WIP move transactions	WIP_MOVE_TXN_INTERFACE
WIP Scheduling Interface	Loads operation schedules, resources.	WIP_SCHEDULING_INTERFACE

Appendix D: Vendor Interface (Pseudo Code)

Since no standard vendor interface/API exists in Oracle Applications, the following steps help programmers to develop their own vendor interface.

1. Create temporary interface tables: PO_VENDORS_INTERFACE, PO_VENDOR_SITES_INTERFACE_ALL, PO_VENDOR_CONTACTS_INTERFACE tables.
2. Load the data into these interface tables using SQL*Loader, Pro*C, or PL/SQL (recent version) tools.
3. Write three different cursors for selecting vendors, vendor sites, and vendor contacts information from the interface tables.
4. Select the necessary information such as SET_OF_BOOKS_ID, TERMS_ID, FOB_LOOKUP_CODE etc., from FINANCIALS_SYSTEM_PARAMS_ALL table.
5. Validate the TERMS_ID against AP_TERMS table.
6. Validate the CURRENCY_CODE for the vendor against the FND_CURRENCIES table. If the Currency code does not exist for the vendor in FND_CURRENCIES table, you can get currency code information from FINANCIALS_SYSTEM_PARAMS_ALL.INVOICE_CURRENCY_CODE and PAYMENT_CURRENCY_CODE columns.
7. Determine if the vendor already exists in the PO_VENDORS table. If the vendor already exists, update the vendor information.
8. If the vendor does not exist, create a new vendor record in the PO_VENDORS table.

9. Determine if the vendor site already exists in the PO_VENDOR_SITES_ALL table. If the vendor site already exists, update the vendor site information.
10. If the vendor site does not exist, create a new vendor site record in the PO_VENDOR_SITES_ALL table.
11. Determine if the vendor contact already exists in the PO_VENDOR_CONTACTS table. If the vendor contact already exists, update the vendor contact information.
12. If the vendor contact does not exist, create a new vendor contact record in the PO_VENDOR_ CONTACTS table.
13. Repeat steps 7 through 12 for each vendor record within a cursor loop.

Appendix E: Environment variables file (APPLSYS.env)

The following environment file contains various types of environment variables, such as base path variables for each application and its definition, Oracle database definitions, and operating system variables definitions.

```
OA_JAVA=/u01/app/oraprod/product/805/forms45/java
REPORTS25_TMP=/tmp
LUSRLIB=/u01/app/applprod/1103/fnd/11.0.28/usrxit/libusr.a
FNDNAM=APPS
PATH=/u01/app/applprod/1103/fnd/11.0.28/bin:/u01/app/appl-
prod/1103/ad/11.0.28/bin::/u01/app/oraprod/product/805/bin:/u
sr/ccs/bin:/usr/sbin:/u01/app/oraprod/local/java/jre1.1.6/bin
:/u01/app/applprod/1103/admin/PROD/scripts:/usr/bin:/utils:.
OA_HTML=/u01/app/applprod/1103/html/html
ORACLE_BASE=/u01/app/oraprod
APPLPTMP=/usr/tmp
STAGE_HOME=/stage_home
ORACLE_SID=PROD
PS1=applprod $
APPLFULL=FND AD AX AK GL RG AP FA AR PO CE AZ
GL_TOP=/u01/app/applprod/1103/gl/11.0.28
APPLSHAR=AU ALR OE AS PAY FF DT INV BOM ENG MRP CRP WIP
ORA_NLS=/u01/app/oraprod/product/805/ocommon/nls/admin/data
NLS_DATE_FORMAT=DD-MON-RR
MFG_TOP=/u01/app/applprod/1103/mfg/11.0.28
TNS_ADMIN=/u01/app/oraprod/product/805/network/admin
```